THE VIETNAM WARS
1945–1990

THE VIETNAM WARS
1945-1990

Marilyn B. Young

HarperCollins*Publishers*

Permissions and illustration credits on page 373.

FIRST EDITION

Designed by Alma Orenstein

Library of Congress Cataloging-in-Publication Data
Young, Marilyn Blatt.
   The Vietnam Wars 1945–1990 / Marilyn Young.—1st ed.
      p.   cm.
   Includes bibliographical references and index.
   ISBN 0-06-016553-7
   1. Vietnamese Conflict, 1961–1975.   2. Vietnam—History—1945–1975.
3. Vietnam—History—1975–   4. United States—Foreign relations—Vietnam.   5. Vietnam—Foreign relations—United States.   I. Title.
DS557.7.Y678   1991
959.704′3—dc20   959.704   90-37427

91 92 93 94 95 CC/RRD 10 9 8 7 6 5 4 3 2 1

For Mollie and Aaron Blatt,
Carole Gonshak,
Leah Glasser,
Lauren Young,
and Michael Young

Contents

Illustrations follow pages 50 and 242.

Preface

WHY ARE WE IN VIETNAM?" Through a decade in which the United States was divided perhaps more deeply than at any other time since the Civil War, the question became a refrain, the inquiring voices more and more discordant and demanding. In the end, "Why are we in Vietnam?" was no longer a question but an accusation addressed beyond the war to the nation's very identity.

There were many explanations offered and these will unfold over the course of the book. At first we were in Vietnam for the sake of stability in France, which held the American plan for European security and recovery hostage to its colonial war in Indochina. We were also there to provide Japan with Southeast Asian substitutes for the China trade the United States had embargoed. In the largest sense, the United States was in Vietnam as a crucial part of the enterprise of reorganizing the post–World War II world according to the principles of liberal capitalism.

Each of these explanations explains something, and together they add up to a pretty fair account of things; indeed, in retrospect, the war does not seem so inexplicable after all. But over the years of contention, the question came to demand more than an explanation, a justification. When an interviewer posed it late in the war to former national security adviser Walt Rostow, he fumed: "Are you really asking me this goddamn silly question?" Though the question was hardly "silly," the interviewer may not have been "really" asking it, for by then those who so queried public officials were sure they knew the answer: There was no conceivable justification for the horrors daily inflicted on and suffered in Vietnam.

While this book discusses the standard explanations and justifications, it interprets the "why" as "how." How did we get to Vietnam? How did we keep expanding the war, and how did we get out? Paralleling the development of the question "Why are we in Vietnam?" from inquiring about motives to denouncing the acts of war, I have come to believe that in the daily, weekly, monthly, yearly progress of the war lay many of its most decisive reasons and irrationalities.

Official justifications for the war changed with the political season, although the climate was always that of the Cold War. As I was finishing this history of the Vietnam–American war, the Cold War was, astonishingly, ending. There is no way to know what this will mean for the next era of world history. But events in the summer of 1990 suggest that peace with the Soviet Union has not necessarily lessened the American propensity to wage war elsewhere. The Iraq crisis is the post–Cold War era's first approach to war. It would be simply foolish, as this book goes to press in August 1990, to attempt any analysis of the crisis or to speculate about its outcome. But in its progress it has already raised old spectres.

Why are we in the Middle East? As of now, President Bush and his administration have told us that we are there to control the source of "our" oil and through that to protect our very way of life. They have invoked Munich and transcendent principles of territorial integrity. I do not suggest any comparison between Southeast Asia and the Middle East or between Vietnam and Iraq. But we had better look very closely at how we approach this or any other intervention. Watching the Iraq crisis unfold as I read the galleys of this book seemed to provide it with a new, harsher, and unwanted conclusion: that war continues to be a primary instrument of American foreign policy and the call to arms a first response to international disputes.

We have been at war since the end of World War II. The Vietnam War itself has not ended. As of this writing, the U.S. still declares Vietnam an enemy nation, prohibits or restricts travel, trade, humanitarian aid, and exchange visits by U.S. citizens, and exerts heavy pressure on its allies to discourage any constructive relations with Vietnam. The ongoing war in Cambodia that came to an uneasy truce in July 1990 received U.S. support throughout. One way the Vietnam war might at last end, and the post–Cold War peace begin, would be for an American president to acknowledge, as a Soviet foreign minister did with respect to Afghanistan, that the United States invaded Vietnam against our stated values and ideals and that it did so secretly and deceptively, fighting a war of immense violence in order to impose its will on another sovereign nation. Otherwise only the name of the country changes, and Americans will continue to ask, "Why are we in Vietnam?"

Marilyn B. Young
Union Village, Vermont
August, 1990

Acknowledgments

THIS BOOK is a work of synthesis that could not have been attempted without the extraordinary work of scholars and writers on both the history of the American war and the history of the Vietnam war of resistance. My narrative has relied heavily on the published work of William Conrad Gibbons and the staff of the Congressional Research Service, James William Gibson, George Herring, James P. Harrison, George Kahin, Huynh Kim Khanh, Ngo Vinh Long, David Marr, Edwin E. Moise, Gareth Porter, Jeffrey Race, and Christine Pelzer White, and I gratefully acknowledge them here. In the history of the Vietnam-American war, the work of journalists has been as important as that of scholars, and the books of Nayan Chanda, Gloria Emerson, David Halberstam, Seymour Hersh, Arnold Isaacs, Jonathan Schell, William Shawcross, and Neil Sheehan have been invaluable.

In addition to their published work, conversation and correspondence with Noam Chomsky, David Hunt, George Kahin, Don Luce, Ngo Vinh Long, Gareth Porter, Jayne Werner, Christine Pelzer White, and Howard Zinn has deepened my understanding of Vietnam and the United States. A trip to Vietnam in January 1988 made concrete what had been until then abstract: Vietnam as a real and wounded country. I want to thank Don Luce, who led the trip, and my fellow travellers, especially Len Ackland, Michael Call, Geoffrey Gates, Carlie Numi, Rick Pyeatt, and Hugh Swift, whose sensitivity to what we were seeing and readiness to talk with me about their wartime experiences in Vietnam brought past and present powerfully together.

I have learned, too, from the work of my friend and colleague, Moss Roberts, with whom I teach a course on the history of Vietnam at New York University. In that course, the Vietnam-American war is only one chapter in Vietnamese history.

The book began as a much shorter project, suggested to me by James Peck, and I want to thank him and all those who read that slimmer version in whole or part: Myra Jehlen, Christina Gilmartin, Gail Hershatter, Carma Hinton, Emily Honig, Myra Jehlen, Mary Nolan, Ernest P. Young, Howard Zinn, and Rosalyn Zinn. As the manuscript grew, some of these good friends read it all again, and others were enlisted to read it in whole or part, including Carolyn Eisenberg, Tom Grunfeld, and Moss Roberts. In its final version the book has benefitted greatly from the careful annotations of Christine Pelzer White. Tom Grunfeld assembled the illustrations and maps, and I am grateful to him for his calm efficiency and excellent judgment.

My understanding of American ideology and its incarnation in foreign policy deepened in the course of long discussions with Myra Jehlen. In the last stages, I took comfort and encouragement from frequent conversations with Sara Ruddick on matters of war, peace and the process of writing.

The book was written, as is often the case, far from the world it describes: during a semester's sabbatical leave from New York University, extended with the help of a friend; in the peace and civility of Fairlee, Vermont; among new and old friends: Don Henderson, Pat Henderson, Suzanne Lupien, Maryssa Navarro, Robert Nichols, Steve Niederhauser, William Noble, Grace Paley, Nora Paley, Dorothy St. Peters, Harold St. Peters, and James Tatum. In addition, the Department of History at Dartmouth courteously extended library privileges to the rich collections of Baker Library; I should like to express particular appreciation to Patricia A. Carter, whose Inter-Library Loan Office supplemented Baker's holdings.

I thank my intelligent and patient editors, Hugh Van Dusen and Stephanie Gunning.

I am grateful to all but alone responsible for the use to which I have put the good advice and help.

List of Abbreviations

AID	Agency for International Development
ARVN	Army of South Vietnam
CIP	Commercial Import Program
COMECON	Council for Mutual Economic Assistance (USSR)
COSVN	Central Committee Directorate for the South
CPK	Khmer Communist Party
DMZ	Demilitarized Zone along the seventeenth parallel
DRV	Democratic Republic of Vietnam
FAC	Forward air controller
GVN	Government of Vietnam (Saigon)
MACV	Military Assistance Command, Vietnam
MAAG	Military Assistance Advisory Group
NLF	National Liberation Front
NVA/VC	North Vietnamese Army/Viet Cong
PAVN	People's Army of Vietnam (North)
PLAF	People's Liberation Armed Forces (South)
POL	Petroleum, oil and lubricants
PRC	People's Republic of China
PRG	People's Revolutionary Government
RVAF	Republic of Vietnam Armed Forces (Saigon)
SEATO	Southeast Asia Treaty Organization
VC	Viet Cong
VVAW	Vietnam Veterans Against the War

MONGOLIA

CHINA

Beijing

Shanghai

INDIA

BANGLADESH
Dhaka

Taipei

BURMA

Hanoi

LAOS
Vientiane

HONG
KONG

TAIWAN

Hainan

PHILIPPINES

Rangoon

Paracel Islands

THAILAND

Indian

Bangkok

CAMBODIA
Phnom Penh

Andaman

Sea

South China
Sea

Gulf of
Thailand

Ho Chi Minh City

Ocean

Spratly
Islands

Bandar Seri Begawan

SABAH

Kuala MALAYSIA
Lumpur

BRUNEI

SARAWAK

SINGAPORE

Kalimantan

Sulawesi

INDONESIA

Jakarta
Java

International
boundary
National capital

0   300 KILOMETERS
0   300 MILES

Boundary representation
not necessarily authoritative

CHAPTER ONE

The Fate of OSS Agent 19 (1945–1946)

Perhaps naively, and without consideration of the conflicting postwar interests of the "Big" nations themselves, the new government believed that by complying with the conditions of the wartime United Nations conferences it could invoke the benefits of those conferences in favor of its own independence.

—ARTHUR HALE,
U.S. INFORMATION AGENCY,
HANOI, OCTOBER 1945

I N AUGUST 1945, most Americans believed their country victorious over the unjust imperialist ambitions of two oppressive nations: Germany and Japan. Peace was lovingly embraced, joyously celebrated, as if it were the natural state in which people had always, and would always, live. Soldiers sailed slowly home, confident of welcome, looking forward to the world promised by the resounding victory over fascism: a world free of want, fear, and war, a world their sacrifices had made safe for democracy.

Two months later, twelve of the U.S. Merchant Marine ships engaged in the pleasant duty of ferrying American troops home were given new orders: they were to transport some thirteen thousand French combat troops halfway around the world to Saigon, capital of what the French called Cochin China. To the people who lived there, it was *Nam Bo,* the southernmost region of Vietnam. Not our war, the American sailors thought, and then wondered what they were doing in the South China Sea. Many objected, as best they could, in letters to Congress and

1

newspaper editors. In November, seamen on the S.S. *Winchester Victory* sent a cable to President Truman in which they "vigorously protest[ed]" the use of "this and other American vessels for carrying foreign combat troops to foreign soil for the purpose of engaging in hostilities to further the imperialist policies of foreign governments when there are American soldiers waiting to come home."[1]

In August 1945, most Vietnamese believed their country was at last independent of all foreign rule and at peace. For over eighty years, the French had effaced the very name Vietnam, ruling it as three separate districts: Tonkin, Annam, and Cochin China. For that entire period, Vietnamese had struggled against French rule in sporadic uprisings that sometimes achieved the intensity of full-scale guerrilla warfare. Resistance to French rule in turn drew upon centuries of struggle against Vietnam's most persistent threat, China. Twentieth-century Vietnamese patriots often quoted, with understandable pride, the fifteenth-century poet Nguyen Trai's boast that Vietnam had "at no time lacked heroes." The corollary was that Vietnam had at no time lacked enemies.

French surrender to Germany in June 1940 had doubled the number of Vietnam's colonial overlords. The new Vichy government acquiesced to the demands of Germany's ally Japan, which seized control of Vietnam's economic resources while leaving daily administration in the hands of the French. In their five-year tenure in Vietnam, Japanese policies devastated the economy, creating a famine in the North that killed between 1.5 and 2 million people.

By 1944, as the war against Germany in Europe merged with the war in the Pacific against Japan, Vietnamese nationalists became, in a formal sense, allies of the United States, Great Britain, and the Soviet Union in a joint struggle against the Axis powers and such collaborationist regimes as Vichy France. The most effective nationalist group, by all accounts, was the League for the Independence of Vietnam *(Vietnam Doc Lop Dong Minh Hoi)*, Viet Minh for short, established in May 1941 and led by Ho Chi Minh.* A founding member of both the French and the Indochinese Communist parties, Ho had lived most of his life outside Vietnam, organizing, mobilizing, agitating, his steady goal the independence of Vietnam. In 1919, wearing a borrowed suit and using the pseudonym Nguyen Ai Quoc (Nguyen the Patriot), he had appealed to Wood-

---

*The best known of the many pseudonyms used by Nguyen Tat Thanh during a revolutionary career that can be said to have begun with his birth in 1890 into a family that had already engaged in one uprising against the French and that would end only with his death in 1969.

row Wilson at Versailles to fulfill the promise of American war aims: self-determination for all peoples. But the conference at Versailles merely dismantled the Austro-Hungarian Empire, without unduly disturbing European colonial arrangements; like hundreds of disappointed nationalists, Nguyen Ai Quoc turned to the writings of Lenin and the history of Russian Bolshevism and there discovered what he called a "path" for his compatriots. A friend had given him the French translation of Lenin's "Thesis on the National and Colonial Questions," Ho recalled many years later.

> There were political terms difficult to understand in this thesis. But by dint of reading it again and again, finally I could grasp the main part of it. What emotion, enthusiasm, clear-sightedness, and confidence it instilled in me! . . . Though sitting alone in my room, I shouted aloud as if addressing large crowds: "Dear martyrs, compatriots! This is what we need, this is what we need, this is the path of our liberation."[2]

Lenin's theses, presented to the Second Congress of the Communist International in 1920, were both a call for national revolution in the colonial world and an offer of help. The establishment of the Communist International (Comintern) gave revolutionaries a headquarters, a network, a source of advice and funds. The advice was not always very good and the funds were limited, but hundreds of colonial subjects concluded, with Ho, that "only Socialism and Communism can liberate the oppressed nations. . . ."

What Ho and those who answered his call to join the Communist Party of Vietnam meant by socialism and communism is reflected in the first Party platform, adopted at a meeting held beyond the reach of the French police in Hong Kong on February 18, 1930. Ten "slogans" summarized the program:

1. To overthrow French imperialism, feudalism, and the reactionary Vietnamese capitalist class.
2. To make Indochina completely independent.
3. To establish a worker-peasant and soldier government.
4. To confiscate the banks and other enterprises belonging to the imperialists and put them under the control of the worker-peasant government.
5. To confiscate all of the plantations and the property belonging to the imperialists and the Vietnamese reactionary capitalist class and distribute them to poor peasants.

6. To implement the eight-hour working day.
7. To abolish public loans and poll tax. To waive unjust taxes hitting the poor people.
8. To bring back all freedom to the masses.
9. To carry out universal education.
10. To implement equality between man and woman.

It was a program that asserted the link between national independence and social revolution but that, in the very ordering of its enemies, insisted as well on the necessity of a broad nationalist coalition. "Reactionary" Vietnamese capitalists must be overthrown and their property confiscated. Nothing was said about those deemed patriotic, and while French plantation owners were obvious targets, the platform was silent on Vietnamese landlords. Indeed, many of the planks of the February program would have been perfectly at home in a liberal, reformist vision of an independent Vietnam. The problem was that liberal, reformist politicians in France had little interest in granting Vietnam independence. And indeed liberal, reformist nationalists in Vietnam, while able to support some of the program, would also find that their own interests inhibited them from accepting all of it.

What Ho felt he had learned in Paris and then at Versailles was that to become independent meant to oppose imperialism, to free Vietnam not only of the taxes the French had imposed but of the financial, agricultural, and industrial institutions through which France profited at the expense of Vietnam. And what he had learned at his father's knee, listening to the nationalist Phan Boi Chau read aloud his patriotic verses, was that the tasks of the national revolution must come first; those of the social revolution would build on that victory.

The Comintern, on the other hand, was of the firm opinion that the revolution must *simultaneously* overthrow both traditional agrarian hierarchical structures and the stunted, dependent Vietnamese commercial class that fed off and sustained French rule. Nationalism without immediate social revolution would only produce new forms of dependency; a Vietnam organized outside the imperialist world order alone could claim true autonomy. That social revolution and nationalism were two parts of the same process was not at issue: the question was one of timing. On October 30, 1930, the eight-month-old Party met again, revised its platform so that it fell solidly in line with Comintern views, and changed its name from Vietnam to Indochinese Communist Party.[3] Over the next few years, Ho Chi Minh's writings were denounced for their "nationalist stench," and his support for a broad alliance that could include even small and medium landowners, provided they were patriotic, was attacked as reformist and collaborationist. A decade would pass before this bitter debate on the relationship between national and social revolution was resolved, along the lines initially urged by Ho, in the formation of the Viet Minh.

Almost at once the infant revolutionary movement was put to the test by a wave of peasant insurrections and worker strikes in two provinces of central Vietnam, Nghe An and Ha Tinh, which culminated in the formation of the shortlived Nghe Tinh soviet. For several months peasant associations and unions, often led by Communist cadres, abolished taxes, shortened the work day, distributed confiscated land, conducted literacy classes, administered justice—in short, they ruled themselves. Begun in the spring of 1930, the movement lasted until mid-1931, crushed in the end by massive French firepower, including bombing raids in the countryside in which several hundred people were killed. Virtually all the leaders of the Party (as well as those who would become leaders later on) were arrested at this time, serving prison sentences that varied from two years (Vo Nguyen Giap) to eleven years (Le Duan). And while Hong Kong may have been beyond the reach of the French police, it was readily accessible to the British, who cooperatively arrested Ho Chi Minh in June 1931. With the help of a British friend, Ho managed to escape. Although his death was reported and even memorialized by the international Communist movement in 1932, he was in fact alive and working in Moscow until he was able to move considerably closer to Vietnam, arriving in China in the late summer of 1938.[4]

As French politics moved to the right after the collapse of the Popular Front in 1938, colonial policies grew harsher. A new wave of arrests began in 1939, and over two thousand were jailed. Vo Nguyen Giap was among those who escaped the dragnet, but his wife, daughter, father, sisters, brother-in-law, and sister-in-law were caught. All were jailed and ultimately killed between 1941 and 1943. In November 1940, a brief and bloody insurrection in southern Vietnam virtually wiped out the Party in that region. "The Air Force bombed the nests of the resistance with great violence," a later report recounted, "in order to terrorize the dissidents." Over five thousand people were arrested, over a hundred executed. Jail cells, handcuffs, chains were all in short supply, but the French improvised, packing "prisoners into dry-docked ships floating in the Saigon River. For want of chains and handcuffs, wires piercing the hands and heels of prisoners were used to hold them in one place."[5] Those deemed ringleaders were shipped to the "tiger cages" of Poulo

Condore—a facility still in use during the American war over thirty years later.

From a constantly shifting base in Cao Bang Province on the Chinese border, Ho gathered together survivors of the ongoing French repression; by the summer of 1941, he had established both the military and the political instruments necessary for a new drive for independence. At a series of meetings held in a cave near the village of Pac Bo in Cao Bang Province in May and June of 1941, the Eighth Plenum of the Indochinese Communist Party gathered to discuss the changing situation in Vietnam. France had surrendered to Germany in June 1940; the Japanese were assuming full economic control of the colony. Ever since the October 1930 rejection of Ho's original Party platform, the governing assumption of the Party had been the indissolubility of the twin tasks: social revolution and national liberation. Now, in a major decision, their relationship was redefined. The revolution on the land would have to wait. "Everyone knows," the Party resolution read, "that, at the present stage, unless the French and the Japanese are overthrown, not only will the nation remain in slavery forever, but the agrarian question will never be solved." All the demands of the Party "which would be beneficial to a particular class but would be harmful to the nation should be postponed." Landlords, rich peasants, Vietnamese entrepreneurs, those who one way and another joined the French in exploiting the majority of Vietnamese were, at this crucial juncture of Vietnamese history, part of the "reserve army of the revolution." Only "local tyrants" and the "few running dogs who flatter and fawn on the Japanese enemy" were excluded.[6] Accordingly, in May 1941, Ho Chi Minh announced the founding of the Viet Minh.

On June 6, in a "Letter from Abroad" whose ringing cadences consciously evoked Vietnam's full roster of heroes, Ho Chi Minh addressed the "Elders! Prominent personalities! Intellectuals, peasants, workers, traders, and soldiers!" of Vietnam:

> Since the French were defeated by the Germans, their forces have been completely disintegrated. However, with regard to our people, they continue to plunder us pitilessly, suck all our blood, and carry out a barbarous policy of all-out terrorism and massacre. . . . Some hundreds of years ago, when our country was endangered by the Mongolian invasion, our elders under the Tran dynasty rose up indignantly and called on their sons and daughters throughout the country to rise as one in order to kill the enemy. . . . The elders and prominent personalities of our country should follow the example set by our forefathers in the glorious task of national salvation. . . . Let us unite

CHINA

Bac Bo

VIET BAC

Tan Trao

Dien Bien Phu

HANOI

Haiphong

LAOS

Gulf

of

Tonkin

0   50   100 KILOMETERS
0   50   100 MILES

N

Viet Minh Base Area, 1941–45.

together! As one mind and strength we shall overthrow the Japanese and French. . . .

Back in 1885, an all-out movement of resistance to the French in the name of the emperor Ham Nghi had begun with an edict calling for those with intelligence to contribute ideas, those with strength to lend their force; "the rich shall give money to buy military supplies," while peasants were instructed "not to refuse hardship or evade danger." Ho Chi Minh's father, among many patriotic scholars, had responded to that call. Now, fifty-six years later, in words that drew upon Ham Nghi's edict but pushed well beyond it, Ho Chi Minh called for every Vietnamese to participate in a movement for national salvation:

Rich people, soldiers, workers, peasants, intellectuals, employees, traders, youth, and women who warmly love your country! . . . Let us unite together. . . . He who has money will contribute his money, he who has strength will contribute his strength, he who has talent will contribute his talent. I pledge to use all my modest abilities to follow you, and am ready for the last sacrifice.
      Revolutionary fighters!
      The hour has struck! Raise aloft the insurrectionary banner and

guide the people throughout the country to overthrow the Japanese and the French! The sacred call of the fatherland is resounding in your ears; the blood of our heroic predecessors who sacrificed their lives is stirring in your hearts! . . . Let us rise up quickly! . . . Victory to Vietnam's Revolution!

     Victory to the World's Revolution.

Ho's passionate nationalist appeal thus concluded with an assertion of the ultimate victory of socialism. But the immediate goal was national unity for the sake of national independence. The joining of Vietnamese national and revolutionary goals empowered the Viet Minh, drawing into its ranks that amazing panoply of types Ho's Letter evokes: the elders, prominent personalities, rich people, soldiers, workers, peasants, intellectuals, youth, and women. Obviously neither the French (Vichy or Free) nor the Japanese accepted either national or revolutionary goals as legitimate. In time, to the perhaps mutual surprise of both Vietnamese and Americans, the United States was to reject them as well.[7]

The Viet Minh was the political arm of liberation struggle; the National Salvation Army, organized in February 1941, its military muscle. But the separation is artificial. The army, for all its proud-sounding name, was a tiny band, armed with homemade weapons; as was often the case in the history of the Vietnamese independence movement, its significance was as much political as military.

Cao Bang, like other border provinces, was home to minority peoples (Nung, Tay, Meo, Man, Yao) who had only a limited commitment to the idea of a Vietnamese nation. Many had been pushed out of richer landholdings and into the mountains by lowland Vietnamese. The French, in addition to seizing tribal land and imposing a heavy array of taxes (head, poll, land and property, alcohol, buffalo, opium, kitchen fire), made good use of hostilities between highland and lowland, deepening and exacerbating them as a relatively inexpensive means of dividing and thus controlling their enemy. If the base in Cao Bang were to survive, it would require not only the tolerance of the people of the region but their active sympathy and support.

Efforts to recruit minority people to the Communist Party had begun years earlier: lowland Vietnamese were encouraged to learn the local languages (Ho himself could manage basic conversation in a number of them), care was taken to promote minority cadres, and, most important, the relevance of Party aims to the lives of minority people was explained. An independent Vietnam would do away with corvée labor, conscription, and colonial taxation. It would eliminate inequities of land ownership and "achieve the unity of all nationalities on the basis of equality and mutual assistance. . . ."[8] In the 1940s, these efforts bore fruit as the base in Cao Bang expanded and small highland guerrilla units merged to form the National Army of Salvation. Led by Chu Van Tan, himself a Nung, the National Salvation Army was the nucleus of the liberation army Vo Nguyen Giap would later lead in successive wars against the Japanese, the French, and the Americans. And like that larger force, the National Salvation Army took as its first premise the intimate, symbiotic relationship between the army and the people in whose name it claimed to fight. Mobile educational units taught literacy and the benefits of supporting the Viet Minh:

> Q: What benefits will we enjoy if the revolution succeeds?
> A: We will have equality; men and women will be equal, there will be no oppression. We will have enough to eat, warm clothes to wear, the peasants will have land to till, and there will be no exploitation. We won't have to pay head taxes. . . . We won't have to do labor conscription work.

Cadres for the Viet Minh, like Party cadres earlier, were instructed to learn local languages, customs, and habits, to help people with their daily work, to "teach the local people to sing, read and write, to win their sympathy and little by little to conduct revolutionary propaganda." Of equal importance were the things cadres were *not* to do: cause damage, deface furniture, buy or borrow what people did not wish to sell or lend, forget promises or violate local customs. It was a list that would serve the army well, first in the highlands and later throughout Vietnam.

In July 1944, the Vichy regime in France collapsed; eight months later, in March 1945, the Japanese unilaterally ended French rule in Vietnam, imprisoned the French civilian and military leaders, and replaced them with a puppet regime of their own. During the five-month interlude between the Japanese coup and the end of the Pacific War, the Viet Minh base in Cao Bang expanded to include six provinces in northern Vietnam. In this "liberated zone," entirely new local governments were established, self-defense forces recruited, taxes abolished, rents reduced and, in some places, land that had belonged to French landlords was seized and redistributed. Above all, the Viet Minh acted to alleviate the famine then raging in the North, by opening local granaries and distributing the rice.[9]

Five months later, in August 1945, the combination of American nuclear war and Soviet ground invasion ended the Japanese Empire in Vietnam as elsewhere in Asia. Throughout the region former colonies (the Philippines, Indonesia, Burma, Malaya, Korea, Taiwan, Vietnam, Laos, Cambodia) sought to renegotiate their status with the victorious powers, only to find that wartime conferences in which they played no role had already made decisions that would prove crucial to them. As early as 1943, for example, Franklin Delano Roosevelt, the American president whom historians have considered uniquely sympathetic to the yearnings of colonial peoples, concluded that Indochina should be held in international "trusteeship" until such time as its population was deemed fit to govern itself; by March 1945, Roosevelt was ready to accept France as the trustee, provided the French agreed that "independence was the ultimate goal." Although American authorities were dubious about the future of European colonialism, they were equally wary of the movements for independence that had begun to gain strength during the Pacific War.[10]

Nevertheless, in the last months of the war, the Viet Minh and the Americans had become allies of a sort. American OSS agents (Office of Strategic Services; father to the CIA) relied on Viet Minh networks for intelligence information and help in rescuing downed American airmen. Americans who met Ho were universally impressed. Agents thought he was an "awfully sweet guy," and the OSS gave him six revolvers and an official appointment as OSS Agent 19. The arms and supplies were appreciated; far more important was the hope such contacts gave that an American connection might provide a shield against the return of the French.[11]

On August 15, 1945, news of the Japanese surrender reached Vietnam, along with word that Chinese and British troops would soon arrive in Vietnam to supervise the surrender. A few days later, having made certain the Japanese would not interfere, the Viet Minh called for mass rallies in Hanoi and later in Hue and Saigon. Thousands of peasants poured into the cities from the countryside, demonstrating their support for the Viet Minh in huge rallies. On August 30, Emperor Bao Dai, who had served the French and then the Japanese and would live to serve the French once more, presented the imperial seal and sword, symbols of Vietnamese sovereignty, to representatives of the Viet Minh and voluntarily abdicated the throne, perhaps his first and last act of genuine nationalism. And on September 2, 1945, in the square in Hanoi where his body now rests, Ho faced a crowd of half a million people and, having checked his translation with an American OSS officer, proclaimed Vietnam's independence in the words of the American declaration of national sovereignty. "All men are created equal. The Creator has given us certain inviolable Rights: the right to Life, the right to be Free, and the right to achieve Happiness." At this point he paused, looked out over the crowd, and gently asked, "Do you hear me distinctly, fellow countrymen?" And the crowd answered that they did indeed hear him. Ho named his source and explained its meaning: "These immortal words are taken from the Declaration of Independence of the United States of America in 1776. In a larger sense this means that: All the people on earth are born equal: All the people have the right to live, to be happy, to be free." In the hush that followed, Ho read a specific indictment of French crimes, listing them one by one:

> In the field of politics, they have deprived our people of every democratic liberty.
> They have enforced inhuman laws; they have set up three distinct political regimes in the North, the Centre and the South . . . in order to wreck our national unity and prevent our people from being united.
> They have built more prisons than schools. They have mercilessly slain our patriots; they have drowned our uprisings in rivers of blood. . . .
> They have robbed us of our ricefields, our mines, our forests and our raw materials. . . .

"We are convinced," Ho concluded, "that the Allied nations which at Tehran and San Francisco have acknowledged the principle of self-determination and equality of nations, will not refuse to acknowledge the independence of Vietnam. . . . Vietnam has the right to be a free and independent country—and in fact is so already."[12]

Giap, describing the scene years later, called it the "first great festival of the country. . . . The beautiful autumn sun bathed Ba Dinh Square which from this moment had entered history." That autumn, the Voice of Vietnam began broadcasting from Hanoi. Each time Giap heard its call letters, he wrote, they left "a trailing echo. Vietnam had been reborn."[13]

By October 1945, it was clear that the only people ready to recognize the freedom and independence of Vietnam were the Vietnamese themselves. In late September 1945, the British, charged with administering the Japanese surrender south of the 16th parallel, paused in the disarmament of the Japanese, rearmed French prisoners of war and, with a few Indian Ghurka troops of their own, participated in a coup against the Viet Minh Executive Committee that had been administering Saigon in the name of the Democratic Republic of Vietnam. Thus not only did one colonial power come to the aid of another in need, but it drew on the resources of its colonies to do so. The Indian nationalist leader Pandit Nehru was enraged: "We have watched British intervention [in Indochina] with growing anger, shame and helplessness that Indian troops should thus be used for doing Britain's dirty work against our friends, who are fighting the same fight as we." Still faced with a shortage of troops, Major General Douglas D. Gracey rearmed the Japanese and, when they expressed some reluctance to return to war, threatened to have them tried as war criminals. The sympathy of Japanese troops for the Viet Minh in some instances extended to the point of active assistance; they were condemned by their officers as "traitors to the Emperor," which must have been confusing for everybody. After several days of fighting, the Viet Minh were forced to flee Saigon and regroup in the countryside, and the French were in a position to reclaim the richest of their Indochinese possessions. "Cochin China," at least, might yet be saved for France.[14]

American policy was succinctly expressed in an October 5 telegram from Dean Acheson, then Acting Secretary of State, to the American chargé d'affaires in China: "US has no thought of opposing the reestablishment of French control in Indochina and no official statement by US Government has questioned even by implication French sovereignty over Indochina." Of course, the cable went on, "the willingness of the US to see French control reestablished assumes that French claim to have the support of the population of Indochina is borne out by future events." It was not a claim the secretary chose to investigate with any care. On October 17, Ho Chi Minh appealed to Truman, as he had to Wilson twenty-nine years earlier, to support Vietnamese independence; once again he was met with studied silence.[15]

Americans in Vietnam at the time were more sympathetic to the Vietnamese than their superiors in Washington. Arthur Hale, an official with the U.S. Information Agency, wandered around Hanoi for thirteen days in October 1945. *Blondie Goes to Town* was still playing in one of the local cinemas and young Vietnamese bombarded Hale with questions about America, from the war record of American movie stars to how to run a newspaper or a sanitation department. "They seemed to feel that every American contained within himself all the virtues and accomplishments of the nation they wanted most to emulate." Based on widespread knowledge of America's intention to grant the Philippines independence, people everywhere seemed to expect American support for Vietnamese independence. Hale was familiar with scenes of enthusiastic crowds greeting Americans as liberators, but "nowhere did the coming of Americans, in this case a mere handful of them, mean so much to a people as it did to the population of northern Indochina. To Anna-mites, our coming was the symbol of liberation not from Japanese occupation but from decades of French colonial rule. For the Annamite government considered the United States the principle champion of the rights of small peoples, guaranteed so promisingly by the United Nations conferences."[16]

Meanwhile, the Viet Minh set about establishing the rudiments of government in a country occupied by the troops of three hostile and anti-Communist countries: Nationalist China, Great Britain, and France. In an effort to disarm suspicion that proved futile in the long run, the Communist Party dissolved itself in November 1945 as a sign that it put the "interests of the nation above class interests." National elections were scheduled for December 23, 1945, but delayed due to the fears of conservative nationalists that none of their candidates could win. A bloc of seats in the National Assembly was therefore set aside for the candidates of non-Communist nationalist parties, and the elections went forth on January 6, 1946. This was the first and, some would argue, the last free election in Vietnamese history. There were irregularities and the secret ballot was not perfectly maintained except perhaps in Cochin China, where the French banned the election altogether and the fact that people voted had to be kept secret. Perhaps, one historian has concluded, an election held in strictest conformity to Western rules would have returned one or two more conservatives; but "the general sentiment in favor of independence—and independence under the men who had already proclaimed it—would almost certainly have been as marked." In the district of Hanoi, where he ran, Ho received 90 percent of the vote—a statistic that is instantly suspect, and yet no historian or contemporary journalist has ever questioned its accuracy.[17]

In the North the new government faced continuing famine and a new menace: 180,000 Chinese Nationalist troops, who treated Vietnam as conquered territory, carted off everything normally movable—and much that was not, such as roof tiles. Careful rationing and a mass campaign for planting food crops brought the famine to an end by March 1946. It was a stunning achievement, and it joined a growing list of reforms in other areas (literacy, taxation, labor legislation) that were not merely decreed but acted upon. Within six months of taking power, under their own government and without assistance from any foreign country, the people of North and Central Vietnam were free of famine and colonial taxation, and on the way to universal literacy.

But there was little the government could do about the Chinese, although it was clear that some sort of agreement with the French would have to be reached quickly, before Chiang Kai-shek become more ambitious for rights and privileges in Vietnam or reached a settlement with the French that might further disadvantage the Vietnamese. There was not much time, for in late February 1946 the Chinese agreed to withdraw their troops from Vietnam in exchange for an end to the privileges China had been forced to grant to France in the nineteenth century. Under the terms of this Sino-French convention, French troops would start landing at Haiphong Harbor on March 8.

Ho Chi Minh renewed his appeals to the United States. On February 16, in a long letter to the president, Ho reminded Truman that it was the Viet Minh, not the French, who had fought the Japanese in Indochina, that all the wartime conferences promised independence to subject peoples, that Vietnam wanted no more than the United States had "graciously granted" the Philippines, that in the five months his government had been in office, peace and order had prevailed. Finally, Ho appealed to an argument the United States would itself find useful in the future. Obliquely referring to the Munich Conference of 1938, which all now agreed had encouraged German aggression, Ho charged that French "aggression on a peace-loving people is a direct menace to world security. It implies the complicity, or at least the connivance of the Great Democracies. The United Nations ought to keep their words [sic]. They ought to interfere to stop this unjust war, and to show that they mean to carry out in peace-time the principles for which they fought in war-time."[18]

It was Ho's last letter to the United States and, like the earlier ones, it was never answered. Now, there was no course left other than direct negotiations with France. The French were worried too. Vietnamese armed resistance to French troops would be at best embarrassing, at worst a serious military concern. At the penultimate moment, on March 6, 1946, Ho Chi Minh and the relatively sympathetic French negotiator, Jean Sainteny, signed an agreement that permitted the peaceful landing of fifteen thousand French troops in the North along with ten thousand Vietnamese troops under French command. French troops would be gradually withdrawn until, by 1952, Vietnam would be free of all foreign soldiers. In exchange, France agreed to recognize the Republic of Vietnam, not as an independent nation but as a "free state" within an Indochinese Federation of the French Union, with its own government and army. The precise limitations on the independence of the republic were left vague, as was the timing of a referendum on reunification with southern Vietnam (Cochin China), where Viet Minh resistance to the French continued. The task was now to explain the necessity of such a compromise to a people still flushed with the triumph of independence. Word of the agreement spread through Hanoi and non-Communist nationalists were quick to accuse the Communists of having sold the country to the French.

The next day, March 7, before a huge outdoor rally in the Place du Théâtre, the leaders of the government tried to explain what they had done. Jean Lacouture, a French reporter, watched as Giap walked out onto the balcony of the theater facing the Place and saluted the crowd with a clenched fist: "a menacing silence came over the gathering." Into that silence Giap explained why returning French troops would have to be welcomed rather than resisted. His speech, another French observer later wrote, "rehearsed the entire drama of Vietnam." Throughout the spring of 1946, as again at Geneva in 1954 and, some would argue, once more in Paris in 1973, the goal of complete and absolute independence was compromised in order to save lives, buy time, consolidate the ground on which an independent Vietnam might one day stand.[19]

The country was isolated, Giap explained, and poor. Immediate long-term resistance to the French would require immense and useless sacrifice, for they could not win. The March 6 convention gave Vietnam control of its internal affairs and reunification in the near future—for the result of the promised referendum was certain. There was no way to have prevented the landing of French troops, but now at least there was a written agreement on how long they would stay. Those who wanted to reject the agreement because it fell short of independence understood independence only as a "slogan."[20]

Giap's speech was frank, open, unemotional. Lacouture thought it stilled the angry restiveness of the crowd. Then Ho got up to speak and Lacouture, recalling the outrage he had heard people direct at Ho when they learned of the agreement, was "completely taken aback by the tremendous ovation which rose to greet him." It was, another reporter wrote, "interminable." Ho began with a simple assertion: "It testifies to our intelligence that we should negotiate rather than fight." After reviewing the provisions of the compromise and its virtues one more time, Ho faced the crowd and swore his fealty to them in direct and personal terms:

> I, Ho Chi Minh, I have always led you on the road to freedom, I have all my life fought for the independence of our country. You know that

I would prefer to die rather than sell out the country. I swear to you
that I have not sold you out.

The March 6 agreement might have worked. It was a moment,
David Marr has written, when both sides seem to have "overcome history" in a set of mutual concessions that provided for French acceptance
of an independent Vietnam and Vietnamese acquiescence in an ongoing
French presence in postcolonial Vietnam. On May 31, before leaving for
Paris to negotiate details deliberately left vague in March, Ho Chi Minh
sent a letter to the resistance in the South to ease their concerns about
the course of negotiations. He reiterated his promise not to betray them
and expressed gratitude for their sacrifices. "You in Nam Bo are citizens
of Viet Nam. Rivers may dry up, mountains may erode; but this truth will
never change."[21] The next day, already en route for France, Ho learned
that Admiral Georges Thierry D'Argenlieu had announced the establishment of a separate Republic of Cochin China.

Ho spent the summer of 1946 negotiating with the French. Almost
everyone who met him, in France or Vietnam itself, seems to have been
charmed by him, though some later dismissed it all as a calculated act.
Sainteny has described the way Ho's "face reflected a mixture of intelligence, guile and subtlety. . . ." He was a "person of the highest caliber,"
whose "intelligence, vast culture, unbelievable energy and total unself-
ishness had earned him unparalleled prestige and popularity in the eyes
of his people." A French reporter who met him around this time describes his "engaging manner and extraordinary gift for making contact,"
which "at once brought a warm and direct exchange of views and gave
a startlingly fresh ring to commonplace words." Truong Nhu Tang, an
upper-class Vietnamese from the South studying in Paris, described
meeting Ho at a reception for students. He "wore a frayed, high-collared
Chinese jacket. On his feet he had rubber sandals . . . he gave off an air
of fragility, almost sickliness. But these impressions only contributed to
the imperturbable dignity that enveloped him as though it were something tangible. . . . Ho exuded a combination of inner strength and
personal generosity that struck me with something like a physical blow."
Gathering the students around him:

"Come, my children," he said and sat down on the steps. We settled
around him, as if it were the most natural thing in the world. . . . [Ho's]
message combined ardent and idealistic nationalism with a moving
personal simplicity. Ho had created for us an atmosphere of family
and country and had pointed to our own role in the great patriotic
endeavor.[22]

Ho talked with the ordinary French people around him as well, argued religion with a priest, did his own laundry, dressed with absolute simplicity, and instructed the French on the power of their political vision and the horrors of their colonial policy:

> If you only knew, monsieur, how passionately I reread Victor Hugo and Michelet year after year! There is no mistaking the tone of their writings: it is the tone of the ordinary people in your country. . . . So different . . . from the Frenchmen who have misrepresented your country here. . . . Ah, monsieur, colonialism must certainly be evil if it has the power to transform men to such a degree!

Yet however sincere, however genuinely loving of small children and the rivers and mountains of his native country, Ho was also determined to retain control over the route to independence Vietnam followed.[23]

The talks, held in Fontainebleau so as to make access to Ho by Vietnamese supporters and a sympathetic press more difficult, broke down altogether in August, when the Vietnamese delegation in France learned that D'Argenlieu had convened a conference in the Vietnamese mountain resort town of Dalat to discuss the "framework of the French Union." Representatives from Laos, Cambodia, "the autonomous Republic of Cochinchina," the minority peoples, and an entirely mythical place called "Southern Annam" were all invited, but not the Republic of Vietnam whose existence France had presumably recognized in the March 6 agreement. Ho's desire to achieve the substance of reunification and independence without war was predominant and he was desperate to return to Hanoi with something, however little, that could "arm [him] against his own extremists." On September 14, Ho woke the Minister of Overseas Territories, Marius Moutet, in the middle of the night and persuaded him to sign a *"modus vivendi"* that might stave off war just a little longer. The broad outlines of the March 6 agreement were reaffirmed, the French were granted new economic concessions in the North and in exchange agreed to protect "democratic rights" in Cochin China. There was to be a cease-fire in the South that would begin October 30. And that was all. No date was set for the referendum; no further steps taken toward defining the relationship between the "free state of Vietnam" and the French Union.

Returning home in October 1946, Ho once again faced the task of explaining to the country why independence and reunification must still wait. And once again, the popular response was overwhelming. A cynical French observer described the train trip from Haiphong to Hanoi, the train stopping every mile or so to receive the cheers of peasants along the route. "Old Ho . . . would bound to the door, take out a red handkerchief and wipe his eyes. . . . What a marvelous actor!"

In a proclamation released on October 23, 1946, Ho appealed to the people of his country for time, patience, and discipline. He reminded them that France had not rescinded its promise of a referendum. Moreover, under the *modus vivendi,* "our southern compatriots are to have freedom of organization, of meeting, of the press, of movement, etc." In exchange, they must refrain from "all acts of reprisal." "Violent actions are absolutely forbidden. This is what you have to do at present to create a peaceful atmosphere, paving the way democratically to reach the unification of our Viet Nam."[24]

But the creation of a peaceful atmosphere was not really up to Ho Chi Minh. Colonial authorities in the South viewed the *modus vivendi* as a disaster. Any recognition of the Viet Minh was, in their view, the opening wedge of a process that would in time end French power throughout Indochina. To safeguard the autonomy of the South, some argued, it would be necessary to carry the war North.[25] All that was wanted was an incident. In late November, a clash over who controlled the customs in Haiphong Harbor proved sufficient. Local French and Vietnamese authorities had finally resolved the issue when the French military commander in Saigon, Jean Valluy, whose plans for a military démarche against the North were already well under way, decided the time had come to make a decisive move. On November 22, he instructed the French commander in Hanoi to "give a harsh lesson" to the Vietnamese, using "every means at your disposal" to seize Haiphong and force the evacuation of Vietnamese troops from the city. When an ultimatum to surrender the city to the French was ignored, Valluy ordered an all-out attack. Bombarded by ships anchored in the harbor, the unprotected city of Haiphong fell to the French. There were at least 6,000 people killed, some 25,000 wounded.

And still Ho Chi Minh attempted to negotiate. But now the pressure for war, both within his own ranks and from an increasingly aggressive French military command, was irresistible. Ho's telegrammed appeals to the new French president for renewed negotiations were deliberately delayed by the French in Saigon; last-minute efforts by conciliatory Parisian authorities were similarly sabotaged in Saigon. On December 19, 1946, at eight o'clock in the evening, the war for independence, already a year old in the South, engulfed the North as well. Years later, Giap described Hanoi that night:

Dusk fell. The whole city was unusually quiet. It was cold and dry. The houses seemed to shrink back and to be standing warming themselves in the yellowish electric light. Outwardly the city seemed to grow lacy in the cold and to go to bed early. But beneath this calm surface, line upon line of surging wave was ready to rise.[26]

The offensive against French positions in Hanoi launched that night by local militia failed. But many of the leaders managed to escape to bases which had already been established outside the city. For however hard Ho Chi Minh may have tried to maintain the peace, he had hardly neglected the possibility that war might come. The army under Giap's command had by now expanded from several thousand in September 1945 to over sixty thousand in December 1946 when the order for "nationwide resistance" was broadcast. It would grow exponentially thereafter. In addition to the army, there were support organizations of youth (1 million Vanguard Youth), peasants (820,000), and the Viet Minh itself (500,000). Strong in popular support, the government lacked everything else: military supplies, economic strength, international allies. In their place Ho appealed to the country for unity, irrespective of ideology, and for struggle: "Those who have rifles will use their rifles; those who have swords will use their swords; those who have no swords will use spades, hoes or sticks. . . . Long live an independent and unified Vietnam! Long live the victorious Resistance."[27]

CHAPTER TWO

The Thirty-Year War Begins (1946–1954)

Question [whether] Ho as much nationalist as Commie is
irrelevant. All Stalinists in colonial areas are nationalists.
—CABLE, MAY 20, 1949,
SECRETARY OF STATE DEAN ACHESON
TO U.S. CONSUL, HANOI

In prison camp we faced the reality of the Vietminh and we
saw that for eight years our generals had been struggling
against a revolution without knowing what a revolution was.
—FRENCH VIETNAM VETERAN TO
LUCIEN BODARD, HANOI, 1954

IN THE WINTER OF 1946, French inability to deal with a recalcitrant colony was only one of a host of problems facing Acting Secretary of State Dean Acheson. In Korea, a major uprising in the American military zone had been crushed, but unrest continued; the outcome of the emerging civil war in China was uncertain at best and there was considerable pressure on Washington to take a more active role in its disposition; the European economic situation remained bleak; there were serious crises in Greece, Iran, and Turkey. Abbot Low Moffat, head of the Division of Southeast Asia, arrived in Hanoi early in December 1946 carrying clear instructions: in all dealings he was to remember that Ho Chi Minh was an unrepentant Communist and that the Department would hardly look with favor on the establishment of a Communist-dominated Vietnam. Indeed, while Moffat was in Vietnam he was to explore the "strength [of] non-communist elements [in] Vietnam." When

20

he met Ho Chi Minh, Moffat was to suggest the possibility of a compromise on the status of Cochin China. Finally, Moffat was to congratulate Ho on the attainments of the people of Indochina in their search for "greater autonomy in [the] framework [of] democratic institutions," and stress how "regrettable" it would be if Ho's government were to "force issues by intransigence and violence." As for the French, Moffat was to suggest that D'Argenlieu's open contempt for the Vietnamese had perhaps made him a less than useful administrator and to urge restraint in the use of force.

Moffat reported back to Acheson after their meeting that Ho might be an unrepentant Communist, but he was, first and foremost, a nationalist seeking to establish an "effective nationalist state" as a "prerequisite to any attempt at developing a communist state—which objective must for the time being be secondary." Moffat's early judgment was echoed by virtually all American officials stationed in Vietnam at the time. While the consul in Saigon, for example, questioned how far one could trust "communist-trained Ho Chi Minh," he recognized that "the majority of natives stoutly maintain that Ho Chi Minh is the man, *and the only one,* who represents them and they will oppose the putting forward of any other candidate as the creation of but another puppet. . . ."[1]

There were moments in 1946 and 1947, before the world began the zero-sum game called the Cold War, when even very senior American officials were able to ask other than rhetorical questions. In July 1947, Secretary of State George Marshall, whose experience in China had alerted him to the complexities of revolutionary nationalism, asked the American consuls in Hanoi and Saigon to think about the likelihood of an unaligned, independent Vietnam led by Ho Chi Minh. While both men insisted that the "Annamites" remained incapable of genuine self-government, neither thought Soviet domination a necessary result of a Viet Minh victory. But Marshall did not pursue the thought.

The State Department's dilemma was evident well before Ho Chi Minh had flattered and embarrassed the United States by declaring Vietnamese independence in the language of 1776, indeed even before the Pacific War ended. While the Southeast Asia desk at the Department urged that some attention be paid to Vietnamese nationalism, the European desk insisted that the stability, prosperity, and goodwill of France in Europe was of paramount interest to the United States. Had the French been content simply to grant Vietnam independence under the auspices of the Viet Minh, it is unlikely the United States would have objected. But France defined its well-being in terms of repossessing its lost colony, not only as a balm to wounded national vanity, but because of a reasonable fear that an independent Vietnam would threaten French interests in the economically far more significant colonies of Algeria, Morocco, and Tunisia. The United States decided it had little choice but to support the French. America's own plans for a healthy postwar order rested on a stable, prosperous France ready to play its proper role in an economic and military world system dominated by the United States, which saw itself acting in the interests of the entire "free world." The electoral strength of the French Communist Party endangered this vision, and if Washington had any doubt about the importance of U.S. support for France in Indochina, de Gaulle made the connection explicit. "If the public here comes to realize that you are against us in Indochina," he had warned Harry Hopkins in 1945, "there will be terrific disappointment and nobody knows to what that will lead. We do not want to become Communist; we do not want to fall into the Russian orbit, but I hope you will not push us into it."[2]

The Truman administration had no intention of pushing. Instead, substantial material aid was made available to France to pursue its war against the Viet Minh, including $160 million in direct credit late in 1946 expressly for use in Vietnam. In addition, Washington acquiesced in the diversion to the war of economic and military aid earmarked for French domestic reconstruction. To France, the reconquest of Vietnam *constituted* reconstruction, and the United States raised no objection despite some discomfort. "Colonial empires in [the] XIX Century sense," the State Department cabled the Paris Embassy in January 1947, "are rapidly becoming [a] thing of the past." At the same time, the United States had "no interest in seeing colonial empire administrations supplanted by [the] philosophy and political organization emanating from and controlled by [the] Kremlin." But was Ho Chi Minh controlled from the Kremlin? If he was, opposition to Ho could reasonably be presented as an aspect of a larger policy directed against Soviet expansionism, rather than as an opportunistic betrayal of American ideals for the sake of a European ally.

From January 1946 until Dean Acheson resolved the issue some three years later, American consuls in Saigon and Hanoi, as well as traveling State Department officials, were repeatedly asked by the Department to measure "how Communist" Ho Chi Minh really was. Over and over, the answer came back that he was certainly a Communist, but that he put nationalism first, had no known direct ties to the Soviet Union, but was relentless in his pursuit of direct ties to the United States. Almost every American who met with Vietnamese officials in these early years reported back constant appeals for aid, capital, technology—and no signs of a Soviet presence. A State Department summary of the situation in Vietnam, compiled in September 1948, noted the continuing lack of any evidence of direct communication between the Soviet Union and Vietnam. Even more problematic was the "unpleasant fact" that Ho Chi Minh remained the "strongest and perhaps the ablest figure in Indochina and that any suggested solution which excludes him is an expedient of uncertain outcome."[3]

In October 1948, the State Department Office of Intelligence Research was chagrined to find Soviet influence throughout Southeast Asia, but not in Vietnam. "If there is a Moscow-directed conspiracy in Southeast Asia, Indochina is an anomaly so far," the report concluded. Hard put to explain its findings, the report listed three possibilities: Moscow had not issued any rigid directives to the Vietnamese; the "Vietnam Communists are not subservient to the foreign policies pursued by Moscow"; or Vietnam had been given "a special dispensation . . . in Moscow." Of these, without feeling the need to argue the case, the report chose the first and third. In short, if there was no evidence Moscow was giving the orders, then obviously the Vietnamese didn't even need orders; that's how obedient they were.[4]

Finally, in May 1949, Secretary of State Acheson abandoned the search for hard evidence. A simple equation could replace all this effort to observe and report. Ho was an "outright Commie" so long as he "(1) fails to unequivocally repudiate Moscow connection and Commie doctrine and (2) remains personally singled out for praise by [the] international Commie press. . . ." All Communists in colonial countries—Acheson cabled consuls in Hanoi, Saigon, and Paris—were Stalinists, and as soon as independence was achieved, their "objective necessarily becomes subordination [of the] state to Commie purposes. . . ." How did Acheson know? "On the basis [of the] example [of] eastern Eur[ope]," his cable of clarification read, "it must be assumed such [would] be [the] goal [of] Ho and men [of] his stamp. . . ." Of course there was a theoretical possibility of the "estab[lishment of a] National Communist state on [the] pattern [of] Yugoslavia in any area beyond Soviet army. However, US attitude [could] take acc[oun]t [of] such [a] possibility only if every other possible avenue closed to preservation area from Kremlin control."[5]

A further refining of theorems, however, was desirable. State Department analysts recognized the power of "militant nationalism" in Asia and deplored the stubborn refusal of European colonial powers like France and the Netherlands to make judicious concessions to Asia's demands. It was that stubborn resistance that had forced the United States into its distressing alliance with anachronistic European colonialism. Yet the real conflict, the State Department insisted, was not between Asian nationalism and the West but between Communism and nationalism. If the French withdrew from Indochina, a 1949 State Department review of Southeast Asia explained, "the false issue of French imperialism," which obscured the "basic conflict between nationalism and Stalinism," would disappear. Should the French withdraw and the Viet Minh take over, civil war would certainly break out. Then, "foreign anti-communists, including ourselves," operating "through a screen of anti-communist Asiatics," could work "to ensure, however long it takes, the triumph of Indochinese nationalism over Red imperialism."

Here was a formula that at one blow met the needs of America's anti-colonial ideology and the reality of its postwar position as hegemon of world capitalism. By definition, Communists could not be genuine nationalists; by definition, America supported genuine nationalism. Therefore, those people the United States supported were nationalists, the rest were Communist stooges.

Vietnam was only one country in which the political geometry of the postwar world was being worked out. Much had been learned, as Acheson pointed out, from the history of Europe, lessons that would now be applied elsewhere. These lessons involved redrawing the demographic map of the world. In the press as in official government statements, the Soviet Union and Eastern Europe, with the exception of Yugoslavia, were referred to only as the domain of the Communists, rather than Russians, Central Asians, Rumanians, Hungarians, Czechs, or Bulgarians. As for China, after October 1949, there were no more Chinese there, only Communists. The remaining Chinese lived on the small island of Taiwan. The same was true of Korea, where the United States fought a war against "Communist aggression" from the North. At its conclusion, Koreans continued to live in South Korea, but only Communists lived in the North. In Vietnam, the French fought Communists, not Vietnamese.

For U.S. leaders in government, business, and the press, Communism had become a culture, a language; it could even define a race of people. Still more frightening was the fact that they could look just like you and me, as anti-Communist loyalty hearings and trials soon made clear. The terrifying thing about Communism, the American people were instructed by their leaders, was the way it spread. "Internal aggression" is what Truman called it when he announced a new foreign policy doctrine in 1947. He had pledged the United States to fight it everywhere. Communism attacked not only from outside a country (as when North Korea attacked South Korea) but also from inside. Communism was a virus, a vicious form of political life much like that newly identified biological form. The task of the United States was to stand by those governments attempting to "root it out," as well as to pose a credible military threat to the main sources of contamination—China and the Soviet Union. Communism could be contained. When it was frozen within its borders, Communism could be prevented from attacking healthy organisms.

Keeping the organism healthy was another aspect of the complex foreign policy arsenal developed to meet the Communist threat. Government analysts and academic observers agreed that misery and poverty were the breeding ground for Communism, whose ruthless and cynical operatives would manipulate people for their own ends. The international system the United States sought to create after the war required constant maintenance and attention. Third World markets must be kept open and available to European customers of American goods; how else would they pay for U.S. imports when the Marshall Plan ended in 1952? Furthermore, American planners, as if extrapolating from Gracey's use of Japanese troops to fight the Viet Minh, concluded that Japanese economic recovery depended on its control of Southeast Asian markets; otherwise Japan would either remain an American ward (impossible) or seek accommodations with Communist China (intolerable). And so the United States, which had fought the Pacific War in the name of ending Japan's Greater East-Asian Co-Prosperity Sphere, now worked to resurrect it in the name of defeating communism.[6]

At Truman's request a number of studies were undertaken on how best to meet the Soviet threat, made more terrible by the knowledge that the Soviet Union had broken the American monopoly on nuclear power in August 1949. In April 1950, a report to the National Security Council by the secretaries of state and defense, best known by its serial number, NSC-68, put it all together in a document that outlined the position of the United States in the world and instructed the president on how to safeguard it.[7] NSC-68 sounded the tocsin: "The issues that face us are momentous, involving the fulfillment or destruction not only of this Republic but of civilization itself." In the past, despite recurrent wars, no one country had been able to achieve world hegemony. Now, in the face of the defeat of Germany and Japan and the waning of the European empires, one state, "animated by a new fanatic faith," had emerged to claim that hegemony. Through violent and non-violent means alike, a nuclear armed Soviet Union intended to "bring the free world under its dominion. . . ." The attack was internal as well as external, a plan to subvert American institutions through "infiltration and intimidation."

Nothing was safe and nothing sacred: "Those [institutions] that touch most closely our material and moral strength are obviously the prime targets, labor unions, civic enterprises, schools, churches, and all media for influencing opinion." The Communists were very clever. "The effort is not so much to make [these institutions] serve obvious Soviet ends as to prevent them from serving our ends and thus make them sources of confusion in our economy, our culture and our body politic." Thus American values of diversity and freedom were actually vulnerabilities that allowed the Kremlin to "do its evil work."

To meet the Soviet threat, NSC-68 called for a policy of aggressive "containment," in which the United States seeks

> by all means short of war to (1) block further expansion of Soviet power, (2) expose the falsities of Soviet pretensions, (3) induce a retraction of the Kremlin's control and influence and (4) in general, so foster the seeds of destruction within the Soviet system that the Kremlin is brought at least to the point of modifying its behavior to conform to generally accepted international standards.

In this report, a policy of containment merges with one of "roll-back." Central to its implementation was a major increase in military spending so as to ensure America's "superior overall power," in conventional as well as nuclear weapons. The plan called for a sharp increase in military aid to U.S. allies, a "militarized version of international Keynesianism," in Thomas McCormick's apt phrase.[8] Programs must also be developed to "build and maintain confidence among other peoples in our strength and resolution, and to wage overt psychological warfare calculated to encourage mass defections from Soviet alliegiance. . . ." Covert economic, political, and psychological warfare would receive funds and attention so as to foment rebellion and unrest in "selected strategic satellite countries." The development and improvement of U.S. internal security and intelligence capacities was an absolute must. Funding all this would require some increase in taxation and the reduction or deferment of federal expenditures "for purposes other than defense and foreign assistance," no matter how desirable the project. Since a parsimonious Congress was unlikely to vote such funds, one official urged a "scare campaign."[9] In the event, the campaign was unnecessary: the Korean War, which began in June 1950, was all the scare Congress needed.

Here then was the blueprint for the Cold War state: one armed ideologically and materially against an evil Kremlin; a democracy able to overcome the vulnerabilities freedom entails and to conduct covert and overt war when and where necessary, short of all-out war, so as to foil "piecemeal aggression," its economy streamlined for the purpose, irrespective of other needs. It was a vision of the United States formed in the mirror Washington held up to the entity that was now almost always referred to in sinister tones as "the Kremlin": America through a glass darkly. Early American support for the French reconquest of Vietnam had been rooted in its concern for French recovery. With Mao's triumph in China and the Korean War, the division between those who put Europe first and those who worried about the rest of the world disappeared. Now, to help France fight to retain its Indochinese colony was to fight communism.

There were some problems with this definition. For example, "internal aggression" as opposed to the more familiar variety was not always easy to identify. Was a large demonstration against a military dictatorship actually an early sign of internal aggression? Or was it merely a symptom of the dictator's growing unpopularity? When a popularly elected president moved to implement a moderate land reform policy (as in Guatemala in the mid-1950s), did that mean he was a captive of the Communists? Or was he simply fulfilling an election promise? For almost twenty years after the end of World War II these reasonable questions were very difficult not only to answer but also to raise; even asking them was taken as a symptom of "softness" on the issue of communism. Although the postwar administrations sometimes disagreed along party lines on the appropriate tactics to be employed, there was a general consensus on foreign policy. By the early 1950s, both parties had accepted a set of axioms derived from NSC-68 as unquestionable as Euclid's. We can summarize these axioms as follows:

1. The intentions of the United States are always good. It is possible that in pursuit of good ends, mistakes will be made. But the basic goodness of U.S. intentions cannot ever be questioned. The intentions of the enemies of the United States are bad. It is possible that in the pursuit of bad ends, good things will seem to happen. But the basic badness of enemy intentions cannot ever be questioned.

2. Communism, on the other hand, is fundamentally bad; indifferent to human life, individual values, ordinary moral scruples. Moreover, in order to solidify its absolute control within the Soviet Union and the Soviet bloc, communism must expand. Quoting NSC-68, the fundamental design of the Soviet Union calls "for the complete subversion or forcible destruction of the machinery of government and structure of society in the coun-

tries of the non-Soviet world and their replacement by an apparatus subservient to and controlled from the Kremlin." Thus the
Soviet Union and communism are inherently aggressive.

3. The most important lesson of recent world history is never to
appease an aggressor. The softness of the democracies at Munich
encouraged Germany and Japan to start World War II. Aggression, "internal" or "external," must be stopped early if it is to be
stopped at all.

4. In the nuclear age all-out war against communism is impossible.
Instead, Communists must be strictly contained. In a shrinking
world, the fate of each country is linked to that of all others. The
free world is only as strong as its weakest link; thus the fall to
communism of any country threatens the security of the United
States and so the fate of the entire world itself.[10]

5. Communists feel no restrictions on the means they use to
achieve their ends; a free society, on the other hand, often feels
itself constrained. Nevertheless, the United States, NSC-68 ad-
vises, should not feel that it has compromised its values by "any
measures, covert or overt, violent or non-violent, which serve
the purposes of frustrating the Kremlin design . . . provided only
they are appropriately calculated to that end and are not so
excessive or misdirected as to make us enemies of the people
instead of the evil men who have enslaved them."

Most Americans, absorbed in their own domestic pursuits, did not
pay close attention to the foreign policy of the United States, except at
times of crisis. There was no large war, but there seemed never to be a
year when the world was entirely at peace. In the main, successive
administrations made foreign policy decisions without undue interference from a public whose sons were drafted or enlisted, whose taxes
steadily rose, and who may have occasionally wondered whether the
sense of peace they had briefly enjoyed in 1945 would ever return.

In churches and schools, the lessons of anti-communism were part
of the religious and secular curricula. Peace could only come from
strength; war could only be avoided if the Communists believed we were
ready to fight. Logically, this war was without physical or temporal
boundaries. It would last as long as the Communists insisted on pursuing
a course of internal and external aggression. To fail to respond to the
challenge was to appease the enemy.

The end of fighting in Korea, then, could only mean a pause between wars, a truce rather than a peace. There could be no full demobili-
zation in the face of such an enemy. In the movies, Korean War veterans

sometimes went on to fight in advance of their government's call. In *China Gate*, released in 1957, several Americans come to the aid of the beleaguered French in Vietnam. One explains that "Korea got cold— Indochina got hot." Another patriotic American, played by Nat King Cole, declares that he hadn't finished what he'd set out to do in Korea. "There are still a lot of live Commies around."

Vietnam was a domino whose "fall" would turn the Pacific into a Soviet lake, denying vital raw materials to the United States and its allies. Throughout both the Truman and Eisenhower administrations, French conduct of the war in Indochina was closely monitored and their needs generously met.[11] The United States supplied the French with war materiel of all sorts, including transport planes and American crews to service them. Apparently, no one in American public life looked directly at the army receiving this aid, which consisted of approximately 80,000 French soldiers; 20,000 Foreign Legionnaires, 10,000 of whom had served in Nazi armies; 48,000 gathered from France's other colonies; and some 300,000 Vietnamese. The use of "native" troops was the subject of endless debate and the decision to "yellow" the Expeditionary Force taken only in the face of dire manpower shortages. The war was too unpopular in France to risk conscription, and the supply of troops from other colonies was limited. Similarly, the casualty rate among French officers (half the graduating class of St. Cyr, the French West Point, for each year of the war) moved the high command to establish a military academy to train Vietnamese officers in 1950.[12] Under the Elysée Agreements, signed in March 1949, this army fought in the name of a State of Vietnam headed by the emperor Bao Dai, who had been recalled from the beaches of the French Riviera into the service of French colonialism. To Bao Dai, whose total dependence was assured, the French granted all they had withheld from Ho Chi Minh.

Opposing this force were Viet Minh troops, ultimately numbering 350,000 plus hundreds of thousands of Vietnamese organized into support groups, fighting a "people's war" in the the name of the Democratic Republic of Vietnam, under President Ho Chi Minh. The strong united front of all classes Ho had called into being in the 1940s against the Japanese was now directed against the French and their colonial army, but after five or six years of war there were severe strains. As control over territory shifted from the French to the Viet Minh and back to the French again, many peasants dropped out of active involvement, and those landlords and richer peasants who sought only to join the winning side abandoned the cause at the first opportunity. But the successful waging of a people's war depends, above all, on the fullest possible mobilization of a committed population.

In February 1951, the Indochinese Communist Party, which had been disbanded in November 1945 out of consideration for the sensibilities of non-Communist nationalists, was resurrected as the Lao Dong (Workers' Party; a separate organization for Cambodia was established later in 1951 and the Laos People's Party was founded in 1955). Over the next two years, land policies that had been generally flouted were now enforced. Effective rent reduction and land redistribution (even of land belonging to landlords allied with the Viet Minh) renewed peasant allegiance to the Viet Minh. In the midst of the bitter military struggle with France, indeed, as an integral part of that struggle, the government conducted an agrarian revolution that transformed the countryside. The twin goals of revolution and nationalism that had marked all of Ho Chi Minh's life were now entirely fused. Out of the power generated by that fusion, the Vietnamese were able successively to defeat the modern industrialized military power ranged against them first by the French and later by the United States.[13]

By 1950, the war had assumed the shape it would retain until its end four years later: Viet Minh control of most of the countryside, north to south; French control of the cities, north to south. But the international context in which the war was fought had changed considerably. Mao Zedong's victory in China gave the Vietnamese not merely an ally but, for the first time, direct material aid. In addition to formal recognition (which the Soviet Union also extended in January 1950), the Chinese shipped across the border a rich supply of American arms captured from Chinese Nationalist troops during the Chinese Civil War. At the same time, the United States increased both its direct military aid to France and its stake in a French victory. To Washington, the war in Vietnam— whose specific historical circumstances had never been of great interest—was now wholly assimilated in the worldwide fight against communism in general and its Asian branch in particular.

As French casualties mounted without any visible sign of an early victory, French public opinion turned vociferously against the war and the government contemplated the possibilities of a negotiated peace. After all, Premier Joseph Laniel reasoned, the Americans were negotiating an armistice in Korea. But first the French must win some signal victory so that they might negotiate, when the time came, from strength. Precisely because of the armistice in Korea, however, the Eisenhower administration felt strongly that the French must hold out in Indochina, which had now become the crucial domino. The loss of Indochina, Eisenhower told a press conference in what was becoming a familiar litany, would bring in its train the loss of Burma, Thailand, Indonesia, Malaya; threaten Japan, Formosa, the Philippines, Australia, and New Zealand. In economic terms it would deprive "the world" of Southeast Asian tin, tungsten, and rubber. Finally, Japan "must have [that region] as a trading partner or Japan, in turn, will have only one place in the world to go— that is, toward the Communist areas in order to live." Thus, "the possible consequences of the loss [of Indochina] are just incalculable to the free world." As careful political analysis, it made little sense; as the expression of axiomatic American policy, it was complete.[14]

The French were assured that every resource, save only American combat troops and nuclear weapons, would be at their disposal. Before the war ended, some American officials were ready to offer both. In pursuit of a victory that would give them an effective negotiating position at least, a solid victory at best, the French launched what turned out to be their last campaign in Indochina. In 1953, in a flat valley surrounded by high hills close to the Lao border, General Henri Navarre positioned twelve well-supplied battalions of troops (13,000 men; over the course of the battle, some 16,500) in the heavily fortified village of Dienbienphu. To this were added a force of six fighter bombers and ten tanks. The central base was further protected by strongpoints established in the surrounding hills, named, some said, by commanding officer de Castries for his mistresses: Beatrice, Gabrielle, Dominique, Éliane, Claudine. Field brothels of Vietnamese and Algerian women were deployed to solace the men.

Confident of his superior resources and certain that the Viet Minh would run out of supplies in less than a week, Navarre dared the commander of the Viet Minh forces, Vo Nguyen Giap, to attack.

The Vietnamese did attack, but in their own time. Through terrain the French had considered impassable, 200,000 peasants hacked trails and moved supplies as far as 500 miles to the battlefront. They laid hundreds of miles of roads. All through the North, women and men mobilized to transport dismantled howitzers and mortars (American in the main, captured by the Chinese in Korea), tons of ammunition, and rice by bicycle and shoulder pole. Troops and equipment, doubly camouflaged by jungle foliage which they attached to themselves and through which they moved, scattered whenever they heard the engines of the French planes searching for them. The combat troops, four divisions strong (49,000 men), carried their own weapons and food supply—a 30-pound bag of rice—as well as water and salt. Daily the column of porters and soldiers was strafed, bombed, napalmed; and daily they ad-

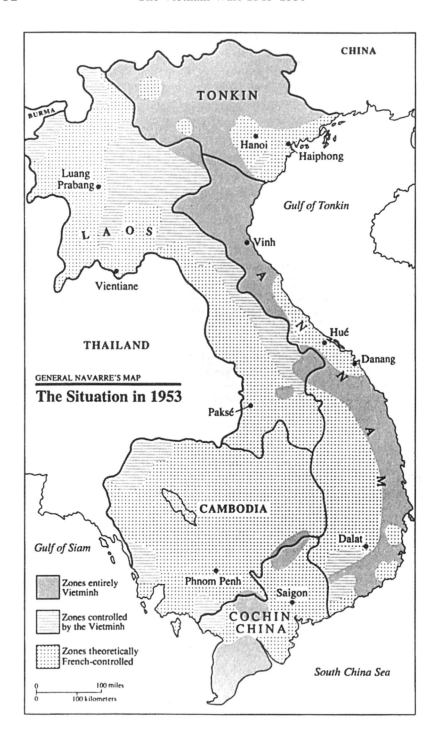

CHINA

TONKIN

BURMA

Hanoi

Haiphong

Luang
Prabang

Gulf of Tonkin

L A O S

Vinh

Vientiane

A

THAILAND

N

Hué

Danang

GENERAL NAVARRE'S MAP

The Situation in 1953

Paksé

N

CAMBODIA

A

Gulf of Siam

M

Dalat

Phnom Penh

Saigon

	Zones entirely Vietminh
	Zones controlled by the Vietminh
	Zones theoretically French-controlled

COCHIN
CHINA

South China Sea

0   100 miles

0   100 kilometers

vanced. Roped to the heaviest artillery pieces, men dragged the guns through the last 50-mile stretch of jungle where no roads could be built. In all, it took three months. When they reached the French base, they reassembled the heavy guns and set them up in caves dug deep into the hillsides so that they were invisible from the air, as was the entire attack force itself. In addition, hundreds of kilometers of trenches and tunnels reached to the very edges of the French position.[15]

Impatient, the French High Command dropped leaflets on the hills and roads surrounding Dienbienphu challenging the Vietnamese: "What are you waiting for? Why don't you attack if you aren't cowards? We are waiting for you." On March 13, 1954, when everything was in place, Giap began the attack. A French Legionnaire recalled the confidence, even relief, with which news of the attack was received: "Indeed we would have to consider as crazy the Viets who would have the idea to try and dislodge us from our Hill Beatrice, well fortified and defended by a whole Foreign Legion battalion. Believe me, it would be no simple walk in the sun for them!" But then Giap's guns opened fire, and "we are all surprised and ask ourselves how the Viets have been able to find so many guns capable of producing an artillery fire of such power. Shells rained down on us without stopping like a hailstorm on a fall evening. Bunker after bunker, trench after trench, collapsed, burying under them men and weapons." By midnight of that first day, strongpoint Beatrice was wiped out; its artillery commander a suicide.[16]

Earlier, despite American opposition, the Laniel government had decided to place the subject of Indochina on the agenda of a major international conference already scheduled for late April 1954 in Geneva. As the siege tightened, parochial schoolchildren all over America prayed for the French Army to defeat the atheist infidel, while in a more practical vein the Eisenhower administration discussed the possibility of direct U.S. intervention.

Air Force chief of staff Nathan Twining and the chairman of the Joint Chiefs of Staff, Admiral Arthur Radford, thought three tactical nuclear bombs dropped carefully on Dienbienphu could save the day. "You could take all day to drop a bomb," Twining recalled years later, "make sure you put it in the right place. No opposition. And clean those Commies out of there and the band could play the Marseillaise and the French would come marching out of Dien Bien Phu in fine shape. And those Commies would say, 'Well, those guys may do this again to us. We'd better be careful.'"[17] An attractive prospect to Radford and Twining perhaps, but not to the Army chief of staff, Matthew Ridgway, nor to Eisenhower and Dulles, who rejected nuclear as well as a recommended

massive conventional bombing attack (code-named Operation VUL-
TURE). Instead, Dulles and Eisenhower looked toward the establishment
of an alliance, called "United Action," which included Great Britain,
Australia, New Zealand, France, Thailand, and the Philippines, as well
as the Indochinese states—Laos, Cambodia, Vietnam. Such a coalition,
acting in the name of the Indochinese states themselves, could, if necessary, pick up the fallen baton from the hand of France; or perhaps, just
knowing of its existence, the Communists would back off or the French
hold on a little longer. In order to provide for all contingencies, the
administration called a meeting with leading members of Congress, seeking advance approval for the use of "air and sea power in the area if he
[the President] felt it necessary in the interest of national security."[18]

But the congressmen, answering to constituencies still absorbing
the shock of Korean War dead and the inconclusiveness of its outcome,
were cautious. They would approve only if it could be guaranteed in
advance that the British would indeed enter the war as full allies.
Morover, the French must grant full and complete independence to
Indochina since, the congressmen argued, the United States could hardly
fight in the name of French colonialism. The British refused, and the
French rejected what amounted to a surrender of French war aims
without an end to French war sacrifices.

Meanwhile, the battle at Dienbienphu was proceeding. After a
week of intense fighting, Viet Minh artillery had successfully targeted the
airstrip, keeping it under constant fire and making bombing runs, resupply, and evacuation of the wounded virtually impossible. Giap's own
forces continued to be supplied by the extraordinary system of civilian
porters that had transported the anti-aircraft guns and howitzers to
Dienbienphu, as well as by an occasional enemy error. In April, for
example, three U.S. supply planes missed the French base altogether and
unloaded 119 tons of howitzer and mortar ammunition behind the lines,
where they were at once put to use against the French. As the siege
moved into its final weeks, the French appealed to the United States for
a saving air strike. At Dienbienphu, Major Bigeard told his men to hold
out just one more day: "The Americans will not let us down; the free
world will not let us down. They may come." But they did not come.
Given congressional scruples, Eisenhower and Dulles could not act without the British, and the British would not act. "None of us in London,"
Eden firmly told Dulles on April 25, "believe that intervention in Indochina can do anything." Nor was Churchill very sympathetic. He had
himself suffered "many reverses," he mused at a formal dinner party
next evening. "I have suffered Singapore, Hong-Kong, Tobruk; the

French will have Dien Bien Phu." How could British citizens be asked to fight for Indochina when they had let India go without a fight?[19]

All through the night of May 6, the survivors on Éliane, one of the last remaining outposts, could hear the Viet Minh, only a few hundred yards away, singing the song of the French Resistance, written to inspire partisans against the Nazi invader. The words, in this setting, were both ironic and exact: "Friend, can you hear the black song of the crow on the plain? Friend, freedom is listening to us in the night."[20]

On May 7, 1954, the French command at Dienbienphu surrendered. It was May 8 in Europe, the ninth anniversary of the German surrender. In Geneva, delegations from France, Great Britain, the United States, China, the USSR, Cambodia, Laos, and Vietnam had been in session for several weeks discussing problems relating to Berlin and Korea. Now the subject turned to Indochina. Georges Bidault, the French foreign minister, in a choked voice announced the fall of Dienbienphu and then proposed an immediate cease-fire in Indochina.

"It was all for nothing," a French survivor of Dienbienphu told the reporter Lucien Bodard, as they sat drinking in the Normandy bar in Hanoi some months later. "In the prison camp the Viets told us they had won because they were fighting for an ideal, and we were not," he went on. "I told them about my paras at Dienbienphu. I told them how they fought. And they said, 'Heroism is no answer.' "[21] The Vietnamese victory at Dienbienphu summarized the entire war. On the basis of a nationalist appeal that was at the same time revolutionary, the government of Vietnam had organized and inspired a poor, untrained, ill-equipped population to fight and ultimately win against a far better equipped and trained army. It had done so through the integration of political and military struggle and through tactics of the utmost flexibility. Initially, the only way to meet the far superior French forces was through classic guerrilla warfare—sharp, fast, disruptive raids. Gradually it became possible to engage in more mobile tactics, engaging units of comparable size and strength, combining the techniques of both guerrilla and conventional warfare. Finally, at Dienbienphu, it all came together: the strength necessary to launch what Giap called a "general counteroffensive" based on the efforts of thousands of committed peasants whose road building and transport had made the revolution possible.[22]

The French recognized the intimate connection between the Viet Minh and the population without bothering to contemplate its meaning. Rather, it was seen as a technical problem, to be dealt with tactically. Early in the war, an effort had been made to separate the people from the Viet Minh through the construction of thousands of forts that would keep the people in and the Viet Minh out. But the forts both tied the army down and proved vulnerable to guerrilla attack, so soon forts were built to protect other forts. General Navarre, taking full advantage of the technological largesse of the Americans, abandoned this static approach in favor of establishing a series of strongpoints (one of which was Dienbienphu), linked by highly mechanized mobile forces intended to seize the strategic initiative and "mop up" the guerrillas. In some villages, mopping up meant arresting the entire male population between fourteen and sixty, and everywhere, a French observer wrote, the military "had a record of pillage, violence, assassination, and of the burning of the villages and the execution of the innocent."[23] In response, the Viet Minh turned their attention to ambushing the new mobile units, and at Dienbienphu Giap directly engaged one of Navarre's "hedgehog" forts by a feat of arms literally beyond the imagining of the French military.

The meaning of Dienbienphu, Giap wrote on its fifth anniversary, was that it established a "great historic truth: *a colonized and weak people once it has risen up and is united in the struggle and determined to fight for its independence and peace, has the full power to defeat the strong aggressive army of an imperialist country."[24] The French journalist Jules Roy, reflecting on the defeat many years later, understood. "Apart from the French high commissioners who supported his government," he wrote, "who indeed would dare imagine that anybody could get himself killed for H[is] M[ajesty] Bao Dai? What soldier in this army could be expected to fight to enrich the big landlords and the provincial governors? . . . what kind of honor could be found in the ranks of H.M. Bao Dai's army, trained by the French and paid by the Americans?" Honor lay elsewhere, in a "faith, which we had contemptuously dismissed as fanaticism, in which our military leaders had refused to believe, and which had broken our battalions, our tanks and our planes." An American aide to President Kennedy, however, after reading Giap's account of the battle, drew the ominously obtuse conclusion that "in Southeast Asia . . . there is no pervasive *national spirit* as we know it."[25]

Today, in the War Museum in Hanoi, the Vietnamese have given an entire room to the Battle of Dienbienphu. A tape in French, English, Russian, or Vietnamese, depending on the audience, explains the action as it unfolds on an enormous diorama of hills, mountains, tiny trails, flashing lights. At the museum shop you can buy a small bag of dirt from the battlefield itself. To the Vietnamese, the French defeat at Dienbienphu was the end of the war for their independence. To the other powers gathered at Geneva, it was only the beginning of negotiations over what they would allow independence to mean.

CHAPTER THREE

A Pause Between the Wars (1954–1956)

Q. You said the other day, Mr. Secretary, that it was the Government's policy to oppose a communist advance in Indochina by whatever means. What would be your attitude toward a victory of Ho Chi-Minh or a coalition in a free election in Indochina? Would you recognize that or would you consider that to also be barred by your formula?
A. I said that I thought the United States should not stand passively by and see the extension of communism by any means into Southeast Asia. We are not standing passively by.

—SECRETARY OF STATE JOHN
FOSTER DULLES, PRESS
CONFERENCE, MAY 5, 1954

ONE EXPECTS a successful war for independence to end with the lowering of the colonial flag, the departure of troops, and the investiture of a proud new national government with its own flag. But a world frozen in Cold War was not one in which colonies might fight against the colonial power and win an uncomplicated independence. The Viet Minh had fought the French to a standstill; Dienbienphu was mutually understood to be the last battle of their nine-year war. Yet the 1954 conference at Geneva ended not in a united, independent Vietnam but in one divided, not with peace but with renewed war. The Geneva Conference reflected neither the aspirations of the Vietnamese nor the military and political victory of the Viet Minh, but rather the hard realities of Cold War power.

The conference itself was the result of French insistence that Indochina be put on the agenda of a Five-Power Conference (France, the

37

United States, Great Britain, China, and the Soviet Union), scheduled to meet in Geneva in April 1954 to discuss problems relating to Berlin and Korea. On May 8, 1954, the day after the fall of Dienbienphu, representatives of the Soviet Union, the People's Republic of China, the United States, France, Great Britain, Laos, Cambodia, the State of Vietnam, and the Democratic Republic of Vietnam turned to the subject of Indochina. Because all sides to the conflict so frequently appealed to the accords signed at Geneva to sanction their actions, it is necessary to understand their provisions in some detail.

By the early summer of 1954, the Viet Minh dominated most of Vietnam politically and militarily, and the Viet Minh-supported Pathet Lao independence movement controlled as much as 50 percent of neighboring Laos. Only in Cambodia had the independence movement (the Khmer Isarak) remained weak. What is remarkable about the Geneva Conference, however, is how little these local realities counted. Each of the major powers—China, the Soviet Union, the United States, and France—had its own agenda, and a united, sovereign Vietnam was not on anyone's list.[1]

The French sought terms that were well short of full surrender to the Viet Minh. Given the domestic unpopularity of the war, however, as well as the decidedly bleak military situation, no French government could respond to the urging of the Eisenhower administration that France fight on. The Americans, disappointed by the reluctance of the French to pursue the war, were loathe to participate in the Geneva Conference at all. But there was a constraint on the ability of the United States to push the French, and this was French participation in the European Defense Community (EDC), an organization the United States considered essential to its design for European security. France, disturbed by the prospect of a Germany rearmed in any fashion, refused to commit itself to the American plan and invoked the possibility of rejecting the EDC to balance U.S. pressure to continue the war, as French leaders had earlier used the promise of participation in the EDC to gain increased American aid to fight the war. Ironically the EDC constrained the Soviet posture at Geneva as well. In hopes of persuading France to stay out of the EDC, the USSR encouraged Hanoi to relax its terms. Moreover, the Russians were in general anxious to pursue détente and had no special concern for Southeast Asia.

The People's Republic of China, mindful of the repeated threats of American military intervention, joined the Russians in urging a moderate negotiating stance on Hanoi. In this, its international debut, China was intent on a policy of "peaceful coexistence." Exhausted by the strain of civil war (1946–49) followed almost immediately by the war in Korea, the Chinese intended to turn their full energy to the problems of internal development. Given this priority, they were relatively indifferent to whether a fraternal socialist state existed in all of Vietnam or only in part of it, so long as one remained in the north to act as a buffer on its southern border. The Soviet Union and China both made it clear that in the face of an American threat to intervene, the Vietnamese would have to compromise; the political reality of Viet Minh power in Vietnam must yield to the larger political reality of its powerlessness in the world at large.

Slowly, over two and a half months of hard negotiating, Hanoi was forced to modify its terms. The long-term political settlement the Vietnamese had hoped for was postponed in favor of an immediate armistice during which the country would be temporarily divided into two military zones. But where would the line be drawn? And for how long would it last? The Vietnamese insisted it be drawn at a line that reflected the reality of Viet Minh military control, and with a fixed date for unification elections. If they could not have their country whole at once, then they would settle for a temporary line of division at the 13th parallel (see map p. 40), with elections fixed for a day six months hence. The French rattled the American military saber and demanded a division at the 18th parallel with no fixed date for reunification. The conference deadlocked. Molotov, the Soviet representative, suggested elections in a year's time; the Chinese were more accommodating to the West—two or two and a half years, and with no fixed date. Finally, a compromise was reached— elections in two years but at a definite time: July 1956.

Now only the line of demarcation remained at issue. The French agreed to a small adjustment at the 17th parallel; but the Vietnamese refused to budge. The area between the 13th and 17th parallels included not only the historical imperial capital city, Hue, but also the port city of Danang, and the major highway linking Laos to Vietnam. As even the French recognized, this was an area that had always, in the words of the new French premier, Mendès-France, "shown allegiance to the Vietminh. . . ." In early July, Ho Chi Minh traveled to China to meet privately with Premier Zhou Enlai. According to CIA reports, Chinese pressure was both intense and effective. Shortly after the meeting, Vietnamese resistance collapsed. It would be the 17th parallel after all.[2]

As the terms of the settlement became clear, there were questions in Hanoi. Was such a partial and endangered peace what they had fought for? In a long report to the Central Committee of the Lao Dong (workers') Party, Ho Chi Minh argued that the terms of Geneva were the best they could hope for. In the light of American enmity, Ho insisted, the old

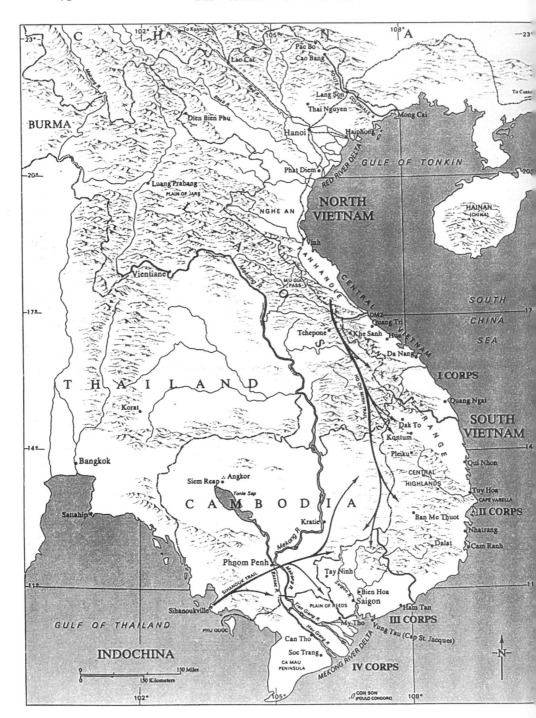

slogan, "Resistance to the end," must give way. Ho acknowledged that people living in the southern regroupment zones (the area south of the 17th parallel) "will be dissatisfied; some people might fall prey to discouragement and to enemy deception." But there was no choice. Regroupment zones were a step toward peace and elections the only route to reunification. "To secure peace," Ho concluded, "is not an easy task; it is a long and complex struggle." For the time being the struggle must be political rather than military; and in terms of political strength, the Viet Minh had little to fear from any rival.[3]

On July 20, 1954, the Geneva Conference ended in two separate, but connected, agreements. First, a cease-fire signed by the representatives of the two combatants: Ta Quang Buu, vice minister of National Defense for the Democratic Republic of Vietnam, and Brigadier General Henri Deltiel for the French Union Forces in Indochina. Under its terms, troops of the People's Army of Vietnam (the Viet Minh) would regroup north of the 17th parallel, while French Union forces would withdraw to the south. Pending general elections for reunification, "civil administration in each regrouping zone shall be in the hands of the party whose forces are to be regrouped there. . . ." Most important, Articles 16, 17, 18, and 19 barred the remilitarization of the conflict. There were to be no troop reinforcements, no augmentation of weapons, no military bases, and no foreign military alliances on the part of the administration of either zone. An International Control Commission comprised of Canadian, Indian, and Polish representatives would supervise the terms of the armistice and investigate any complaints. The Pathet Lao, which was barred from independent representation at the conference, fared less well in its cease-fire arrangements; instead of the 50 percent of Laos to which its military situation entitled it, Pathet Lao troops were confined to two small, underpopulated regroupment zones; Viet Minh units were to withdraw from Laos entirely.[4]

The cease-fire dealt with the military situation. A "final declaration" endorsed by all participants save the United States addressed Vietnam's political future. This declaration took note of the several particulars of the cease-fire barring any increase in troop level, armament, foreign military aid, or alliance. It also stipulated that the 17th parallel was not to be construed in any way as a "political or territorial boundary," and that "free general elections by secret ballot" were to be held in July 1956 under the supervision of the International Control Commission. Representatives of each zone would meet on July 20, 1955, to prepare for the elections.

In a separate protocol, the American representative at Geneva,

Walter Bedell Smith, declared that the United States took note of the agreements and would "refrain from the threat or the use of force" to disturb their provisions. But it could not join the other powers in a blanket endorsement because of the provision that the International Control Commission would supervise elections. Only UN supervision, Bedell Smith insisted, would meet America's exacting electoral standards. Since, as all present knew, the British and French were implacably opposed to UN supervision as an awkward precedent in their remaining colonies, Smith's statement, if it is not to be read as purely gesture, can be understood as establishing a legal basis for future American actions disregarding the accords themselves.

The expectation of all the Geneva participants was that France would remain in Vietnam to oversee the settlement. In the meantime, Vietnam consisted of two military zones, administered by two civilian governments—the Democratic Republic of Vietnam in the North, the State of Vietnam in the South. Military regroupment was to be completed within three hundred days of the signing, during which time civilians could move freely north or south of the parallel. Elections in 1956 would determine which government might legitimately claim to represent the whole country.

The "State of Vietnam" had been the name the French gave the nominally independent government it installed in 1949. The titular head of the State of Vietnam was the Emperor Bao Dai, who had served the French, the Japanese, and then again the French. Always more comfortable in France than in Vietnam (his château outside Cannes was his favorite residence), Bao Dai's lack of popular appeal had worried the United States throughout the war. The American minister to Saigon in 1951, Donald Heath, urged that "American technicians" essentially redecorate Bao Dai to give his government a " 'new look'; uniforms, stamps, seals, government forms, street signs, money, etc. As long as Bao Dai is our candidate," Heath concluded, "he must be ingeniously 'sold'— an American advisor should be stationed with him." But while Bao Dai seemed willing enough to visit Vietnam on occasion, he firmly resisted living there. As a political rival to Ho Chi Minh, the emperor remained rather ephemeral.[5]

This was not a minor problem. A vivid national presence was central to the American formula for the creation of non-Communist nations. In the American view, the French had lost because, to put it bluntly, they were not Americans. Hopelessly corrupted by their own colonialism, the French refusal to grant Vietnam independence had allowed the Communists to "capture" Vietnamese nationalism. But the United States, as its presidents and their advisers understood its history, was uniquely an anti-colonial power, the guardian of all genuine, non-Communist nationalists as it was the implacable foe of all false, Communist ones. (It should be kept in mind that the United States considered the only really safe non-Communist to be an avowed anti-Communist; those claiming neutrality, like India, were not to be trusted.) American analysts compared the unhappy effort of the French to recolonize Vietnam with the exemplary American decolonization of the Philippines.

The difference between France in Indochina and America in the Philippines was perhaps less in terms of policy than in the conditions each faced in its postwar colony. Totally in military control of the Philippines after the defeat of Japan, as France could not be in control of Indochina, the United States moved quickly to disarm the Communist-led Hukbalahap, the largest and most effective anti-Japanese guerrilla movement in the country. To run the civilian government General Douglas MacArthur selected Manuel Roxas, a collaborator closely associated with the most exploitative Japanese occupation policies. Roxas quickly pardoned other notorious collaborators, banned peasant political organizing, refused to seat newly-elected opposition congressmen, and unleashed a campaign of violent repression throughout the country.

Formal independence was granted the Philippines on July 4, 1946 (its terms included American retention of major military bases and "business citizenship" for Americans), but Roxas's policies ensured a revival of the Hukbalahap movement, and crushing the insurgency became a primary goal of the United States. "Victory of the Communist-led and dominated Huks," Secretary of State Acheson insisted, "would place us in a highly embarrassing position vis-à-vis the British, French and Dutch whom we have been persuading to recognize the realities and legitimacy of Asiatic nationalism and self-determination." Failure to hold the line in the Philippines, Dean Rusk warned, would mean writing off all of Asia.

Both Rusk and Acheson felt they had learned valuable lessons about "Asiatic nationalism" from the example of China, where the problem, in their view, was less the deep structure of social and economic inequities than the qualities of the man at the top. Chiang Kai-shek had been incompetent. Roxas and even more so his successor Quirino were similarly incompetent, unable to make such timely reforms as would deny the Communists their appeal. By 1950, a competent man had at last been identified, Quirino's minister of defense, Ramon Magsaysay.

By all accounts, Magsaysay was a charismatic politician attuned to the skillful public relations advice offered by a former advertising executive on loan to the CIA from the U.S. Air Force, Colonel Edward Geary

Lansdale. He was also able to put large quantities of American aid to good use, in contrast to his predecessors who seem simply to have pocketed it. Magsaysay's political, military, and economic reforms were sufficient to halt the insurgency, if not solve the severe problems that had given rise to it. In time these would yield a new insurgency and the United States would search once more for the right man to deal with it; ultimately the mantle would fall on Ferdinand Marcos.

The problem in Indochina would be to find a Vietnamese Magsaysay. In January 1954, Secretary of State Dulles and his brother Allen, head of the CIA, decided to send Lansdale to Vietnam; after a brief delay, he was dispatched to head the Saigon Military Mission and "develop quickly a way to keep [Vietnam] from going Communist."[6]

By the spring of 1954, a likely actor for Magsaysay's role had been selected by the Americans to serve as Bao Dai's prime minister—Ngo Dinh Diem. Although the American ambassador to France found him a "yogi-like mystic," capable of taking charge only "because the standard set by his predecessor is so low," Diem was a natural for the part. An ascetic bachelor from a large, ambitious Catholic family with a long history of government service under the French, he had reliable credentials as a nationalist (in 1933 he resigned a high post under Bao Dai citing nationalist grounds) and an anti-Communist. Indeed, during the war of resistance he had refused to work with either Ho Chi Minh or Bao Dai, and in 1950 left Vietnam altogether.[7]

In Japan, Diem met a young political scientist named Wesley Fishel who invited him to the United States on a trip sponsored by Fishel's university, Michigan State, an ambitious land-grant institution which may have thought to balance its considerable reputation in agricultural science and extension services with more contemporary governmental good works, such as international consulting. Over the next three years, Diem was befriended by a variety of Americans who in 1955 organized themselves formally as the American Friends of Vietnam. The Friends included Supreme Court Justice William O. Douglas, Cardinal Francis Spellman, Senator Mike Mansfield, Joseph Kennedy, and his son John F. Kennedy, and Hubert Humphrey, and they would stand by Diem with remarkable steadfastness for almost a decade.

On June 25, 1954, Ngo Dinh Diem returned to Saigon. The American chargé d'affaires in Saigon was not impressed: "[Diem's] only formulated policy is to ask for immediate American assistance in every form, including refugee relief, training of troops and armed intervention. His only present emotion, other than a lively appreciation of himself, is a blind hatred for the French."[8] But it was precisely for this last quality that Diem had been selected. If the United States were to take over from the French and transform the regroupment zone south of the 17th parallel into a regime capable of rivaling Ho Chi Minh in the North, it would need politicians whose hatred of the French on the one hand and fear of the Communists on the other would make them turn to the Americans.

Covert American subversion of the Geneva Agreements began simultaneously with their final signing on July 21, 1954. Lansdale was already in place. His original mission, to bypass the French and work with sympathetic Vietnamese in unconventional warfare, was now readily redirected to "paramilitary operations in Communist areas." Having witnessed the "grim efficiency" with which silent, sneaker-clad Viet Minh troops vanquished the "clanking armor" of the French, Lansdale was determined to beat the Vietnamese at their own "military-political-economic" game. In Hanoi, his team distributed leaflets that spread disinformation about new economic and monetary regulations, causing some panic among more affluent residents; they poured sugar into the gas tanks of Hanoi buses, impeding public transportation and creating consumer dissatisfaction; they suborned astrologers who predicted dire disasters; they spread rumors of rampaging, raping Chinese Communist troops.

Of particular propaganda value to Diem was the exodus of almost 1 million Catholics from north to south who were said to have "voted with their feet" for freedom. They did not really use their feet, nor was their flight entirely about freedom. Encouraged by the Catholic hierarchy and organized by Lansdale and his team, entire parishes were carried south in American ships, following priests who told them Christ had moved south, as well as making promises of land and livelihood. The usefulness of this refugee population did not end with their much-photographed arrival in the South. In effect they were an imported political resource for Diem, a substantial and dependent bloc of loyal supporters.

One of the more effective rumor campaigns Lansdale developed was that the United States would back a new war, one in which atomic weapons would certainly be used. Widely believed, this added to the flow of refugees south. With boyish enthusiasm, Lansdale reported these triumphs, all of them in direct violation of the Geneva Accords, to the CIA. In the South the team was equally busy, smuggling in arms, ammunition, radios, some for use on the spot, the rest destined to be shipped north. Lansdale took particular pleasure in the work of an agent he code-named Trieu Dinh. Under the guidance of a Captain Arundel, Trieu Dinh had written a "Thomas Paine type series of essays on Vietnamese patriotism against the Communist Vietminh." These clarion essays ran on the front page of Saigon's leading newspaper, whose publisher "found it profitable to heed our advice on the editorial content of the paper." Apparently genuinely unaware of any contradiction, Lansdale's cheerful brutalization of democratic values (newspaper fraud was among the more pacific tactics employed) earned him immortality as the model for Colonel Hillendale in Eugene Burdick's novel *The Ugly American.*[9] Lansdale was the man of the hour, filled with energy and conviction, confident he could fulfill Dulles's mandate to "help the Vietnamese much as [he] had helped the Filipinos."[10]

On the whole, Secretary of State Dulles was pleased with the way things were turning out in Vietnam. "We have a clean base there now," he told a friend in 1954, "without a taint of colonialism. Dienbienphu was a blessing in disguise."[11] U.S. policy rested on two firm pillars: a government led by the nationalist politician Ngo Dinh Diem would serve as a viable political instrument for the creation of an anti-Communist state; and a regional mutual security pact would supply the legal grounds for military intervention should that prove necessary.

Dean Acheson had cut the politics of Indochina to the procrustean bed of Eastern Europe. Now Dulles drew upon a Western European model (and indeed Western European countries) to serve his conception of Southeast Asian security. The Southeast Asia Treaty Organization (SEATO; signed in Manila in September 1954) would parallel the North Atlantic Treaty Organization (NATO), neatly binding much of the world into explicitly anti-Communist alliances. Indeed, although the language of SEATO referred to deterrence against "massive military aggression" as such, a statement in the final paragraph of the treaty specifically limited U.S. intervention to cases of Communist aggression. Something like the United Action approach Eisenhower and Dulles had proposed to Great Britain and France in the closing days of the French war against the Viet Minh, it was now expanded to include New Zealand, Australia, the Philippines, Thailand, and Pakistan, as well as France, Great Britain, and the United States. (The more powerful neutral countries in the region, India, Burma, and Indonesia, refused to join.) France resisted Dulles's effort to bestow full membership in SEATO upon Laos, Cambodia, and Vietnam as too direct a violation of the Geneva Accords, which barred their participation in a military alliance. Instead, the treaty adhered to the letter though hardly the spirit of Geneva, in a separate protocol in which the member nations extended their protection to Laos,

Cambodia, and "the free territory under the jurisdiction of the State of Vietnam." Cambodia, under the wary leadership of Norodom Sihanouk, refused the courtesy.[12]

The terms of SEATO required nothing more than consultation of the membership in cases of subversion or insurrection (as opposed to cases of external aggression, to which a member nation could respond immediately and on its own). Uneasy about the range of responsibilities the United States was assuming, some senators questioned Dulles carefully during hearings on the treaty in 1954. Did SEATO mean the United States was obliged to "put down revolutionary movements?" Senator Theodore Green asked. Certainly not, Dulles responded.

> If there is a revolutionary movement in Vietnam or in Thailand, we would consult together [with other members of SEATO] as to what to do about it, because if that were a subversive movement that was in fact propagated by communism, it would be a very grave threat to us. But we have no undertaking to put it down; all we have is an undertaking to consult together as to what to do about it.[13]

It was on these limited grounds that the treaty passed the Senate in February 1955. In the years that followed, however, SEATO became the justification and the explanation of the American commitment to defend an anti-Communist state in South Vietnam. Indeed, SEATO was part of the early definition of such a state, since at the time it was signed there was only one Vietnam, explicitly banned from participation in any military agreement, whose political shape would be determined by elections to be held in 1956. By throwing a "mantle of protection" over the "free territory under the jurisdiction of the State of Vietnam," Dulles denied the terms of Geneva and gave himself the legal grounds on which to do so. The 17th parallel was beginning to assume the dimensions of a national boundary rather than the temporary cease-fire line negotiated only two months earlier at Geneva.

In Saigon, Diem set about organizing a government. Drawing on family resources, Diem placed one brother, Ngo Dinh Can, in charge of Hue and its environs, while another, Ngo Dinh Thuc, was its archbishop and the primate of Vietnam. A third brother, Ngo Dinh Nhu, became Diem's principal adviser and co-founder of the only legal party in the South, the Can Lao (Personalist Labor Revolutionary Party), through whose secret membership the Ngo brothers exercised control over the police, the officer corps of the army, and the civil bureaucracy. On the distaff side, Diem's sister-in-law, Mme Nhu, founded and trained a women's militia and served as hostess in the palace.

But government organization meant nothing without actual power, and in the summer of 1954 Diem did not even control the city of Saigon, much less its environs. Among the many contenders for power were two armed religious sects with followers numbering in the hundreds of thousands (the Cao Dai and the Hoa Hao);[14] the Binh Xuyen, an armed gang controlling major sectors of the Saigon drug and sex trades; French-trained Vietnamese Army officers with large ambitions; and the French themselves, who were less than eager to yield their place to the Americans and had their own ideas as to who should dominate the new government. Against all these rivals, Diem could use a mighty American weapon: money. As early as August 1954, the Eisenhower administration directed the Joint Chiefs of Staff to undertake the training and payment of the Vietnamese Army. "What we want," Eisenhower told the National Security Council, "is a Vietnamese force which will support Diem . . . the obvious thing to do is simply authorize [General] O'Daniel to use up to X millions of dollars to produce the maximum number of Vietnamese units which Prime Minister Diem can depend on to sustain himself in power."[15]

As important as the military skills of such a force were the political skills involved in the further disbursement or withholding of American dollars. The French, for example, dropped their support for Prince Buu Hoi, their alternative to Diem, when it became painfully clear that they could expect no help from the United States in their new colonial war against Algeria if they opposed Diem in Saigon. Vietnamese Army officers who favored Buu Hoi were simply informed there would be no funds to pay their troops. Toward the religious sects, whose militia the French had subsidized in exchange for their services against the Viet Minh, Diem was less flexible. His refusal to share political power with them and his insistence that their militia be disbanded created the first crisis of American confidence in his ability to control the situation in the South. By the spring of 1955, sect leaders, some of whom had accepted handsome bribes in exchange for supporting Diem, were threatening to join forces with the Binh Xuyen crime army in a direct military challenge to Diem's administration. When fighting broke out between Diem and the Binh Xuyen on April 27, 1955, Eisenhower's special representative in Saigon, General Lawton Collins, whose doubts about Diem's capacity to hold things together had grown through the spring, insisted that Diem would have to be replaced. Accordingly, that same day a reluctant Dulles cabled the embassy in Saigon to begin looking around for a new leader, taking care however that "the Vietnamese in Saigon should appear to be the framers of a new government."[16]

But Lansdale's bribes held his constituency, and with close CIA support, military units loyal to Diem were able to drive the Binh Xuyen from the city. Dulles countermanded his cable, and U.S. support for Diem was resoundingly reaffirmed.

The French called America's dedication to Diem an "addiction" and understood its source: Diem was "the only Vietnamese politician who would absolutely never enter into contact with the Vietminh under any circumstances." Eight years later, when Diem had lost that distinction, he would also lose his life, but in the spring of 1955 the Americans were well pleased. By the following spring, all French forces had withdrawn from Vietnam and, with close support from the United States, Diem set about the task of eliminating the last obstacle to his total control over a separate nation in the South: the tracking down and annihilation of those who had fought in the anti-colonial war against the French. For while Diem had been preoccupied with establishing control over Saigon, in the countryside the order established by the Viet Minh during the war against the French still held.

For all Vietnam, the crucial question was the extent to which the agreements reached at Geneva would be honored. So long as the promise of nationwide elections in 1956 was not violated, the possibility, though not the certainty, of peaceful reunification remained. Although American actions were hardly reassuring, Hanoi would do nothing to precipitate the cancelation of the elections. Southerners in the armed forces (some 130–150,000 soldiers, cadres, and their families), who had regrouped north of the 17th parallel in accordance with Geneva requirements, waited patiently for the time when they could return home. Some remained in the military, in units made up entirely of southerners; others received technical training or further education. All thought themselves to be participating in the further course of the Vietnamese revolution, one that allowed for the immediate construction of socialism in the North even as they awaited the day when the nation as a whole would be united.[17]

For Ho Chi Minh and the Lao Dong (Workers' Party), independence from France was only the ground on which revolution in Vietnam could take place; it was hardly the revolution itself. This was to be an economic, political, and social transformation of the country, one that would result, the leadership believed, in a fully developed modern socialist state, sovereign throughout its territory. Land reform and industrial development were the main priorities, the twin pillars of socialist construction, according to the model set decades before in the Soviet Union. Land reform had been a demand of Vietnamese reformers since the 1930s, consistently ignored by the French colonial authorities. Although ownership was by no means as concentrated as in the South, poor peasants and agricultural laborers, 60 percent of the population, held only 11 percent of land.[18] During the war against France, rent reduction and a modest amount of land redistribution had made a significant contribution to the mobilization of the countryside in support of the war effort.

In 1955, a more thoroughgoing land reform campaign began under the control of land reform cadres sent out by a central land reform committee, who worked outside the ordinary channels of the Party hierarchy and in close cooperation with local village committees. Careful Party guidelines distinguished between productive and unproductive landlords, patriotic and traitorous rich peasants, but these distinctions were increasingly ignored as the campaign gained a radical momentum of its own. Ancient village grievances, religious differences, petty spite, and a growing paranoia frequently left villages not transformed, but deeply embittered. By mid-1956 the campaign had ended. In an exceptionally stringent self-criticism, Party leaders reexamined the entire course of the reform and set out to correct its abuses.

The most careful historian of the land reform, Edwin Moise, estimates that between three thousand and fifteen thousand people were executed during the land reform campaigns. For Western propagandists, however, the real errors of land reform were not bad enough. Inflated statistics, from Bernard Fall's relatively modest 50,000 executions to Richard Nixon's charge of 500,000 dead, 500,000 in slave camps, helped create the myth of a Communist "bloodbath," one which only an American military effort could keep at bay. In the mid-1960s, American interrogators of prisoners of war and defectors who had been in the North during the land reform sought confirmation of the myth—without much success. Instead, many described satisfaction with the way in which errors and abuses had been corrected. As one "VC physician" put it:

> My conviction is that, if a thorn pricks you on a path and you bleed, that is not a reason to discontinue; it is a lesson for avoiding future thorns.
>   Grave faults in agrarian reform were admitted before everyone. That is more of a reason for showing that the North will benefit from the lesson.[19]

The presidents responsible for U.S. involvement in Indochina. The final tearful figure is the last president of South Vietnam, Nguyen Van Thieu. (Drawing by David Levine)

The American presidents as a Vietnamese cartoonist saw them. The Vietnamese reads: "The 'traditional burden' of American presidents." (Courtesy Ngo Vinh Long Collection)

NICH XƠN   GIÔN XƠN   KEN NƠ ĐI   AI XEN HAO

"Truyền thống ưa nặng" của các ngài tổng thống Hoa kỳ!

Vo Nguyen Giap (in derby hat) reviews Viet Minh troops. (Courtesy Ngo Vinh Long Collection)

Members of the OSS pose with Agent Number 19 (aka Agent Lucius, aka Ho Chi Minh) and Vo Nguyen Giap (*in white suit, third from left*) in the summer of 1945. (Photograph by Allan Squiers)

Stamp of His Majesty Bao Dai, emperor from the age of twelve in 1925 until his abdication in 1945; emperor once again when the French returned him to putative power in 1949; exiled in France in 1955 after his election loss to Ngo Dinh Diem.

Indochinese leaders, *Left to right:* Prince Norodom Sihanouk, President Nguyen Huu Tho of the NLF, North Vietnamese Premier Pham Van Dong, and Prince Souphanouvong of Laos.

RESISTANCE WAR
AGAINST THE
FRENCH

Ho Chi Minh observing the Dong Khe Battlefront. (Courtesy Ngo Vinh Long Collection)

Like the Americans later on, the French built blockhouses to control the rural population. Here one burns in 1951 near Cu Chi, twenty miles northwest of Saigon in the area the Vietnamese called "The Iron Land," the Americans, the "Iron Triangle." (Courtesy Ngo Vinh Long Collection)

American "volunteers" flew supplies into the besieged French base at Dienbienphu. Here pilots for the CIA-run airline, Civil Air Transport, pose for a photograph in front of the briefing shack at Haiphong Airport, March 1954. (UPI/Bettmann Archive)

Supplying Dienbienphu by bicycle transport. (Courtesy Ngo Vinh Long Collection)

An exhausted lieutenant in the French Foreign Legion during the battle of Dienbienphu, November 1953 to March 1954. (UPI/Bettmann Archive)

The dramatis personae at the Geneva Conference, May to July 1954, *top, left to right:* Pierre Mendès-France, Ho Chi Minh, Zhou Enlai; *bottom, left to right:* Walter Bedell Smith, Anthony Eden, V. M. Molotov. (UPI/Bettmann Archive)

Guerrilla leader Ta Thi Kieu. (Courtesy Ngo Vinh Long Collection)

Ngo Dinh Diem and his family. *Left to right:* Diem, Ngo Dinh Nhu, Madame Nhu, and Archbishop Thuc. (Courtesy Michigan State University Archives and Historical Collection)

Madame Nguyen Thi Dinh, organizer of the Ben Tre uprising, 1960, and later the deputy commander of the National Liberation Front, inspects a guerrilla unit. (Courtesy War Resisters League)

Vice President Lyndon B. Johnson and Nguyen Ngoc Tho, vice president of South Vietnam, during Johnson's May 1961 visit. According to the original AP Wirephoto caption, LBJ "has a big smile for the crowd that lined the Saigon airport road." (AP/Wide World Photos)

Malcolm Browne's photograph of the self-immolation of Thich Quang Duc sits atop the hood of the car that took Quang Duc to the intersection of two busy streets in downtown Saigon on June 11, 1963. Both on view in the garden of a pagoda in Hue. (Photo by Geoffrey Gates)

Johnson and the National Security Council—*(left to right)* George Ball, Dean Rusk, and Robert McNamara—discuss events in the Gulf of Tonkin, August 4, 1964. (UPI/Bettmann Archive)

After the assassination of Diem and Nhu in November 1963, a military junta led by Duong Van Minh *(second from the left)* was briefly in charge. A coup in January 1964 replaced the junta with a "Military Revolutionary Council" under Nguyen Khanh *(third from the left)*, seen here taking an oath of unity with other members of the Council. Nguyen Van Thieu, face obscured by his upraised arm, is on the far right. (UPI/Bettmann Archive)

American Marines landing at Danang, March 1965. (Courtesy Department of the Army)

THE AMERICAN INVASION

OF VIETNAM

In June 1965, Air Vice Marshal Nguyen Cao Ky became prime minister in the ninth cabinet since the fall of Diem. Here he inspects a battlefield with his wife. (Photograph by Nguyen Thanh Tai; UPI/Bettmann Archive)

GIẤY THÔNG-HÀNH

SAFE-CONDUCT PASS TO BE HONORED BY ALL VIETNAMESE GOVERNMENT AGENCIES AND ALLIED FORCES
이 안전보장패쓰는 월남정부와 모든 연합군에 의해 인정된 것입니다.
รัฐบาลเวียตนามและหน่วยพันธมิตร ยินดีให้เกียรติแก่ผู้ถือบัตรผ่านปลอดภัยนี้.

SAFE-CONDUCT PASS TO BE HONORED BY ALL VIETNAMESE GOVERNMENT AGENCIES AND ALLIED FORCES

MANG TẦM GIẤY
THÔNG HÀNH
nầy về cộng tác
với Chánh Phủ
Quốc Gia các bạn
sẽ được :
● Đón tiếp tử tế
● Bảo đảm an ninh
● Đãi ngộ tương xứng

NGUYỄN VĂN THIỆU
Tổng Thống Việt Nam Cộng Hoà

TẦM GIẤY THÔNG HÀNH NẦY CÓ GIÁ TRỊ VỚI TẤT CẢ CƠ - QUAN
QUÂN CHÍNH VIỆT-NAM CỘNG - HÒA VÀ LỰC-LƯỢNG ĐỒNG - MINH.

A safe conduct pass, part of the *chieu hoi* (open arms) surrender program, illustrating as well the results of the Johnson administration's "more flags" effort: Korea, Thailand, the Philippines, Australia, New Zealand. Pictured is Nguyen Van Thieu, who outmaneuvered Ky to become head of the government in 1967; Ky stayed on as vice president. The Vietnamese reads: "If you carry this pass and cooperate with the government, you will receive a warm welcome, a guarantee of safety and proper treatment." (Courtesy Don Luce)

Buddhist demonstration against the Ky government, May 1966. Troops broke up a demonstration of ten thousand people in Saigon and strung barbed wire around the group pictured here. (AP/ Wide World Photos)

A 1966 cartoon by Jules Feiffer explaining the American presence. (Universal Press Syndicate)

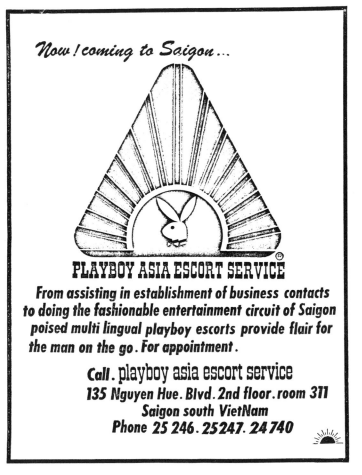

"Playboy" flyer, Saigon. (Courtesy Don Luce)

Saigon. (Photograph by Mark Jury)

Fire Support Base Fuller, which overlooked the DMZ. There were hundreds of such bases throughout South Vietnam from which every inch of the country could be hit by artillery fire. This base was supplied entirely by air. (Photograph by Mark Jury)

The war was more personal for Marines fighting the ground war: A marine carries a suspected guerrilla captured southwest of Danang in January 1966. (Photograph by Nguyen Thanh Tai; UPI/Bettmann Archive)

The NLF's homemade weapons of war: Villagers plant sharpened bamboo "punji sticks" (Courtesy Ngo Vinh Long Collection); perfume bottles are refashioned into lights for night operations and knapsacks are made from gift sacks of American wheat. (Courtesy International Publishers)

Using the side of a disabled U.S. military vehicle, an NLF instructor teaches recruits how to operate an antitank grenade launcher. (Courtesy Ngo Vinh Long Collection)

Carrying supplies South.

Stamps celebrated particular military achievements. Villagers near Cu Chi, "the Iron Land," fashion "naily-board" mines. The number of American planes shot down over the North was marked by a regular issue of stamps.

A militia fighter named Kim Lai and the American pilot she captured after his plane crashed over the North. (Courtesy Ngo Vinh Long Collection)

Instead of alienating the population, as contemporary American analysts had expected, land reform (which increased the holdings in land, tools, and farm animals of 60 percent of the population) and the public rectification of its campaign excesses deepened popular support for the government. As even defectors to South Vietnam tried to instruct the unbelieving Americans who questioned them, "the North has the support of the people." One Vietnamese from a Central Highlands tribe described a life in the North that was

> very wonderful compared to previous years. There have been many changes in the North. The living conditions of the people were getting better and better every day. The people were well off. They had enough to eat. They were able to attend school. They were free with no oppression from anyone. There were no imperialist foreigners in the North. They had land to work and buffaloes to help them plow the land. There were no more cruel landlords to lord it over them.[20]

Determined not to repeat the mistakes of land reform, the Party's approach to the establishment of cooperatives was slow and cautious. "One does not form a cooperative just for fun," Ho Chi Minh observed. Party cadres relied on persuasion and the demonstration effect of rising food production to convince household farmers to join their neighbors in village cooperatives. By 1960, 86 percent of the rural population was engaged in some level of cooperative farming, and eight years later some 90 percent belonged to full-scale collectives (in which land, tools, and animals were collectively owned and rewards were based on the amount of labor contributed).[21]

French industrial development of Vietnam had accomplished very little; everything remained to be done. With independence, French-owned enterprises in coal, steel, and textiles were nationalized, but the significance of this may be measured by the fact that industrial output amounted to only 1.5 percent of total material output in 1954, while out of a population of thirteen million, Melanie Beresford estimates, "only a few thousand were employed in modern industrial enterprises. . . ." The urban economy was overwhelmingly artisanal and by 1960 had been reorganized into cooperatives. Soviet and Chinese economic aid supplied crucial raw materials as well as consumer goods. In 1961 a Five Year Plan, dedicated to the rapid development of heavy industry, was promulgated and Hanoi could begin to look forward to the rewards—and the severe problems—its model of development entailed.[22]

In short, in 1956–57 the Democratic Republic of Vietnam was an exceedingly poor country, determined to achieve both social equity and prosperity for as much of its population as international politics and the limits of its own vision allowed.

In the South too there was poverty, but it was differently distributed and the initial efforts of the Diem government were focused less on fundamental economic issues than on political control, military strength, and the enrichment of selected segments of the population. One immediate political problem was how to respond to Hanoi's insistent requests for consultations (set by the Geneva Accords for July 1955) on procedures for the agreed-upon 1956 countrywide elections. The possibility of such elections had troubled the United States from the start. During the Geneva negotiations, Dulles's concern was clear: " . . . since it was undoubtedly true that elections might eventually mean unification [of] Vietnam under Ho Chi Minh this makes it all [the] more important they should be held as long after cease-fire agreement as possible and in conditions free from intimidation to give democratic elements [their] best chance."[23] The problem, as the State Department intelligence analysts saw it in 1955, was that ironically such conditions would probably benefit the Communists. "Almost any type of election," the report observed, "would . . . give the Communists a very significant if not a decisive advantage." Conditions of "maximum freedom and the maximum degree of international supervision might well operate to Communist advantage and allow considerable Communist strength in the South to manifest itself at the polls." It would be best, therefore, that neither Diem nor the United States make too big an issue of "free political conditions in the period preceding and during whatever type of elections might finally be decided for Vietnam."[24]

Fully alert to these dangers and assured of American support, Diem reminded Hanoi that his government had never subscribed to the election plan and had no intentions of abiding by it. Instead, a referendum to ratify Diem's presidency (formally, he remained Emperor Bao Dai's prime minister) and to proclaim a republic would be held in October 1955. Diem and the Eisenhower administration argued a delicate logic. Both depended on the cease-fire and temporary partition provisions of the Geneva Accords to provide the time and space within which a separate "nation" might be built south of the 17th parallel: therefore they insisted the Democratic Republic of Vietnam adhere to these provisions strictly. On the other hand, neither Diem nor the Eisenhower administration had been signatories to the accords; thus they claimed freedom to act outside the accord strictures. Technically, France was responsible for supervising the Geneva provisions with the help of an International Control Commission comprised of representatives of Canada, Poland, and India. But in the words of the government officials who later compiled a history of the war for Defense Secretary Robert McNamara, despite the French determination "to carry out the Geneva elections," they eventually "were obliged to choose between the U.S. and the DRV, so firmly did the U.S. foreclose any adjustment to the DRV's objectives."[25]

Voters in the South would, however, be given a choice: Diem or the distant Bao Dai. The experienced Lansdale advised against outright fraud, but was otherwise full of positive suggestions. Diem's ballot depicted the very model of a modern democratic statesman, and was to be printed on red paper, "the Asian color of happiness," while Bao Dai, wearing traditional robes, appeared on paper in "an uninspired shade of green." The range of choice was narrow. Voters could support the deposing of Bao Dai and "recognize Ngo Dinh Diem as the Chief of State of Vietnam with the mission of installing a democratic regime," or they could refuse to support that proposition. More significant, perhaps, were the police agents who went "from door to door explaining the unpleasant consequences which failure to vote would be likely to entail," the police presence at the polling booths, and the unsupervised ballot count by Diem's men. Lansdale had urged modesty: "I said, all you need is a fairly large majority." Instead, Diem rolled to victory with 98.2 percent of the vote. In Saigon, out of a total of 450,000 registered voters, an astonishing 605,025 voted for Diem.[26]

Hanoi was alone in protesting Diem's refusal to hold consultative talks. Neither Great Britain nor the Soviet Union, co-chairmen of the Geneva Conference, showed much interest in the implementation of its provisions. Indeed, by 1957 the Soviet Union seemed ready to ratify a permanent division between North and South Vietnam: in response to an American effort to allow the Republic of Vietnam into the United Nations, Khrushchev, anxious to strengthen détente, suggested the admission of both, since "in Vietnam two separate States existed, which differed from one another in political and economic structure."[27]

Southern members of the Viet Minh resistance, awaiting their promised return home, despaired. The scheduled date for nationwide elections, July 20, 1956, "arrived noiselessly, nothing stirred. . . . We were worried and watchful; we asked for explanations. . . ." There were demonstrations and Prime Minister Pham Van Dong sent yet another note of protest to the International Control Commission, but in the end they were told by senior officials only to be "patient in our struggle" for reunification.[28] Recovery from the land reform campaign was still under way, industrial reform was just beginning. Internationally, no country would support a direct military challenge to the United States and Diem. In time, Hanoi felt certain, the Diem government would collapse of its own ineptitude and venality. Meanwhile, as Ho Chi Minh advised the regroupees in an open letter, "everything we are doing in the North is aimed at strengthening both the North and the South. Therefore, to work here is the same as struggling in the South: it is to struggle for the South and for the whole of Viet-Nam." The struggle would be not military but political and because it was just, "although long and hard [it will] certainly be victorious."[29] What Ho Chi Minh left unsaid, however, was that as far as the rest of the world was concerned, the de facto division of Vietnam was now permanent. Years later a high-ranking defector bitterly remembered the final violation of the hopes of Geneva:

> When the Geneva Accords were signed, there was already much ill will against the Central Committee and Ho Chi Minh, because people felt that the South was always treated as a sacrificial animal. ... Now the Southerners were called upon to sit by and tolerate more sacrifices. They felt that the Party and Ho Chi Minh had turned out to be more stupid than the French, the Americans, or even Diem himself. ... People had sacrificed heavily in the Resistance and had been told by the Party that the Geneva Accords would be carried out. Now they saw that the Geneva Accords were ignored.[30]

The October 1955 referendum and a subsequent and even more fraudulent election for a Constituent Assembly in March 1956 satisfied American requirements that a stable government had been created in Saigon. The first necessity was money. From January 1955 until the final collapse of the Saigon government in April 1975, the economy of the South was sustained almost entirely through American aid. The aid did more than just keep the government going: it was designed to build an urban middle class, dependent on the steady flow of American dollars and loyal to Diem and his successors. Through the operations of the Commercial Import Program, which was intended to inject large quantities of American aid into the economy without creating runaway inflation, a select group of Vietnamese entrepreneurs was able to realize windfall profits of up to $600 million a year. His social base in the cities thus secured, Diem turned to the countryside, where the majority of the population lived.

However firm Diem's control was over the city of Saigon, it did not extend much beyond, as Joseph Alsop, touring former Viet Minh areas of the Mekong Delta in December 1954 as a guest of the "Vietminh Committee of the South," discovered to his evident chagrin: "I would like to be able to report—I had hoped to be able to report—that on that long, slow canal trip to Vinh Binh I saw all the signs of misery and oppression that have made my visits to East Germany like nightmare journeys to 1984. But it was not so." Traveling in an old wooden canal boat in company with fifty passengers of every sort, Alsop described an idyllic landscape of emerald rice fields, tiny villages along canal banks thick with mangoes, palms, bamboo, papaya. Here, during the war against the French, the Viet Minh had established a "strong, self-contained state, with a loyal population of nearly two million, a powerful regular army, a complete civil administration, and all the other normal apparatus of established governmental authority." Under the terms of Geneva this "palm-hut state" had been dismantled, but the appeal of the Communists was undiminished and it was in pursuit of understanding that appeal that Alsop found himself in that crowded canal boat.

> This was no easy region to defend. . . . Yet the Vietminh had success-fully defended it, with no more elaborate artificial defenses than guerrilla traps around the villages and blockades on the canals to stop the passage of French armed launches. And here, after the long war and the hasty rebuilding of the bombed-out villages, the countryside looked perceptibly more prosperous—with larger palm huts, better vegetable gardens, and more pigs and chickens running in the village streets—than the French-controlled territory north of Phung Hiep.

Alsop's fellow passengers confirmed his observations, expressing their contentment and boasting of the Viet Minh victory over the French. Reluctantly, he believed them, for "there was no hint of the bleak, guarded, totalitarian atmosphere, flavored but not leavened by drilled enthusiasm, that I had imagined I would find." Instead, if you could forget "the inevitable character of the Communist future," the scene before him, land and people, "were both intensely pleasing, as smiling countrysides and happy people always are." "At first," Alsop confessed, "it was difficult for me, as it is for any Westerner, to conceive of a Communist government's genuinely 'serving the people.' I could hardly imagine a Communist government that was also a popular government and almost a democratic government. But this is just the sort of government the palm-hut state actually was. . . ."[31]

In the Delta, as elsewhere in rural Vietnam, the war against the French had brought significant gains: land reform, an end to heavy colonial taxation, to forced labor (corvée), and to assorted abuses by the landlord-controlled village councils. A peasant in Long An, recalling the period before the Viet Minh had driven out the French, couldn't remember exact details: "just mostly that the people here were poor and life was very difficult. . . . We had to do whatever [the village authorities] told us, if not we'd be called communists and sent . . . to be tortured." "For a large part of the population," Jeffrey Race observed of that province, "the war had actually meant an immediate, or at least a prospective improvement in their condition. . . ." Not surprisingly, then, a "significant part of the population was either indifferent or strongly embittered towards the new government, both as sponsor of the returning landlords and village councils, and as the successor to the French."[32]

The Diem campaign against former Viet Minh activists had begun in late 1955. Tens of thousands of those who had, one way or another, fought against the French under the banner of the Viet Minh were arrested, jailed, sent to "reeducation camps." In January 1956, the process was regularized when Diem issued Ordinance No. 6, under which anyone the regime considered a security threat was subject to arrest. Agitation for the 1956 national elections was taken as proof of subversion, and perhaps as many as twelve thousand people were executed, upward of fifty thousand imprisoned.

But control of the countryside required more than widespread arrests. Suppose Viet Minh sympathizers were elected to local village councils? To avoid this problem, Diem abolished the councils and substituted appointed officials—many of them Catholic refugees more dependent on the central government than on their village constituencies. One requirement for holding any administrative post in the village was an "anti-Communist and anti-rebel" background: not only the individual appointee but his entire family had to have either remained neutral or fought with the French against the Viet Minh. These measures gave the Diem government administrative levers for political/military control from above. What could be done to bind the countryside more positively to Diem?

In the Philippines, land reform had assumed the status of one of the more effective weapons in the counterinsurgency arsenal. With this in mind, Lansdale requested the services of Wolf Ladejinsky, an anti-Communist New Deal Democrat and the architect of conservative land reform in Japan, Taiwan (where it was credited with preventing the rise of insurgencies), and the Philippines (where it was presumed to have won Hukbalahap supporters to the government side).[33] The structure of land tenure in the Delta and the Central Lowlands made South Vietnam a natural for land reform efforts. In the Delta, the overwhelming majority of the farming population owned little or no land, subsisting as tenants paying rents of 50 percent or better of the estimated annual yield. In bad years, this might well amount to more than the actual harvest, in which case anything of value the tenant owned was subject to seizure by the landlord or his agent. Where landholding was less concentrated, as in the Central Lowlands, landlords made their money through usurious interest rates of 100 percent or more a year. The only problem, really, was that the Viet Minh had already conducted an extensive program of rent and interest reduction and land redistribution during the war of resistance against the French. To win the loyalty of the countryside, Diem's reforms would have to match or surpass the earlier program. And this created a larger problem: Diem's slender social base leaned heavily on the absentee landlords who crowded Saigon, awaiting armed support to return them—or at least their rent-collecting bailiffs—to the land.

Ladejinsky's land reform program, however, was moderation itself. Only holdings over 115 hectares would be subject to confiscation (in Japan, the figure was 3 hectares; the Viet Minh maximum in the South was 5 hectares). This left about 30 percent of the rice land in the South available for purchase by tenants, if they had the money. In addition, rent was to be held at a maximum of 25 percent of the actual harvest. At that only a small fraction of the land targeted was actually ever expropriated and redistributed, and the implementation of rent reduction was less than strict.

Such meager returns on Ladejinsky's efforts would perhaps have been bad enough, but in fact the overwhelming majority (87.5 percent) of the tenants who did not benefit from Diem's land reform actually suffered from it. Landlords or their agents returned to the villages in the Jeeps of Diem's army and, under the provisions of his land reform, the police evicted farmers who had received land from the Viet Minh and sold their holdings to the highest bidder. Tenants could buy it back or lose it; if they remained on the land they had been farming as theirs for a decade, they would have to pay a back rent at 25 percent. Some tenants borrowed from a special bank established to offer agricultural loans in order to buy back their holdings. However, CIA field investigators reported cases of farmers selling their farm animals in order to get out of the prisons into which they were thrown if they defaulted on repayment. As a Stanford Research Institute study put it, the "reinstatement of the landlord, combined with the apparent ineffectiveness of rent controls, would seem to detract seriously from the psychological appeal of a return to GVN [Government of Vietnam] control."[34]

*   *   *

With the departure of the last French soldier in 1956, the United States was no longer tied to the history of French colonialism in Vietnam and could return, as General Bonesteel of the National Security Council said, to "our traditional role of supporting the 'independence and legitimate national aspirations' of people." Vietnam, Senator John F. Kennedy announced to a symposium sponsored by the American Friends of Vietnam in June 1956, was the "cornerstone of the Free World in Southeast Asia," a "proving ground of democracy," and a "test of American responsibility and determination in Asia." The United States were the "godparents" of "little Vietnam." At peril of its reputation, the United States must never abandon it or fail to meet its needs. Vietnam was taking its "first feeble steps toward the complexities of a republican form of government." What it needed, what the United States could offer it as a gift, was a "revolution . . . far superior to anything the Communists can offer. . . . A revolution of their own making." Allan Nevins, a dean of American historians, joined Kennedy in praise for the "little republic" that had become a "proving ground for democracy. It has produced in its President, Ngo Dinh Diem, one of the true statesmen of the new Asia."[35]

The United States had succeeded in creating a new government that would now call itself a nation, the Republic of Vietnam. To confirm its nationhood, Diem was invited to pay a state visit to Washington. For some years Diem had employed Harold Oram, a New York public relations expert, at $3,000 a month plus expenses to polish his image.[36] In May 1957, Oram earned his fee. Flown to Washington in the presidential jet, met at the airport by Eisenhower himself, Diem pledged to a joint session of Congress to continue the fight against Communists and to prevent "the raw material of the area from falling into Communist hands."

A New York Times profile of Diem, entitled "An Asian Liberator," praised his efforts to "save his country from falling apart," the way he "tirelessly toured the countryside so that the people would get to know him and perhaps like him more than they did Ho Chi Minh." The Republic of Vietnam, the anonymous author assured Times readers, grew stronger as "the Vietnamese learn to respect their new Government and their new leader." In New York, Mayor Wagner greeted him as a man "to whom freedom is the very breath of life."[37]

The United States had created South Vietnam and its leader; it was now clear that any opposition to Diem would be understood as a hostile act, an attack on America's baby. "This is our offspring," Senator Kennedy said in 1956, "and if it falls victim to any of the perils that threaten its existence—Communism, political anarchy, poverty and the rest—then the United States, with some justification, will be held responsible; and our prestige in Asia will sink to a new low." But, in fact, what the United States had labored mightily to produce was not a democratic, independent new nation-state but an autocratic ruling family held in place by foreign power.

CHAPTER FOUR

The War for the South Begins (1956–1962)

The truth is that the population of South Vietnam, like any other, is more responsive to fear and force than to an improved standard of living. The conclusion is clear: The paramount consideration is to gain and maintain a superiority of force in all parts of the country. This is done by developing the military and police potential as the most urgent objective of our national program in Vietnam.

> —GENERAL SAMUEL T. WILLIAMS
> TO AMBASSADOR ELBRIDGE DURBROW,
> FEBRUARY 1960

Most of [our] efforts are political and the poor people must learn how to advance the revolution through political means, thus avoiding the risks of regrettable losses which hurt the revolution and discourage the people. Above all, we must keep the masses from becoming passive.

> Captured document: "Experiences in turning XB village in Kien Phong province into a combatant village."

I N THE AFTERGLOW of his successful trip to the United States, Diem moved toward a further consolidation of his regime through a second wave of repression in both urban and rural areas. A French reporter described the "classical" sequence of events that prevailed in the countryside in 1957–58: "denunciation, encirclement of villages, searches and raids, arrests of suspects, plundering, interrogations enlivened sometimes by torture (even of innocent people), deportation, and 'regrouping' of populations suspected of intelligence with the rebels, etc." The American press at the time in effect served as a branch of the U.S. enterprise in South Vietnam, cheering Diem's successes and praising his efforts to defeat communism in his country. The critical news reports of Scripps-Howard correspondent Albert Colegrove, which led to congressional hearings on Vietnam in the summer of 1959, focused almost entirely on the inefficient and wasteful use of American aid. Colegrove, like many members of Congress, called for closer supervision of funds rather than a reexamination of policy. Even such limited criticism drew the ire of Diem's loyal supporters. Wisconsin Democratic Representative Clement Zablocki, for example, wondered aloud if the public shouldn't be informed of the way in which Colegrove's criticism had given aid to the Communists.[1]

While Congress chided Diem for misusing American aid, experts from the Michigan State University School of Police Administration (working under a secret contract with the CIA for which it received a total of $25 million) trained and equipped the forces of repression: the Civil Guard, a paramilitary police force made up primarily of Catholic refugees from the North; a Vietnamese FBI; and, on the softer side, Civic Action teams designed to "get close to the people" in order to "explain why the communists were bad and why the people must follow the government." All three agencies were involved in implementing repression in the countryside.[2]

In the provincial capital of Quang Ngai, some six thousand prisoners were jailed during the 1957 "denounce Communists" campaign, and the cells of Poulo Condore, the old French prison island, were filled once more. "Every arrest," a Viet Minh veteran reported, "was synonymous with barbarous tortures—this was an absolute rule. Even if an arrested person was ready to turn traitor, to cooperate from the first moment, he could not escape the preliminary torture." Relatives of former Viet Minh members were regularly arrested and tortured: "They poured water in my nose, and then later hooked up a generator to my fingers and toes and cranked so hard I collapsed and wanted to die. . . . I told them, 'Stop, stop, I confess, I haven't done anything but I confess anyway. . . .' " A man who had once belonged to the Viet Minh but since 1954 claimed loyalty to Saigon was arrested in 1958 and sentenced to five years without trial; his sister was assassinated by government agents; his home village twice swept by government troops. The first time his wife was shot; the second, his house was torched and his fourteen-year-old daughter "died of illness and sadness, or else committed suicide," her father never learned which. In the Delta province of Ben Tre, those known to have fought in the resistance were systematically hunted down. The future deputy commander of the South Vietnam Liberation Armed Forces, Nguyen Thi Dinh, who had followed her older brother into the Viet Minh when she was a teenager, was able to hide in the home of sympathetic villagers, but her nephew was arrested, tortured, and executed.[3]

In May 1959, Diem increased the scope of state terror through Law 10/59. Under its terms, anyone charged with the crime of committing or attempting to commit acts against the security of the state would be arrested, tried by military tribunal, and executed within three days. There was no process of appeal. Nor could there be any doubt as to how the law would be applied. Roving military tribunals rounded up former Viet Minh and their families, as well as members of Viet Minh support groups (the Association of Resistant Catholics, the Association of Buddhists for National Salvation, the Association of the Fighters' Mothers) in order to determine which were patriots, which "slaves of Red Imperialism." The Geneva Accords explicitly prohibited retaliation against those who had fought on either side of the resistance war against the French, but Section B of Law 10/59 reserved to the government the right to determine "who is a Resistance member and a patriot, who is a Vietcong saboteur."[4]

Terror compounded other problems in the countryside: the return of land to the landlords so that, as under the French, a majority of the peasantry were once again landless or land poor; the reimposition of old taxes and exactions, including forced labor (corvée); the glaring and open corruption at all levels of the bureaucracy; conscription into local self-defense forces; extortion and arbitrary arrests. It was the accumulation of grievances, large and small, that angered villagers and moved many of them to respond to those who sought to resist the government. Even more than the return of onerous taxes and high rents, one man complained, was the constant drain of small bribes: "five piasters here, five piasters there. We were obliged to take national lottery tickets, which we then threw away because we didn't know how to find out about the results." Some years after the fall of Diem, a village chief in Long An Province described the situation to an interested American adviser:

> During the Diem period the people here saw that the government was no good at all. That is why maybe 80% of them followed the VC. I was village chief then, but I just had to do what the government told me. If not, the secret police would have picked me up and tortured me to death. Thus I was the very one who rigged the elections [for National Assembly] here. . . . But even if you offered me a million

piasters, I would not have said a word, because in those days if you opened your mouth you were put in jail immediately. But believe me, I am telling the truth—I know because I did it myself.[5]

As Diem tightened the screws in the South, Party leaders in Hanoi debated the appropriate response. The question of elections for unification had become moot; good behavior on the part of Hanoi could not bring them about. What sense then did it make to unilaterally honor the Geneva provisions? In Le Duan, who had fought the French in the South from the 1930s on, proponents of forceful and immediate action had a powerful advocate. Yet his 1956 analysis of the situation, "The Path of Revolution in the South," continued to hold consolidation of the North as the preeminent revolutionary task and political struggle as the only permissible weapon against Diem.[6] An all-out attack on the Diem government risked increased American intervention, even an attack on the North. Without foreign allies ready to support a more forceful response, the only sensible policy was to carry on the most vigorous political struggle possible, delaying for as long as possible the resort to arms.

With repression thinning the ranks of southern Party members and outrage against Diem's rural policies growing in the countryside, keeping the struggle strictly political became increasingly difficult. In some villages, Party chapters of four hundred or five hundred people had been reduced to ten or fewer—and the survivors were on the run. A Party member captured in 1962 described how difficult it was to "talk of political struggle while looking down the gun barrels of the government." A few of the younger draft-age men, enraged at this pacific policy, "became so angry that they took weapons the Party had hidden and came out of the jungle to kill the officials who were making trouble for them or their families."[7]

In the Delta, some hunted Party members fled to base areas they had used against the French and picked up where they had left off in 1954: organizing self-defense forces, making crude weapons, occasionally attacking a government outpost in order to improve their arsenal and frighten their adversaries. Remnant Cao Dai, Hoa Hao, and Binh Xuyen units, survivors of Diem's 1955 attack on the sect armies, joined them so that, by the end of 1958, a small "armed force of the people" lived a precarious and independent life. This was the mix of forces (along with their sympathizers) that Diem labeled the Viet Cong—the Vietnamese equivalent of "Commie."

From Hanoi flowed a litany of communiqués that insisted that full-scale armed struggle was premature, doomed, unnecessary, irrelevant.

But in the villages, as Saigon government troops and security police hunted down both real and imaginary Communists, local Party members increasingly took matters into their own hands, assassinating detested village chiefs, attacking local garrisons. By 1957, with the appointment of Le Duan to the Politburo, Party policy sanctioned the arming of anti-Diem propaganda teams that were permitted to use their weapons in self-defense. As unauthorized assassinations of government officials mounted, a program called the "extermination of traitors" was authorized that gave Central Committee legitimation to what was taking place anyhow. In the main, however, even when arms were available, Party discipline was maintained. In one account of village-level activity in this period, the desire of young recruits like Ta Thi Kieu to take military action against particularly villainous local officials was held firmly in check. After successfully leading a large protest demonstration at an army post, Kieu urged an immediate attack against the handful of soldiers at the base. Told the demonstration was enough, she disagreed. "We were far more numerous, and each of us had a pole in our hands. How can you speak of success when none of the mercenaries was killed?" But the Party secretary of her unit criticized her: "This is a political struggle. You always think of armed struggle only."[8] Yet in many places political struggle came to a halt under the pressure of the terror. In one district, the Party secretary, having watched helplessly as members were rounded up and executed, despaired and committed suicide. In another, the numbers shrank from 1,000 in 1954 to 385 in 1957 to a single individual in 1959.[9] "In my heart I still mourn the many comrades who fell in battle—with weapons in their hands but not daring to fire," a military leader of the National Liberation Front wrote years later, "and mourn the many local movements that were drowned in blood."[10]

Not all the officials Diem appointed were venal; not all governed through terror. The honest ones would agree that corrupt local officials should be punished; brutal army or police agents dismissed. What remained invisible to them—and to their American advisers—was that the order and stability they sought to maintain in the countryside inevitably rested on precisely such officials and on the landlord class they served. Beyond this, order and stability for a small segment of urban society meant disorder and instability for the majority of the population—tenant farmers, landless laborers, the urban poor, and all those to whom Diem had denied a political voice or security of livelihood. Long An Province, for example, was administered from 1957 to 1961 by Mai Ngoc Duoc, a native of Central Vietnam who had fought on the side of the French during the Resistance war. Personally honest and considered an able administrator, Duoc thought he could get close to the people of his province by conducting regular inspection tours during which he would meet with the population of three or four villages assembled for that purpose by the district officials. "I would tell the people that I was there to help them," Duoc explained, "and if they had any problems, they should come up to the microphone and tell me the whole truth." They tried, complaining about the daily abuses of local civil and military authorities, "a lot of little things," according to Duoc.

When some peasants protested that a section of public land they had cleared and worked for several years had been taken away from them, Duoc "explained this situation clearly" so that they "did not ask further." And when several peasants "got up to say that the government should give out one hectare of land for each poor family in the village to live on," Duoc explained "that this was impossible because most people in the province were poor." The task of governing, as Duoc seems to have practiced it, consisting of explaining to the farmers why things were the way they were rather than how they might be changed. Perhaps he found the problems brought to him either insignificant or impossible of solution; at any rate his efforts went to sustain the social order in the countryside, not to challenge it. As for his many tours of inspection:

> Whenever Major Duoc visited our village, he didn't come like a province chief or even the president—he came like a king . . . he would be escorted . . . to the market, where all the people and local officials in their best clothes would have been waiting for him for hours. He organized it that way so that the government would think people liked him, but it was just a sham.

And as for how much he learned about what was going on:

> suppose a Cong An [internal security] agent forced you to give him 10,000 piasters. Then there would be a big meeting called by the province chief. The village council and hamlet chiefs would order all the people to come, like herding ducks to market. When you got there, would you stand up and denounce the Cong An? Of course not, nobody dared to say anything—you figure you can always make another 10,000 piasters, but once you're dead, you're dead for good.[11]

By 1959, the Party in the North could no longer ignore the toll of the Saigon terror nor the independence of local southern activists. At the Fifteenth Plenum of the Central Committee, which met in Hanoi in January 1959, approval was extended from arming propaganda teams to the use of armed force to support political actions; the establishment of base camps in the Central Highlands; cooperation with surviving units of Cao Dai and Hoa Hao troops and the limited return of regroupees to the South (by 1960, this amounted to some 4,500 cadres whose tasks remained primarily political). Far from a call for the armed overthrow of Diem, the Fifteenth Plenum was nevertheless a sanction for a considerable array of armed actions.

Encouraged by the Plenum's decisions, local Party leaders in the South strained the guidelines to their limits. Uprisings in Long An, Quang Ngai, Tay Ninh, and Ben Tre provinces moved the situation to the very edge of a direct attack against the Saigon regime itself. In January 1960, Nguyen Thi Dinh led a small unit into action against government outposts in three districts of Ben Tre Province. Eighteen village committees had contributed 162 women and men, some homemade explosives, and four ancient rifles. By the end of the campaign, the following September, Nguyen Thi Dinh could boast a company-sized unit fully equipped with captured weapons, the withdrawal of government troops from large sectors of the province, and the return to peasant cultivators of thousands of acres of rice fields confiscated by Saigon authorities.[12] In Tay Ninh Province the "Liberation Army," as it now styled itself, overran an ARVN (Army of the Republic of Vietnam) base in battalion strength, helping itself to U.S.-supplied weapons in the process.

The most significant aspect of these feats of arms was that they made possible, and were made possible by, the organization of villages for their own defense. Nguyen Thi Dinh's initial success in Ben Tre Province was followed by concerted Saigon army action. Thirteen thousand soldiers surrounded her small band and, as she put it in her memoirs, "the villagers became worried and demoralized." Dinh's unit was able to escape encirclement by a ruse that required the cooperation of villagers and whose success seems to have relieved the villagers' anxieties and renewed their confidence in the guerrilla forces. In these engagements recruits were armed with homemade weapons, some quite innovative, such as the "sky horse" rifle, a primitive mortar firing steel pellets and glass shards dipped in snake poison. Captured weapons were studied for reproduction in small village armories. And everywhere the land and its resources—bamboo sharpened into deadly points, thick screens of hedges, the earth itself fashioned into tunnels and shelters—provided the basic means of both defense and attack. The maps of the Liberation Army, a defector later told an American, showed "every creek, trail and path going through the orchards"; and unlike government maps, "they bear no foreign words. Everything was written in Vietnamese."[13]

When the use of force was not possible, Party cadres devised ways to continue to act so that villagers did not give way to despair. Nguyen Thi Dinh's group may have escaped encirclement, but retaliation was swift and ferocious. In March 1960, the village of Phuoc Hiep was occupied by the army, which arrested and executed twenty young men, burying their bodies conspicuously around the army post. The outraged villagers asked Nguyen Thi Dinh's group to rid them of the post.

> We also wanted to destroy this gang badly and relieve our anger, but our armed forces were still weak. So we discussed ways to put a stop to the enemy's killing while still maintaining the initiative and the legal status of the masses [so as to avoid mass arrests]. Everyone unanimously agreed that we should organize immediately a large group of women who would push their way into Mo Cay district town to denounce the crimes of the soldiers in Phuoc Hiep.

Five thousand women from six different villages, wearing mourning bands and carrying their children, poured into Mo Cay demanding compensation for the dead and an end to the soldiers' brutality. "The district chief was scared out of his mind and shouted at the soldiers to shut the gates tightly and not to allow anyone to enter. The people stayed in front of the district headquarters, defecating and urinating on the spot, and refused to go home." For five days and five nights, singing revolutionary songs and appealing to the soldiers to desert, the women camped in front of the district headquarters, their numbers constantly reinforced, until finally their demands were met and the army outpost was withdrawn from Phuoc Hiep.[14]

Not always so dramatically, organization of the population proceeded hamlet by hamlet, village by village, incorporating ever-larger numbers into associations of Peasants, Women, Youth. Techniques devised by Diem to control the villages were reversed into means of defiance. Thus when the Saigon government required individual households to signal the presence of the "Viet Cong" in the village by knocking on a wooden block, the resistance organized a general drumming, uniting the villagers and frightening the local army post. At night, one young man recalled, "sounds coming from the knocking on everything that could produce a sound, arose from the dark countryside all around my hamlet. This created a diabolical concert which gave all of us a frightening thrill. It made me think the whole population had decided to stand behind the Front and that huge manpower would give the Front the necessary punch to overcome anything."[15]

Such village organization, unlike government efforts to control the rural population, had immediate implications. It meant reduced rent, the distribution of land, freedom from both corvée labor and conscription into the army, protection from extortion and the casual brutality of appointed village chiefs, security police or the army—in short, a resumption of the Viet Minh program. One police report records how the guerrillas disabled the government through a blend of violence (in this instance threatened; often actual) and redistributive justice:

> A platoon of armed Vietcong called a meeting of the residents of Binh Loi and Binh Thuan hamlets, Nhut Ninh village. In front of the meeting the Vietcong warned our soldiers, hamlet chiefs, and police that they must cease work immediately under penalty of death. . . . The Vietcong also forbade landowners to recover land from their tenants. In addition, those who bought land were forbidden to remove the current tenant or to allow anyone else to work the land.

The pace of the return of land to the farmers was reflected in the increasing number of government arrest sheets in which the charge was "accepting land distributed by the Vietcong."[16]

Robert Sansom, analyzing the impact of the land policies as a staff member of the Economic Office of the U.S. Mission in Vietnam, found that "the Viet Cong land reform program possessed the universality and mass appeal that the Diem land reform lacked."

> It is difficult to overestimate the extent of these reforms. Every landlord in the Delta, including those in GVN secure areas, was conscious of Viet Cong policies, interests, and desires. Those who collected rents above 10 or 15% [Diem's infrequently implemented reform required rents of 25%] did so at the risk of their lives. . . . From all the benefits it brought to the peasantry, it can probably be said that the impetus behind the Viet Cong land reform was not in the general case terror but the sanction of implied force supported by the general will.[17]

Nor was popular support only about the land. A team of American social scientists interviewing prisoners and defectors under contract to the Department of Defense explained that the guerrillas saw themselves "as the legitimate rulers of an independent Vietnam." "They certainly do not regard the present war as a struggle between North and South Vietnam," the report continues, "or between Communists and anti-Communists, but as a struggle between the legitimate leaders of an independent Vietnam and the usurpers protected by a foreign power." "Our findings," the team concluded,

> give the lie to the old cliché . . . that all the Southern peasant wants is his *'petit lopin de terre et qu'on lui fiche la paix'* (little piece of ground and to be left alone). We found in our sample many poor peasants with no formal schooling who were eloquent in the expression of their aspirations for education, economic opportunity, equality and justice for themselves and especially for their children. They were equally eloquent in expressing their indignation at the injustices they knew.[18]

During 1959 and 1960, the attacks on government military posts grew bolder. In July 1959, while the nightly movie played, the headquarters of the American advisers to the 7th ARVN Infantry Division at Bien Hoa (17 kilometers north of Saigon) was attacked and two American officers killed. The CIA judged that the "VC" controlled all of the Ca Mau region of the Mekong Delta and its strength was constantly rising. It was on the basis of such successes that northern Party leaders believed that full-scale warfare might still be avoided. Diem could perhaps be overthrown by the progressive loss of control in the countryside combined with the weight of the urban political coalition that had begun to organize against him.

As if to confirm this judgment, in April 1960, an elite group in Saigon, including ten former cabinet ministers, met at the Caravelle Hotel across from the Opera House that now served as a meeting place for the newly installed National Assembly. Impeccably anti-Communist and confident that their high status would protect them from reprisal (it did, but only for six months), the group issued a respectful but nonetheless devastating criticism of Diem. His elections were anti-democratic, his National Assembly a farce. "Continuous arrests fill the jails and prisons to the rafters . . . public opinion and the press are reduced to silence." The country was staggering under the weight of an incompetent bureaucracy, a clannish army, a corrupt economy. The signatories appealed to Diem to institute an immediate program of reforms. Otherwise, "truth shall burst forth in irresistible waves of hatred on the part of a people subjected for a long time to terrible suffering and a people who shall rise to break the bonds which hold it down. It shall sweep away the ignominy and all the injustices which surround and oppress it."[19]

A week earlier, in March 1960, a coalition which described itself as the Former Resistance Fighters and included representatives of the Buddhists, Cao Dai, Hoa Hao, former Viet Minh, and "independents," had already appealed to the people of the South to overthrow Diem, expel the Americans, and fulfill the promise of Geneva. In contrast to American assumptions about North Vietnamese policy, this open call for the direct overthrow of Diem was not entirely welcome in the North. Things were going too far, too fast, worried the Party: "We have not yet reached the stage of direct revolution; that is to say, we have not yet reached the period of direct overthrow of the American-Diem government. . . ." To sanction armed struggle meant risking expanded American intervention—the devastation visited upon both North and South Korea after U.S. intervention must certainly have been prominent in Ho Chi Minh's mind. And Diem seems to have made the same estimate, for feeling secure in American support, he ignored the appeal of the Caravelle group and intensified the struggle against the resistance fighters past and present.[20] But by the fall of 1960, the strength of the southern movement could no longer be contained, whatever the risks. Finally, in September 1960, the Central Committee in Hanoi called for the formation of a coalition organization to "liberate the south."

On December 20, 1960, at a secret base near Saigon, the National Front for the Liberation of South Vietnam was duly announced. Its ten-point program remained remarkably constant for most of the next fifteen years. This program is what the United States and the Diem regime fought against; it is also the basis on which the NLF recruited supporters. Like its chairman, the anti-Diem lawyer Nguyen Huu Tho, the founders of the Front were independent professionals, architects, lawyers, doctors, school teachers, along with members of the Communist Party, Buddhists, and one or two Catholics. They framed a set of demands that would appeal to all sectors of southern society that had been hurt by the Diem regime: not only the overthrow of Diem, but higher wages for civil servants including soldiers, jobs for workers and refugees (or a return home if they so wished), promotion of domestic industry over foreign imports, land rent reduction and redistribution, equality between men and women and among national minorities, a neutral foreign policy, the end to American military advisers, their bases, and their "enslaving and depraved U.S.-style culture." Finally, they wanted the establishment of normal relations between the "two zones"—North and South—"pending the peaceful reunification of the fatherland."[21]

Was the National Liberation Front Communist? Communist members of the southern branch of the Vietnam Workers' Party (Lao Dong) did openly dominate the Front. But, as it claimed, the NLF was an umbrella organization that included non-Communist individuals and organizations. The NLF is best described as a coalition led by Party members but held together by a common program. Did the Front take its orders from Hanoi? If only because of often insuperable difficulties of communication, units of the NLF at all levels frequently operated independently of Hanoi and sometimes even of one another. This was certainly true at district and village levels. Nevertheless, overall strategy, the design of the struggle and its timing, was certainly set by Hanoi, whose leadership group, of course, included southerners. Truong Nhu Tang, by 1984 an embittered exile living in Paris, was one of the founding members of the Front. Upper class, French-educated, urban and urbane, Tang stepped over these contradictions to explain in his memoirs:

> For better or worse, our [Tang refers here to the non-Communist founding members of the NLF like himself] endeavor was meshed into an ongoing historical movement for independence that had already developed its own philosophy and means of action. Of this movement, Ho Chi Minh was the spiritual father, in the South as well as the North, and we looked naturally to him and to his government for guidance and aid. . . . And yet this struggle was also our own.

"Had Ngo Dinh Diem proved a man of breadth and vision," Tang insists, people like himself "would have rallied to him. As it was, the South Vietnamese nationalists were driven to action by his contempt for the principles of independence and social progress in which they believed."[22] Though he joined the Front, Tang did not confuse himself with those he called "ideologues." But peasant recruits to the NLF were unlikely to concern themselves with the differences among its constituents. To them, as oral histories repeatedly demonstrate, the NLF was only the latest name for the Viet Minh, for Ho Chi Minh's party, for the organization that had been fighting for Vietnamese independence—and social change in the countryside—since the 1940s. This sense of things was reinforced by the return to their home villages of the southern Viet Minh partisans who had been regrouped north. (About 4,500 came south between 1959 and 1960; by 1961, the number had risen to over 6,200.) "Some of us thought they had died. We were surprised to see them return, and we were very happy to hear them say that they wanted to organize the Liberation in the area," a peasant from a village near Hue recalled. In this peasant's village and thousands like it, a Front committee was established by former Viet Minh activists—a combination of returnees and those who had survived the repression at home.[23]

In essence, as Jeffrey Race has observed, by "loosening the restraints on the use of violence, the Party eliminated the previous asymmetry between government and Party agents in the rural areas." Before, government agents moved with impunity, while the opposition hid. Now, "the threat was equalized for both sides, and rather than meet this challenge the government apparatus largely withdrew into outposts . . . thus conceding freedom of movement in the rural areas to the Party." In large sections of the fertile, double-cropping province of Long An, whose security was crucial to that of Saigon itself, the NLF had replaced the authority of Saigon even before the end of 1960.[24]

From 1960 on, the dialectic of resistance and repression intensified, although Hanoi continued to apply the brakes. Protracted guerrilla warfare was *not* to be the order of the day, and although the NLF was functioning like a government, its intended role was to reach out to all anti-Diem factions for the purpose of forming a coalition government rather than aspiring to full power for itself. The Party in the South was instructed to pursue a policy of "special war" by means of which local uprisings and small-scale engagements would cause "the Saigon administration [to] disintegrate part by part . . . mak[ing] striking at the center unnecessary." A January 1961 directive laid down guidelines for this special war, which called for the balance between political and military actions to be fine-tuned to the local situation.[25]

In February 1961, the armed forces established in 1958 were formally organized into the People's Liberation Armed Force (PLAF) operating under the Liberation Army Command of South Vietnam. This move was accompanied by considerable political reorganization: the Southern and Central branches of the Lao Dong Party merged into a Central Committee Directorate for the South, which the Americans transliterated as COSVN. Having domesticated it by an acronym of their own invention, the Americans imagined COSVN as a Viet Cong Pentagon, a place that could be found and smashed. But COSVN was a leadership group, not a fixed headquarters. It functioned as an extension of the Central Committee in Hanoi, in charge of the overall direction of the struggle in the South, without fixed headquarters, an elaborate bureaucratic structure, or a research and development wing.[26]

Now everywhere in the South the Front's military force expanded. In late 1961, U.S. intelligence estimated PLAF strength at 17,000; by 1962, the estimate was 25,000. Expansion of a force that had been operating in independent local units brought the possibility of greater differentiation. Small groups were combined to form "main force" regiments, which operated like a regular army throughout the country. Equally important were the regional forces, which fought outside their villages but within their home regions, and the guerrilla militia organized at both village and hamlet levels. As William Turley has explained, hamlet self-defense forces were the crucial base of the pyramid, setting mines and traps, supporting small armed actions, collecting and distributing intelligence about the whereabouts of government forces, training recruits for service at the regional or main force level.[27] When the government responded to small engagements with massive displays of force, villagers who might otherwise have been hesitant to support the Front were enraged. "Everywhere [Diem's] Army came," a peasant remarked, "they made more friends for the V.C." "Cruel," a friend who overheard him agreed, "like the French." Indeed, the divisions within villages reproduced those that had existed against the French: 75 percent support for the Front, 20 percent trying to remain neutral, and 5 percent firmly pro-government.[28]

By October 1961, the Front was so successful that government troops or officials could not drive more than a few kilometers out of any given provincial capital without running into sniper fire. As NLF control expanded, the rich fled to the cities, "leaving the poorer element as almost the sole dwellers in the countryside," an American analysis conducted a few years later concluded, "and the war became in a real sense a class war." This was because the "poor came under the control of the Front." What was so difficult for American observers to understand, although hundreds of prisoners, defectors, and suspects said so in thousands of pages of transcript interviews, was that the Front included the poor, who interpreted the support they received from Hanoi neither as contradiction nor contamination but as affirmation that Vietnam was one country.

No wonder that in the countryside Diem's forces seemed to venture out only to fall into ambush. In one month of 1960, to the disgust of General Williams, the Saigon army lost over one thousand weapons.[29] But the Armed Forces of the Republic of Vietnam, 150,000 strong—wearing American uniforms, helmets, packs, carrying the latest in American military hardware—looked good on the parade ground, and the money that poured in to keep the army looking good was a resource Diem could distribute to loyal commanders. As other sources of support were limited, keeping the army loyal was crucial. It was an army trained to deal with an invasion from the North rather than an uprising in the South. Indeed, since the possibility that the southern insurrection was locally motivated had been ruled out, an uprising in the South could only signal an invasion from the North. The U.S. military believed that this had been the case in Korea, where guerrillas were taken as adjuncts of the North Korean Army and an early warning sign that a large conventional invasion was on its way. Having misunderstood Korea (where a locally supported southern insurgency had operated without support from the North from 1945 to 1950), the military proceeded to misunderstand Vietnam as well.[30]

But in a sense this was a necessary misunderstanding. To have acknowledged the popular southern base of the NLF, to have abandoned Diem in favor of a coalition government in the South, would have required a complete reversal of U.S. policy. It would have meant that the terms of the Geneva Accords, so firmly resisted by the Eisenhower administration, would be fulfilled. And while there was no question of such a policy reversal, the failure of the ARVN to fight effectively against the guerrillas became a matter of growing concern. In April 1960, a high-level U.S. military conference in Okinawa agreed that an effective counterinsurgency capacity had to be developed, and in May three American Special Forces teams arrived in Vietnam to train Vietnamese Special Forces for counterinsurgency warfare. Conceptually, U.S. counterinsurgency planning at this point was entirely focused on establishing control of the population through military and administrative means. The Vietnamese in the countryside, the Okinawa plan noted, "are willing to support whichever side is in momentary local control. . . ."[31] The objective was to make sure it was Diem's side.

To the extent that local dissatisfaction with Diem was acknowledged by the United States, it was limited to the discontent of urban political groups or the slowness with which the very modest land reform policy of Wolf Ladejinsky was being implemented. A growing concern was that Diem was alienating the very people that the United States assumed would be the bulwark of his regime. The model remained the Philippines, and while comfort could yet be found in the hope that Diem would develop into the Vietnamese Magsaysay, time was short.

In the fall of 1960, Ambassador Durbrow urged Diem to act quickly to reform his government or face the possibility that the United States would "begin consideration [of] alternative courses of action and leaders in order to achieve our objective." Specifically, Diem should open the political process to the sort of people who signed the Caravelle Manifesto rather than arrest and harass them; his brother Nhu's secret party, the Can Lao, must consider going public; Nhu himself should leave the government, perhaps even the country; the legislature should be allowed to initiate legislation rather than just approve it; press censorship, however warranted by the military emergency, could nevertheless be eased; the return of elected village councils on some limited basis might lessen alienation in the countryside; and Diem himself should change his aloof image by giving "fire side chats" to explain the ways of his government to the people.[32]

Diem was unresponsive, and relations between his government and the Americans become increasingly tense. Then, in November 1960, shortly after the American election and with the probable foreknowledge and possible support of American officials, several elite military units surrounded the Presidential Palace in Saigon, seized the airport and the radio station, and seemed on the very edge of a successful coup. But Diem was able to draw on loyal troops in the Delta to fend off the threat. The coup was aborted and its leadership exiled. Diem's presidency was saved in time for the newly elected American President, John Fitzgerald Kennedy, to renew his 1957 vow to protect the Republic of Vietnam against all threats. When Kennedy, having called on his compatriots to answer any call for freedom anywhere in the world, sat down to read the cable traffic on Southeast Asia, the news was far from encouraging. In South Vietnam the Communist-led insurgency spread apparently at will; the American-trained South Vietnamese officer corps was doubtfully loyal and observably incompetent; the president of Vietnam, even after his near overthrow, remained stubbornly resistant to American advice.

Among the first reports to capture Kennedy's attention was a review growing out of the Okinawa conference by the military and civilian agencies in Vietnam, entitled the "Basic Counterinsurgency Plan for Viet Nam." In a manner that was to become characteristic of reports from the field, the plan began with a sober assessment of the current situation. The general trend was "adverse," with Viet Cong activity widespread and dissatisfaction with Diem "prevalent" in all sectors of Vietnamese society. To meet this situation, the report recommended that Diem's army be increased from 150,000 to 170,000 men, and the Civil Guard Force from 32,000 to 68,000. The cost to the United States would be $42 million over the $225 million per annum already budgeted for Vietnam. Yet there were only an estimated 9,800 guerrillas operating in the country at the time. At a meeting to discuss the plan held a week after his inauguration in January 1961, Kennedy asked the logical question: why did it take such a vast force to meet such a small threat? The increase was necessary, came the answer, to enable the ARVN to meet both the reality of guerrilla warfare in the South and the possibility of a formal invasion from the North. No one asked if this was a likely event. Nor were very probing questions raised about the reasons for Viet Cong success. The Counterinsurgency Plan attributed their support to "terror or sympathy" but apparently no one asked which, nor what might be the source of Diem's unpopularity. Instead, assured that these financial and military increments would indeed enable the ARVN to take the offensive in the field, Kennedy approved the plan with a marginal notation, "Why so little?"

The question was rhetorical; Kennedy's response to its implication was to dramatically expand a number of programs concerned with South Vietnam, in particular those addressed to counterinsurgency. In Vietnam, Kennedy argued, the free world faced "another type of war, new in its intensity, ancient in its origins—war by guerrillas, subversives, insurgents, assassins; war by ambush instead of combat; by infiltration, instead of aggression, seeking victory by eroding and exhausting the enemy instead of engaging him. . . ."[33] Khrushchev, Kennedy believed, had thrown down the gauntlet in a speech in January 1961 which, in the midst of a passionate appeal for peaceful co-existence, expressed generalized support for national liberation movements in the colonial world. Ignoring Khrushchev's call to end the Cold War, Kennedy instead read the passages about national liberation aloud to the first meeting of his National Security Council, insisting on a strong American response.[34]

Whatever Khrushchev's actual intent, the speech was a suitable launching pad for policies Kennedy had embraced throughout his campaign for the presidency. Under Eisenhower's sclerotic administration, Kennedy had charged, American prestige and military strength declined at a shocking rate. Eisenhower's strategic reliance on "massive retaliation" to deal with Soviet threats meant the United States could not act effectively in the very arena Khrushchev had named—the colonial world—for clearly nuclear weapons were inappropriate to wars like the one in South Vietnam. What was needed was an overall increase in American military capacity, both nuclear (to seal an alleged missile gap) and conventional. In the three years of the Kennedy presidency, the largest peacetime increase in U.S. military history was accomplished at a cost of a $17 billion increase in the defense budget.

Part of the non-nuclear military buildup was devoted to techniques of counterinsurgency, and to this end Kennedy ordered all the services to study guerrilla warfare and contemplate how they might restructure their forces to meet its challenge; he authorized a large increase in the Army Special Forces Group (it was on this occasion that they acquired green berets), and a Special Group Counterinsurgency (CGI) was established, chaired by the President's Special Military Representative, General Maxwell Taylor (who had retired from the Army in 1959 because he disagreed with the strategy of massive retaliation), and attended by the Secretary of Defense, the Chairman of the Joint Chiefs of Staff, the director of the CIA, the heads of the United States Information Service

(USIS) and the Agency for International Development (AID), the Special Assistant for National Security Affairs, and the Attorney General, Robert Kennedy. Counterinsurgency would not suffer from want of high-level attention. In addition, the President encouraged covert missions against North Vietnam and an immediate increase in the number of U.S. military personnel in South Vietnam in explicit and acknowledged violation of the Geneva limit. A memorandum from Robert Komer, who had moved from the CIA to the National Security Council in 1960, noted that such increases would "require circumvention of the Geneva Accords," but, he added laconically, "we should not let this stop us."[35]

The academic experts Kennedy brought with him to the White House were equally enthusiastic about counterinsurgency and certain they understood how insurgencies arose and operated: they were the toxic byproduct of the disruptive process of modernization, in the course of which a small band of ruthless outside agitators were able to exploit the poverty and confusion of a passive population through propaganda and intimidation in order to seize state power on behalf of communism. At this point, they became a direct threat to the national security of the United States. Deputy Special Assistant for National Security Affairs Walt Whitman Rostow, an economist and anti-Communist polemicist who had offered the Third World a "non-communist Manifesto" as a guide to its development, was convinced that guerrilla warfare was a "systematic attempt by the communists to impose a serious disease on those societies attempting the transition to modernization." To Roger Hilsman, Kennedy's director of the Bureau of Intelligence and Research at the State Department (like Rostow a graduate of the OSS, but also of the CIA and the Princeton Center for International Studies), guerrilla war was "a new kind of aggression in which one country sponsors internal war within another." Therefore, by definition, Vietnamese guerrillas were not villagers seeking independence or social justice. They could only be Communist agents. Their movement was not a social revolution but a tactic to gain state power. Fortunately, the operative principles of insurgencies could be studied and combated; and the analysis suggested the remedies. First, establish physical security for villagers threatened by insurgent forces; second, install honest local government officials; and third, improve the living conditions of the population. Of course neither the second nor the third step could be taken until the first, physical security, had been successfully established. What if the insurgents had already installed honest local officials and improved the living conditions so that the population did not feel threatened by them but, in fact, only by the way in which government forces pursued "security"? On this, counterinsurgency doctrine was silent.[36]

The first few months of Kennedy's administration were difficult. In April, an unsuccessful American-directed invasion of Cuba exposed the new administration to criticism from every political quarter. In June, Kennedy felt humiliated by Khrushchev in Vienna. He might promise the survivors of the Bay of Pigs they would one day return to Havana and reassure the citizens of a divided Berlin that he too was a Berliner, but he knew this was bravado.

From Eisenhower he had inherited not only Diem's beleaguered regime but an even shakier right-wing government in Laos. On leaving the White House, Eisenhower advised Kennedy that it might be necessary to send U.S. troops to Laos to prevent a Communist takeover by the Pathet Lao. The Joint Chiefs of Staff, however, were reluctant to consider military action unless the administration was prepared to consider a major intervention in Laos—sixty thousand troops at minimum and a possible expansion of the war to China, which might necessitate the use of nuclear weapons. Kennedy nevertheless authorized preparations for a limited U.S. ground intervention while Hilsman expressed contempt for the Joint Chiefs who "beat their chests until it comes time to do some fighting and then . . . start backing down. . . ." But defeat in the Bay of Pigs intervened and Kennedy told Arthur Schlesinger he was grateful: "If it hadn't been for Cuba, we might be about to intervene in Laos."[37] And Laos, Kennedy's advisers agreed, was a terrible place to take a stand—it was a "non-country," NSC staff member and former CIA analyst Chester Cooper wrote. "It [was] clear that the Laotians in their good-humoured lassitude were reeds too thin to support a heavy American commitment against Communist expansion in Southeast Asia." (Although not all Laotians were so good-humored. In the fall of 1960, the CIA began to train and equip a secret army of Meo tribespeople under the leadership of Vang Pao, who had fought with the French at Dienbienphu.)[38] By May, after extensive British and Soviet mediation, a conference on Laos convened in Geneva, and Kennedy's delegate, Ambassador at Large Averell Harriman, began delicate negotiations toward neutralization. Republicans watched these negotiations closely, ready to pounce should the Democrats "lose" Southeast Asia as they had "lost" China.

To the Kennedy administration, the importance of sustaining Diem and defeating the NLF in Vietnam rose in direct proportion to the slings and arrows of international politics elsewhere. Vietnam was a better place than Laos to take a stand. "It was an articulated, functioning nation," Averell Harriman's deputy William H. Sullivan thought. "Its troops were tigers and real fighters. And, therefore, the advantages would be all on our side to have the confrontation and showdown in Vietnam. . . ." "If the line was to be held," Chester Cooper agreed, "Vietnam rather than Laos was the place to hold it."[39]

But it had better be held. McGeorge Bundy warned the State Department that Kennedy was "really very eager indeed that [Vietnam] should have the highest priority for rapid and energetic action. . . ."[40] Fact-finding missions were dispatched, studies undertaken, training speeded up. Vice President Lyndon B. Johnson was sent to Saigon in May 1961 to bolster Diem's spirits—and his reputation. Hailing Diem as the "Winston Churchill of Southeast Asia," Johnson delivered a letter from the president that elevated the American commitment from supporting Diem in his efforts against communism to a readiness to engage in a "joint campaign" with him. On his return, Johnson reported his conviction that a stand must be taken over Vietnam or "throw in the towel . . . and pull back our defenses to San Francisco. . . ." To secure congressional support for the necessarily costly and long-term effort to enable Diem to win in Vietnam, Johnson urged Kennedy to allay the "paralyzing fears" that American troops might have to fight there. Diem didn't want them and would not call for them except in the case of an "open attack" (from the North), which Johnson thought unlikely.[41]

But the infusion of Johnsonian energy left the military and political situation unchanged. The reported strength of the NLF military force continued to grow—to sixteen thousand, according to U.S. intelligence, back in 1960, armed with homemade or captured weapons; overwhelmingly southern in origin. Some members of Kennedy's cabinet urged the immediate dispatch of ground combat troops, but there was no unanimity on policy nor even on the appropriate military target. Rostow wanted to send 25,000 soldiers recruited from the SEATO countries to seal the border between North and South Vietnam, and if that didn't work, begin large-scale U.S. guerrilla operations in the North, possibly followed by the capture of Haiphong, North Vietnam's major port. But Deputy Undersecretary of State U. Alexis Johnson called Kennedy's attention to the most recent national intelligence estimates, which continued to show insignificant amounts of infiltration; the overwhelming majority of the guerrillas (80 to 90 percent) were southern.[42]

In October 1961, Kennedy sent his personal military adviser, General Maxwell Taylor, to Vietnam. Within a week Taylor cabled an urgent "eyes only" message to the President recommending the immediate dispatch of American troops so as to establish a "military presence capable of showing to Southeast Asia the seriousness of the US intent to resist a Communist take-over." The Pentagon historian of this period describes the report as combining "urgency" with "optimism." The situation was deteriorating, but rapid U.S. action could "buy time" and save the day.[43] Taylor's recommendations included: the introduction of a force of eight thousand ground combat troops, disguised as a "flood control team" in order to overcome Diem's sensitivity on the issue of foreign combat troops; American advisers to be assigned at all military and governmental levels (a measure in particular urged by Lansdale, with whom Taylor had consulted); intensive training of local self-defense forces; and a hefty increase in the number of helicopters, fighter bombers, and reconnaissance aircraft, along with the crews to operate and maintain them.[44]

Since policy rather than empirical data was at issue, it is not surprising that the debate over the Taylor report echoed debates that preceded his trip. Hilsman, rushing to complete a four-month study of counterinsurgency, recommended the development of a "sophisticated combination of civic action, intelligence, police work, and constabulary-like counter-guerrilla forces" rather than the use of regular troops. Walt Rostow called for the dispatch of five thousand U.S. soldiers to the 17th parallel as an unambiguous statement of America's commitment. If the "[enemy] goes to war because of what we do on our side of the line . . . it means he had already determined to face war rather than forego victory in South Viet Nam, and that only our surrender of South Viet Nam could prevent war." Robert Komer also argued for an immediate, decisive military commitment. "True," Komer wrote, "we may end up with something approaching another Korea, but I think the best way of avoiding this is to move fast now before the war spreads to the extent that a Korean type commitment is required." Not that Komer looked forward to the United States "getting involved in another squalid, secondary theatre in Asia. But we'll end up doing so sooner or later anyway because we won't be willing to accept another defeat." McNamara and the Joint Chiefs of Staff spelled out what was required. A clearcut commitment to South Vietnam must be made, which could begin with Taylor's recommended eight thousand men "in a flood relief context" but should extend to "punitive retaliation" against North Vietnam if it continued to support the Viet Cong. Such a commitment might ultimately require a U.S. ground force of as many as 205,000. McGeorge Bundy argued that sending combat troops had "become a sort of touchstone of our will." Therefore, the United States should make a limited commitment of one division, after which "the odds are almost even that the commitment will not have to be carried out."

But not all voices were so bellicose. Averell Harriman, Undersecretary of State Chester Bowles, John Kenneth Galbraith, the ambassador to India, and Abraham Chayes, the State Department legal adviser, thought that a negotiated settlement in Vietnam, perhaps by including the country in negotiations already under way on Laos, was both possible and desirable. The basic causes for the near collapse of the Diem regime, Chayes pointed out, were political, not military, yet "the remedies proposed [by Taylor] would undertake to cope with the situation principally by military and semi-military means." If the President authorized the introduction of U.S. combat troops, Chayes warned, he must be prepared to "escalate, if necessary, to the dimensions of a Korea-type conflict." And Chayes was less sanguine about such an outcome than Komer:

> In assessing the prospects for this course the long history of attempts to prop up unpopular governments through the use of foreign military forces is powerfully discouraging. The French experience in this very area, as well as our own efforts since 1955, reveal the essential inadequacy of the sort of program now proposed. The drawbacks of such intervention in Viet-Nam would be compounded, not relieved, by the United States penetration and assumption of co-responsibility at all levels of the Vietnamese Government suggested in the Taylor Report.

At the National Security Council meeting on November 15, 1961, Kennedy's reluctance to send American troops was evident. Korea, the president argued, had been a case of "clear aggression." But the "conflict in Viet Nam is more obscure and less flagrant." He could "even make a rather strong case against intervening in an area 10,000 miles away against 16,000 guerrillas with a native army of 200,000, where millions have been spent for years with no success." There was considerable discussion, but then, according to the notes of the meeting, the president dropped the matter, returning "the discussion to the point of what will be done next in Viet Nam rather than whether or not the U.S. would become involved." Facing the full measure of his own doubts, Kennedy had turned away.[45]

The president's final decision on the Taylor Report reflected both his hesitations and his determination to act. Negotiations were rejected because, Chayes reflected long afterwards, "we didn't have enough people for it. . . . We had all the non-power in the Department, and so it just never flew." But the immediate dispatch of combat troops was also rejected. Other elements in Taylor's report were accepted and implemented: the Military Assistance and Advisory Group was upgraded to the U.S. Military Assistance Command, Vietnam (MACV), two fully armed helicopter companies were sent over, and a steady increase in the number of advisers authorized. American advisers, including those training Vietnamese fighter bomber pilots, were authorized to participate in combat, though Kennedy and his aides repeatedly denied that this was the case. In Kennedy's calculations, these were interim steps that left him free to expand or contract the U.S. military commitment. There were eight hundred "military personnel" serving in South Vietnam when Kennedy took office; the number increased to three thousand by December 1961, eleven thousand in 1962. There had been some suggestion of a quid pro quo with Diem: U.S. assistance in exchange for reforms that might make his government more popular. But when it came to it, Diem did not deliver and the United States did.

In tandem with this increase in U.S. military activity, Vietnam began to serve as a laboratory for counterinsurgency techniques and weapons. In the spring of 1961, a joint U.S.-Vietnamese testing center was established whose first project was an evaluation of herbicidal warfare: the use of chemicals to poison food crops and strip the foliage in areas in which guerrillas were known to operate. Operation RANCH HAND (whose motto was "Only We Can Prevent Forests") started flying in January 1962; over the next eight years, one hundred million pounds of herbicides would be dropped on over four million acres of South Vietnam.[46]

The most prominent new approach to counterinsurgency was the "strategic hamlet" program suggested to Diem in 1961 by Robert Thompson, a member of the British Advisory Mission, who had developed this tactic in Malaya. Strategic hamlets were a variation of the "agrovilles" with which Diem had experimented in 1959.[47] The pilot project, "Operation Sunrise," took place in March 1962 in the Ben Cat district of Binh Duong Province, long an NLF stronghold. The 5th ARVN Division, reinforced by Vietnamese Special Forces and a psychological warfare company (which distributed a pamphlet prepared by the U.S. Information Service entitled *Toward the Good Life*), first cleared the area. "The Viet Cong simply melted into the jungles," the Pentagon historian of the operation noted. Then the population was rounded up and moved, the majority at gunpoint. Their new home, located so far from the nearest market town as to ensure hardship, consisted of cleared ground and a few concrete administrative buildings. American funds ($300,000) to pay for the move and the construction of new housing were withheld "until the resettled families indicated they would not bolt the new hamlet." "The operation," Bernard Fall wrote, "was hailed as a vast success," but by August 1962 the NFL had taken over the whole settlement.[48] In the Delta, sprawling villages strung out along canals were bunched toward the middle, bulldozing houses at either end and herding farmers into a smaller, more defensible area. Here, too, the relocated villagers were required to pay the government for the building material for their new houses and for the barbed wire inside which they were now to live—though both had been generously donated by the United States. Inside the enclosure, farmers were closely guarded by government troops.

American counterinsurgency experts like Roger Hilsman were enthusiastic. Hilsman's "Strategic Concept for South Vietnam," submitted to Kennedy in February 1962 and widely circulated within the government by Hilsman himself, envisioned secure villages under Saigon control in which varieties of civic action programs would take place. In contrast to Rostow, Hilsman believed the Viet Cong had no more than "a limited need for outside resources. Our main effort must therefore be directed at cutting the links between the Viet Cong and the South Vietnamese villagers." The problem was "by no means just a military problem. It is more accurately described as a problem in effectively coordinating military action with political and economic and social measures." The first essential, however, was "physical security, so that [the farmer] has a choice of refusing to cooperate with the Viet Cong. . . ." The military "guts" of the program, Hilsman wrote, was for the ARVN to "clear and hold" an area, "pushing regular Viet Cong out of a district or at least holding them at bay so that the civic action teams could go to work in the hamlets," and "providing the teams and hamlets protection for the weeks or months it took to turn the area into a solid bloc of strategic hamlets capable of defending themselves." Thus the popular rural revolutionary axiom that guerrillas were the fish in the ocean of the people would be reversed; with the ocean walled off, the fish would surely die. It was here that Hilsman felt himself to be most at odds with the American military, who disliked the static defense of clear-and-hold operations. Aggressive "search and destroy" tactics were more to their taste. In the absence of U.S. combat troops, however, both tactics perforce depended upon the skills of the Vietnamese military.[49]

Diem's brother Ngo Dinh Nhu was put in charge of the strategic hamlet program, which he pursued with enthusiasm. By the summer of 1963 Nhu listed over two thirds of the population safely ensconced in fortified hamlets. In reality, fewer than 10 percent of the camps constructed had any security at all; in many places the families herded behind the fortifications were oddly lacking in young men, who had already joined the NLF. Promised supplies and social services never reached the peasants, however lavishly the Americans supplied them to provincial officials. Living in hovels, farming under the impossible restrictions of curfews, subject to searches, arrests, and extortion, many peasants secretly left the "security" of these hamlets to farm their old lands, look after their fruit trees (if they had not been bulldozed), and meet with Front friends and relatives even at considerable risk to their lives. And when government troops withdrew for the night, local guerrillas and Front officials often visited to collect food, taxes, and information, conduct meetings, and in general carry on the business of government. Sometimes hamlet-level guerrillas and the hamlet militia recruited by the Saigon government were one and the same, grateful for the U.S. carbines to which the militia were entitled.

The NLF version of strategic hamlets were fortified or combat villages equipped for self-defense and serving as bases for small-scale offensive operations. The difference between strategic hamlets and combat villages can be expressed in their central physical features. Strategic hamlets were guarded by army posts and tall watchtowers from which suspicious activity both inside and outside the camp could be observed. By contrast, a guerrilla explained to a sympathetic reporter, "we build our fire positions as close to the ground as possible and the rest underground, because our people are defending their own homes." Thus the two sides fought not just with different tactics but in different dimensions.[50]

How combat villages were organized provides an even more dramatic contrast to the strategic hamlets and illustrates as well how differently each side conceptualized its relationship to the people and the meaning of "control." A captured document described the transformation of one such village it called "XB" in Kien Phong Province, with a population of six thousand. Significantly, the report begins with an account of the landholdings in the village, for any mobilization effort would have to start there, at the center of people's concerns. During the Resistance war, the land of absentee landlords had been distributed to villagers by the Viet Minh; but with the establishment of Diem's government, the landlords had returned accompanied by troops who seized the land and helped to collect back rent. Efforts to resist this process were quickly crushed through arrests and executions; nor did fellow villagers automatically defend the endangered cadres. Indeed, they offered no help at all.

In 1959, however, the surviving Party members, with the help of a few senior cadres, began to rebuild their base in XB, hiding in the fields and marshes during the day and emerging at night to meet with villagers in their houses. As a first step in reestablishing a base in the village, the report explains in a section titled "Means and Methods of Our Success," the cadres "began agitation of farmers to seek their own interests—the right of owning land or reduction of land rent." The campaign attracted considerable support, but not enough to form the "mass base" necessary to struggle against Diem and the Americans (the "My-Diem" clique). However, the village Party group, strong enough now to risk exposure, called mass meetings at which the crimes of the Diem government were "discussed." After a few of these, the Diem-appointed village administrators left; "no village council could be maintained there." At this point, the local Party group became the effective government of the village.

As for the landlords, the cadres encouraged the farmers to go beyond demands for rent reduction and tenancy rights to claim the land itself. The slogan "Kill the land robbers" gained popularity, and local landlords decided to join the Diem-appointed administrators in the nearest town. (The document does not mention executions of landlords; apparently the threatening slogan was enough.) All public and private land was distributed except for plots near Siagon army posts. With the land problem taken care of, attention turned to improving public health, sanitation, education, and maternity facilities. Efforts were made to help farmers market their produce. "The people pay for these services," the report noted, "and they also have a voice in the management of them."

The most difficult part to envision is that the village, now totally removed from Diem's administrative control, was nevertheless still entirely part of the country Diem ruled. There were nearby ARVN posts, the local market town was government controlled, and so on. A description of how funds were raised for the village school illustrates the integration: on the advice of the cadres, the villagers successfully petitioned the Diem-appointed district chief for an appropriation to build one in the village.

In December 1960, the village held a ceremony to celebrate the establishment of the National Liberation Front. Houses were whitewashed and the NLF flag flew from some six hundred homemade flagpoles. When ARVN soldiers came to remove them, according to the report, people protested: "This is a flag of peace. It is not a Viet Cong flag. This flag means that the people, some of whom are your relatives or even your families, have land to till." The soldiers retreated, taking some but not all of the flags.

Having helped the villagers achieve gains they would then wish to defend, the cadres turned to the military problem. At first villagers, fearing government retaliation, resisted all appeals. Cadres tried to explain that organizing for self-defense would protect the villagers, not endanger them, keeping away tax and rent collectors as well as soldiers. After considerable persuasion, villagers began to help construct "naily boards," hidden traps with sharpened bamboo and metal spikes; one farmer invented a bottle grenade, and these preparations seem to have paid off, for a government attack led by some six hundred soldiers decided to withdraw when it became clear that XB village was fortified.

The report on XB village ended with a reflection on a paradox of mobilization: once the programs that won people's support had been successfully established, everyone tended to want to just go about their business. In peace, this would of course have been possible. But there was no peace.[51]

In time, combat villages would become the basis for the integrated political/military struggle the NLF was able to maintain for over a decade. Moving at night, main force units in battalion strength (500+) would camp for short periods of time in villages like XB, gathering food and information and then moving so as to avoid straining village resources or attracting the notice of government troops. Soldiers relied on village militia at every stage of an operation, from initial intelligence to help in retreating from a battlefield, caring for the wounded, and a safe refuge.[52]

To defeat such an enemy required taking rural Vietnam apart, village by village. For this reason, the American military wanted not merely to contain the ocean but to dry it up. After a successful NLF raid in the Central Highlands in 1962, the ARVN cleared an entire valley of its population. The French anthropologist Georges Condominas observed "haggard people, 'uprooted' in the true sense of the word, torn forcibly from a land the smallest corner of which they knew and with which they were accustomed to commune as if that land were human; they had been transplanted to terrain where they knew nothing of the religious taboos or those . . . having to do with planting, moving about, etc.; they were prisoners, not shackled in irons but broken by illness and despair, in what the organizers of their death delicately called 'refugee camps.' " In addition, the Americans had established two Special Forces camps, and the area in between them was declared a free-fire zone. The choices of the Mnong Gar, the minority tribe in that area, were now stark: they could try to survive in the bush or they could submit, live in the Special Forces camps, and become either "beggars or hirelings." It was a choice Diem and the Americans seemed intent on presenting to the population of South Vietnam as a whole.[53]

The helicopter companies Kennedy had authorized in the fall of 1961 were deployed in 1962, bringing napalm and vastly increased firepower to the village battlefield. David Marr, a young Marine intelligence officer, was one of the 550 Marines who made up the first Marine helicopter squadron assigned to duty in Vietnam. In the summer of 1962, he accompanied a division-sized ARVN search and destroy operation. The NLF troops, having observed the helicopters, fighter bombers, and armored personnel carriers that accompanied the ARVN, faded away, and Operation BINH TAY (Pacify the West) succeeded only in "leaving behind smoking villages, plowed-up rice fields, and several hundred dead citizens—the NLF battalions resumed their operations with more success and public support than before."[54]

Nevertheless, the mobility American helicopters gave ARVN troops, the enormous firepower they could now bring to bear by calling for U.S. bombing strikes, and the new weapons with which they had been equipped slowly began to change the war. At first, the PLAF was caught off balance, especially by the helicopters and the enormous M-113 armored personnel carriers. Each M-113 carried a dozen heavily armed ARVN infantrymen and was protected by a .50 machine gun capable of firing ammunition that could shred trees and earthworks. Nothing available to the PLAF could penetrate the armor of the M-113s, whose machine guns, by contrast, could smash through anything. Immense and terrifying machines of war, the initial impact of the M-113 was as demoralizing to the guerrillas as the American military hoped it would be. Villagers, and the guerrillas themselves, had to be convinced their army could cope with state-of-the-art military technology. In part, weapons captured from the ARVN helped to narrow the weapons gap. The guerrillas had carefully observed how the M-113s operated, and although not all their observations were accurate, enough of them were to prove effective when tested in battle. Similarly, careful study of the aerodynamics of helicopters and how the Americans used them, while hardly equalizing matters, rendered the guerrilla far from powerless. Properly directed small arms could bring them down, landing parties could be surprised and ambushed, while mastery of the local environment meant the NLF could still choose when to engage the ARVN, when to disperse. In time, it was hoped, tactics rather than technology could be brought to bear against whatever new machine the Americans gave the ARVN. Meanwhile, NLF troops made careful decisions about when and where to engage in combat, breaking off contact when ARVN strength was too great, ambushing smaller ARVN units and then safely withdrawing when the bombs began to fall. The frustration of the American advisers was almost palpable. In Saigon, General Harkins and the embassy were convinced the Viet Cong were on the run and all that was necessary was to finish them off. Like the French at Dienbienphu, the American military was certain that if the enemy would only stand and fight, the American-trained, -equipped, and helicopter-assisted ARVN troops would smash them.

CHAPTER FIVE

The Fall of Diem
(1963)

Neither you nor I . . . know the Americans well, but what we
do know of them, what we have read and heard about them,
suggests that they are more practical and clear-sighted than
other capitalist nations. They will not pour their resources into
Vietnam endlessly. One day they will take pencil in hand and
begin figuring. Once they really begin to analyze our ideas
seriously, they will come to the conclusion that it is possible
and even worthwhile to live in peace with us. Weariness,
disappointment, the knowledge that they cannot achieve the
goal which the French pursued to their own discredit will lead
to a new sobriety, new feelings and emotions.

> —HO CHI MINH TO MIECZYSLAW
> MANELI, POLISH DELEGATE TO THE
> INTERNATIONAL CONTROL
> COMMISSION, AUTUMN 1963

It's true that working with the Americans sometimes sends a
chill up the back.

> —FORMER EMPEROR BAO DAI TO
> LUCIEN BODARD, PARIS, 1966

I N JANUARY 1963, the Americans got their wish; the NLF did stand
and fight, determined to demonstrate to its own supporters that the
tactics developed to withstand U.S. technology could work. On January 2, a small NLF force of about 350 lightly armed guerrillas faced 2,000
ARVN soldiers, their American-operated helicopter gunships, fighter
bombers, armored personnel carriers, and advisers in the Delta village

of Ap Bac, 40 miles southwest of Saigon. The Front forces inflicted heavy casualties (61 dead, including three Americans, over 100 wounded) and then managed to escape with comparatively light damage themselves. To the astonishment of the American advisers, the guerrillas had even learned how to deal with the terrible and terrifying M-113 armored personnel carriers, thirteen of which were deployed at Ap Bac.

At Ap Bac, American advisers had instructed, demanded, pleaded with their ARVN colleagues to pursue a more offensive strategy, to no avail. Instead, it was the NLF that had given the Americans the battle they asked for and won. "The Viet Cong," Neil Sheehan wrote, "had accomplished the impossible," although one would never know it from the after-action reports distributed by the U.S. military and embassy press officers, which insisted the ARVN had carried the day. The dispute between high American officials in Saigon and the small corps of young American reporters in the field came to a head over the Battle of Ap Bac, though it had been simmering for some time. As Harkins blandly announced an ARVN victory in Saigon, reporters who had been to the battlefield and talked with American advisers were incredulous and said so. The reporters were armed with the evidence of their own eyes and the expertise of John Paul Vann, a senior adviser to an ARVN infantry division operating in the Delta. Vann was convinced the war was being slowly lost, however optimistic the reports Saigon sent home to Washington. Vann persuaded the reporters of something else as well: there was a right way to fight this war, if only senior officials, military and civilian, could see it.

It was a message bound to attract the press corps, much as Vann himself did, with his persuasive insights into the NLF and his corruscating impatience with fools of whatever rank. Ten and more years older than most of the reporters, Vann took them into his confidence, leaking documents that would help them to understand the war as he understood it. Relentlessly masculine, Vann talked war to the reporters as if they were comrades in arms. And the world of the war at field level could be intoxicating. David Halberstam of *The New York Times* found in Vietnam a "marvelous and rare combination of constant excitement, some danger, the exhilaration that comes from being around brave men, beautiful countryside, good food and lovely women . . . and recurrent bitter fights with American officialdom." On his twenty-eighth birthday he joined an eagle flight:

> In an eagle flight you load up a helicopter with a small number of picked troops and circle around until someone shoots at you. Then

you swoop down, land your troops and try and police up a hamlet. This had been a particularly successful day and we had made several strikes, capturing about 15 Vietcong and killing about 10 others. . . . Going into combat [in a helicopter] is a bit like watching a football game from a good press box seat. . . . There was one particular moment when we flushed a Vietcong out and he started running desperately along a dry paddy, stumbling and jerking as he went. Our helicopter pursued him relentlessly, machine after man . . . and I might have felt some sympathy if I had not carried out bodies of dead government defenders from an outpost earlier in the week.[1]

Vann taught Halberstam and many other acolytes how to understand the war in terms that confirmed their own experience without disturbing their fundamental assumptions. Increasingly, those experiences were at odds with official pronouncements from both Washington and Saigon, raising a problem of credibility for the Kennedy administration and of conscience for many Americans. "This is a political war," Vann instructed them, "and it calls for discrimination in killing. The best weapon for killing would be a knife, but I'm afraid we can't do it that way. The worst is an airplane. The next worst is artillery. Barring a knife, the best is a rifle—you know who you're killing." Vann did not doubt his mission to kill, albeit with a rifle; neither did the press corps, though their weapon would be the honest report: "We thought it our duty to help win the war by reporting the truth of what was happening in order both to inform the public and to put the facts before those in power so that they could make the correct decisions," Neil Sheehan explains in his biography of Vann.[2]

The more insistent was official American optimism about the course of the war, the more energetically the press called that optimism into question. Reporters like Halberstam, François Sully, Neil Sheehan, Malcolm Browne, and Charles Mohr described in detail the fragility and corruption of the Diem regime and the failure of its military to profit from nine years of American training and mountains of equipment. "People keep writing me," the newly appointed ambassador, Frederick Nolting, complained, "asking, 'Fritz what's going on out there all of a sudden? I thought we were doing so well.' "

To Nolting and to General Paul Harkins, as to Diem and his family, any story in the American press that deviated from the official account of success and optimism gave material aid and comfort to the Viet Cong, and every investigative journalist was a potential traitor to the cause. "The first time I saw [Ambassador] Nolting," one reporter told fellow correspondent Stanley Karnow, "he told me that Diem's real strength lay in the countryside. After hearing that I figured there was no point in questioning him again." (A cautious man, Nolting once delayed a TV interview while he had the office portrait of Thomas Jefferson replaced by one of George Washington, whom he considered "less controversial.")

For a time, State Department instructions for handling the press explicitly attempted to limit press access to "military activities of the type that are likely to result in undesirable stories" by denying military transport. But Saigon was full of cars for hire, and the enterprising reporter could often manage to get to the scene of battle (as Sheehan had at Ap Bac) without a helicopter.[3]

Press management, how the war *looked* at home and abroad, was a central concern of Kennedy administration policymakers. Hanoi must be publicly warned of America's unswerving commitment to South Vietnam so that Hanoi would end the war that, in the first place, the American public must be convinced there was no danger of America entering, and in the second, the South Vietnamese were anyhow winning. It was equally important for the United States to avoid looking like a new colonial power to the population of the South while at the same time persuading them to support the government chosen for them.

In an effort to harness the power of the word against NLF charges that Diem was an American puppet, John Mecklin, the new head of the U.S. Information Service (USIS) in Saigon, announced a "Name the Enemy Contest" to his Vietnamese staff in the spring of 1962. Inspired by a suggestion from Robert Thompson (well known to American officials because of the strategic hamlet program), Mecklin offered a top prize of 3,500 piastres (U.S. $47) for a name that would "describe the enemy in his true light, and will tend to turn the people against him." The enemy did not deserve to carry the national appellation, "Viet," and "Cong" was perhaps less than telling to illiterate peasants. What was needed was something that would

> influence the Vietnamese people to regard the enemy in the most important (in your view) of the following ways: with contempt, as arrogant bullies, as foreign and/or Chinese puppets, as common criminals, with ridicule so the enemy loses face, with hatred, as traitors, as hypocrites, as crackpots or madmen, as children playing soldier, or as bloodthirsty murderers. Or perhaps the right answer is something that a Westerner would never think of? Maybe the term should be related to the way they dress . . . or the way they behave, or address each other, that can be made to look ridiculous or evil. Perhaps a colloquial peasant term implying disgust or ridicule? Or a term about the way they lecture everyone for hours and make the villagers under their control learn silly songs and slogans?[4]

Mecklin's contest was only one of hundreds of such efforts. In Phu Yen Province, for example, 100,000 matchbooks were distributed with a message extolling the strategic hamlet program on the cover and "kind words for the various government forces" on the inside. PsyWar Adviser Captain McCarthy was delighted with the ploy: "multiplying 100,000 × 20 matches and you have a message exposure of two million!" But it was frustrating work. Like other American advisers, those engaged in "psy-war" were often disappointed in their Vietnamese students. "Colonel Chuong," a staff member wrote Mecklin, "head of ARVN Psywar, got caught the other day bringing in 5 million piastres worth of pornography from Taiwan."[5] Yet the all-important task, as a RAND report summa-rized it several years later, was to "enlist nationalistic sentiment on the side of the South Vietnamese government, and to establish in the minds of the people the conviction that the Saigon regime is the legitimate government of the country." Colonel Chuong did not make the job any easier.[6]

The administration response to the bad press the war and Diem were receiving was to dispatch another fact-finding mission. "Our overall im-pression," Roger Hilsman and Michael Forrestal reported to the presi-dent in February 1963, "is that we are probably winning, but certainly more slowly than we had hoped." Strategic hamlets continued to be a good idea, but it was difficult to know how villagers really felt about them, or "how many of the 20,000 'Viet Cong' killed last year were only innocent, or at least persuadable villagers. . . ." There was a problem as well with air strikes, which were currently running at one thousand each month. During the month of November 1962, Hilsman and Forrestal learned, about 32 percent of the strikes were attacks on "installations" that photo reconnaissance indicated were enemy-held; 53 percent were in direct support of an attack; and 15 percent occurred in the course of other sorts of missions. "There is no doubt," the report continued, "that the Viet Cong fear air attacks. . . . On the other hand, it is impossible to assess how much resentment among persuadable villagers is engendered by the inevitable accidents."[7]

The report troubled Kennedy, whose first response, as Forrestal recalled it many years later, was to try to restrict the "heavy military activity of the ARVN—the use of napalm, the use of herbicides, the use of too many mines." But he didn't get very far, Forrestal went on, "be-cause our Army supported all those activities, and thought they were necessary and militarily justified." After Kennedy's death, several of his close friends and supporters reported that the President considered withdrawing from Vietnam before the end of his first term, but decided that to do so would mean he wouldn't have a second. He would do it after 1965, Ken O'Donnell remembers being told. "I'll be damned everywhere as a Communist appeaser. But I don't care. If I tried to pull out completely now from Vietnam we would have another Joe McCarthy red scare on our hands, but I can do it after I'm reelected." Lyndon Baines Johnson, when he became President, professed a similar fear. No one thought it odd that the United States should continue to conduct an anti-Communist war in Vietnam in order to prevent a resurgence of domestic anti-communism in the United States.[8]

Like Kennedy, the American Friends of Vietnam, the organization of Diem supporters and admirers that had brought Diem to the attention of the Eisenhower administration, were beginning to lose faith, not in South Vietnam, but in Diem as its savior. Founding members spoke out against Diem publicly, and some American reporters were quietly advising friends in Congress that a coup would be a good idea—provided it was initiated by the Vietnamese. Joseph Buttinger, one of Diem's original supporters, went even further, directly urging Diem's overthrow in a secret proclamation (written in cooperation with a former Vietnamese official) for distribution in South Vietnam. In Washington, Buttinger lobbied the Kennedy administration, arguing that the war could only be won without Diem. While senior White House aides and State Department officials tended to agree, the military, including McNamara, resisted. The effort to replace or even reform Diem was misguided, they argued; best to concentrate on the military front and win the war.[9]

American dissatisfaction with Diem's performance was matched by Diem's displeasure with the United States. To the French ambassador, he complained of the sheer number of advisers around: "All these soldiers I never asked to come here," he said. "They don't even have passports."[10] The American effort to bypass the central government by giving U.S. advisers control over the distribution of aid to the provinces and hamlets infuriated Diem, and he requested the removal of two thousand province-level advisers currently in the field. The issue was sovereignty, he explained; what sort of independent nation allowed a foreign country to so dominate its internal affairs? Ambassador Nolting, a longtime supporter, was worried. In April he sent a cable, warning that the Vietnamese seemed on the verge of "repudiation of concept of expanded and deepened U.S. advisory effort." Nolting urged that new military aid be suspended to convince Diem "that we mean business."[11] But instead of pressure making the regime more amenable to U.S. advice, Diem and his brother grew ever more resistant, complaining to reporters about the number of advisers and their behavior; making it clear that any increase in their number would be resisted. Indeed, the exact number of American troops in the country was a closely guarded secret for precisely this reason. Diem was under the impression there were twelve thousand, though the actual number had reached sixteen thousand.[12]

It was the 2,527th birthday of the Buddha on May 8, 1963, that brought the tensions between Diem and the Americans to a point of crisis. For almost a decade, the Catholic Diem and his family had given favors and patronage to Vietnam's Catholic minority (southern-born as well as those who arrived from the North in 1954), alienating the Buddhist majority. In the villages and towns around Hue, whose Buddhist organizations had begun to speak out politically against Diem's favoritism, government troops conducted sweeps each spring at the time of Buddha's birthday, "to show the V.C. that the Government was strong," a Catholic priest in the district told an American, "and to make the opponents of the Government afraid."[13]

On this particular birthday, the government decided to demonstrate its strength by enforcing a law against the display of flags other than the national flag. In Hue, where Vatican flags had recently blanketed the city in honor of Diem's brother, Archbishop Ngo Dinh Thuc, Buddhist flags were flown in conscious defiance of the ban and nine people died when troops opened fire on the celebrating crowd. Diem's claim that the Viet Cong was responsible convinced no one. Two days later, ten thousand Buddhists marched to protest the killings; to which Diem responded by jailing leading Buddhist monks and their supporters. As distressed American advisers stood by helplessly, the Ngo Dinh family denounced the Buddhists as a Communist front organization and placed an armed guard around the most active pagodas. The American press, which had on the whole ignored political dissent in South Vietnam in favor of war stories, now focused on the crisis, and U.S. officials who felt the time had come to apply maximum pressure on Diem leaked stories of Washington's immense distress with his handling of the situation.[14]

On the morning of June 11 the struggle reached a new stage. Quang Duc, a sixty-six-year-old Buddhist monk, sat peacefully in the back of a 1960 Austin sedan. When the car reached the intersection of Le Van Duyet and Phan Dinh Phung Streets, the driver stopped. Thich (Reverend) Quang Duc got out, sat down in the middle of the street, and assumed the lotus posture. A chanting crowd of monks many rows deep observed as two helpers slowly doused the seated figure with gasoline. Quang Duc lit the match himself and sat motionless and silent as the flames consumed him. As he burned, a young acolyte with a microphone repeated, in Vietnamese and English, "A Buddhist priest burns himself to death. A Buddhist priest becomes a martyr."[15] Only Quang Duc's heart did not burn, a phenomenon not much commented on in the West but of considerable import to his followers, who placed it reverently in a container to be displayed as a relic.[16] Today, the Austin occupies a position of honor in the garden of a pagoda in Hue, Malcolm Browne's photograph of the priest engulfed in flames propped against the windshield.

In America, this image of self-immolation had an enormous impact. It cut across the political debates over Diem with its demonstration of just how much the Ngo Dinh family was hated, how passionate was the Buddhist opposition. The sympathy that poured out to the martyred monk was culturally specific, however; it was understood as the sort of thing that was done in the Orient. When an American, Norman Morrison, immolated himself in protest against the war some years later, the Vietnamese honored him, but his compatriots thought him simply mad. Madam Nhu, misjudging the American public, mocked the event, calling it "a barbeque." Protests spread beyond the Buddhist religious community to high school and university students throughout South Vietnam, creating the potential for a massive urban anti-government movement.

The Kennedy solution to the crisis was better management. First, Henry Cabot Lodge, a man whose ancestral and personal Republican Party credentials offered the Kennedys cover on their right (the only side on which American politicians seem ever to feel exposed), was appointed ambassador to replace Frederick Nolting, whose history of friendship with Diem had become problematic. Secondly, Diem's brother Nhu must go. It was Ngo Dinh Nhu who had alienated the country and oppressed the Buddhists. If Diem would only rid his top governing councils of Nhu and his wife, the country would rally to his support. Blaming Nhu exempted the rest of American policy from close examination, and Nhu was such a convincing villain. In August, instead of conciliating the Buddhists as the Americans urged, he ordered elite American-trained troops to raid pagodas throughout the country, brutally expelling and arresting resident monks. Vietnamese of all political persuasions were appalled; the Vietnamese ambassador to Washington and the observer to the United Nations (respectively, Madame Nhu's father and mother) resigned.

With each new outrage, Nhu confirmed Washington's judgment that he was an intolerable liability. By mid-September 1963 he had moved in a direction that made his removal not only desirable but absolutely necessary if the United States intended to remain active in Vietnam affairs. Either as a ploy to pressure Washington or because he really meant it (and the closest examination of the documents has failed to resolve the issue with any degree of certainty), Nhu was probing the possibility of a rapprochement with Hanoi. The one condition that had long ago made Diem so attractive—that he was a Vietnamese nationalist who could be counted on never to cut a deal with Hanoi—was forfeit. In the spring of 1963, Nhu was discreetly exploring the possibility of a cease-fire; in August, Ho Chi Minh indicated his readiness to negotiate the terms of a cease-fire, provided American troops withdrew and negotiations were followed by a freely elected government in the South. Hanoi and this new government might then discuss the form reunification could take. Rumors of contacts between Saigon and Hanoi multiplied along with rumors of an American-sponsored anti-Diem coup.[17]

In Washington, Roger Hilsman, who had been arguing for months that the time had come to force Diem's hand, drafted a cable to Lodge instructing the ambassador to give Diem one last chance to get rid of his brother and sister-in-law. "We wish," an August 24 cable instructed Lodge, "[to] give Diem [a] reasonable opportunity to remove Nhus, but if he remains obdurate, then we are prepared to accept the obvious implication that we can no longer support Diem. You may also tell appropriate military commanders we will give them direct support in any interim period of breakdown [in the] central government mechanism." The cable has been the subject of some controversy; McNamara's deputy signed it for the secretary of defense, as did John J. McCone's deputy for the CIA, and Victor Krulak for the Joint Chiefs, the principals being out of town at the time. Kennedy and Rusk approved it by telephone. Later, Taylor, McNamara, and McCone all expressed considerable distress over the cable, and Kennedy himself may have had second thoughts. Nevertheless, it was not rescinded and Kennedy's major reservation, as he expressed it to Lodge in a private cable on August 29, was that a U.S.-backed coup succeed. With the Bay of Pigs much in mind, Kennedy told Lodge that in his experience, "failure is more destructive than an appearance of indecision." He would count on Lodge to warn him "if the current course begins to go sour. When we go, we must go to win, but it will be better to change our minds than fail."[18]

In Saigon, CIA agent Lucien Conein passed the word along to the Vietnamese generals, only to find them nervous, unsure they could command the necessary forces, anxious for even more explicit American help. Some of their hesitation may have been due to their knowledge that the Kennedy administration was divided on the entire question of a coup. Harkins, on whom the Saigon generals might have to depend in the event of a coup, as well as McNamara, McCone, and Taylor, continued to oppose the overthrow of Diem. Without for a moment abandoning the idea, Lodge advised Rusk that a coup would have to wait until "some other group with the necessary strength and lust for office comes forward. . . ."[19]

Coup planning now paused and a National Security Council meeting on August 31 attended by Dean Rusk, Robert McNamara, Maxwell Taylor, Lyndon Baines Johnson, Robert Kennedy, and Roger Hilsman reviewed the possibility of working with Diem. Rusk reminded his colleagues that above all it was necessary to determine what measures the government should take to *improve the Vietnamese position wherein [sic] U.S. public opinion is concerned"*(italics in original).

Paul Kattenburg, the State Department coordinator of an interdepartmental working group on Vietnam, who had just returned from Saigon, was also there. "I listened for about an hour or an hour and a half," he recalled many years later, "before I was asked to say anything at the meeting and they looked to me absolutely hopeless, the whole group of them. There was not a single person there that knew what he was talking about. . . . They were all great men. It was appalling to watch. . . . They didn't know Vietnam. They didn't know the past. They had forgotten the history. They simply didn't understand the identification of nationalism and Communism, and the more this meeting went on, the more I sat there and I thought, 'God, we're walking into a major disaster.' " At that point Kattenburg did an extraordinary thing: he dissented. If the United States continued to support Diem, he predicted, "we are going to be thrown out of the country in six months. . . . it would be better for us to make the decision to get out honorably." His outburst was "very imprudent and also very presumptuous. . . . And the reaction to it was sort of what I had invited. They all just disregarded it or said it was not backed by anything."[20]

Kattenburg's superiors did more than just disregard what he said; they explicitly rejected it. Rusk called the meeting sharply back to order: it would be best if the discussion proceeded "on the firm basis of two things—that we will not pull out of Vietnam until the war is won, and that we will not run a coup." McNamara, Taylor, and Vice President Johnson agreed. Without specifying how they differed, Johnson declared that it would be a "practical and political" disaster to pull out of Vietnam. The time had come "to stop playing cops and robbers" and restore communications with the Diem government, though it might be necessary for "someone to talk rough to them. . . ."

Lodge received the results of the meeting in two cables, one from

Rusk, one from Hilsman, both instructing him to remind Diem that the continued presence of the Nhus in his government "eroded our capacity to . . . support the effort in Viet-Nam. . . . [Diem] must make . . . a demonstration to the American people that we were not asking Americans to be killed to support Madame Nhu's desire to barbeque bonzes."[21] The problems were tactical: how to rid the Saigon government of the Nhus short of a coup; if a coup proved necessary, how to make sure it succeeded without assuming responsibility for it; if it failed, how to make sure the United States would not be blamed; finally, how to make sure the right people took over. As Lodge pointed out in a cable to Kennedy, "We do not want to substitute a Castro for a Batista."[22]

What to do with Nhu became the subject of much discussion. Could he be persuaded to resign, leave the country, silence his wife? Edward Lansdale, now a general, urged Harriman "to create a place for Nhu up at Harvard. . . . I said, 'Kick him upstairs. Tell him he's an intellectual. Listen to him and give him a job there.'" John Kenneth Galbraith, on leave from the Harvard Department of Economics to serve as ambassador to India, demurred, and while Harriman thought it a splendid notion, Harvard never made an offer.[23]

Debate on how hard to press Diem to reform continued throughout September 1963. Should some or all aid be cut off? What would happen to the war effort if such sanctions were applied? Hilsman railed at the way in which Diem and Nhu led the "U.S. around by the nose" and insisted there must be some way to show "the Vietnamese people that the U.S. could not be made a puppet." An effort to demonstrate which way the lines of control ran was made on September 17 in a cable from the White House to Lodge, authorizing him to apply aid sanctions at his own discretion. Lodge could "delay any delivery of supplies or transfer of funds by any agency until you are satisfied that delivery is in U.S. interest. . . ." It might be particularly desirable to limit or reroute money flowing to Nhu and his associates. In addition, Diem should be presented with a list of "helpful" reforms which included, in order of priority,

A. Clear the air—Diem should get everyone back to work and get them to focus on winning the war. He should be broadminded and compassionate in his attitude towards those who have . . . found it difficult under recent circumstances fully to support him. A real spirit of reconciliation could work wonders. . . .
B. Buddhists and students—Let them out and leave them unmolested. This more than anything else would demonstrate the return of a better day and the refocusing on the main job at hand, the war.
C. Press—The press should be allowed full latitude of expression.

...While tendentious reporting is irritating, suppression of news leads to much more serious trouble.

D. Secret and combat police—Confine its role to operations against the VC and abandon operations against non-Communist opposition groups. . . .

The list projects an idea that Diem and Nhu had somehow wandered into error, lost their way on the path to good government, and resisted American advice out of willfulness rather than self-interest. Cut off the money and then perhaps they would behave. Lodge was less sanguine. In his September 19 reply to the president, Lodge pointed out that he had suggested the entire package of reforms to Diem on many occasions and been rejected. "[Diem and Nhu] think that most of them would either involve destroying the political structure on which they rest or loss of face or both." It would be foolish to expect any substantive changes from them. Nor was there any way to apply economic sanctions without seriously damaging the war effort. "If a way to do this were to be found," Lodge wrote, "it would be one of the greatest discoveries since the enactment of the Marshall Plan in 1947 because, so far as I know, the U.S. had never yet been able to control any of the very unsatisfactory governments through which we have had to work in our many very successful attempts to make these countries strong enough to stand alone." In Lodge's view, a coup remained the best hope if the war was to be won. Sanctions would work only in concert with a "promising coup d'etat." And time was running out. General Duong Van Minh had warned the ambassador privately that

> the Viet Cong are steadily gaining in strength; have more of the population on their side than has the GVN; that arrests are continuing and that the prisons are full; that more and more students are going over to the Viet Cong; that there is great graft and corruption in the Vietnamese administration of our aid; and that the "Heart of the Army is *not* in the war." (italics in original)[24]

Lodge understood that self-interest, not whim, shaped the Diem regime. But he believed the problem to lie in the particular family the United States had chosen to lead South Vietnam rather than the social and economic structure of the country itself. A shuffle of the Vietnamese deck could yet produce the right man (or men) for the job.

Uncertain of what course to take, Kennedy dispatched new observation missions. General Victor Krulak, the Joint Chief of Staff Special Assistant for Counterinsurgency, and Joseph Mendenhall, of the State

Department Far East Planning Office, reported back on September 10 after a four-day trip. "Were you two gentlemen in the same country?" Kennedy asked after their report. Not really, Krulak replied. He'd been to the countryside, where the war was, and there things were going quite well. Krulak "believed strongly we can stagger through to win the war with Nhu remaining in control." Mendenhall, on the other hand, insisted that "the disaffection with the regime had reached the point where a breakdown of civil government was threatened. . . . The war could not be won with the present regime."[25] And in the midst of this ongoing debate, Washington received word that Nhu was once again publicly discussing the possibility of direct negotiations with Hanoi. According to Roger Hilsman, Nhu's minimum goal was to "sharply reduce the American presence"; his maximum goal was "a complete removal of the US presence, and a 'neutralist' or 'Titoist' but still separate South Viet-Nam."[26] No member of Kennedy's staff wondered why this could not be an American goal as well.

In late September, Kennedy sent Maxwell Taylor and Robert McNamara to Saigon for yet another assessment of the situation. Although they brought back assurances from Harkins of tremendous military success (sufficient to warrant the withdrawal of one thousand American troops), Lodge had convinced them of Diem's political fragility. They recommended continued economic pressure on Diem, including an end to funds supporting the Vietnamese Special Forces under Nhu's control. While not expecting that these measures would actually succeed in forcing Nhu out of the administration, they stood a chance of deterring Diem from "resuming large scale oppressions." The report did not recommend a coup "at this time."[27]

But whatever the report's intention, cutting off aid to Nhu's elite troops was the signal of U.S. support the hesitant Saigon generals sought. On October 5, 1963, in full knowledge of how it would be received, Kennedy approved the move. That very day, General Duong Van Minh met with Conein in Saigon to discuss various approaches to a change of government, including the assassination of Nhu and the retention of Diem as a figurehead. The local CIA team preferred this to an all-out military battle in Saigon, and CIA director John McCone, though loath actively to condone assassination, told the Saigon station not to act to prevent it either. For three weeks the plotters plotted and Washington waited anxiously. In late October, Kennedy's anxiety about a failed coup or, equally, a successful coup for which the United States would be held responsible, prompted Lodge to reassure him. A coup was entirely desirable. It was at least "an even bet that the next government would not bungle and stumble as much as the present one has." And anyhow, "this is the only way in which the people of Vietnam can possibly get a change in government."[28] It was, at any rate, the only way in which the United States could get a change in Vietnam's government.

While the energies of the administration were occupied with how to continue the war with or without Diem, some attention was diverted to fend off the threat of a negotiated peace. It would have been possible, for example, to allow Nhu to go ahead with his Hanoi dealings and use them as a suitable excuse for dignified disengagement. Or, less problematically, Kennedy might have responded to Charles de Gaulle's offer to mediate. In late August 1963, de Gaulle proposed a comprehensive approach to Vietnam, which included the withdrawal of American troops, the neutralization of South Vietnam, and the resumption of North-South relations: in effect, a return to the basic provisions of the Geneva Accords.

Reactions from both Hanoi and Saigon were positive; only the United States rejected the suggestion out of hand. There was both ironic reversal and considerable consistency here. Throughout the French war against the Viet Minh, American observers were convinced the United States could do it better if it had the chance. When the French decided their war was over, Eisenhower and Dulles urged them to fight on, explored the possibility of joining them in combat, attended peace negotiations with utmost reluctance. In 1963 and 1964 a French president who understood imperial longings was suggesting that it was time for the Americans to suppress these in their own bosom, and end the war they had seized from the French.

Instead, although some senior military and CIA officials continued to argue against a coup on the grounds that the war was going well enough, on October 27, 1963, in the casual setting of the Falls Road public golf course, Averell Harriman and Roger Hilsman caught up with Acting Secretary of State George Ball, who interrupted his round of golf to sign a "green light" cable. Funds were allocated to Conein for distribution to the relevant generals so that troops might be paid and the coup begin. On November 2, Diem and his brother were dead. "Like all assassinations," a staff member of the Joint Chiefs of Staff observed, "it had just happened. Nobody in Washington had said, 'Shoot Diem.' You don't do an assassination that way. The way people are assassinated is by taking away the power that has been created to keep them there." Three weeks later, Kennedy was dead, assassinated. "We had a hand in killing him," Johnson told Hubert Humphrey, gesturing at a portrait of Diem. "Now it's happening here."[29]

* * *

There were 800 American military personnel in South Vietnam when Kennedy took office and 16,700 when he died in November 1963. The National Liberation Front controlled the majority of villages in the South when Kennedy took office; they continued to do so in the year of his death, and basic American policy was also unchanged. After a decade of intense engagement in Indochina, the categories of America's understanding of the Third World remained pristine of historical experience. The abstract mythological model, applicable to any nation, upon which United States policy based itself, reflected not so much ignorance of the history, culture and society of others as indifference. This in turn reflected American history, culture and society, which had always denied that traditions or social constraints had to matter. The United States had created itself and it could help other nations to do the same. The United States declared South Vietnam a new nation, born in 1954, and did not take seriously the evidence that this new nation was really half of an old one, whose long struggle for independence against outside invaders informed the social and personal imagination of every Vietnamese. Vietnamese society was insubstantial to U.S. policymakers except as it must be overcome, its cities modernized, its passive peasantry urbanized, its government placed in the hands of strong men, though not too strong to be removed when necessary. In time, no doubt, South Vietnam would even be ready for democracy. Meanwhile, there were technological an swers for every problem and managerial solutions for every crisis.

To understand Hanoi, furthermore, policymakers peered into the mirror. Since the United States was determined to create an anti-Communist state in South Vietnam, it followed that it was the intention of Hanoi to build a Communist state there. And this ambition, far from growing out of the history of a revolutionary independence movement that had been Communist-led since the 1930s, was an assault on both South Vietnam and the national security interests of the United States. And continuing this reasoning, if the NLF grew in strength, the only possible explanation was that it was receiving increased support from Hanoi; for that, of course, was how the ARVN grew. Hanoi, having created the NLF as the United States had created the Republic of Vietnam, could dissolve it at will. Had the United States not just rid the South of Diem? The soldiers of the PLAF were outsiders as were the American advisers. The fact that they were known to be locally recruited did not signify—in the act of joining the NLF a villager became a Viet Cong, and thus an outsider. American reporters, like American government officials, never referred to the members of the NLF, civilian or military, as

South Vietnamese. That appellation was strictly reserved for the officers and officials of the Saigon government, though more often than not they were born in the North. It was also extended to villages under government control. All others were Viet Cong and not South Vietnamese villages. The final leap of this logic cast Vietnamese who lived and worked north of the 17th parallel as more foreign to South Vietnam than the Americans, for the Americans were invited guests, while North Vietnam was an enemy country.

It was not only its Vietnamese enemies that the United States saw thus abstracted from their national identities but its Vietnamese friends as well. The repressive policies of the Ngo Dinh family were seen as inspired by clan and cultural loyalties that they could expunge if they really tried. The failure of ARVN troops in "aggressivity" was seen as cowardice, local cease fire arrangements remaining quite invisible to American advisers. And since Vietnamese realities were irrelevant to American policy, failures of policy were generally analyzed as merely tactical. Thus Diem was a tactical failure, readily replaceable by a junta whose origin, far more than was the case with Diem, made it entirely dependent on the United States and therefore ready to follow its advice without a quarrel. Now at last, the Americans thought, the war could proceed in earnest.

CHAPTER SIX

Taking the War North (1963–1964)

In order to achieve . . . victory, the Joint Chiefs of Staff are of the opinion that the United States must be prepared to put aside many of the self-imposed restrictions which now limit our efforts, and to undertake bolder actions which may embody greater risks.

—GENERAL MAXWELL TAYLOR TO
SECRETARY OF DEFENSE ROBERT
MCNAMARA, JANUARY 1964

O N HIS SECOND DAY in office, Lyndon Baines Johnson met with Kennedy's top advisers to discuss Vietnam. He had inherited the policy and the men who made it—as he had the office of the presidency itself. And he was worried, his friend and aide Bill Moyers recalls, that "they'll think with Kennedy dead we've lost heart. . . . The Chinese. The fellas in the Kremlin. They'll be taking the measure of us." Johnson insisted that the generals in Saigon be informed "that Lyndon Johnson intends to stand by our word."[1] That word now meant full U.S. support for the new government and accelerated planning for military action against the North in order to pressure Hanoi to call off its war in the South.

Vietnam was a large nettle Johnson seized with both hands. What he really wanted, he said repeatedly at the time and thereafter, was to focus on domestic reform in civil rights and social welfare. Instead, he found himself in charge of a war he claimed he could not abandon:

I knew from the start that I was bound to be crucified either way I moved. If I left the woman I really loved—the Great Society—in order to get involved with that bitch of a war on the other side of the world, then I would lose everything at home. All my programs. . . . But if I left that war and let the Communists take over South Vietnam, then I would be seen as a coward and my nation would be seen as an appeaser, and we would both find it impossible to accomplish anything for anybody anywhere on the entire globe.

Complaining that he could do no other, Johnson chose the war, whose definitions he never questioned. "Losing the Great Society was a terrible thought," he told a biographer, "but not so terrible as the thought of being responsible for America's losing a war to the Communists. Nothing was worse than that."[2]

The generals in Saigon, ironically, could think of worse things, though few of the American Vietnam policymakers understood that. However desperately they might wish to secure and control a separate state in the South, the members of the junta that deposed and assassinated Diem were nevertheless not quite ready to make all-out war against their own country, especially when they thought they might lose. "Our requirements," the assistant secretary of state for Far Eastern affairs, William Bundy, said, "were really very simple—we wanted any government which would continue to fight." Yet the new junta, despite the fact that it was entirely military in composition, was determined to shift the arena of struggle to politics. The jailed Buddhist leaders were released and a Buddhist Congress Diem had banned was encouraged. The junta reasoned that the success of the NLF was correlated to the repression and corruption of the Diem administration. The new government planned to build a base of support among groups in the society Diem had alienated, members of the Cao Dai and Hoa Hao sects, the Buddhists, students, and urban professionals, minority peoples displaced by Diem's Catholic clients—in short, all those the junta guessed had made common cause with the NLF not out of commitment to communism but out of despair and anger directed at Diem.

The junta was non-Communist rather than anti-Communist. "You must understand the distinction," General Duong Van Minh, one of the leaders, said later, "because it is an important one." What he sought, Prime Minister Nguyen Ngoc Tho explained to the historian George Kahin, was a "government of reconciliation, which would be one wherein all elements of the NLF would be welcome to participate in an electoral process. . . . We would have striven for a neutral government—not a government without an army, but one without foreign troops or bases and one whose neutrality in international affairs would incline towards the West." The government of reconciliation would then work toward a "relationship of peaceful coexistence between Saigon and Hanoi."[3]

There is every reason to believe that both the NLF and Hanoi would have welcomed these moves, though of course no certainty that a permanent peace would have followed. One can imagine such a neutral, non-Communist government of reconciliation resisting the revolutionary transformation in land ownership the NLF had instituted and repressing those responsible for it; in time, a new insurgency might well develop. Possibly, Hanoi would have eventually tired of peaceful coexistence with a neutral South that nevertheless leaned to the West, and demanded full unification and integration. Yet whatever the dangers, Tho's surely was a vision of peaceful resolution that the newly installed American president might have explored.

The opening months of Johnson's presidency thus gave him the opportunity to disengage from Vietnam and devote his energies entirely to the Great Society. Duong Van Minh's Military Revolutionary Council looked forward to American disengagement; de Gaulle was ready to help in negotiations leading to the neutralization of all the Indochinese states; the majority leader of the Senate, Johnson's friend and colleague Mike Mansfield, appealed directly to Johnson to pursue the possibilities of peace. But others worked equally hard to keep "that bitch of a war on the other side" alive. Don't even *think* about neutralization, Kennedy's former top aide, McGeorge Bundy, instructed the president. Neutralization would only mean unification on Communist terms; Japan, Thailand, and the Philippines would all shift toward neutrality; U.S. prestige would drop so low in South Korea and Taiwan as to "require compensating increases in American commitment there—or else further retreat." And he would lose the next election. Rostow stoked the fire: neutralization of South Vietnam would be "the greatest setback to US interests on the world scene."[4] The secretary of defense, the head of the CIA, and the Joint Chiefs of Staff agreed.

Even before learning of Duong Van Minh's conciliatory efforts, American officials had expressed grave disappointment in the junta both for its reluctance to pursue the war in the South with sufficient aggression and for its resistance to American plans for bombing the North. In response to U.S. prodding, Minh complained about excessive American interference. At a meeting on January 10, 1964, between Ambassador Lodge, Duong Van Minh, and several other members of the Military Revolutionary Council, the "extreme undesirability of Americans going into districts and villages" was raised. U.S. military advisers should not be assigned below the regimental level; otherwise, there "would be a colonial flavor to the whole pacification effort," the generals argued. And Minh stressed that "even in the worst and clumsiest days of the French they never went into the villages or districts." Indeed, the Americans should back off everywhere: United States Information Service teams should work at the provincial level only; Americans should stop training Cao Dai and Hoa Hao militia. When Lodge protested that the USIS teams were mostly made up of Vietnamese nationals, Minh replied: "Yes, but they are considered the same as the Vietnamese who worked for the Japanese and the same as the Vietnamese who drive for Americans and break traffic laws."[5]

Taylor's first report to Kennedy, in November 1963, had called attention to the vulnerability of the North to conventional bombing.[6] Now Johnson's advisers argued that a simple cost-benefit analysis would persuade Ho Chi Minh to give up his war of aggression in the South on pain of losing everything his government had worked so hard to build since 1954. Yet at a meeting with McNamara, General Harkins, and Ambassador Lodge in Saigon, Duong Van Minh strongly objected, arguing that bombing the North was wrongheaded on almost every conceivable count: it would harm innocent people; it might provoke a substantial movement of northern troops to the South; it would alienate popular opinion in the South; and it was unlikely to have any effect on NLF troops fighting in the South.

Since the U.S. military had on the whole opposed their coup against Diem, relations between senior American officers and the Military Revolutionary Council were distant. The Council itself was divided: some of its members looked toward both a negotiated settlement of the war and a thoroughgoing reform of military corruption; others, feeling threatened by both policies, began to entertain thoughts of another coup. They found members of the U.S. military sympathetic to their plans, and on January 30, 1964, a coup against Duong Van Minh and his supporters in the Council (later sometimes referred to as the "Pentagon's coup") was successfully conducted by General Nguyen Khanh.[8]

Diem had been overthrown because of his almost universal unpopularity, his resistance to American guidance on how to prosecute the war, and the threat that he might choose not to prosecute it at all but instead reach an agreement with Hanoi. Duong Van Minh and his colleagues were on their way to achieving a modicum of popularity, but they too resisted American guidance on how to prosecute the war and had begun to design ways not to prosecute it at all but instead to make peace. What the United States found in Khanh was a Vietnamese government that would follow orders. Now McNamara, returning to Washington in early March 1964 from another trip to Vietnam, reported that the government led by General Nguyen Khanh would do very well. Khanh was entirely in favor of U.S. advisers at all levels of both the civilian and military hierarchies; he even consulted with Lodge on whom to appoint to his cabinet. McNamara described him as "highly responsive to American advice," and Ambassador Lodge doubted if "anywhere in the world the United States has a better relationship with a chief of staff than exists here."[9]

However satisfactory Khanh may have been, McNamara thought that the situation in Vietnam was "unquestionably . . . growing worse." ARVN draft dodging and desertion rates were high and rising, "while the Viet Cong are recruiting energetically and effectively." Most disturbing to McNamara was the behavior of village and hamlet self-defense forces. In some areas, the militia had "turned in" their weapons; in others, the militia had to be disarmed because their loyalty was suspect; in two major provinces, the number of strategic hamlets under government control had dramatically decreased. Throughout the Delta, "security . . . has deteriorated badly. The Viet Cong control virtually all facets of peasant life in the southernmost provinces and the government troops there are reduced to defending the administrative centers." In the face of this situation, McNamara's overall recommendation was to begin planning for carrying the war north: "To prepare immediately to be in a position on 72 hours' notice to initiate the full range of Laotian and Cambodian 'Border Control actions' . . . and the 'Retaliatory Actions' against North Vietnam, and to be in a position on 30 days' notice to initiate the program of 'Graduated Overt Military Pressure' against North Vietnam." In addition, the ARVN should be increased by fifty thousand, to be paid for with $50 million more in aid; paramilitary forces must expand and receive U.S. training; and Khanh should be urged to institute national conscription.[10] The political failure of successive Saigon governments was to be solved by means of new and more energetic military action.

The Pentagon was delighted. Well before McNamara's March trip, the Joint Chiefs had been urging overt attacks on North Vietnam as well as an expansion of covert actions already under way. In late February and early March, an interagency study group working under the State Department Vietnam Committee developed detailed proposals to extend the war to the North. Its March 1 recommendations to McNamara reasoned that military pressure on the North would take advantage of "North Vietnamese concern that their industrialization achievements might be wiped out or could be defended (if at all) only at the price of Chicom [Chinese Communist] control." And if the Chinese did not come to their aid, even better, for this would demonstrate "that their more powerful communist allies would not risk their own interests for the sake of North Vietnam." While no amount of pressure on the North would "substitute for successful counterinsurgency in South Vietnam," bombing the North would, in contrast to the expected passivity of the Soviet Union and China, "demonstrate U.S. power and determination, along with restraint, to Asia and the world at large."

For all its enthusiasm, the study group sounded a note that could have been read—had Johnson or his aides been so minded—as a warning not to do any of the above:

> It is not likely that North Vietnam would (if it could) call off the war in the South even though U.S. actions would in time have serious economic and political impact. Overt action against North Vietnam would be unlikely to produce reduction in Viet Cong activity sufficiently to make victory on the ground possible in South Vietnam unless accompanied by new U.S. bolstering actions in South Vietnam and considerable improvement in the government there.

What would be gained by bombing, then? At most, "some time and opportunity by the government of South Vietnam to improve itself."[11]

In addition to its military discussion, the interagency study group had drafted a congressional resolution that would make the war it advocated safely non-partisan. The need to draw Congress into the process was patent as Vietnam increasingly became the subject of debate in both the House and Senate. In a passionate speech to the Senate on March 4, 1964, Democratic senator Wayne Morse of Oregon declared that the United States "should never have gone in. We should never have stayed in. We should get out." And he warned that "when the casualty lists of American boys in South Vietnam increase until the mothers and fathers of those boys—and, yes, the American people generally—start crying 'Murder,' no administration will stand." But in the House, Republican representative Gerald Ford of Michigan baited McNamara during his testimony before the House Appropriations Committee. Ford sensed a "reluctance on the part of Administration officials to commit U.S. forces to combat for a Vietnamese-United States victory, and I don't think this is a proper or prudent attitude."[12]

By the spring of 1964 the war was becoming sufficiently divisive to warrant public review in the form of a full-dress CBS television documentary. With an accuracy its producers could only have guessed at, "Vietnam: The Deadly Decision" concluded that Washington was on the brink of a major decision: whether to find an "honorable way out" of the war, or "as a nation, as a people, to continue to accept the cost, the casualties, the frustration and the uncertainty, not for just a little while longer, but perhaps for many years." The program illustrates the context in which journalists most often set the war and the distortions endemic to that context. But it also illustrates the contradictions these same journalists exposed, and while they may have mostly turned away from fully exploring them, many Americans, watching and trying to understand, did not. The narrator, Charles Collingwood, described the victory of the North Vietnamese over the French, followed by the Geneva Accords which, in this version, "divided [Vietnam] along the 17th Parallel." Ho Chi Minh ruled in the North and then—Collingwood's syntax suddenly becoming passive—"Ngo Dinh Diem was brought to power in the South." At first, with American help, South Vietnam seemed stable; but then, the "Viet Minh of the North . . . created an underground in the South and won the confidence of many villagers." Diem might have prevailed had he conducted the necessary reforms, but he didn't, and so in 1961 the Kennedy administration "decided on a massive effort to save South Vietnam. From that time on we have become more and more deeply embroiled." The account is seamless: the United States had decided to save from North Vietnam a country created at Geneva in 1954, South Vietnam. The unpopularity of Diem is squarely stated but simultaneously rendered irrelevant by not being addressed.

After hinting at American complicity in the overthrow of Diem, Collingwood turned to the present and the regime of Nguyen Khanh, young, unknown, and "with no political following." The program had opened with clips of McNamara's embrace of Khanh during his March tour of South Vietnam: "We are prepared to furnish whatever economic aid, whatever military training and logistical support, whatever military equipment is required, in whatever quantities are required and for as long as that is required." Collingwood answered the implicit question (why was such a commitment made to a man with no political following in his own country?) with the assertion that Khanh "at least moved with resolution to get the country back on its feet and to pursue the war against the Viet Cong."

At several points in the broadcast Collingwood insisted that the United States "got into South Vietnam through the best of motives." The point had to be stated firmly if the audience was not to lose its way in the Vietnam footage that followed, an account of a government assault on two hamlets in the Delta in which four hundred prisoners had been taken. "Are these bonafide Viet Cong or the frightened population of two hamlets, or both?" correspondent Peter Kalischer asked, and concluded that most likely "they're from the 300,000 so-called 'true believers,' part time or regional guerrillas, farmers, fishermen, bus drivers, school teachers, or your hotel room boy in the city." If "guns and gadgets" could win the war, Kalischer concluded, it would have been won: "but men and motivation, not machines, are the basic ingredients of victory, and not enough Vietnamese men have wanted hard enough to win that war." The corollary, that there were enough Vietnamese on the other side who wanted it hard enough, could not be fully voiced. To do so would immediately call into question Collingwood's first premise: that the United States, with the best of intentions, was saving Vietnam.

Why, then, was the United States in Vietnam? Collingwood turned to Henry Cabot Lodge, who explained: "if you take a piece of string and put one end of it in Saigon on the map and measure off a thousand miles and make a circle, you'll find that within that circle are 240 million people, which is Southeast Asia. . . . Loss of this area would be a catastrophe. That would make a lot of Americans think that we'd better resign from the human race, so to speak, and fall back on a fortress America and gird ourselves up for a fight with guided missiles." Collingwood did not protest the explanation but only asked: Can the war be won? Lodge answered yes, but would make no time commitment.

The reporters were then asked for their recommendations. They talked tactics. Kalischer complained of the abuse of firepower: "I've been witness to too many times when . . . in trying to kill a handful of Viet Cong in a village, why, we've made at least a hundred recruits by indiscriminate bombing or strafing." There must be more attention to civic action and psychological warfare. Marvin Kalb agreed: "it's exceedingly difficult, if not impossible, to beat an ideology with technology. You cannot do that." Instead, thoroughgoing reform in Saigon was necessary, as well as officials who "make the peasants feel that they are identified with this war. . . ." Kalischer did not foresee a clearcut military victory, but argued that denying South Vietnam to communism would be enough: "Coldbloodedly, we really don't care what happens here providing the Communists don't get it and with it Southeast Asia." It had been a cheap war, so far, only seven hundred and fifty American casualties in the past two and a half years. Korea had cost 53,000 lives, after all, and the stakes here were higher.

Finally, Collingwood confronted McNamara. For years the United States had been trying to increase the effectiveness of the South Vietnamese government and still the situation deteriorated. "How do you reconcile those two?" McNamara's answer was brief: "Because we now have a leader in South Vietnam, General Khanh, who himself is ready to put that nation on a war footing." It would be almost a year before the United States sought a replacement for Khanh.[13]

On the CBS program, McNamara had hinted at the possibility that war might be carried to North Vietnam. In May 1964, the Joint Chiefs of Staff worked out a detailed thirty-day "scenario," which incorporated elements of the recommendations made by the interagency study group in March and provided for consultation with allies, a congressional resolution authorizing the president to do "whatever is necessary with respect to Vietnam," and a set of speeches written for General Khanh to deliver that threatened "unspecified military action." The plan climaxed with "D-Day": the mining of North Vietnamese ports, destruction of bridges, railroads, and such targets as would have "maximum psychological effect on the North's willingness to stop insurgency." Yet in a general discussion of the "scenario" led by the Board of National Estimates of the CIA, State Department, and Defense Intelligence, all agreed that none of these measures would affect "communist *capabilities* to continue that insurrection" because "the primary sources of communist strength in South Vietnam are indigenous." The goal therefore was to affect the *"will"* of the DRV leaders"[14](italics in original).

    This was war as performance, albeit deadly performance, and Johnson's senior advisers preferred it to Air Force General Curtis LeMay's call for bombing North Vietnam "back to the Stone Age." The limited nature of American intentions was to be clearly signaled to the enemy, who would be given an opportunity to surrender at each stage. Bureaucratic prose ("the U.S. will use selected and carefully graduated military force against North Vietnam") and political science calculations ("military action [which] will not trigger acts of terror and military operations by the Viet Cong") masked reality. However modern and reasonable it sounded, the logic of calibrated pressure was the logic of the rack, articulated in the language of games theory and the accountant's spread sheet.

    Perhaps to balance this cool abstraction, an effort was undertaken to improve the image of the Saigon government, in whose name, after all, this "scenario" was to be enacted, through a campaign to make General Khanh popular and attractive to his fellow countrymen. Ambassador Lodge, who boasted of having performed similar duties for General Eisenhower, coached Khanh in the art of the fireside chat, or more precisely in its delivery, since the talks themselves were written by U.S. Information Agency staff members. In Washington the head of USIA, Carl Rowan, looked to more "sophisticated" techniques, and urged that an effort be made to "find a Vietnamese who can write a GVN [Government of Vietnam] version of 'God Bless America.' "[15]

Johnson was not ready to approve the direct bombing of the North and the wider war it threatened. Instead, he authorized an increase in the pace of the covert action campaign he had initially approved in January 1964. OPlan 34-A was a series of punitive but covert operations carefully calculated to intensify the pressure on Hanoi. At its most pacific, OPlan 34-A involved air and naval surveillance of the North. More provocative were commando raids against bridges, railways, and coastal fortifications. As part of a declared effort to disrupt NLF supply lines that ran through Laos, and to discourage North Vietnamese support for the Communist-led Pathet Lao, American pilots began routinely to bomb and strafe Pathet Lao positions. In early August 1964, North Vietnamese villages on the Lao border were bombed as well.[16]

Lyndon Baines Johnson was a politician rather than a political scientist. He understood, none better, a world in which deals were made, compromises reached, backs mutually scratched, and the general interest, as defined by benevolent powerholders, generally served. Even as his advisers prepared lists of military targets in the North, at Johnson's direction they also worked on propositions Ho Chi Minh couldn't refuse. At Lodge's suggestion, J. Blair Seaborn, the Canadian representative on the International Control Commission, was asked to serve as the intermediary between Washington and Hanoi.[17] Seaborn made his first trip in June 1964; there would be four more over the next twelve months.

Seaborn delivered a simple message: the United States intended to "contain the DRV to the territory allocated it by the Geneva Agreements," but it had no desire to "overthrow the DRV" or acquire permanent military bases in the South. If Hanoi would end the insurgency in the South, for which Washington held it fully responsible, the benefits of "peaceful co-existence" could follow. But Hanoi must beware: "[U.S.] patience was growing thin." Premier Pham Van Dong was equally direct: the United States must withdraw from the South, after which a "neutral" regime should be established that would include the National Liberation Front. What happened next "was up to the people of the region."[18]

Whether administration officials expected anything to come of the Seaborn mission or not, by early June the president had before him a fully worked out schedule for bombing the North, as well as a draft for a congressional resolution that would sanction any military actions he ordered in Vietnam. But Johnson continued to hesitate. Passage of the resolution might prove difficult; bombing the North was hardly the act of a peacemaker. Best to wait until after the elections, the president decided. And when the Republican Party nominated Barry Goldwater in July, Johnson's caution seemed to have been rewarded. Let the Republican nominee propose "extremism in defense of liberty." The Democratic incumbent ran as a moderate, a peace candidate. But not too peaceful, or Johnson might face those charges that have made all Democratic presidents since Truman wake sweating in the middle of the night: that in their sleep they had somehow lost a country. On the other hand, a warlike posture carried its own dangers, such as reproducing the Chinese intervention in Korea, a memory that haunted the American military and political world equally.

The problems that summer seemed overwhelming. Nothing had come of Seaborn's effort to end the war in the South by threatening the North with condign punishment. In the field, the war continued to go very badly indeed. General William Westmoreland, who had replaced Harkins, requested an additional 900 military advisers in June 1964 and a month later asked for another 4,200. William Sullivan, now head of the interdepartmental Vietnam Working Group, was convinced that the long slide of General Khanh's government into terminal demoralization could be halted only by giving him a "confident sense of victory," and that could be achieved only "from an act of irreversible commitment by the U.S." In 1967, the Pentagon historians summarized the logic of this moment for McNamara:

> Khanh had not been able to provide the necessary leadership, despite all the aid and support the U.S. had given. No level of mere aid, advice, and support short of full participation could be expected to supply this deficiency. . . . [Khanh] would not be able to feel that assurance of victory until the U.S. committed itself to full participation in the struggle, even to the extent of co-belligerency. If the U.S. could commit itself in this way, the U.S. determination would somehow be transfused into the GVN. The problem before the assembled U.S. policy-makers, therefore, was to find some means of breakthrough into an irreversible commitment of the U.S.[19]

"Co-belligerency," Johnson was advised, must await some overt act of war on the part of Hanoi, and none seemed to be forthcoming.

*   *   *

For its part, the government in Hanoi had developed its own set of contingency plans. In December 1963, shortly after the deaths of both Diem and Kennedy, the Central Committee of the Lao Dong Party met to consider the situation in the South. Party Secretary Le Duan spoke of the need to increase the commitment to the struggle in the South. The problem he faced was more than how to deal with ARVN forces, more even than the constant flow of new and more powerful firepower made available to the Saigon government. As the Battle of Ap Bac had demonstrated, outgunned and outnumbered NLF troops could defeat an ARVN force. But what if the United States chose to land its own troops in the South and make it an American war? Contingency plans would have to be made in terms of this danger, for an American ground invasion would fundamentally change the nature of the struggle.

For Hanoi, American support for a South Vietnamese government, even with incremental increases in advisory support and weaponry, was far less dangerous than full American participation. The governments the Americans supported were vulnerable both politically and militarily. Coalitions with anti-government groups and even direct negotiations, such as Duong Van Minh had seemed to invite, were possible in these circumstances. But if the United States itself entered the war, Saigon governments could survive almost any amount of domestic dissent, almost any degree of local military defeats. The situation would then become what it had been from 1946 to 1954: a colonial war that could only be defeated, as France had been, by protracted warfare. North Vietnam would have to become a "revolutionary base for the whole nation," vastly expanding both land and sea supply lines to the South and preparing for the movement south of regular combat units. Such conclusions were not uniformly applauded. There was, among some Central Committee members, a deep reluctance to expose the North to an American onslaught. But it was difficult to argue against Tran Van Tra, who had fought the French in the South, that it was the South that would bear the brunt of what was, after all, a war of national defense.[20]

At the same time that plans were made to increase support for the military effort in the South, Hanoi actively sought openings for a negotiated settlement. In a major concession, Hanoi let it be known through French Communist Party circles that even a North/South separation of indefinite duration was acceptable provided the United States withdrew, and normal trade and diplomatic relations between the two parts of the country were permitted. There was no response from the United States.

Instead, under the general auspices of OPlan 34-A, South Vietnamese commando raids against North Vietnamese coastal targets increased and DE SOTO naval surveillance operations, introduced in 1962 to gather information as well as to give a "show of force," continued. In mid-July, for reasons that remain unclear, the destroyer *Maddox* was ordered to the Gulf of Tonkin on a DE SOTO mission. Then, on July 30, South Vietnamese commandos accompanied by American advisers conducted heavy raids against two islands in the Gulf of Tonkin. The very next day the *Maddox* reached the Gulf, and as it entered, exchanged greetings with the gunboats carrying the commando party back to base in Danang. *Maddox* crew members also waved at the North Vietnamese fishing boats they passed, laden with nets and families; but no one, the sailors complained, not even the children, waved back.[21]

On August 2, as the destroyer cruised close to offshore islands that were again under attack by South Vietnamese commandos, the *Maddox* was pursued into the middle of the Gulf by three North Vietnamese patrol boats which, according to Commodore Herrick, Commander of Destroyer Division 192, kept charging at the ship in a V formation and then rapidly veering off. In response, the *Maddox* opened fire with its huge five-inch guns. The North Vietnamese held their course and Captain Ogier was pleased: "Of course, you know, if they had just turned and run away after we'd started firing at them, then we could have been in trouble. Because they could have said, 'Here we are in international water, too, and you went and fired at us.' But they came on and fired torpedos at us, which was good."[22] The torpedos missed their target and the Vietnamese PT boats, damaged by the guns of the *Maddox,* turned back toward port, briefly pursued by jets from the aircraft carrier *Ticonderoga.* And that was it; the first and only incident in the Gulf of Tonkin.

The exchange was reported to Washington in a key of alarm and anger. Johnson personally ordered a second destroyer, the *Turner Joy,* into the Gulf; he also used the "hot line" to Moscow for the first time, informing the Kremlin that the presence of two U.S. destroyers in international waters off the coast of North Vietnam was no cause for alarm. The Joint Chiefs also responded. U.S. combat troops were placed on alert and a fighter bomber squadron in Thailand strengthened. Admiral U. S. Grant Sharp, Jr., Commander-in-Chief Pacific Command (CINCPAC), ordered a second aircraft carrier to the area and instructed the destroyers already in the Gulf to "assert the right of freedom of the seas." And the South Vietnamese commandos returned to the Gulf once again to attack mainland coastal fortifications.

American officials consistently denied any connection between the presence of the destroyer and the commando raids, and it is possible that the two were indeed unconnected and that no special provocation was intended. But a hostile response from Hanoi was certainly welcome, even solicited. Radio intercepts informed U.S. officials that Hanoi linked the presence of the *Maddox*, South Vietnamese commando raids, and the bombing of North Vietnamese villages on the Lao border on August 1 and August 2 as signaling a new level of American involvement. Did Hanoi want a war, Johnson asked his National Security Council about North Vietnamese actions in the Gulf. Not at all, McCone answered. "[They] are reacting defensively to our attacks on the off-shore islands. They are responding out of pride and on the basis of defense considerations." Rather than reassure Hanoi, Rusk professed himself delighted that Hanoi was "rattled" and informed the Saigon Embassy that larger commando raids were planned for the near future.[23]

On the hot summer night of August 4, the sonarmen of the destroyers detected a sea alive with hostile torpedos, and for several hours the guns of both the *Maddox* and the *Turner Joy* blazed into the night. A few hours later no one was sure there had been anything at all out there. James B. Stockdale, overflying the action from the deck of the *Ticonderoga*, "with the best seat in the house from which to detect boats," failed to see anything at all. "No boats," Stockdale recalls, "no boat wakes, no ricochets off boats, no boat impacts, no torpedo wakes—nothing but the black sea and American firepower."[24] Commodore Herrick, on board the *Maddox*, immediately radioed Sharp's headquarters urging daylight reconnaissance. "Review of action makes many reported contacts and torpedos fired appear very doubtful. . . . No actual sighting by *Maddox*. Suggest complete evaluation before any further action." Stockdale was relieved. "At least there's a commodore up there in the Gulf who has the guts to blow the whistle on a screw-up," he thought before going to bed. But next morning he was woken early with orders to retaliate against targets in North Vietnam. "And I said, 'Retaliate for what?' " Nevertheless, Stockdale "led this big horde of airplanes over there and we blew the oil tanks clear off the map."[25]

In between the first alarming report from the *Maddox* and the subsequent, more hesitant cables, the president's men had met to select targets in the North and to work on the precise wording of the long-contemplated congressional resolution. A resolution would avoid the problem Truman faced when he went to war in Korea without soliciting prior congressional approval, and it was certainly preferable to a declaration of war—provided one could have been passed—especially in an election year.

Herrick's message did not go entirely unnoticed. McNamara cabled Sharp to be absolutely sure the second attack had taken place, and the admiral duly answered that it had, though there remained a "slight possibility" that it hadn't. McNamara requested a further check but even as that was taking place, the order to retaliate was given. At the same time, Johnson called together congressional leaders of both parties to inform them of events. They were told of an unprovoked attack against American ships in international waters and asked for their support for a resolution that would sanction the retaliatory attack already under way.

On August 5 the resolution was placed before Congress. After two days of debate it passed the Senate by a vote of 88–2 (ten affirmative absentees; Senators Wayne Morse of Oregon and Ernest Gruenig of Alaska opposed) and the House by a resounding 416–0. It was a resolution, its preamble stated, to "promote the maintenance of international peace and security in southeast Asia." There followed a set of propositions which, whatever their relationship to Vietnamese reality, accurately summarized the legal and moral case on which the Johnson administration intended to prosecute the war:

> Whereas naval units of the Communist regime in Vietnam, in violation of the principles of the Charter of the United Nations and international law, have deliberately and repeatedly attacked United States naval vessels lawfully present in international waters . . . and Whereas these attacks are part of a deliberate and systematic campaign of aggression that the Communist regime in North Vietnam has been waging against its neighbors and the nations joined with them in the collective defense of their freedom; and
>
> Whereas the United States is assisting the peoples of southeast Asia to protect their freedom and has no territorial, military or political ambitions in that area, but desires only that these people should be left in peace to work out their own destinies in their own way. . . .

In the light of these self-evident truths, then, Congress pledged its approval and support for "the determination of the President . . . to take all necessary measures to repel any armed attack against the forces of the United States. . . ." A second section asserted that "peace and security in southeast Asia" was vital to American national security and therefore the president, acting in accord with the Charter of the UN and as a member of SEATO, would "take all necessary steps, including the use of armed force," to assist member states of SEATO "in defense of [their] freedom." Finally, the resolution would expire when the president determined that "peace and security had returned to the area"; it could also be terminated by a subsequent congressional resolution.[26]

Wayne Morse, working on a tip from a source in the Pentagon that the Vietnamese attack was far from unprovoked, tried to interest fellow senators in the information, with no success. "Hell, Wayne," one of them told him, "you can't get in a fight with the President at a time when the flags are waving and we're about to go to a national convention. All Lyndon wants is a piece of paper telling him we did right out there, and we support him, and he's the kind of president who follows the rules and won't get the country into war without coming back to Congress."[27] At very brief hearings on the resolution, members of the administration lied when asked if the United States had done anything to provoke an attack (no one knew enough to ask whether the attack had taken place at all). The attacks, McNamara told the House Foreign Affairs Committee, were "deliberate and unprovoked" against a ship on "routine patrol in international waters." When Morse raised the possibility of a connection between the *Maddox* and the South Vietnamese commando raids, McNamara flatly denied it: "our Navy played absolutely no part in, was not associated with, was not aware of any South Vietnamese actions, if there were any."[28]

Years later, as the lies were exposed and Congress tried to distance itself from the war it had sanctioned in 1964, many senators claimed that had they known the facts, they would have opposed the resolution. But Johnson's Deputy Attorney General, Nicholas Katzenbach, may have been closer to the truth when he told an interviewer that the Tonkin Gulf incident in itself "was an absolute nothing." If it hadn't been that incident, something else would have come around. "I don't think it made one iota of difference in any congressman's or senator's vote as to what happened or didn't happen in the Tonkin Gulf." Representative Dante B. Fascell of Florida remembers it that way, too: "The President needed the authority. Who cared about the facts of the so-called incident that would trigger this authority? So the resolution was just hammered right on through by everybody."[29]

Still, some senators did express concern about the degree to which they were abandoning the constitutional authority, solely invested in them, to declare war. Senator Sherman Cooper, a Kentucky Republican, asked if the resolution meant that "if the President decided that it was necessary to use such force as could lead into war, we will give that authority by this resolution?" Fulbright said it would, though a subsequent resolution could withdraw the authority, and in any case the president would not use the power the resolution gave him "arbitrarily or irresponsibly," and would certainly consult with Congress "in case a major change in present policy becomes necessary." Cooper was not entirely satisfied. He expressed confidence in Johnson but urged that the administration keep in mind the "distinction between defending our own forces, and taking offensive measures in South Vietnam which could lead progressively to a third world war."

Gaylord Nelson, Democrat of Wisconsin, suggested a friendly amendment to the resolution that would express congressional anxiety about escalation by stating explicitly that U.S. policy was limited to the "provision of aid, training assistance and military advice." The modesty of the limitation is expressed in the convoluted language of its conclusion: "it is the sense of Congress that, *except when provoked to a greater response,* we should continue *to attempt to avoid* a direct military involvement in the southeast Asian conflict" (italics added). And in any case the floor manager of the resolution, Senator Fulbright, talked Nelson out of formally presenting his amendment, arguing that the resolution was harmless, that any opposition would only aid Goldwater, and that Congress was "just backing the President on his Tonkin response, not giving him a blank check for war." In this Fulbright was passing on the assurances he had received from his good friend and former colleague Lyndon Baines Johnson that the resolution was about Tonkin and nothing else.[30]

Yet the most important aspect of the resolution was not what it authorized Johnson to do but the completeness with which it accepted administration reasoning about *why* it was doing it. With few exceptions, indeed only two, Congress shared the world view of the administration, debating the edges of the issue but never questioning the basic premises. Senator Charles Mathias, a Republican from Maryland, explained to an interviewer how deeply he had believed that "merely by enacting a resolution which seemed, at least, to show a high degree of national unity, we could in some way dissipate the forces which we at that moment, saw as a threat." What Congress was saying, Mathias thought, was "we'll sign this blank check, but we don't have any expectation that it will ever have to be used. All you'll have to do is wave it in front of your creditors and they'll all go away." In a similar vein, Fulbright, who later bitterly regretted his role in ensuring passage of the resolution, said at the time he had believed the administration account of the second attack: "I don't normally assume a President lies to you." And he had agreed with the "theory of the resolution," which was that "this was the way to avoid and to stop the war. . . . These people would give up if we would just bomb them in a serious way, and they could see what we could do. Then they would stop."[31]

But why did Congress think bombing the North would end the war in the South? Because, like the executive branch itself, they were convinced that Hanoi had the power to stop that war and would do so if the United States made it too costly for them to continue. James Thomson, a wry participant–observer of the scene (he was then on the staff of the National Security Council), told Senate hearings in 1968 that the alleged second incident in the Gulf had been useful as a way of showing "our will or our resolve, regardless of the absence of a clear *causus belli.*"

> *The Chairman [Senator Fulbright]:* And this was interpreted to mean if we showed the will then the North Vietnamese would surrender. I mean, being faced with such overwhelming power, they would stop. Is that really the way they were thinking?
> *Mr. Thomson:* "Would be brought to their knees" was the phrase that was used.
> *The Chairman:* And, in effect, be willing to settle it on our terms; is that correct? Is that a fair summary?
> *Mr. Thomson:* That was the hope, yes.

That had been a "serious mistake in judgement," Fulbright concluded. But it was far more than that. The notion that Hanoi could be "brought to [its] knees," first by the threat of U.S. actions and then by successive and selected punishments, was at the heart of Johnson administration policy. This was "coercive diplomacy," the use of violence short of all-out war. It was not only legitimate but even humane, for it fell far short of the total destruction the United States could unleash if it wished.[32]

No major American newspaper questioned either the official version of the events or the appropriateness of the American response. AMERICAN PLANES HIT NORTH VIETNAM AFTER 2D ATTACK ON OUR DESTROYERS, *The Washington Post* announced. MOVE TAKEN TO HALT NEW AGGRESSION.[33] It is likely that Johnson himself believed an attack against American warships had taken place. Yet there can be little doubt that he responded to the possibility of such an attack with stunning alacrity. No one suggested waiting a bit, probing Hanoi's intentions, or seeking mediation. Whatever happened in the Gulf of Tonkin, its successful presentation to Congress and the public as an overt act of hostility by Hanoi was precisely what Johnson's advisers had told him he needed: a way to justify direct American participation in the war, a "breakthrough into an irreversible commitment."

Johnson's advisers expected that bombing would get results. After all, Walt Rostow pointed out reasonably to Rusk, "Ho has an industrial complex to protect; he is no longer a guerrilla fighter with nothing to lose."[34] But apparently Rostow's and Ho Chi Minh's calculations of what there was to lose differed. And Washington's anticipation of how Hanoi would react to so powerful a signal of its commitment to Khanh was equally inaccurate. The bombing was read as a prelude to the dispatch of U.S. ground troops to the South. It was understood that the North might be invaded as well as the South, and some members of the Central Committee expressed considerable anxiety at the prospect. "If you are determined to win," Ho Chi Minh is reported to have said, "you will have all the wisdom to win; if you are determined to run away, you will have all the wisdom to run away." Hanoi chose to master the wisdom to win. The decision was now taken to send regular combat troops to the South; by October 1964, a total of three regiments (some 4,500 soldiers) had left for the front.[35]

On August 10, J. Blair Seaborn met with Pham Van Dong for the second time. The Vietnamese premier informed the Canadian intermediary that the Democratic Republic of Vietnam was "extremely angry" over the events in the Gulf. The United States, he charged, sought to extricate itself from a failed policy in the South by expanding the war to the north. Seaborn should make it clear to Washington that Hanoi would "fight a war if it came." The first flexing of America's air muscle against the North had produced not immediate surrender but the wider war Johnson, the peace candidate in 1964, had promised the American people he would not seek.[36]

CHAPTER SEVEN

A Wider War
(1964–1965)

There is no indication . . . that any of the major intelligence
agencies believed that the bombing of the North could or
would reduce the level of support for the war in the South. . . .
Rather, the agencies placed their hopes in punishing North
Vietnam and in possibly breaking her will.
—"BOMBING AS A POLICY TOOL IN
VIETNAM: EFFECTIVENESS,"
SENATE FOREIGN RELATIONS
COMMITTEE STAFF STUDY,
OCTOBER 12, 1972

I N WASHINGTON, the failure of Blair Seaborn to extract a promise
from Hanoi to call off the war in the South was read as proof of
Communist determination to defy the United States. It was time to
consider increasing the pressure. The post-Tonkin debate revolved
around the means of increasing pressure on the North: initiation of systematic air war against North Vietnam; the intensification of the air and
ground war in the South, including the introduction of U.S. combat
troops; or a renewed focus on counterinsurgency, rather than conventional war, and the pacification of the countryside through "civic action."
Negotiating American withdrawal was never a serious option.

In Hanoi, the authorities read Seaborn's request as itself proof that
Washington had no interest in compromise but was determined to create
a separate anti-Communist state in the South whatever Hanoi did. Given
the political and military strength of the NLF, the time seemed right for

an all-out effort—on both the military and the political fronts—to induce the government of General Nguyen Khanh to negotiate in the hope that such negotiations would make it difficult for the United States to escalate its intervention.

There was a terrible irony in the continuing success of the NLF. Demonstrations of popular political support, which should have persuaded the United States to give up its support for an incompetent, dictatorial, minority anti-Communist government in the South, instead intensified Washington's conviction that it must do more to prop it up. What the NLF and its supporters saw as its expanding, increasingly stable, organization of the South was seen in Washington as increased instability and "deterioration," to be halted by the application of yet new increments of force. Early in 1964 the Front had organized a broad-based Self-Determination movement, which could operate openly in Saigon. Truong Nhu Tang, one of the non-Communist members of the NLF, knew that the vested interests of the businessmen and professionals who joined the Self-Determination movement made them suspicious of the NLF. "But at the same time," he wrote, "they were horrified at the prospect of American intervention and all-out war." The movement's manifesto insisted on "America for Americans. South Vietnam for South Vietnamese. We demand that the NLF and the Government negotiate peace between the two brothers. South Vietnam must have the right to determine its own future."[1] This was not a welcome message in Washington, where the abiding fear had become the emergence of a government in Saigon that would make its own peace with the Communists and ask the United States to leave the country. In September, the CIA Board of National Intelligence Estimates warned Johnson that "the odds are against the emergence of a stable government capable of effectively prosecuting the war in Vietnam." There was a grave danger that in the absence of such a government, "neutralist sentiment would almost certainly increase, together with the danger that a loosely organized coalition would emerge which could take advantage of frustration and war weariness to seek a neutralist solution."[2]

The United States claimed not to oppose neutralism as such, though of course it preferred firm allies. But everything depended on the definition of neutralism. Two definitions had been circulating with respect to Vietnam: an end to both North Vietnamese and U.S. intervention in the South, and/or the opening of the political system to NLF participation. At a high-level meeting on the situation in South Vietnam in late November 1964, there was general agreement that "unless the VC was defeated ... neutralism either in the sense of no more external assistance or in the sense of a free political system could not be maintained. . . ."³ Secretary of State Rusk had put the matter very clearly in a Voice of America interview. As it was currently used, all neutralization meant was "getting Americans out," which would expose South Vietnam to Communist takeover. Once South Vietnam was "independent and secure, it would be perfectly free to pursue its own policy. It can be unaligned, as far as we are concerned."⁴ An "independent and secure" Vietnam, of course, was what Hanoi and the NLF also claimed to be fighting for.

The dilemma Johnson faced was painfully clear; Kennedy had faced it before him, Nixon would after him. Any government in Saigon that aspired to popular support was likely to seek peace with the NLF and in time probably reunification as well. All the reports Johnson received made the same point. When Henry Cabot Lodge resigned the Vietnam ambassadorship in order to participate in the presidential election campaign, Johnson appointed General Maxwell Taylor to take his place. Three years had passed since Taylor urged Kennedy to increase troop strength to eight thousand under cover of flood-control aid. Now there were over 27,000 American soldiers in South Vietnam, with authority to accompany South Vietnamese units on offensive combat patrols. In a somber report to Rusk on September 6, 1964, Taylor observed that only "the emergence of an exceptional leader could improve the situation and no George Washington is in sight." The president, Taylor's report continued, had only two choices:

> (A) passively watching the development of a popular front, knowing that this may in due course require the U.S. to leave Vietnam in failure; or (B) actively assuming increased responsibility for the outcome following a time-schedule consistent with our estimate of the limited viability of any South Vietnamese government.

The first was obviously unacceptable. "If we leave Vietnam with our tail between our legs," Taylor wrote, "the consequences of this defeat in the rest of Asia, Africa, and Latin America would be disastrous." Therefore the only choice was (B) and the only question, how to implement it.⁵

Only one voice urged caution. George Ball had served in the Kennedy administration as an undersecretary of state for Economic Affairs, and had warned the president then that the advisers he was about to dispatch to Vietnam were the beginning of a commitment that could well lead to sending 300,000 soldiers to Vietnam in a few years. "George, you're crazier than hell," Kennedy scoffed. Now an undersecretary of state in the Johnson administration, Ball thought it should be possible to preserve American credibility, prestige, power, and influence, even if the 14 million inhabitants of South Vietnam were to form a government that included elements of the NLF and possibly reach some accommodation with their 16.5 million fellow countrymen to the north.

In early October 1964, Ball wrote a lengthy memo addressed to McGeorge Bundy, Rusk, and McNamara that expressed his "sceptical [sic] thoughts on the assumptions of our Viet-Nam policy." To the usual list of options presented to the president (continuation of current policy; air war against North Vietnam; U.S. takeover of ground war in the South) Ball added a fourth: "a course of action that would permit a political settlement without direct U.S. military involvement. . . ." All the military options carried unacceptable risks:

> It is in the nature of escalation that each move passes the option to the other side, while at the same time the party which seems to be losing will be tempted to keep raising the ante. To the extent that the response to a move can be controlled, that move is probably ineffective. If the move is effective, it may not be possible to control—or accurately anticipate—the response. Once on the tiger's back we cannot be sure of picking the place to dismount.

A political solution would require the withdrawal of U.S. military forces; the objection posed by Ball's colleagues was that it would humiliate the United States in the eyes of the world and damage U.S. credibility among its allies. Ball argued to the contrary that the European nations would "applaud a move on our part to cut our losses"; Japan, so far as could be determined, favored a political solution; the attitude of the eternally pragmatic Thais would depend on "what we were prepared to offer as a guarantee of our willingness to assist Thailand against aggression." The Philippines might initially support escalation but they were unlikely to support it over the long haul. Finally, withdrawal would cost the United States little in the eyes of the "less-developed countries, particularly if it appeared . . . we were responding to the wish of the South Vietnamese people to bring a halt to the war." Bombing the North, on the other hand, would have a decidedly negative effect as the "element of race would have a strong influence, as well as the disparity in strength and size between ourselves and the Vietnamese." Thus, in the world at large, only Taiwan and South Korea were opposed to a political solution; hardly the stuff of global humiliation.

A political solution would begin with a cease-fire, followed by negotiations in a number of possible contexts, from a localized settlement between the government of Saigon and the NLF to the sort of large-scale international conference de Gaulle professed himself eager to convene. The result of local negotiations, Ball acknowledged, "might well be an uneasy coalition in which the Communists would presumably be the most aggressive and dominant component. But the full effect of a Communist takeover would be diffused and postponed for a substantial period of time." Nor was "Communist takeover" a foregone conclusion. A government that included elements of the NLF functioning in a country free of external military intervention could well make a claim on the international community. It had been impossible to interest America's allies in its war in Vietnam, but it might well be possible to solicit their support for a genuinely neutral government in the South, one which, as it joined the ranks of the non-aligned nations, could be presented as the fulfillment rather than the defeat of U.S. goals.

As a first step, Ball suggested that the United States reaffirm that it was in Vietnam because "the South Vietnamese people, speaking through their Government, have asked us to help them resist Communist aggression." Moreover, the United States had made it clear that it would stay in Vietnam *"so long as the Vietnamese people wish us to help"* (emphasis in the original). But if it developed, as now seemed likely, that the government in Saigon did not represent the will of the people and moreover the people themselves did not wish to risk their lives to avoid a Communist takeover, then the United States should "put other governments on notice that we do not intend to remain in South Viet-Nam." Rather than an expression of failure and defeat, the United States "should, so far as possible, seek to make a virtue out of this position, emphasizing that, unlike the Communists, we never seek to impose our will on another country."[6]

Ball recognized that he was offering only a "sketchy outline of the possibilities," but then no experts had been assigned to study how to achieve a political solution:

> We have spent months of concentrated effort trying to devise ways and means to advance the present policy of winning the war in the South.
> We have spent weeks trying to devise an effective strategy for applying increasing military pressure against the North.
> But we have given almost no attention to the possible political means of finding a way out without further enlargement of the war.

Ball's views were briefly debated and then dismissed. Rusk, McNamara, and Bundy, Ball wrote, "regarded me with benign tolerance;

to them, my memorandum seemed merely an idiosyncratic diversion from the only relevant problem: how to win the war." Indeed, it was only through the efforts of Bill Moyers that Johnson got to see the memo at all, a month after Ball had written it. And Ball remained a single voice in a wilderness of warmakers.[7]

Other peacemakers were ignored as well. In June and July 1964, de Gaulle renewed his call for the neutralization of Indochina and urged the reconvening of the Geneva Conference of 1954; in August, U Thant, Secretary General of the UN, urged direct negotiations between the United States and North Vietnam and in September began the process of arranging for them to take place. Johnson seems not to have been informed of these actions until much later, and U Thant himself, advised that nothing would happen until after the American election, paused in his efforts. In December 1964 he was pleased to inform Rusk that Hanoi was ready to begin secret discussions, but when another two months passed without a response, an angry U Thant issued a public denunciation of the United States on February 24, 1965:

> I am sure the great American people, if only they knew the true facts and background to the developments in South Viet-Nam, will agree with me that further bloodshed is unnecessary. And that the political and diplomatic methods of discussions and negotiations alone can create conditions which will enable the United States to withdraw gracefully from that part of the world. As you know, in times of war and of hostilities the first casualty is truth.

But the American people did not learn of these 1964 possibilities until March 1965, after the first combat troops had already landed; and the interest of the government of the United States in a graceful withdrawal was, in any case, minimal.[8]

On the war front, on the other hand, things were more active. As early as 1962, Brigadier General Rollen Anthis had devised a scheme to keep his pilots in the air in the absence of obvious targets. "Free-fire zones" were areas designated by Saigon-appointed province chiefs as NLF-dominated; within such a zone anything that moved, anything at all, was a fair target. By 1964–65 the zones had multiplied to encompass ever larger sections of the countryside, including those most heavily populated. In late September 1964, restrictions on the weapons used in the air war in the South were lifted. In addition to napalm, which had been available for some time, white phosphorous and cluster bombs were added to the arsenal. The Vietnamese called the cluster bombs *bom bi* ("mother bombs"), which exploded in midair and released from 350 to

600 baby bombs. When these hit the ground, each one exploded into thousands of metal pellets. (Later, fiberglass—invisible to X-rays and thus harder and more painful to remove—was used.) The advantages of white phosphorous were described by an American pilot:

> We sure are pleased with those backroom boys at Dow. The original product wasn't so hot—if the gooks were quick they could scrape it off. So the boys started adding polystyrene—now it sticks like shit to a blanket. But then if the gooks jumped under water it stopped burning, so they started adding Willie Peter [WP—white phosphorous] so's to make it burn better. It'll even burn under water now. And one drop is enough, it'll keep on burning right down to the bone so they die anyway from phosphorous poisoning.[9]

Yet despite this increased firepower, the NLF continued to score military victories, increasingly directing its attacks against Americans. On October 31, 1964, the NLF used captured American mortars against the U.S. air base at Bien Hoa, destroying five B-57s and badly damaging thirteen more; four Americans were killed and thirty wounded. The attack occurred only three days before the American election. From Saigon came Taylor's call for retaliation against North Vietnam. Johnson's immediate response was political. Would failure to retaliate cost him votes; he asked the pollster Lou Harris. Not at all, Harris responded; voters in favor of increased military action in Vietnam would be voting for Goldwater anyway.

On the day of his landslide victory, derived in large part from the popular perception that he was less likely to wage war than the bellicose Goldwater, Johnson appointed an interagency Working Group of the National Security Council to consider American options in Vietnam. According to the chairman of the Working Group, William Bundy, Johnson was "thinking in terms of the maximum use of a Gulf of Tonkin rationale. . . ." The first draft of the group's report to Johnson affirmed American aims in South Vietnam: "to protect US reputation as a counter-subversion guarantor; to avoid domino effect especially in Southeast Asia; to keep South Vietnamese territory from Red hands; to emerge from crisis without unacceptable taint from methods." The situation in November 1964, as in September and October, was "deteriorating." Sometime soon—anywhere from six months to two years—the President could expect the emergence of a "popular front government which will invite the US out. . . ." What choices did the President have? There were three. George Ball said there were always three; the "Goldilocks principle," he called it: one too soft, one too hard, one just right, and all of them military. His own fourth alternative, a political settlement with no prior military action, was notably absent from the list.

Option A would maintain the current level of covert operations in the North and Laos ("secret" bombing of Laos had begun in earnest in May); reprisals against the North would occur only in response to "VC spectaculars" in the South, such as the attack on Bien Hoa. Basic to this option was the "continued rejection of negotiating in the hope that the situation will improve." Option B was the "fast/full squeeze"—a rapid escalation of military actions against the North "without interruption until we achieve our central present objectives." Option C was "progressive squeeze and talk," a combination of offers to talk with Hanoi and a "crescendo of additional military moves" against targets in Laos and North Vietnam. In the words of John McNaughton, assistant secretary of defense, it would demonstrate that the United States was " 'a good doctor' willing to keep promises, be tough, take risks, get bloodied and hurt the enemy badly." All three options were intended to yield negotiations on American terms: a "mutual withdrawal" by the United States and Hanoi from the conflict, leaving South Vietnam free from "Red hands." Bombing was a "bargaining chip," something the United States had to do so that it could promise *not* to do it if Hanoi would cooperate.[10]

After consultation with Taylor and a review by the National Security Council, the group presented their recommendation to the President: a combination of Options A and C; reprisal and steady escalation.[11] Bombing the North, the Joint Chiefs argued, would destroy its capacity to carry on the war in the South, though all agreed that the overwhelming majority of arms and ammunition used by the NLF were bought or captured from the ARVN. Taylor disputed the rationale but not the policy. Bombing the North, Taylor argued, would raise morale in the South and perhaps reduce the amount of infiltration, though all agreed troops from the North made up no more than 5 percent of the insurgent forces. Never mind, Walt Rostow insisted, the whole point of bombing the North was to demonstrate America's iron resolve. Everyone thought some level of bombing of the North would be salutary. In a brief discussion of the possibility of using nuclear weapons, McNamara said he could not imagine the circumstances that would justify them, McGeorge Bundy thought there might be pressure to deploy them nevertheless, and General Wheeler suggested that they might be considered *"in extremis. . . ."*[12] There was no debate on the appropriate level of force to be used south of the 17th parallel.

*   *   *

Indeed, the violence of the air war against the South Vietnamese countryside increased once again at the turn of the new year when General Westmoreland received approval for the regular use of B-52 bombers. Originally designed to deliver nuclear bombs, the B-52 flew too high to be heard until the bombs were already falling. Each plane carried a payload of 30 tons of explosives. A single mission of six B-52s would devastate an area one-half mile wide by three miles long.[13] *The New York Times* reported that the number of armed helicopters had risen from one hundred to three hundred. Ten operations a day were conducted in which a single helicopter might deliberately draw fire and then "radio for armed helicopters and fighter bombers . . . with heavy fire-power to blast at the positions of the Viet Cong. . . ." World War II bombers known as "Skyraiders" were reoutfitted for Vietnam, with four 20-millimeter cannon that together fired over 2,000 rounds per minute; under its wings the Skyraider could carry a bombload of 7,500 pounds.

Bernard Fall flew in a Skyraider that carried 750- and 500-pound napalm bombs; the wing plane carried 7,500 pounds of CBUs. The target of the mission was a Communist "rest center," but, as Fall pointed out, "a rest center could be anything, any group of huts, or it may be just a normal village in which Viet Cong troops have put down stake for, perhaps, 48 hours." The village looked entirely peaceful to Fall as the pilot banked the Skyraider and went into a steep dive, driving people into the open by dropping napalm first so that they became targets for the wing plane. Fall's plane made three passes until the village was completely engulfed in flames. Not surprisingly, as American combat activity increased, so did the casualties, with 356 dead in 1964, 1,546 wounded, and 19 missing. The number of civilian Vietnamese deaths was not counted; the NLF was said to have lost about 100,000 dead since 1961.[14]

In Washington, Johnson mulled over the options presented to him by the Working Group. They had been reduced to two and were significantly no longer called options but "phases." Phase I entailed bombing selected targets in the North as a reprisal against any major NLF action ("VC spectaculars") in the South. Phase II would be the initiation of systematic, graduated military pressure against the North. Johnson endorsed the plan but made it subject to a marked improvement in the Saigon government. His reluctance to move against the North was based on his lack of confidence in the Saigon government. Suppose it collapsed, or was taken over by neutralists? What was the point in pressuring the North if the government in Saigon was unstable, unrepresentative, and incapable of making a serious effort to defend itself? In a perverse echo of George Ball's approach, which suggested that Johnson use the evident unrepresentative nature of the Saigon government as a way of negotiating itself out of Vietnam with honor, Johnson instructed Maxwell Taylor on December 3, 1964, to tell General Khanh to *make* his government representative if he expected any new military departure from the United States.[15]

Taylor delivered a clear message, but the general's government grew weaker almost hourly. This was intensely frustrating since Johnson had made any new American military move dependent on stability in Saigon. When Khanh and a group of younger officers moved against the vestiges of civilian government in Saigon in late December, Taylor angrily called them together. "Do all of you understand English?" he asked.

> I told you all clearly . . . we Americans were tired of coups. Apparently I wasted my words. Maybe this is because something is wrong with my French because you evidently didn't understand. I made it clear that all the military plans which I know you would like to carry out are dependent on governmental stability. Now you have made a real mess. We cannot carry you forever if you do things like this.[16]

In an acrimonious exchange the next day Taylor demanded Khanh's resignation, while for their part the Vietnamese threatened to ask for Taylor's recall as ambassador.

As if to underline the impotence of Khanh's government, on Christmas Eve an NLF sapper unit destroyed the American officers' billet in the heart of Saigon, killing two Americans and injuring thirty-eight. This was the sort of "VC spectacular" to which Phase I was addressed, but Johnson refused to authorize the air strikes against the North urged by the Pentagon, Taylor, and General Westmoreland. The political situation in Saigon was too precarious, the president pointed out. And besides,

> I have never felt that this war will be won from the air, and it seems to me that what is much more needed and would be more effective is a larger and stronger use of Rangers and Special Forces and Marines, or other appropriate military strength on the ground and on the scene. I am ready to look with great favor on that kind of increased American effort, directed at the guerrillas and aimed to stiffen the aggressiveness of Vietnamese military units up and down the line. Any recommendation that you or General Westmoreland make in this sense will have immediate attention from me, although I know that it may involve the acceptance of larger American sacrifices. We have been building our strength to fight this kind of war ever since 1961, and I myself am ready to substantially increase the

number of Americans in Vietnam if it is necessary to provide this kind of fighting force against the Viet Cong.[17]

Johnson was mistaken. The military, wedded to more conventional tactics, had not noticeably improved its counterinsurgency capacity. And Taylor, who in any case consistently opposed an American ground war in Vietnam, did not make the request. Taylor's answer to Johnson, on January 6, 1965, was that American troops were not only unnecessary, they were counterproductive. The Vietnamese had all the manpower they needed. What they lacked was motivation. "The entire advisory effort has been devoted to giving them both skill and motivation. If that effort has not succeeded there is less reason to think that U.S. combat forces would have the desired effect." Instead, the Americans would take on an ever-increasing burden of the fighting while the majority of Vietnamese "would actively turn against us . . . until, like the French, we would be occupying an essentially hostile country." Nevertheless, some action would have to be taken, and Taylor proposed "an old recipe with little attractiveness," the initiation of "graduated air attacks against the will of the DRV."[18]

The problem, William Bundy told Rusk early in January 1965, was that morale in Saigon was plummeting because of a "widespread feeling that the US is not ready for stronger action and indeed is possibly looking for a way out." (William Sullivan had made the same argument in June 1964, when the Working Group he chaired urged the administration to make a "breakthrough into an irreversible commitment" in order to buoy Khanh's morale and get the Tonkin Gulf resolution and retaliatory air strikes against the North.). Things were "coming apart" Bundy warned, more rapidly than had been anticipated in November. And then Bundy described the "most likely form of coming apart"— a sharp articulation of what the United States should most fear:

> a government of key groups starting to negotiate covertly with the Liberation Front or Hanoi, perhaps not asking in the first instance that we get out, but with that necessarily following at a fairly early stage. In one sense, this would be a "Vietnam solution," with some hope that it would produce a Communist Vietnam that would assert its own degree of independence from Peiping and that would produce a pause in Communist pressure in Southeast Asia. On the other hand, it would still be virtually certain that Laos would then become untenable and that Cambodia would accommodate in some way. Most seriously, there is grave question whether the Thai in these circumstances would retain any confidence at all in our continued support.

Here was the full answer to George Ball's appeal for a political settlement: "the outcome would be regarded in Asia, and particularly among our friends, as just as humiliating a defeat as any other form." (A month later, John McNaughton quantified this for McNamara: "US aims: 70%— To avoid a humiliating US defeat (to our reputation as a guarantor). 20%—To keep SVN (and then adjacent) territory from Chinese hands. 10%—To permit the people of SVN to enjoy a better, freer way of life. ALSO—To emerge from crisis without unacceptable taint from methods used. NOT—to 'help a friend,' although it would be hard to stay in if asked out.") The American public, Bundy acknowledged "would probably not be too sharply critical" of a "Vietnam solution", but they were not the relevant audience. A Communist Vietnam, probably independent in its orientation and even serving as a bulwark against Chinese expansion, was unacceptable if it occurred at the expense of a perceived American defeat. The alternative, Bundy continued, was stronger U.S. military action in South Vietnam, which had only a "faint hope of really improving the Vietnamese situation," but would "put us in a much stronger position to hold the next line of defense, namely Thailand."[19]

It is worth pausing a little here to excavate the assumptions that underlie Bundy's reasoning. His analysis makes sense only if the legitimacy and stability of the Thai government in fact depends not on its capacity to govern Thailand but rather on its confidence that the United States would support it in the face of an insurrection. This assumes, however, that the Thai people have no analysis of their own about their society but await the judgment of the United States, the *primum mobile* of a universe in which other peoples look to America to know what is good for them. Put another way, for Bundy, American power and prestige lay in the extent to which it could forge such a world—one in which governments were sustained by the fact of American support and fell at the first hint of American dissatisfaction. Withdrawal from Vietnam exposed American impotence.

Bundy concluded his memo with a recommendation that Johnson take an early occasion for a reprisal air attack against the North. On February 7, while his brother McGeorge was in Vietnam, just such an occasion arose. The NLF attacked a U.S. helicopter base at Pleiku in the Central Highlands, killing 8, wounding 126, and destroying 10 planes. In response, 132 American jets struck pre-selected targets in North Vietnam. The raid occurred while Soviet Prime Minister Kosygin was in Hanoi, so the CIA informed the president, to urge that "North Vietnam avoid actions which might provoke US reprisals. . . ." Since McGeorge Bundy himself remarked that there would be no lack of occasions for a reprisal raid—"Pleikus are streetcars"—it seems clear that the administration decided not to wait for another one to come along because it *wished* to punish Hanoi in the presence of its Soviet ally and thus derail the possibility of negotiations. On February 11, another reprisal raid against the North was authorized after an attack on U.S. military housing in Qui Nhon. Moving closer to Phase II bombing, this raid was announced as a necessary response to a "general pattern of aggression" on the part of Hanoi rather than as retaliation for a specific incident. In the North, Hanoi's leaders hastened efforts to evacuate children, disperse factories, build air-raid shelters, and in general prepare for the expected all-out air war.[20]

On February 13, almost a year after McNamara had first urged "graduated overt military pressure against North Vietnam," Johnson finally authorized ROLLING THUNDER, the sustained bombing of the North; but he left the timing of its implementation open. Even if ROLL-ING THUNDER failed, McGeorge Bundy argued in a memo to the president, it would have been worthwhile. "At a minimum it will damp down the charge that we did not do all that we could have done, and this charge will be important in many countries, including our own." Of equal importance, it "set a higher price for the future upon all adventures of guerrilla warfare, and it should therefore somewhat increase our ability to deter such adventures."

Bundy expressed no hesitation about recommending extensive aerial warfare as a demonstration of American resolve and on the off chance that it might deter a future insurgency somewhere in the world. Moreover, he was certain bombing the North would improve the situation in the South, specifically the "minds of the South Vietnamese and the minds of the Viet Cong cadres." The CIA, Bundy assured the president, was of the strong opinion that even low-level bombing of the North would have a "substantial depressing effect upon the morale of Viet Cong cadres in South Vietnam."[21]

At interrogation centers in South Vietnam, however, American social scientists working under a RAND contract for the Department of Defense found that the bombing did just the opposite.

> *Q:* What effect did the attacks [on the North] have on your unit's morale?
> *A:* As I have told you before, the attacks have no effect on the Front members, for they have realized that the stronger the Front is, the more attacks the North will have to endure. . . . We are somewhat concerned about the fruits of ten years labor. . . . These attacks will

destroy the fruits of our labor. This thought pushed us to fight harder
so the South would soon be entirely liberated and the North would
thus be spared further destruction.[22]

And instead of discouraging all thoughts of peace and neutrality in Sai-
gon, the bombing seems to have inspired bolder efforts to achieve them.
A Committee to Defend the Peace was established and Pham Van
Huyen, a refugee from the North and a former minister in Diem's cabinet, agreed to head it. A petition campaign gathered thousands of signatures denouncing the attacks on the North and calling for negotiations.
A press conference was set for February 16, 1965. When Pham Van
Huyen was arrested, the conference was held anyhow, and his daughter,
Madame Ngo Ba Thanh, an American-educated lawyer, rose to denounce her father's arrest and to call for a march against the government. The government's response was a wave of arrests. Given the composition of the Committee, those arrested comprised a substantial
proportion of Saigon's professional and business class. The police station,
Truong Nhu Tang remembers, took on an odd appearance, as if "the
city's elite had somehow mistaken the address of an upper-crust social
gathering."[23]

Still, above all else, Johnson's advisers feared negotiations. Peace on
terms not dictated by the United States must be avoided if the demonstration effect on future insurgencies was to work. The United States,
McGeorge Bundy wrote, must not "accept the idea of negotiations of any
sort except on the basis of a stand down of Viet Cong violence." In the
future, he advised, a "neutral non-Communist force may emerge perhaps under Buddhist leadership, but no such force currently exists, and
any negotiated U.S. withdrawal today would mean surrender on the
installment plan." This was disingenuous: such a force obviously did exist,
and that was the problem.[24]

Vietnamese realities had little to do with the world of memos that
increasingly became the sole context of American policy choices. Events
could occasionally force tactical adjustments and reconsiderations, of
course. But the structure of the debate and its limits were set by the goal
that the Bundy brothers, Rusk, MacNamara, Rostow, and the military
had set themselves when they first came to Washington with John F.
Kennedy. The goal was the creation of a separate anti-Communist state
south of the 17th parallel. Failure to achieve it represented that humiliation it was their paramount duty to avoid. Any doubts that might have
been suggested by the growing difficulty in mobilizing the Vietnamese
in pursuit of this goal were ruled out by reference to an overarching

axiom: a world ordered by the principles and practices of the liberal capitalist system that governed America was good for America and good for the world.

Ambassador Taylor fully supported ROLLING THUNDER. His only worry was that it required a compliant government in Saigon. Khanh had given his approval for bombing targets in the southern region of North Vietnam; but could he be relied upon? What of his increasingly close relationship with the Buddhists? More and more, the embassy feared that Khanh saw himself as a Vietnamese Sihanouk, the Cambodian royal prince whose daring high-wire act among the powers still kept his country peaceful. The CIA had learned that Khanh had contacted the NLF in December 1964, and they reported renewed and more serious exchanges in January and February of 1965. McGeorge Bundy and McNamara now agreed with Taylor that Khanh was no longer a suitable instrument of American policy. It was more important to get rid of him than to worry about the bad publicity certain to follow renewed evidence of political instability in Saigon.[25]

After weeks of prodding, pushing, encouragement, and some financial threats, the desired result was finally achieved. Six days after Johnson approved ROLLING THUNDER, but before its actual implementation, a coup was launched in Saigon, its details finely tuned by Taylor and the commander of the American forces in Vietnam, General William Westmoreland. Khanh left the country, and power was now in the hands of a military triumvirate, Generals Ky, Thi, and Thieu, all of whom were in considerable debt to the American Embassy. On March 1, the Saigon government pledged itself not to negotiate with the enemy. The next day, one hundred U.S. planes took off for targets in the North. "A guarantee by the [Saigon] government that the war would continue," Jack Langguth reported to *The New York Times* that day from Saigon, "was considered here to be a necessity for a U.S. decision to proceed with further air strikes against the north." The same story noted a further step-up in the war—reports that a contingent of Marines would be dispatched as a security force to guard U.S. installations.[26]

Taylor's resistance to the dispatch of U.S. combat forces had finally collapsed in the face of a concerted effort by the Joint Chiefs of Staff, McGeorge Bundy (who had suggested such a course in June 1964), and above all a worried General Westmoreland. With air attacks against both North and South Vietnam being launched from bases in the South, airfields were a logical target for NLF forces, and no one placed much confidence in ARVN protection. But Taylor was full of warnings. To deploy the Marines in Danang, Taylor cabled the State Department on February 22, 1965, would be

> a step in reversing long standing policy of avoiding commitment of ground combat forces in SVN [South Vietnam]. Once this policy is breached, it will be very difficult to hold the line. . . . Once it becomes evident that we are willing to assume such new responsibilities, one may be sure that GVN [Government of Vietnam] will seek to unload other ground force tasks upon us. Increased numbers of ground forces in SVN will increase points of friction with local population. . . .

As for the use of the Marines in mobile operations rather than static defense,

> White-faced soldier armed, equipped and trained as he is [is] not suitable guerrilla fighter for Asian forests and jungles. French tried . . . and failed; I doubt that US forces could do much better. . . . Finally, there would be ever present question of how foreign soldier would distinguish between a VC and friendly Vietnamese farmer. When I view this array of difficulties, I am convinced that we should adhere to our past policy of keeping ground forces out of direct counterinsurgency role.

In the event of a conventional cross border attack from the North, Taylor was entirely ready to call for American troops to help the ARVN defend the country; but no one expected that in any near future. Nevertheless, Taylor deferred to Westmoreland's concern, and on March 8, 1965, 3,500 Marines (two battalions) landed at Danang. In mid-April, two more were dispatched; the following month the first U.S. Army units arrived.[27]

Anxious to limit the number of ground troops, Taylor urged an increase in the bombing of the North. Military estimates had expressed confidence that intensive bombing would work to bring Hanoi to its knees in a matter of weeks; a few months at most. But in the summer of 1965, five months later, McNamara reluctantly informed the president that its impact remained unclear—except on one score, whose logic was murky. Although the morale in South Vietnam was actually lower than before the bombing began, to halt the bombing now would further damage morale in Saigon; therefore the bombing must continue. The Joint Chiefs remained convinced that more massive bombing would do the trick. In June 1966, intensive bombing of North Vietnam's fuel supplies was finally authorized. Now Hanoi would sue for peace, surely; anyhow, it would stop its infiltration. It took one month to eliminate 70 percent of Hanoi's fuel supplies. And still the war continued. The JCS demanded an end to restricted targeting, and in the spring of 1967, almost all restrictions on the bombing were lifted. Pentagon analysts concluded that "except for the port of Haiphong and a few others, virtually all of the economic and military targets in NVN [North Vietnam] had been hit. Except for simply keeping it up, almost everything bombing could do to pressure NV had been done."[28] Since pressure against Hanoi was only one of the many reasons for bombing, Hanoi's failure to respond in a manner satisfactory to the United States was never in itself reason to stop.

On the other hand, public criticism of the air war against the North began with the first reprisal raid in February and increased in volume along with the tonnage dropped. In late February, *The New York Times* published a map of worldwide demonstrations against U.S. policies, and the size and passion of domestic protests mounted. Johnson, who prided himself on his powers of persuasion, scheduled large numbers of conferences with congressmen, press people, visitors from abroad to describe, as dramatically as possible, the careful mix of carrot and stick he was judiciously applying in Vietnam. To the popular syndicated columnists

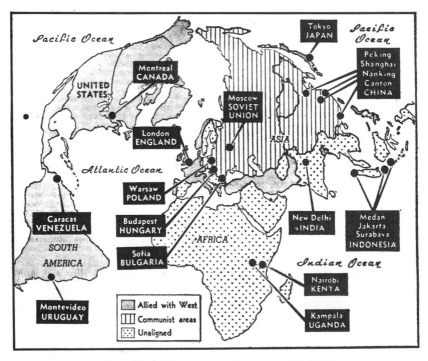

New York Times map, February 21, 1965.

Evans and Novack, for example, he "pointed out the targets he had approved for attack, and the many more targets he had disapproved." And anybody worried about Chinese intervention, Johnson told the reporters, should just relax:

> the slow escalation of the air war in the North and the increasing pressure on Ho Chi Minh was seduction, not rape. If China should suddenly react to slow escalation, as a woman might react to attempted seduction, by threatening to retaliate (a slap in the face, to continue the metaphor), the United States would have plenty of time to ease off the bombing. On the other hand, if the United States were to unleash an all-out, total assault on the North—rape rather than seduction—there could be no turning back, and Chinese reaction might be instant and total.

Senator George McGovern met with Johnson that same spring to protest the bombing on the grounds that it might lead to Chinese intervention and was almost certain to increase the number of soldiers North Vietnam sent south. Johnson reassured him: "I'm watching that very closely. I'm going up her leg an inch at a time . . . I'll get to the snatch before they know what's happening, you see."[29]

The president's personal reassurance, however, had a limited range. To answer its critics, the government released a White Paper on February 17, 1965. Chester Cooper, now an aide in McGeorge Bundy's office, had been working on it for several months, and the intention was to put U.S. bombing raids in the context of North Vietnamese aggression. In the event, this was not an easy task. As Cooper wrote Bundy three weeks before the release of the White Paper: "we will have a catalogue of sins and Hanoi's culpability by the end of the week, if possible. Meanwhile D.O.D. [Department of Defense] is preparing a justification for further early strikes in the event there are not additional spectaculars in the next few days." But everyone chipped in. The CIA, for example, having provided all the props, then arranged for journalists to look over a ship filled with Chinese and Eastern-bloc ammunition said to have been on its way from north to south when caught by alert ARVN naval units and sunk in conveniently shallow water off the coast. Max Frankel of *The New York Times* duly published an account of the cargo, calling it "conclusive proof" of Hanoi's escalation of the war.[30]

The White Paper itself, written in militant bureaucratic prose, claimed that South Vietnam was "fighting for its life against a brutal campaign of terror and armed attack inspired, directed, supplied, and controlled by the Communist regime in Hanoi." Northern aggression had been going on for years, but "recently the pace has quickened and the threat has now become active." Two weeks after its publication, the dissident journalist I. F. Stone analyzed the White Paper in detail in his weekly newsletter, arguing, on the basis of the government's own evidence, that the pace of escalation had indeed quickened, but as a consequence of American rather than Vietnamese action. "For four years after Geneva," Stone concluded, "both North Vietnam and China followed the 'peaceful coexistence' policy while the U.S. turned South Vietnam into a military base and a military dictatorship. It is in this story the White Paper does not tell, and the popular discontent it does not mention, that the rebellion and the aid from the North had their origins."

The senior military correspondent for *The New York Times,* on the other hand, was pleased. The Sunday before, he had offered Johnson his own version of the Goldilocks choices in a featured Sunday Magazine piece. " 'Bug Out', Negotiate or Fight," Hanson Baldwin told the president. Negotiation, however, could only be from strength, which left just two choices. Vietnam, Baldwin explained, "is a nasty place to fight. But there are no neat and tidy battlefields in the struggle for freedom. . . . And it is far better to fight in Vietnam—on China's doorstep—than fight some years hence in Hawaii, on our own frontiers."[31]

On the ground in South Vietnam, the news remained decidedly discouraging to the White House. The number of desertions from the Saigon army was steadily rising, for a grand total of 113,000 by the spring of 1965, a more than 50 percent increase over the 73,000 who had deserted in 1964. In April, General Thieu had even more discouraging news for the Americans. "The Communists controlled seventy-five per cent of the countryside," he told officials. "We controlled only the chief towns. We had the impression we would be overrun. There was a crucial need for American troops."[32] Moreover, McGovern was proving right. ROLLING THUNDER convinced Hanoi that nothing it could do would change the determination of the United States to divide Vietnam permanently. The number of infiltrators sent down the growing complex of roads that constituted the "Ho Chi Minh Trail" increased in the spring of 1965, though the confirmed total of North Vietnamese combat troops in the South, about one thousand in April, was only half the number of South Koreans the United States had persuaded Seoul to send to South Vietnam. Even the total number of Vietnamese from the North since 1959, most of them returning southerners, which MACV set at 39,517, was now outnumbered by the 56,000 Americans soldiers in Vietnam (23,000 advisers; 33,000 combat troops).

*   *   *

By the spring of 1965 the American policymakers who saw victory in Vietnam as essential to the credibility, power, and might of the United States had achieved many of their ends. The war had been carried north, demonstrating the determination of the United States to achieve its goals in the South, even at the risk of a wider conflict. After many coups and much effort, a government had been established in Saigon eager to invite the American military to fight the war as it saw fit, including the use of large number of U.S. combat troops. No longer need U.S. advisers complain that ARVN officers would not fight aggressively. Now they would have their own troops to command: aggressive Americans ready to do the job, whatever it might be, for shortly after their arrival the task of the Marines shifted from static defense to just the sort of mobile warfare whose consequences Taylor had predicted in February. "The only thing they told us about the Viet Cong," a Marine told a reporter later, "was they were gooks. They were to be killed."

On August 5, 1965, Private First Class Reginald "Malik" Edwards was in an Amtrac heading for the village of Cam Ne. A helicopter was supposed to have preceded his unit of Marines, telling everyone to evacuate. "If you're left there you're considered VC."

> They told us if you receive one round from the village, you level it. So we was coming into the village, crossing over the hedges. It's like a little ditch, then you go through these bushes and jump across and start kickin' ass, right? Not only did we receive one round, three Marines got wounded right off. . . . So you know how we felt.

Ordered to shoot an old man running by, Edwards misses, but another Marine fires at him with a grenade launcher.

> Caught my man as he was comin' through the door. But what happened was it was a room full of children. Like a schoolroom. And he was runnin' back to warn the kids that the Marines were coming. And that's who got hurt. All those little kids and people.

The village of Cam Ne was burned to the ground, although CBS reporter Morley Safer said there had been, at most, one sniper: two of the three wounded Marines were hit by "friendly fire." Safer had been disturbed by the Marine mission, had personally tried to rescue villagers who failed to understand the command, given in English, to leave their homes. In the smoking ruins of Cam Ne, Safer gave the TV news audience an intimate accounting of the day's events:

The day's operation burned down 150 houses, wounded three women, killed one baby, wounded one marine [sic.] and netted these four prisoners. Four old men who could not answer questions put to them in English. Four old men who had no idea what an I.D. card was. Today's operation is the frustration of Vietnam in miniature. There is little doubt that American firepower can win a military victory here. But to a Vietnamese peasant whose home is a—means a lifetime of backbreaking labor—it will take more than presidential promises to convince him that we are on his side.[33]

In marked contrast to Safer's account, the Marine after-action report described a heated battle during which enemy fire had been received from "fortified Vietcong bunkers." In fact there had been no battle, but there were a few modest bunkers, for Cam Ne was actually part of the U.S. strategic hamlet program. Months later Safer learned that it had been selected for destruction by a province chief who wished to punish the villagers for their tax delinquency.[34]

Safer drew no larger conclusions from what he had witnessed. That Vietnamese peasants could nevertheless be persuaded the United States was on their side remained the conviction of Edward Lansdale and others who continued to insist that pacification and counterinsurgency rather than bombing the North or an American takeover of the ground war was the only way to win in Vietnam. Before retiring as ambassador, Henry Cabot Lodge had outlined a pacification program he called "Hop Tac" (Cooperation), which would focus on the provinces immediately surrounding Saigon. The basic goal of pacification, according to CIA agent Douglas Blaufarb, was to "create a base of popular support in the countryside."[35] After the ARVN had cleared out the enemy, able Vietnamese administrators, with American help, would be brought into the area to create a "counter-terrorist organization" whose purpose would be to "create security for the local government." Of course, Lodge urged, the military "must also behave itself so well that the people like the Army. . . ." This was a grave problem, as Americans who had witnessed South Vietnamese military behavior in the field knew. One U.S. adviser made a partial list of the methods South Vietnamese Rangers used to interrogate prisoners and suspects. It began: "Wrap in barbed wire," and continued through the stripping of the prisoner's skin to beating until the stomach collapsed and was vomited out.[36]

Lodge's "ten point program for success" included:

1. Saturate the minds of the people with some socially conscious and attractive ideology, which is susceptible of being carried out.

2. Organize the people politically with a hamlet chief and committee whose actions would be backed by the police or the military using police-type tactics. . . .
3. With the help of the police or military, conduct a census.
4. Issue identification cards.
5. Issue permits for the movement of goods and people.
6. When necessary, hold a curfew.
7. Thanks to all these methods, go through each hamlet with a fine tooth comb to apprehend the terrorists.
8. At the first quiet moment, bring in agricultural experts, school teachers, etc.
9. The hamlet should also be organized for its own defense against small Viet Cong attacks.
10. After all these things have been accomplished, hold elections for local office.

Although there would be much discussion of pacification for the next eleven years of U.S. involvement in Vietnam (and in the many postmortems since 1975), the program was never conceptually much more sophisticated than Lodge's 1964 formulation, itself a product of the intense consideration pacification received from Hilsman and other Kennedy staff people. Clear an area, give the people something to believe in, card every inhabitant and control their movements, locate and assassinate the "terrorists," hold an election. The most striking element in Lodge's formulation was his confidence in the ability of the United States to concoct and distribute—not unlike a vaccine—an "attractive ideology." As if Americans could give a people as rooted in history as the Vietnamese a ready-made set of "beliefs" for which they would be willing to die.[37]

There were elements in Lodge's plan, those that dealt with the establishment of physical control over the population, which were within the capacity of the United States to achieve. In 1965, a CT (counterterror) program run by the CIA was established whose function was to "use the Viet Cong techniques of terror—assasination, abuses, kidnappings and intimidation—against the Viet Cong leadership." A Prisoner Interrogation Center was established in each of South Vietnam's forty-four provincial capitals. Here torture was routinely administered to extract information. The Agency for International Development concentrated on the police aspect of Lodge's plan, taking over the work of the Michigan State Group in police training. An effort was made to develop a tamper-proof identification card for every South Vietnamese citizen; a new paramilitary police force was organized; road checks were instituted to hamper NLF access to resources.

Assessing the impact of these programs, Blaufarb notes the criticism that the United States was "fastening a police state upon the communities of rural Vietnam," but argues the need for greatly expanded law enforcement, given the nature of the crisis. And no one could really expect observance of the "niceties of the civil rights of suspected insurgents." Still, one was entitled to expect "that the police would not generally behave toward the public in a manner that contradicted and negated the basic goal of pacification"—building support for the government in the countryside. Yet they did, and did so not occasionally or accidentally but inevitably, for the police were part of a general political system whose reform

> threatened to undermine the arrangements, the deals, and the political understandings that precariously held the regime together. . . . And so with American help, [the police forces] expanded and improved in technical capability, but, because of their weaknesses, each expansion and technical improvement brought them into contact with more of the public and presented more opportunities for misbehavior. The dilemma was not easily solvable under the circumstances.[38]

Johnson's December offer to Taylor and Westmoreland to send more Special Forces and Rangers to Vietnam looked toward a reinvigorated, American-directed, pacification effort. Although the offer of troops was rejected at the time, Westmoreland did launch "Hop Tac" in September 1964, and it is helpful to an understanding of the tactical choices the United States faced in 1965 to take a closer look at how it functioned. At the request of MACV, a RAND staffer, R. Michael Pearce, studied a single village as it passed from NLF to government control over an eight-month period ending in April 1965.

Duc Lap village was part of a newly created province, Hau Nghia, whose boundaries had been drawn in December 1963 in an administrative effort to disrupt NLF control over the entire area. It was in this area that Operation SUNRISE created the first strategic hamlet in January 1962; in the spring of 1965, a conservative estimate of Hau Nghia's population of 228,707 people listed 35 percent in open support of the NLF and 15 percent in favor of the government; 50 percent were said to be uncommitted.

According to its oldest inhabitant, Duc Lap village consisted of 25 hamlets, but in his account Pearce included only the six (a total of about 4,385 people) for which the local military commander had assumed responsibility. Of the six, several were inhabited by people relocated from their native hamlets; each was surrounded by three strands of barbed wire. The people who had been relocated claimed to have felt perfectly secure where they were and did not understand why they had been moved. The cost of relocation was borne entirely by the farmers themselves, but more than money was involved. Once, as he waited for the plane to take him back to Saigon, Pearce saw an old woman coming from the direction of one of the hamlets which made up Duc Lap. She stopped in the middle of the runway and would not move: "She claimed she had lived on this land for 70 years, and the government had taken her land without asking. Furthermore, they did not even allow her to remove the bones of the nine family graves under the spot where she stood."

Not one of the hamlets was completely secure; two could not be visited by government officials even in the daytime despite their location hard by an ARVN battalion headquarters and the provincial airfield, and the Duc Lap village head estimated that 70 percent of the village supported the insurgency. Duc Lap, Pearce pointed out, was a place created by the war, not the

> product of the so-called social revolution that is supposed to sweep the country on the tide of the government pacification plan and leave in its wake a unified and determined people. The government information sources have thus far not been competent enough to reach the people in Duc Lap and tell them they are the source of this revolution. The only revolution of which they are aware is the bloody one going on in their midst every day.

Despite the technological and material superiority of the government, Pearce complained, the "crude printing presses and poor paper" of the NLF had been extremely effective in getting its message—liberating Vietnam from the American imperialists and corrupt government officials—across. What impressed Pearce most was the speed and specificity of NLF propaganda. After the government had accidentally bombed a Duc Lap hamlet, NLF leaflets appeared almost at once denouncing the government for its failure to compensate the villagers for their losses.

The people of Duc Lap, the village policeman told Pearce, "will do what we force them to do," but they believe the "Vietminh" (as they routinely called the NLF) who "have been here before, much longer than the government." And the village chief added that every family "has someone in the insurgent ranks. If one does not, then perhaps his wife, or her husband, or a neighbor has a relative fighting for the National Liberation Front. They have not seen the government people who have been truthful to them. . . ." In a follow-up report, Pearce found that by April 1966, after two years of four different pacification programs, the "villagers' attitude towards the [government of South Vietnam] appeared, in general, to be worse than it was before pacification began."[39]

This is what American soldiers and civilian officials meant by a war without a front. Duc Lap had a government-appointed village chief, finance officer, policeman, and a full complement of militia. Yet the NLF operated in two of its six hamlets with complete impunity and seem to have dominated the nights of all six.

John Paul Vann, who had retired from the Army in 1963, returned to Vietnam in 1965 to work with AID as a civilian province-pacification officer. At around the time Pearce was preparing his report for MACV, Vann arrived in Hau Nghia to take charge of a variety of Civic Action projects. But as Neil Sheehan has written, Vann's real hope was to "take Hau Nghia back from the Vietcong." Shortly after he arrived in the provincial capital, a Vietnamese Ranger company in a hamlet only two miles away was annihilated in a concerted attack. When it was over, "women and children from the hamlet had come with torches . . . to collect the Rangers' weapons and to help carry away wounded and dead guerrillas. The local people had been abused by the Rangers and detested them." And Vann noticed, Sheehan writes, that in marked contrast to the norm on government operations, "the guerrillas had been careful not to harm any of the other houses in the hamlet [than the one occupied by the Rangers] with their fire."

A perhaps deeper problem, from the point of view of Americans determined to prosecute the war, was the extent to which ARVN units made their peace with local guerrillas. Just outside the district town of Cu Chi, for example, Vann learned that an NLF entertainment troupe had given a performance across the street from the billet of an ARVN company. When the soldiers refused their lieutenant's order to attack, the officer sensibly went off to get drunk with the district chief. Americans routinely characterized such behavior as cowardice and incompetence. It was nothing of the kind. These local cease-fires instead were part of that larger movement toward peace and a coalition government American policymakers most feared. Vann saw the ARVN as "ridiculous little Oriental play soldiers." What was necessary was to "take over the command of this operation lock, stock, and barrel—but maintaining Vietnamese front men."

Like Lodge, only on a far grander scale, Vann believed the United States could give the Vietnamese people what they needed. "Behind the shield of the United States Army and Marine Corps," Sheehan writes, "the United States would take over the regime and gradually turn it into a government whose leaders were not fundamentally corrupt." American troops would secure the cities and ports of the South, while the ARVN did most of the fighting in the countryside under a joint U.S.-Vietnamese command in which the Americans gave the orders. In September 1965, Vann summarized his views in a proposal entitled "Harnessing the Revolution in South Vietnam." The United States must put its fear of appearing to be a colonial nation behind it. For fear "of tarnishing our own image, we have refused to become overtly involved in the internal affairs of governing." Patriotic non-Communists had been "literally forced to ally themselves with a Communist-dominated movement in the belief that it was their only chance to secure a better government." The United States should give them a better choice, a program for social change that would win the "true patriots and revolutionaries" away from the NLF to the U.S. side. Vann was fond of saying that if he were a Vietnamese he would have joined the Viet Cong. What he could not allow himself to believe was that enough Vietnamese, sharing his values, had taken that very option, making his dream of an American-delivered revolution irrelevant.[40]

By mid-1965 the tactical debate over whether to bomb the North, intensify the war in the South using U.S. troops, or concentrate on pacification of the countryside had been resolved. The Johnson administration would pursue all three, since no single tactic held the promise of victory.

CHAPTER EIGHT

The American Invasion of South Vietnam (1965–1966)

The incredible thing about Vietnam is that the worst is yet to come.

—BERNARD FALL, DECEMBER 1965

There is an urgent need for a credible explanation of U.S. aims in Vietnam and the role of American forces there.

—RAND VIET CONG MOTIVATION
AND MORALE STUDY, DECEMBER
1965, L. GOURE, A. J. RUSSO,
AND D. SCOTT

I wanna go to Vietnam
I wanna kill a Vietcong
With a knife or with a gun
Either way will be good fun

But if I die in the combat zone
Box me up and send me home
Fold my arms across my chest
Tell my folks I done my best

—ARMY MARCHING CADENCE

THE GROWING DISASTER of Vietnam was somewhat offset by what the administration considered its sizable success in the Dominican Republic. Late in April 1965, a month after the first battalion of Marines landed at Danang, reformist officers in the armed forces of the Dominican Republic mutinied in the name of the civilian liberal politician Juan Bosch and appealed to the public at large to support them. Senior Dominican military authorities opposed Bosch, and so too did the American Embassy, whose power in the Dominican Republic as elsewhere in Central America and the Caribbean was substantial. Even before the political nature of the rebels could be determined, the American ambassador had decided they were Communist-dominated or soon would be. Later, when pressed, the embassy released a list of fifty-eight "Communists" (included some deceased as well as several children) salvaged from the archives of the assassinated dictator Trujillo. On April 28, 1965, conservative Dominican officers formally requested a Marine landing, the first in their country since 1933, to put down a movement they claimed was Communist-led. Several hours later, at the request of the State Department, General Wessin y Wessin added that American lives were endangered, the legal basis for the Marine landing that was already under way. That night, having briefed congressional leaders on his decision, Johnson explained to the American people why the Marines were landing in another foreign country: "The United States Government has been informed by the military authorities in the Dominican Republic that American lives are in danger."

Ultimately 23,000 American troops were sent to the Dominican Republic; 2,850 Dominicans died in the unsuccessful uprising, as did 26 Americans. Despite his low opinion of the Organization of American States ("The O.A.S. couldn't pour piss out of a boot if the instructions were printed on the heel"), Johnson managed to engage member nations in a joint peace-keeping mission. Fourteen months later, American troops were withdrawn and the Dominican Republic left to the mercies of a handpicked "moderate rightist." Despite domestic criticism, Johnson had gambled on quick military action and won. Whatever the Dominican Republic might have been if the reformist officers had succeeded, after the American intervention there was no fear it would be another Cuba.[1] To the president and his men, their effort in the Dominican Republic had been successful.

But people had begun to question the definition of success. John Mecklin, on the lecture circuit to promote his book on his years with USIA in Saigon, *Mission in Torment,* was dismayed to find that "a significant portion of the U.S. population, especially among young people, is no longer persuaded that Communism is a threat to the security of the United States." This was probably why his own book had failed to become a best seller, Mecklin mused, and why McGeorge Bundy "fails to sway the campus left. We have overlooked the fact that the premise of U.S.

policy was in doubt."[2] Doubt for instance that it was really in the interest of the majority of Americans that the majority of Dominicans be subject to a corrupt, military dictatorship; or that American soldiers should be sent abroad to kill Dominicans whom even *The New York Times* thought were "fighting and dying for social justice and constitutionalism." And if such activities seemed dubious in the Dominican Republic, one of the many countries in America's "backyard," then they were altogether puzzling thousands of miles away in Vietnam.

The Gallup Poll rated presidential handling of the Dominican crisis comfortably high, but that was usually the case in the midst of a military action. On Vietnam the voices of protest were growing louder, building on and merging with a black movement that was itself turning from civil rights to "black power," and a student movement energized by the campaign for "free speech" at Berkeley, led by a new national left-liberal organization, the Students for a Democratic Society (SDS). In December 1964, SDS had issued a call for a demonstration against the war to be held in Washington, D.C., on April 17, 1965. Expecting only a handful of people, the organizers were stunned by the twenty-five thousand who attended. The initial assumption of many of the protesters was that the government had simply gotten it wrong. Neither Johnson nor his advisers fully understood Third World nationalism, the link between nationalism and social revolution, the specific history of anti-colonialism in Vietnam, the impact of the raging Sino-Soviet split on the world Communist movement, or the history of the Cold War. Mired in hopelessly anachronistic concepts that saw the beginning of all evil in "appeasement," and communism as monolithic, militaristic, and ruthlessly expansionist, the leaders of the United States had foolishly pursued a misguided policy in Vietnam. It was time to educate them and the American public. Who better to do so than professors? At the University of Michigan, a group of faculty and students organized to hold a "teach-in," its name recalling the tactics of the labor and civil rights movements, that would begin after classes and go on through the night. From eight in the evening of March 24 until eight the next morning, three thousand students participated in workshops, listened to lectures, rallied under banners. The success of the Michigan teach-in led to similar events at colleges and campuses across the country.

White House response was swift. An Inter-Departmental Speaking Team on Vietnam Policy was assembled and dispatched to college campuses.[3] FBI director J. Edgar Hoover needed no prompting from White House aides; his agents were already keeping close watch on student organizations, a logical extension of their duties in black communities. At the President's request, the FBI ran name checks on anyone signing anti-war telegrams or letters and briefed congressmen on the probable Communist source of demonstrations. Johnson was insistent that Communist governments were financing the growing protest movement. When CIA director Richard Helms failed to come up with any proof, Johnson was furious. "Johnson shook that gigantic finger in Helms's face," a reporter remembered, "and said, 'I simply don't understand why it is that you can't find out about that foreign money.' "[4]

Whatever his assumptions about the loyalty of his critics, Johnson recognized that domestic anxiety about Vietnam was sufficiently widespread to require a presidential response. In late March, Johnson announced his readiness to "go anywhere at any time, and meet with anyone whenever there is promise of progress toward an honorable peace." But, as Chester Cooper, then on the staff of the National Security Council, later observed, Johnson's offer was "merely rhetoric, a public relations holding action." None of his advisers devoted any time to thinking about either the form or the substance of the talks Johnson claimed to be ready to conduct anywhere and with anyone. Then, in a major speech at Johns Hopkins University on April 7, 1965 (a few days after he had quietly authorized a change in the Marine role in Vietnam from static defense of base facilities to active combat patrols),[5] Johnson repeated his desire to hold "unconditional discussions." In addition he suggested a grand development scheme that would include North Vietnam and a TVA for the Mekong Delta, to which the United States, Congress willing, would contribute $1 billion. The April speech, like the March offer, contained a host of hidden conditions and was made while ROLLING THUNDER continued to pound North Vietnam. Hanoi unexpectedly responded, and in terms somewhat more moderate than those of the NLF. (The NLF had initially demanded U.S. withdrawal as a precondition for negotiations; Hanoi asked only for a pledge to withdraw.) The week following Johnson's speech, Hanoi Radio broadcast the government's negotiating position. Since it remained Hanoi's position for the next three years, it is worth examining closely:

1. Recognition of the basic national rights of the Vietnamese people—peace, independence, sovereignty, unity and territorial integrity. According to the Geneva agreements, the U.S. Government must withdraw from South Vietnam U.S. troops, military personnel, and weapons of all kinds, dismantle all U.S. military bases there, and cancel its military alliance with South Vietnam. ... According to the Geneva Agreements, the U.S. Government

must stop its acts of war against North Vietnam and completely cease all encroachments on the territory and sovereignty of the DRV [Democratic Republic of Vietnam].

2. Pending the peaceful reunification of Vietnam, while Vietnam is still temporarily divided into two zones the military provisions of the 1954 Geneva agreements on Vietnam must be strictly respected. The two zones must refrain from entering into any military alliance with foreign countries and there must be no foreign military bases, troops, or military personnel in their respective territory.

3. The internal affairs of South Vietnam must be settled by the South Vietnamese people themselves in accordance with the program of the [NLF] without any foreign interference.

4. The peaceful reunification of Vietnam is to be settled by the Vietnamese people in both zones, without any foreign interference.[6]

It was clear to Washington that the four points were intended as the basis for negotiations, rather than as either preconditions for or the expected outcome of such negotiations. A memorandum prepared for McGeorge Bundy was clear about this: "If we choose to make them so, Pham Van Dong's proposals could provide the basis for a negotiating dialogue." George Ball seized the opportunity to restate his modest October proposals—this time directly to Johnson. Ball urged Johnson to respond with a broad negotiating proposal of his own, one which essentially returned Vietnam to the provisions of the Geneva Agreements and explicitly recognized the Liberation Front as a political party "permitted to present candidates and conduct an election campaign by peaceful means." The apparent rigidity of Point 3 in the Hanoi text ("the internal affairs of South Vietnam must be settled . . . in accordance with the program of the NLF") dissolved upon examination, for fundamental to the Front position was the demand for the formation of a new government through elections.

McGeorge Bundy, McNamara, and Rusk strongly advised against a positive response. For them the iron law of diplomacy was "negotiation from strength," which meant that negotiations must await some signal improvement in the military situation. In the interim, the task was to devise ways of "buying time" until there had been sufficient military success to ensure that negotiations would decisively favor the American side. This logically ruled out any *political* solution to the conflict.

Increasingly, it was not the war itself but the American public that made such buying of time necessary. From its inception, ROLLING THUN-

DER had been a particular target of anti-war protest. How could Hanoi be expected to negotiate while it was being bombed by the United States, the critics demanded. Early in May, Johnson considered the possibility of using a pause in the bombing to put the onus on Hanoi. In a personal cable to Ambassador Taylor, Johnson explained that a brief halt in the bombing would "clear a path either toward restoration of peace or toward increased military action, depending on the reaction of the Communists." On May 13 and for the next five days, the bombing of the North stopped (the bombing of the South continued unabated). This was the perfect time-buying device: Hanoi seemed to be at fault for not responding immediately; yet in Hanoi the pause could only be understood as an ultimatum. The reward for negotiating on U.S. terms was not being bombed; refusal meant a return to punishment. Since Hanoi was not bombing the United States, and the pause was unrelated to the level of NLF activity in the South, no reciprocal action was available to Hanoi.

The message announcing the pause was drafted by William and McGeorge Bundy; the American public did not learn its terms until Hanoi Radio broadcast the text in December 1965. Rather than the response to Hanoi's four points proposed by Ball, the message ignored the possibility of negotiations altogether:

> The United States Government remains convinced that the underlying cause of trouble in Southeast Asia is armed action against the people and government of South Vietnam by forces whose actions can be decisively affected from North Vietnam. The United States will be very watchful to see whether in this period of pause there are significant reductions in such armed actions by such forces. . . . In taking this action, the United States is well aware of the risk that a temporary suspension of these air attacks may be understood as an indication of weakness, and it is therefore necessary . . . to point out that if this pause should be misunderstood in this fashion by any party, it would be necessary to demonstrate more clearly than ever, after the pause has ended, that the United States is determined not to accept aggression without reply in Vietnam.

The message went on to point out that while the United States could reverse its decision at any time during the period of aerial peace it was giving the people of North Vietnam, it remained hopeful of a positive response so that a more extended bombing pause could be instituted. Thus Hanoi was made responsible for the bombing to which it was subjected: an approved response would extend the pause, which even then would remain a pause, not a halt. Failure on the part of Hanoi meant the rain of bombs would resume. In effect, the terms were identical to those presented to Pham Van Dong in the summer of 1964 by Blair Seaborn: call off the war in the South. The United States offered nothing in return except an end to the bombing.

In April, Johnson had stated American goals as non-negotiable: "Our objective is the independence of South Viet-Nam and its freedom from attack. We want nothing for ourselves—only that the people of South Viet-Nam be allowed to guide their own country in their own way. We will do everything necessary to reach that objective, and we will do only what is absolutely necessary."[7] To those who opposed the war, the task was obvious: if that indeed was the American objective, then it was necessary to patiently explain that an independent South Vietnam, free from attack and guided only by its own people, meant, precisely, the complete withdrawal of the United States, negotiations among the South Vietnamese participants, and, ultimately, between North and South. It was good tactics for the critics to take the president at his word and then demonstrate how far he was from his own mark.

Some believed Johnson to be sincere; and the American faith that everyone can be educated runs deep. To educate the nation, and its government, a national Vietnam Teach-in, on the model of those held on college campuses earlier in the spring, was planned for mid-May 1965. On May 15, a telephonic hook-up linked one hundred twenty-two college and university campuses to the Sheraton Hotel in Washington, D.C., where several thousand people had gathered to listen to the debates. Each session featured speakers for and against government policy, as well as "opposition resource people" to match the government's State Department researchers who, from a rented room in the hotel, stood by to feed facts and figures to their side. Sessions covered the "realities of North Vietnam," the "domino theory," the issue of Chinese expansion, the American record in South Vietnam, the question of aggression from the North, a review of military policy, and whether or not the war could be won.

Arthur Schlesinger, Jr., historian to the Kennedy administration, spoke as a member of the loyal opposition to introduce an argument that soon became standard; it was not goals he wanted to question, but tactics. ROLLING THUNDER, for instance, was bound to fail; the World War II Strategic Bombing Survey had shown that bombing only stiffened the will to resist. Instead of bombs, Schlesinger argued, the United States should send troops. "Indeed if we took the Marines now in the Dominican Republic and sent them to South Vietnam we would be a good deal better off in both countries." But the Marines already were in South Vietnam.

The featured event of the national teach-in was to have been McGeorge Bundy debating Professor George Kahin, director of the Cornell University Southeast Asia program, but Bundy backed out at the last minute, citing the current crisis in the Dominican Republic. His statement of regret was remarkable for its implicit threat:

> It has been argued that debate of this kind should be avoided because it can give encouragement to the adversaries of our country. There is some ground for this argument, since it is true that Communists have little understanding of the meaning of debate in a free society. The Chinese will continue to pretend that American policy is weaker because 700 faculty members have made a protest against our policy in Vietnam. The American people know better. They know that those who are protesting are all a minority of American teachers and students. . . . We cannot let the propaganda of . . . totalitarians divert us from our necessary arguments with one another any more than we can let them be misled by such debates if we can help it.[8]

Bundy's replacement was Professor Robert Scalapino, a Berkeley political scientist whose standard Cold War views Kahin answered in a careful dissection of the government's rationale for the war, pointing out the deceptive nature of Johnson's spring offer to negotiate. If containment of China were the issue, then the United States should support Hanoi rather than attack it, for Vietnamese communism and nationalism were inseparably blended in the North and would not bend to the Chinese. Most important, Kahin said, the American public should realize that Johnson's offer to open "unconditional" discussions was ringed with conditions: "on condition that the Vietcong cease all operations immediately, and on condition that the state of South Vietnam continue its separate existence, in permanent violation of the Geneva Agreements"; and on condition that "the Vietcong and its political arm, the National Liberation Front, cannot be party to negotiations [which is] not only one more condition, but flies squarely in the face of political reality."[9] In the mainstream press, however, Johnson continued to be presented to the American public as having offered to "negotiate unconditionally" with the enemy, the hidden conditions apparently as irrelevant to the reporters as they were to the White House. For most of those who participated in the national teach-in, it now seemed clear that the goal must be all-out opposition to the administration rather than its education.

While protesters began to dog Johnson's heels, even to his ranch along the Perdernales, and Johnson continued to proclaim himself anxious to negotiate ("I have searched high and wide, and I am a reasonably good cowboy, and I can't even rope anybody and bring them in who is willing to talk and settle this thing by negotiation"), the military situation in South Vietnam continued to "deteriorate." On April 20, senior military and civilian officials met in Honolulu to review a request from Westmoreland for additional troop assignments to augment the 33,500 already assigned to protect base installations. On the 21st, Johnson approved their recommendations for an additional thirteen U.S. combat battalions (82,000 soldiers). Such action would not mean victory, but it would hold the line for now. The remaining questions were no longer whether to send troops, but how many? So many that the reserve would have to be called up? Congress asked for new taxes? The continuing expansion of the war admitted?

Before answering these hard questions, the first step was to see if more allied troops could be induced to join the war, obviating the need for an increase in American ground units. Chinese Nationalist troops from Taiwan were already involved, but any great increase in their numbers would surely upset Beijing in ways Washington was anxious to avoid. There were small contingents from Australia and New Zealand, but these were unlikely to grow. The real hope lay in Thailand, the Philippines, and South Korea. Assiduous bargaining and steady pressure did yield another five thousand by June 1965 from all sources, but they were extremely expensive. In addition to paying their costs in Vietnam, there was the question of remuneration of the allied governments: new economic and military aid for Marcos; the same for the Koreans; as well as lucrative civilian contracts in Saigon, including the standby of organized crime, garbage collection.[10]

An invasion of the North itself was regularly discussed and as regularly rejected. The risk of Chinese intervention was a major constraint; no one wanted "another Korea." But for five weeks in the summer of 1965, the possibility of a major American troop commitment to fight in South Vietnam was debated in the White House. And at the end of that time Lyndon Baines Johnson committed the country to a major ground war in the South, as earlier he had to the air war against both North and South. Johnson would later insist that he refused to be pushed into choosing between being a "leader of war" and a "leader of peace." "I wanted both, I believed in both, and I believed America had the resources to provide for both. After all, our country was built by pioneers who had a rifle in one hand to kill their enemies and an ax in the other to build their homes and provide for their families."[11] Only the enemy Indians in this

case were in someone else's country, and how killing them was connected to providing for American families was difficult to explain.

George Ball was the most clearsighted of the President's men. To
send major ground forces would amount to starting a "new war—the
United States directly against the Viet Cong." Possibly not even half a
million American soldiers would suffice. "Before we commit an endless
flow of forces to South Vietnam," Ball argued, "we must have more
evidence than we now have that our troops will not bog down in the
jungles and the rice paddies—while we slowly blow the country to
pieces." Yet, as in the discussion of ROLLING THUNDER, even Ball could
not simply recommend total withdrawal; nor did he ever take his case
to the public. Instead, he urged sending a test group of 100,000 soldiers
for a three-month period. His expectation was that at the end of that
period the President would realize the futility of a military solution and
turn to negotiating the United States out of Vietnam. When he saw he
was outnumbered, Ball remained loyal. "I have great and grave appre-
hensions. . . . But let me be clear. If the decision is to go ahead, I am
committed."

McNamara, McGeorge and William Bundy, Rostow, Rusk, the Joint
Chiefs of Staff, Taylor, Lodge (who returned as ambassador in June), all
insisted that the goal, a separate anti-Communist state in South Vietnam,
must be pursued and that American troops would have to pursue it. It
would be a long war. The odds were daunting: 200,000 to 400,000+
troops had only a 20 percent chance of success by 1966, a 70 percent
chance of stalemate and a 10 percent chance of total collapse. By 1968,
the chance of winning increased to 50 percent. The chances of achieving
a satisfactory compromise with 200,000 to 400,000 or more troops was
only 40 percent in 1966, though it rose to 70 percent by 1968. With any
fewer troops, there was little chance of ever winning.

Johnson polled his delegation and the support for sending troops
was overwhelming. Ball's pessimism was dismissed. Remember Munich,
Lodge urged. The threat of World War III came from inaction, not
action. How could America lose? "We have great seaports in Vietnam.
We don't need to fight on roads. We have the sea." If the Communists
found out the United States reneged on its commitments, Rusk predicted, "I don't know where they will stay their hand." Ball observed that
General Thieu thought the Communists could still win any election held
in South Vietnam. "I don't believe that," Johnson exclaimed. "Does anyone believe that?" Apparently no one did.

The military was equally firm. The chief of naval operations thought
the situation improved, and anyhow, "we are committed to [the] extent

we can't move out." The assistant secretary of the Air Force agreed: "It's worth taking a major step to avoid [the] long-run consequences of walking away from it." And the Army chief of staff, putting the matter in the familiar three-option Goldilocks formula, said: "The least desirable alternative is getting out. The second least is doing what we are doing. Best is to get in and get the job done."

Johnson delayed. The more his advisers told him it was impossible any longer to retreat, the more Johnson worried: would Congress and the people support hundreds of thousands of troops and billions of dollars? He had committed himself, true, but "if you make a commitment to jump off a building and you find out how high it is, you may withdraw the commitment." No one denied it was a high building. "This is a major change in U.S. policy," McNamara pointed out. "We have relied on South Vietnam to carry the brunt. Now we would be responsible for satisfactory military outcome."

On July 28, the president decided to go with the majority of his advisers. He would fight this war, but fight it on the side, without asking for an increase in taxes or a declaration of war, or risking a congressional debate. The country was rich enough for guns and butter, for the Vietnam War and the Great Society; the Tonkin Gulf Resolution would function, in Undersecretary of State Nicholas Katzenbach's phrase, as the "functional equivalent" of a declaration of war.[12] Rifle in one hand, ax in the other, Lyndon Baines Johnson went forward, announcing at the end of July that 50,000 more soldiers would be sent to Vietnam, bringing the number of troops there from 75,000 to 125,000. The existing draft call would have to be doubled, but there was no mention of calling up the reserves. The American invasion had begun.

American histories of the war frequently refer to the "mutual escalation" that began in late 1964. Although the disparity in the level of force involved on each side makes the phrase suspect, Hanoi did respond to the new stage of the war militarily as well as politically. It had been clear as early as 1963 that if U.S. troops were committed to combat in the South, marking the transition, as Hanoi analyzed it, from "special" war to "limited" war, it would be necessary to send North Vietnamese regular troops south. In April 1964, as we have seen, several units of the People's Army of Vietnam (PAVN) were prepared for possible use in the South, and in the aftermath of the Tonkin Gulf incident the decision was taken to send some 4,500 men South. By May 1965, when U.S. combat strength in South Vietnam stood at over 46,500, there were approximately 6,500 North Vietnamese soldiers in the South. Their senior officers were either southern regroupees (like Tran Van Tra and Nguyen Don) or northerners who had fought in the South against the French. Bases were established in the Central Highlands by the fall of 1964, and the quantity and quality of arms available to NLF main force units increased substantially as work began to expand the Ho Chi Minh Trail. These changes on both sides meant that sooner or later American troops would directly engage PLAF units, rather than just supporting and advising ARVN troops; they were likely as well to encounter regular North Vietnamese.

Two large-scale military engagements, one in August 1965 against PLAF forces and one in October 1965 against North Vietnamese regulars, illustrate this new stage of the war and also demonstrate why U.S. forces imagined themselves always on the brink of final victory, while always finding themselves back where they started.

The first engagement, code-named STARLIGHT, began as troops poured in to satisfy Westmoreland's requests. The general decided to launch an offensive against the Battangan peninsula, an old Viet Minh stronghold 15 miles north of the Marine base at Chu Lai in Quang Ngai Province. In a combined air, sea, and ground assault, using massive firepower (6,000 Marines, Phantom and Skyhawk jets, two destroyers, ground artillery from Chu Lai firing over 3,000 rounds; liberal use of napalm), the Marines killed 573 defenders, took 122 prisoners, lost 46 of their own, and suffered 204 wounded. Over three quarters of the PLAF regiment engaged in the battle escaped, and only 127 weapons were recovered. General Westmoreland counted STARLIGHT a great success, for it proved that American troops could defeat "any Viet Cong or North Vietnamese forces they might encounter." But Nguyen Chi Thanh, commanding general of PAVN and PLAF forces, counted it a victory as well. And while one might dismiss as boasting his claim that "the Southern Liberation Army is fully capable of defeating U.S. troops under any circumstances," William Turley points out that indeed the "PLAF and local guerrillas had engaged U.S. troops at a time and place chosen by U.S. commanders, yet had lived to fight another day." When the Marines moved out of the peninsula back to their base at Chu Lai, the NLF moved right back in.[13]

STARLIGHT was fought in and around heavily populated villages. A report after the battle noted that a number of villages had been "severely damaged or destroyed by napalm or naval gunfire, wherein the military necessity of doing so was dubious." The second engagement, the Battle of the Ia Drang Valley in the Central Highlands, which pitted the 1st Air Cavalry against regular PAVN troops, raised no such doubts. Westmoreland was convinced that the Communists intended to defeat Saigon by cutting the country in two at the Central Highlands. In fact, they already dominated the ground in the highlands and intended now to secure a road that would link supply lines running through Cambodia with the lower highlands. In late October, three regiments of regular North Vietnamese troops attacked ARVN outposts along Route 19. Their move was answered by the 1st Air Cavalry, whose orders were to "find, fix, and defeat the enemy forces. . . ." In over a month of fighting, during which the Air Cavalry conducted "reconnaissance by fire," drawing enemy fire and then swooping in for the kill, the PAVN lost well over fifteen hundred dead, the Americans more than two hundred. U.S. firepower was expended even more lavishly than at Chu Lai: B-52s dropping 500-pound bombs, 33,108 rounds of 105-mm howitzer ammunition, 7,356 aerial rockets, 50,000 helicopter sorties (with only four shot down). As an example of the success of Westmoreland's strategy of attrition, Ia Drang seemed an obvious victory. But some American military officers thought that on the contrary, Ia Drang was where the North Vietnamese began to learn how, despite the apocalypse of American firepower, they might yet defeat the United States: by fighting at extremely close quarters, the North Vietnamese could make American air and artillery support far less effective.[14]

STARLIGHT and Ia Drang represented two different approaches to the use of American troops. The approach exemplified by STARLIGHT and strongly supported by Maxwell Taylor was an "enclave" strategy, in which major cities and towns and well-placed U.S. military bases (mainly along the coast) would be secured by aggressive patrolling. Whenever the American war seemed to reach a stalemate, the enclave approach would be revived by those who both resisted complete withdrawal of American troops and despaired of the most popular alternative, "search and destroy" operations. Westmoreland and General Earle G. Wheeler, chairman of the Joint Chiefs of Staff, on the other hand, were impatient of anything that seemed to tie U.S. troops down in a posture of static defense, even one that allowed for offensive patrolling in a 50-mile radius of any given "enclave."[15] They envisaged battles like Ia Drang, finding the enemy and eliminating him; counting the dead bodies in a war of attrition in which U.S. firepower would inevitably win.

The phrase "search and destroy" was a creation of Westmoreland's own staff, whom the general had directed to find "expressive terms . . . to serve as a common terminology among the South Vietnamese and their American advisers." This particular expressive term indicated operations "designed to find, fix in place, fight and destroy . . . enemy forces and their base areas and supply caches. . . ." It was a tactic to be accompanied by two others: "clearing" operations, in which large enemy units were driven from populated areas in preparation for pacification of the area; and "securing operations," undertaken to protect pacification troops, wipe out remaining local guerrillas, and "uproot the enemy's secret political infrastructure." Later, Westmoreland complained, the phrase "search and destroy" was taken to mean "aimless searches in the jungle and the random destroying of villages and other property." And he wondered angrily why some "friendly critic" had not warned him how bad it sounded.[16]

In "search and destroy" as Westmoreland meant it, U.S. ground patrols, protected by heavily fortified fire bases, would issue forth to locate the enemy and then call in artillery and airpower to eliminate him. Sweeps were to be conducted in the Central Highlands and along the border of the demilitarized zone between North and South, presumably far from heavy concentrations of population. Search, destroy, count the bodies, move on. But as Taylor had predicted, the Saigon generals had little incentive to deploy their own forces and none to tie their troops down in the dangerous and unrewarding business of attempting to control areas "cleared" of Viet Cong by American troops. No place stayed cleared for very long.

The problem emerges very clearly in one exemplary "search and destroy" operation that took place in a heavily populated area of Central Vietnam only two months after the Ia Drang battle. In late January 1966, Operation MASHER/WHITE WING was launched in Binh Dinh Province, like Battangan, an old Viet Minh stronghold, which had been governed by the NLF since at least 1964. MASHER/WHITE WING owed its double name to Johnson's irritation over the naming of operations. "I don't know who names your operations," Johnson complained to senior military officials in Honolulu in 1966, "but 'Masher.' I get kind of mashed myself." So WHITE WING was added, presumably to soften the effect.[17] In combined amphibious and airborne assaults, which lasted almost six weeks, twenty thousand ARVN, South Korean, and American troops engaged PLAF and PAVN troops who had thoroughly fortified the area under attack. By the end of the first week, the Americans counted 603 enemy bodies and 119 of their own (42 in the crash of a transport plane). No one counted the civilian dead, though fifteen hamlets had been destroyed in the fighting and it was obvious to Neil Sheehan, who reported on the battle, that at least one hundred had died and many more were seriously wounded.

When it was over, the Americans withdrew. "It never occurred to me," Sheehan wrote, "that an American general would get so many of his own soldiers killed and inflict such horror simply to walk away." Sheehan asked the commanding officer, Major General Stanley Larsen, why he had swept through the hamlets if he didn't intend to stay there "and achieve something permanent." He learned that neither Larsen nor the ARVN were interested in pacification (though the ARVN officer was able to make a quick commercial killing in the copra market for the brief period the area was secure):

> I had heard these American generals speak of a war of attrition, but its meaning for the people and the country of South Vietnam had not registered with me. Did Larsen realize that the Viet Cong and the NVA were going to move right back into those hamlets? I asked. "Then we'll go back and kill more of the sons of bitches," he said.[18]

Indeed, 1st Air Cavalry intelligence reported signs that the enemy had returned to the area soon after MASHER/WHITE WING finished its search and destruction. Nevertheless, the official military history of the 1st Air Cavalry called the operation a success. The province itself was virtually occupied by the Americans. "But year after year," Gloria Emerson reported, "Binh Dinh never became a place they could overwhelm and change to be what they wanted. The number of dead Vietnamese and the refugees grew; Binh Dinh was never pacified."[19] On this first test, Westmoreland's war of attrition, however devastating to the Vietnamese countryside, would seem to have fallen short of a final solution.

In practice, whatever meaning it had for Westmoreland, "search and destroy" became the generic term for Vietnam combat. Instead of indicating sweeps through sparsely populated areas in search of regular North Vietnamese or main force guerrilla troops, it came to describe for the troops themselves their patrols through heavily populated areas; certainly to any village from which there was sniper fire or upon whose paths a GI tripped a mine. It was Cam Ne over and over again. Sometimes there was no provocation from the village. Kenneth Campbell was an artillery scout observer whose job it was to "spot villages." One day he spotted two villages north of the demilitarized zone. Had he seen any troops? No, Campbell answered, to the disappointment of his superior officer. "I told him, you know, they were working the fields and stuff. And I asked him if I should fire on them, you know, if I should call in artillery on these villages. He stopped for a few seconds, thought about it, and said yes, go ahead. He said they were probably feeding the NVA [North Vietnamese Army] with rice anyway, so therefore they are the enemy."[20]

"Search and destroy" applied as well to helicopter gunships as they swooped over the countryside. David Bressem flew with a reconnaissance unit whose function was to "find the enemy." Testifying before a congressional committee in 1971, Bressem, by then a college student in Springfield, Massachusetts, described the rules under which he fought. One rule concerned evasive action:

> Anyone taking evasive action could be fired upon. Evasive action was never explained to me. It normally entailed someone running or trying to evade a helicopter or any fire. My unit . . . had installed MP sirens on the helicopter and we used these for psychological effect, to intimidate the people. There is one incident I recall where we flew over a large rice paddy, and there were some people working in the rice paddy, maybe a dozen or fifteen individuals, and we passed a couple of times low over their heads and they didn't take any action, they were obviously nervous, but they didn't try to hide or anything. So we then hovered a few feet off the ground among them with the two helicopters, turned on the police sirens and when they heard the police sirens, they started to disperse and we opened up on them and just shot them all down.[21]

Later, when it was all over, some would criticize Westmoreland's strategy, and insist that his "war of attrition" had been woefully misguided; the policy should have been counterinsurgency and pacification. But it all came down to search and destroy in the end. Marine lieutenant general Lew Walt, for example, favored an "inkblot" approach in which domination over an area would gradually spread as small units on twenty-four-hour patrol would enlarge secured areas, leaving North Vietnamese units in the highlands to whistle for a battle. "General Walt stressed that the objective of the war was to win the loyalty of the populace to the government, and the only way to obtain this objective was to eradicate the Viet Cong in the villages and hamlets." Search and destroy then, but intimately, in small units. "It is our conviction," Lieutenant General Victor Krulak, now Commanding General Fleet Marine Force Pacific, wrote, "that if we can destroy the guerrilla fabric among the people, we will automatically deny the larger units the food and the intelligence and the taxes, and the other support they need . . . the real war is among the people and not among these mountains."[22] Therefore search for and destroy the "guerrilla fabric," which, as Krulak knew, was intricately interwoven with the fabric of rural life itself. And then, who would maintain the "security" of the cleared villages? Certainly not the ARVN, who had after all tried to do so from 1959 to 1965 and failed. In time every approach to clearing and holding, searching and destroying, would be employed.

The situation in late November 1965, despite the heavy increment of U.S. troops, was not encouraging. McNamara, returning from a two-day trip to Vietnam, reported to Johnson on November 30 that the Saigon government was "surviving, but not acquiring wide support." Pacification had come to a complete halt, with "no guarantee that security anywhere is permanent. . . ." Air Force General Ky, at this point serving as prime minister, estimated that Saigon controlled no more than 25 percent of the population, though he looked forward to doubling that in the next two years. That was the good news; McNamara went on to describe the military situation in more dire terms. While ARVN desertion rates rose, local NLF recruitment, especially in the Delta, had increased, as had infiltration of North Vietnamese troops; and despite the bombing, more than enough supplies continued to get through. The 220,000 U.S. troops already in place would clearly not suffice, nor would the additional 112,000 already approved.[23]

There were, then, only two options: seek a compromise solution, or "stick with our stated objectives and with the war, and provide what it takes in men and material." This would mean approximately 400,000 troops by the end of 1966 and perhaps another 200,000+ in 1967. Americans killed in action would probably reach one thousand a month, and even so, "we should be aware that deployments of the kind I have recommended will not guarantee success." On Pearl Harbor Day, December 7, 1965, McNamara's grim prognosis was that the "odds are about even that, even with the recommended deployments, we will be faced in early 1967 with a military standoff at much higher level. . . ."[24] Yet the new deployments were approved. Under Kennedy, U.S. troops had armed, advised, and supported the ARVN in combat against its Vietnamese opponent; now the ARVN was an auxiliary in an American war against the NLF and the North Vietnamese.

Until 1965, almost every South Vietnamese government had either resisted a vast increase in the American military presence or threatened to begin talking with the enemy or both. The Saigon government in place from mid-1965 on, however, looked for the fullest American participation and had no intention of discussing anything at all with the NLF or Hanoi. It was, in McNamara's phrase, a "government of generals." Premier Nguyen Cao Ky, born in Hanoi, had been trained as a pilot by the French in Algeria. He shared power with Nguyen Van Thieu, also northern-born, who after fighting with the French against the Viet Minh, had gone on to graduate from the United States Command and General Staff College in 1957. No one in Saigon imagined that the government could outlive American support for even one day. Nor was it only a matter of military security.[25]

Victory, the secretary of the Military Directorate told George Kahin in 1966, had both a political and a military expression, but General Pham Xuan Chieu explained: "We are very weak politically and without the strong political support of the population which the NLF have." So great was NLF political strength that even if it was defeated militarily, Chieu argued, they could still come to power. Thus it would be necessary "to destroy [the NLF] political organizations and political infrastructure among the people." For this reason it was foolish to think that U.S. troops would be able to withdraw in the aftermath of a cease-fire. American troops would have to guarantee Saigon's *political* as well as military predominance before they were free to go home. "Frankly," a Saigon official confided to a reporter late in 1966, "we are not strong enough now to compete with the Communists on a purely political basis. They are organized and disciplined. . . . We cannot leave the Vietcong in existence."[26] The prospect was endless war.

The opposition was equally aware that it depended on the United States. Buddhist leaders told Kahin that peace was only possible if the United States withdrew its life support system from the Ky/Thieu government and allowed it to be replaced by a more representative government that could then negotiate with the NLF from a position of popular strength. The American Embassy condemned this Buddhist vision as naive and Buddhist leaders as "pro-Communist." But over the years the Buddhists had gained in political sophistication. Rather than move directly into the political arena, the leadership took advantage of some vague and incautious promises by Ky that elections for a constituent assembly would take place in 1966. It was difficult for the Americans to oppose free elections outright, and yet it was obvious that free elections posed a serious threat to the entire American enterprise. As *Newsweek* reported the views of top embassy officials, "if any elected assembly sits in Saigon, it will be on the phone negotiating with Hanoi within one week."[27]

What made Buddhist opposition to Ky and Thieu significant in mid-1966 was its connection with a powerful military figure, General Nguyen Chanh Thi, a commander generally respected by the American military, himself a Buddhist, and in charge of "I Corps," the five northern provinces that included both Hue and Danang. To returning Ambassador Lodge, who had replaced Taylor in the summer of 1965, Thi was a dangerous man, who was "considering the possibility of establishing a government in the south which would be of such a character that the bulk of the population including the Vietcong would support it—and presumably neutralization of the country and possibly federation with the North would be possible. . . ."[28] No one asked Lodge why this was not a desirable outcome. Instead, the United States approved a move to dismiss Thi altogether, though the commander of the U.S. Marines in I Corps strongly disapproved and actually sustained Thi in his refusal to accept dismissal. The Buddhists too moved quickly, launching a "Struggle Movement" that began by demanding, first, the cancelation of Thi's dismissal, and then went on to call for the restoration of civilian government. The Saigon government restored Thi to I Corps with orders to quiet things down but instead he apparently joined the Buddhist movement. The pressure on Saigon yielded promises of political reform and a responsive relaxation of the Struggle Movement. When it became clear that the government would not fulfill its promises, demonstrations resumed, with thousands marching in the streets of Saigon, Danang, Hue. In Saigon, Catholic leaders marched in solidarity with the Buddhists and, most alarming, troops of the ARVN 1st Division joined the civilians. In Hue and Danang, even the police and civil service were reported to be sympathetic to the Struggle Movement.[29]

Nor was political reform the only demand. The banners were explicit: "Stop Killing Our People," "Foreign Countries Have No Right to Set Up Military Bases on Vietnamese Land." As they marched up and down in front of the American Embassy in Saigon, seven thousand farmers shouted: *"Da Dao My!* (Down with Americans!)" Daniel Ellsberg, writing intelligence reports for the Department of Defense, emphasized the problems: there was "almost total absence of *any* organized popular *support,* or even sympathy for the American-backed regime." George Kahin, on the basis of his own observation at the time as well as recently declassified reports, concludes that never "had any South Vietnamese government stood more naked of indigenous backing."[30]

On April 3, 1966, with the approval of both Lodge and Westmoreland, Ky announced that the Struggle Movement had fallen into Communist hands and requested American aid in shuttling loyal troops to Danang. In Washington, Johnson and his advisers discussed the situation and how to keep U.S. troops out of it. How could they intervene in favor of Ky without exposing American troops to hostile fire from dissident ARVN troops (armed, as they were, with high-power American weapons)? But what would happen to the war if a truly representative constituent assembly came to power? Ky himself was not trouble-free and had recently expressed a desire to have the mayor of Danang shot. Johnson complained to his advisers that this showed "bad judgment" and wanted to know if the premier had made other "bad judgments." Maxwell Taylor recalled an occasion on which Ky had professed great admiration for Adolf Hitler, "but I thought he had matured."[31]

Despite worries about Ky in Washington, in South Vietnam Lodge and Westmoreland supported him fully. Yet even with U.S. Air Force transport and Marine protection, Ky's early April move against the military units that supported the Buddhist movement in Hue and Danang collapsed. By itself it is unclear what the Buddhist movement, however strengthened by other civilian elements in the cities, would have accomplished. But once the movement had attracted the loyalty of key units of the army, Washington had to pay attention. Although some advisers now urged compromise and negotiation, Walt Rostow, who had recently replaced McGeorge Bundy as national security adviser, took a characteristically harder line. As Johnson was fond of telling Kennedy loyalists, Rostow was "my intellectual. He's not your intellectual. He's not Bundy's intellectual. He's not Galbraith's intellectual. He's not Schlesinger's intellectual. He's going to be my goddamn intellectual and I'm going to have him by the short hairs." Unfortunately, this seems to have resulted in Rostow's having the country in the same hold. "He played to Johnson's weaker side," George Ball recalled, "always creating an image of Johnson standing against the forces of evil. He used to tell him how Lincoln was abused by everybody when he was at a certain stage of the Civil War. . . . He spent a good deal of time creating a kind of fantasy for the president."[32]

When domestic history failed to yield persuasive examples, Rostow enlarged to world history. To persuade Johnson in the spring of 1966 to support Ky and Thieu against the Buddhists, he explained that "We are faced with a classic revolutionary situation—like Paris in 1789 and St. Petersburg in 1917." If they could, the Viet Cong would use the Buddhist leadership as Lenin had used Kerensky. Only this time there was a significant difference, a factor absent from Russia in 1917. This time the cavalry was already there: "In the face of defeat in the field and Kerensky's weakness, Lenin took over in November. This is about what would happen in Saigon if we were not there; but we are there." One of Rostow's own aides also recalled Russia: "Rostow was like Rasputin to a tsar under siege."[33]

Yet the force of the Struggle Movement was so great that Ky had to respond. This time the promise of elections seemed to carry with it an American guarantee and, despite some trepidation, the Buddhist leadership agreed to halt the demonstrations as an earnest display of their goodwill. And now, rather muddying Rostow's Russian analogy, the stage was set for betrayal. In early May, Ky simply canceled his agreements, flew heavy troop reinforcements to Danang and launched his attack against both Buddhists and dissident army units. The local U.S. Marine commander, General Lew Walt, was unhappily surprised; but orders came from the top to support Ky. A Marine named Leo Cawley was on duty in Danang and remembered what happened:

> Tanks were brought in by sea on U.S. vessels while U.S. marines blocked the routes from the south keeping pro-Buddhist units from reaching Danang. On or about May 15 the Buddhist strongholds in the city were reduced in a violent effusion of blood. The Ranger (ARVN) company near our position on a bridge fired an anti-tank round at a bus of demonstrators coming up from Hoi An, a town 50 km. south of Danang. . . . Everywhere there were dead and, spattered with blood, tatters of their bright nice clothing and banners for the demonstration. . . . What did it all mean? These were the Vietnamese that we were supposed to be defending. It was some gook hassle the gunnery sergeant explained. But then the ARVN Rangers were pulled back toward Danang and U.S. Marines were given responsibility for the road block and what we might have thought of it didn't matter. We had freed up the ARVN to crush the Buddhists. Besides there was a war on and the Buddhists should really hold off until it was over. . . .

Bombing and strafing Struggle Movement headquarters at will, Ky's forces, aided by the U.S. Marines, brutally crushed the Buddhists and their supporters. An American reporter described the pagoda headquarters of the movement as a "charnel house."[34] In June, with Danang under control, Ky turned against the city of Hue and, once more aided by American troops, succeeded in ending that opposition. Later that month, pockets of the movement that had survived in Saigon were similarly eliminated.

In 1963, Diem's clumsy handling of the Buddhist crisis had provided the occasion for eliminating Diem. The object then had not been to support the Buddhists but to achieve a government in Saigon that would fight the Communists as the United States saw fit. By 1966, such a government was in place and the United States was determined to keep it there, against all its enemies, not just the Viet Cong. The self-immolation of Buddhist monks had disturbed the American public in 1963 and turned many against Washington's Vietnam policy. But the immolation of Buddhist monks by Saigon troops was a more familiar and acceptable sort of news. The government of Ky and Thieu had been saved.

American troops could clear territory, evacuate populations, drop napalm, defoliate crops, transform the landscape with bomb craters, take Vietnamese mistresses, vaccinate Vietnamese children, train troops, supervise interrogations and the administration of prisons. They could expend, in a single day, more firepower than the French had during the entire fifty-six-day Battle of Dienbienphu. They could flatten cities in the North, as they did the city of Vinh; they could destroy villages in the South. But they could not make the South Vietnamese love the government the United States had brought to power in Saigon, nor could they govern the country themselves. There were now only two options: American troops could be withdrawn, or they could stay on and kill. They stayed.

CHAPTER NINE

An American War
(1966–1967)

Asked if he would fight to final victory, Ho Chi Minh said: "If by 'final victory' you mean the departure of the Americans, then we will fight to final victory. Everything depends on the Americans. If they want to make war for 20 years then we shall make war for 20 years. If they want to make peace, we shall make peace and invite them to tea afterwards."

—HO CHI MINH TO MARTIN
NIEMOELLER, DECEMBER 1966

THE AMERICANS sent to Vietnam fought different wars depending on when they arrived and where (and whether) they were in combat. The Central Highlands, where encounters were often with regular North Vietnamese troops, differed from the Delta, where main force, regional, or local militia bore the brunt of the fighting, and the difference between friendly farmer and enemy guerrilla was not always apparent, or attended to. And because—in contrast to earlier American wars—the tour of duty was a single year, men who fought in the same areas but in different years fought different wars. One thing only the Americans held in common: they would all eventually leave. Vietnamese on both sides were in the war for the duration.

Americans might come in greater and greater numbers but they would always be aliens in a strange land. This basic fact was incarnate in Westmoreland's tactic of "search and destroy," both in its conception and in its repeated failures. Once any battle was over, the Americans returned to their bases; the NLF, indigenous and ubiquitous, would move back in, recruiting among the ruins. To deal with this problem, Westmoreland and his staff devised a new approach in 1966 and 1967: destroy everything in an area known to be largely under NLF control, whether or not there had been an attack—trees, houses, crops—and then withdraw, taking the population out with the troops, leaving the burned-over district as a free field for bombs and artillery. The tale of Ben Suc, told by Jonathan Schell in *The New Yorker* not long after the events it narrated took place, dramatized the nature of this sort of warfare. In 1964, NLF forces made up of Ben Suc villagers drove out the ARVN outpost that had been set up by the Saigon government in 1955 as a symbol of government authority. From 1964 to 1967 the villagers participated in the war against Saigon, and then against the Americans, principally by defending themselves against attack, paying taxes (which were sharply graduated), and helping to supply regional Front troops. At the same time, children went to school, crops were planted and harvested, young people married, children were born. "In short, to the villagers of Ben Suc," their American chronicler, Jonathan Schell, has written, "the National Liberation Front was not a band of roving guerrillas but the full government of their village."

The ARVN had tried and failed to retake Ben Suc in 1964, and the NLF simply chose not to engage an American airborne brigade that probed the area in October 1965. It is difficult, but important, to see the village not as an isolated place "controlled" by the NLF, but as the same village it had been for generations, run by villagers who were also members of the Front. Several village families had relatives in the ARVN, and though they were kept under surveillance, there was no question of driving them out of their homes. Such benefits as could be derived from Saigon were duly exploited. ARVN medical teams, for example, were welcome guests.

The center of Ben Suc was bombed once, in mid-1965, and twenty people were killed. But otherwise the village itself was not directly involved in the fighting, although the surrounding area was heavily contested and subjected to constant artillery bombardment and bombing. The village council organized the construction of bomb shelters, and key points in and around the village were booby-trapped, but no direct assault on Ben Suc occurred.

Then, in January 1967, the village found itself included as a small part of a much larger scheme—Operation CEDAR FALLS, sentimentally named for the Iowa hometown of a posthumous Medal of Honor winner from the 1st Division. CEDAR FALLS was one of a number of sweeps through known NLF enclaves, this one directed against the so-called

Iron Triangle, a center of NLF activity 35 kilometers (about 22 miles) northeast of Saigon that the Army thought harbored a full division of main force NLF troops.

The entire Iron Triangle area, within a 32-mile perimeter, was first to be pulverized by B-52 and artillery fire, then flattened with giant bulldozers. Three villages in the area would be evacuated and then destroyed. Finally, American soldiers would move in behind the bulldozers to engage whoever remained alive. Ben Suc was the first scheduled to go. Schell was present at the military briefing offered reporters shortly before the attack. The problem, as explained by Major Allen C. Dixon of the 173d Airborne Brigade, was that whatever you did to kick out the VC, they always returned. "Now, we realize that you can't go in and then just abandon the people to the V.C. This time we're really doing a thorough job of it: we're going to clean out the place completely. The people are all going to be resettled in a temporary camp. . . ." And the major was as good as his word. Five hundred soldiers were airlifted into the village, whose surrounding woods, for good measure, were pounded by air strikes while the village itself was entirely cordoned off. Villagers were herded into the center of Ben Suc and then ARVN troops flown in. Separately, Americans and Saigon troops divided the villagers into two categories, "people" and "Viet Cong suspects," to be interrogated. ARVN interrogation tactics routinely employed torture, which the Americans observed. One American officer explained the importance of cultural relativism to Schell: "You see, they *do* have some—well, methods and practices that *we* are not accustomed to . . . but the thing you've got to understand is that this is an Asian country, and their first impulse is force. . . . It's the Asian mind. It's completely different from what we know as the Western mind. . . ."

Major Charles A. Malloy discussed with Schell the problem of differentiating between an innocent farmer and a Viet Cong suspect: "What're you going to do when you spot a guy with black pajamas? Wait for him to get out his automatic weapon and start shooting? Anyway, sometimes they throw away their weapon. They'll throw it in the bushes. . . . You can't always tell if they were carrying a weapon." Malloy had a simple yardstick. When a prisoner was brought before him wearing the black shirt and pants of all Vietnamese peasants, he turned to Schell: "There's a V.C. Look at those black clothes. They're no good for working in the fields. Black absorbs heat. This is a hot country. It doesn't make any sense." The man's bare and muddy feet were further proof: "They're all muddy from being down in those holes."

The "people" of Ben Suc and several other villages, now designated "hostile civilians," were evacuated by truck to an ill-equipped refugee camp. Then Ben Suc itself was annihilated: "G.I.s moved down the narrow lanes and into the sunny, quiet yards of the empty village, pouring gasoline on the grass roofs of the houses and setting them afire. . . ." Then came the bulldozers. "There were very few dwellings in Ben Suc to make a bulldozer pause. The bulldozers cut their own paths across the backyard fences, small graveyards, and ridged fields of the village. . . ." Finally, "jets sent their bombs down on the deserted ruins, scorching again the burned foundations of the houses and pulverizing for a second time the heaps of rubble, in the hopes of collapsing tunnels too deep and well hidden for the bulldozers to crush. . . ." Six months later, using a vast network of tunnels that extended throughout the area, the NLF was once more operating in the Iron Triangle.[1]

A Japanese reporter, Katsuichi Honda, understood the distance between American soldiers and the ordinary scenes of Vietnamese rural life they witnessed daily without ever comprehending. It was hard to see a house of mud and thatch as more than a temporary dwelling; hardly a home in the American sense. Rice cultivation—labor-intensive, backbreaking, closer to gardening than any farming even soldiers from farm country had ever seen—simply did not register with the troops, for whom neither the labor, nor the crop, nor the people who planted and depended on it were real. Honda described five tanks driving right into

> the golden waves of rice paddies. The ripe ears of rice, now ready to be harvested, were mercilessly trodden and kneaded in the muddy field under the caterpillars as they took their capricious way over the paddies. They did not even have the kindness to make one tank follow the wake of the preceding one. The seed beds of rice plants, and the newly planted paddies—all these were nothing in their eyes. . . . In the heart of the American soldiers there was a hopeless lack of an element common to rice cultivating peoples. This lack makes it impossible for them to understand the mind of these peasants. The gulf lying between the two makes one despair.[2]

There were American soldiers who bridged the gulf, at the cost of their own despair. "This is what the war ended up being about," Bryan Alec Floyd wrote:

> we would find a V.C. village,
> and if we could not capture it
> or clear it of Cong,
> we called for jets.

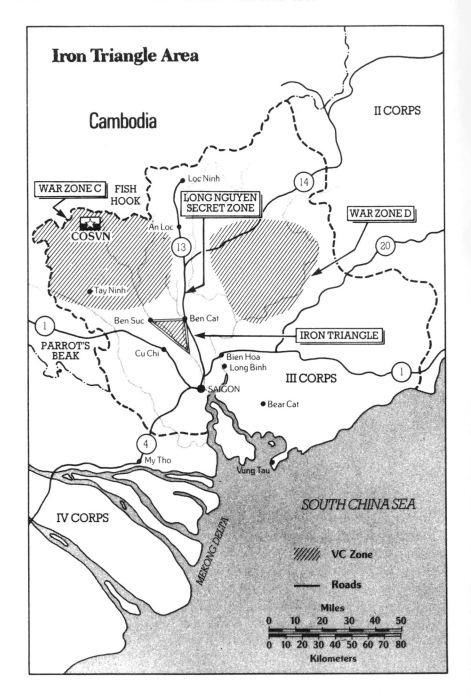

Iron Triangle Area

Cambodia

II CORPS

Loc Ninh

14

WAR ZONE C   FISH
            HOOK

LONG NGUYEN
SECRET ZONE

WAR ZONE D

COSVN

An Loc

13

20

Tay Ninh

Ben Suc   Ben Cat

IRON TRIANGLE

1

PARROT'S
BEAK

Cu Chi

Bien Hoa
Long Binh

III CORPS

1

SAIGON

Bear Cat

4

My Tho

Vung Tau

SOUTH CHINA SEA

IV CORPS

MEKONG DELTA

///// VC Zone

──── Roads

Miles
0   10   20   30   40   50

0 10 20 30 40 50 60 70 80
Kilometers

The jets would come in, low and terrible,
sweeping down, and screaming,
in their first pass over the village.
Then they would return, dropping their first bombs
that flattened the huts to rubble and debris.
And then the jets would sweep back again
and drop more bombs
that blew the rubble and debris
to dust and ashes.
And then the jets would come back once again,
in a last pass, this time to drop napalm
that burned the dust and ashes to just nothing.
Then the village
that was not a village any more
was our village.[3]

Within a very short time, the American war against the NLF and
its northern ally transformed every aspect of Vietnamese society and
became a war against Vietnam as such, North and South, urban and rural,
elite and non-elite, Viet Cong, Buddhist, Catholic, Cao Dai, Hoa Hao,
"neutral." Normally a rice-exporting area, South Vietnam had to import
750,000 tons of rice in 1967. By 1968, the urban population of South
Vietnam had increased from 15 to 40 percent of the total population (it
would be 65 percent urban in 1974); out of a population of 17 million,
5 million people were officially classed as refugees.

Driving the farmers out of the countryside into refugee camps or
cities was seen by some civilian pacification advisers as a "modernizing
experience," and by Harvard political scientist Samuel P. Huntington as
a legitimate instrument of overall U.S. policy. The Viet Cong, Huntington explained, is a "powerful force which cannot be dislodged from its
constituency so long as the constituency continues to exist." Huntington
went on to argue logically that if force were applied "on such a massive
scale as to produce a massive migration from countryside to city the basic
assumptions underlying the Maoist doctrine of revolutionary war no
longer operates. The Maoist inspired rural revolution is undercut by the
American-sponsored urban revolution." For those who did not like to
think the United States was condemning hundreds of thousands to life
in a refugee slum, he prescribed a dose of cultural relativism: "The urban
slum, which seems so horrible to middle-class Americans, often becomes
for the poor peasant a getaway to a new and better way of life. For some
poor migrants, the wartime urban boom has made possible incomes five
times those which they had in the countryside."[4]

General Westmoreland also found positive side effects to the American military operations. From a manufacturer in Rome, Georgia, the military purchased the giant bulldozers known as "Rome plows" that were used to level villages like Ben Suc. These martial plows, the general reported, were "a device much admired by the Vietnamese, for in addition to eliminating enemy hideouts, [they] cleared a vast acreage for cultivation."[5] A dubious gain but a sure measure of how little Westmoreland had observed the actual landscape of the country, which had been cleared and intensely cultivated long before his arrival.

As U.S. casualties mounted, Johnson agonized about the war he commanded, though his image of fighting in Vietnam seems to have been inspired by a World War I flying epic:

> I would . . . begin to picture myself lying in Da Nang. I could see an American plane circling above me in the sky. I felt safe. Then I heard a long, loud shot. The plane began to fall faster, faster, faster. I saw it hit the ground, and as soon as it burst into flames, I couldn't stand it any more. I knew that one of my boys must have been killed that night. I jumped out of bed, put on my robe, took my flashlight, and went into the Situation Room.

There in the middle of the night, with CIA and Pentagon staff monitoring the Telex, learning how many planes had been shot down, how many had hit their targets, and marking the giant map of North Vietnam accordingly, the president recovered his calm.[6] Ramsey Clark, Johnson's attorney general, was familiar with these 3:00 A.M. trips to the Situation Room. "But I never sensed any concern for the other side. How many did the Vietnamese lose? How many people were killed in the village? How many South Vietnamese, how many North Vietnamese, how many Vietcong? It was *our* lives, *our* country; and they didn't figure, those people."[7]

Indeed, the war had become America's war. This arose partly from the logic of the American intervention, which cast North Vietnam as a separate country that had started a war in the neighboring country of South Vietnam. North Vietnam fought in part through the Viet Cong, a wholly dependent subsidiary lacking either political or military autonomy. The United States was in Vietnam to aid its ally, South Vietnam; when aid was not enough, direct military intervention had become unavoidable. Thus McNamara, deploring in 1966 the Communists' claim that they had more "staying power" than the Americans, apparently never thought to wonder how the reverse could obtain—what else would

Vietnamese, Communist or not, do but stay? Where else would they go?

This confusion contributed to reducing the war, for McNamara and other top American military and civilian officials, to a contest of will, resolvable only by force. Hanoi, McNamara wrote, intended to "test U.S. capabilities and will to persevere at a higher level of conflict and casualties." General William DePuy believed the United States must pound away until it had reached the enemy's "threshold of pain"; Henry Kissinger was confident that "every society, like every human being, has a breaking point." Westmoreland shared that confidence. "We'll just go on bleeding them until Hanoi wakes up to the fact that they have bled their country to the point of national disaster for generations. Then they will have to reassess their position." Johnson took it all personally. He hated bombing pauses, David Halberstam writes: "Oh yes, a bombing halt, he would say, I'll tell you what happens when there's a bombing halt: I halt and then Ho Chi Minh shoves trucks right up my ass. That's your bombing halt." Much later, in 1966, exhausted by the lack of progress in the war, McNamara confessed to a *Newsweek* reporter that he had "never thought it would go on like this. I didn't think these people had the capacity to fight this way. If I had thought they would take this punishment and fight this well, and could enjoy fighting like this, I would have thought differently at the start. . . ."[8]

What could not be acknowledged was that Vietnam was one country, that the war in the South was between contending Vietnamese forces, the weaker of which had in large measure been created by the United States itself, and that it was to ensure the triumph of its creation that over 400,000 American combat troops were now fighting in Vietnam. Since none of this could be admitted without irreversible damage to the American rationale for intervention, a basis for negotiations—much urged by America's Western allies—was difficult to discern. Ho Chi Minh insisted that Hanoi would not negotiate while it was being bombed; the United States replied that the bombing would end when Hanoi stopped carrying on the war in the South. (The bombing of the South was not at issue; it just went on.) The American position was not absolute: reciprocal deescalation was a possibility. Yet for Hanoi to formally grant such reciprocity would amount to granting the premise of the American intervention. And for Washington to agree that there were no grounds for reciprocity was to brand itself an aggressor in Vietnam. Since the United States would not grant the legitimacy of the aims of the NLF, nor the interest of Hanoi in the attainment of those aims, the only understanding of the struggle available to Washington was that it was a test of willpower, credibility, prestige. For Hanoi and the NLF, the struggle was about how Vietnamese would live in Vietnam; increasingly, it was about survival as such.

The Johnson administration announced a number of "peace initiatives" in late 1965 and early 1966. In every case they seemed to founder on the issue of timing: the Johnson administration adamantly refused to stop bombing until Hanoi had demonstrated that it was scaling down its military effort in the South. Hanoi refused to talk while it was being bombed or under an ultimatum. But the issue of timing, of course, was basic to the war aims of each side. What Washington was ready to offer in December 1965 was both an ultimatum and a public relations ploy. This much is clear from a late November 1965 memorandum prepared for the president by Secretary of Defense McNamara, urging another bombing pause:

> It is my belief that there should be a three- or four-week pause . . . in the program of bombing the North before we either greatly increase our troop deployments to Vietnam or intensify our strikes against the North. The reasons for this belief are, first, that we must lay a foundation in the mind of the American public and in world opinion for such an enlarged phase of the war and, second, we should give North Vietnam a face-saving chance to stop the aggression.[9]

After much debate, Johnson approved a bombing pause that began on December 24, 1965. Yet indications that military operations in the South had been scaled down in apparent response to the pause were studiously ignored in Washington while the U.S. ground war in the South markedly intensified.[10] Instead, Washington focused on Ho Chi Minh's formal response, which insisted on an unconditional end to the bombing. This enraged the president, whose resistance thereafter to bombing cutbacks seems to have been encouraged by Clark Clifford and Abe Fortas, two old political friends who told him the pause had been a terrible mistake. Efforts by the Canadian diplomat Chester Ronning in the spring of 1966 yielded nothing but acrimony. A more extended effort at mediation through the Polish delegation to the International Control Commission in the summer and fall of 1966 was broken off when a series of heavy bombing raids caused extensive damage to Hanoi even as preliminary meetings were being scheduled. "The series of bombings," White House aide Chester Cooper wryly noted, "seemed to suggest to the Poles, presumably to the North Vietnamese, and even to a few people in the State Department, that the United States had little interest in serious negotiations."[11]

Dean Rusk claimed that his "delicate antennae" would enable him to discern when Hanoi was sincere and when it was deliberately lying. But U.S. intentions were more difficult to sort out. In September 1966 and again on New Year's Eve of that year, UN Ambassador Goldberg pledged that Washington was "prepared to take the first step toward peace: specifically, we are ready to order a prior end to all bombing of North Vietnam the moment there is an assurance, private or otherwise, that there would be a reciprocal response toward peace in North Vietnam." And at a February 2, 1967, press conference, the President repeated that the United States remained ready to open "unconditional discussions" on every aspect of the war. Sadly, he was "not aware of any serious effort that the other side has made . . . to bring the fighting to a stop and to stop the war." Asked what steps the "other side" should take in order to achieve the suspension of bombing and the beginning of talks, Johnson answered, "Just almost any step."[12]

Hanoi seems to have taken Johnson at his word. In early February 1967, with Soviet Premier Kosygin and British Prime Minister Harold Wilson acting as intermediaries, a delicate series of negotiations began in which an effort was made to finesse the issue of reciprocity. The scenario, first discussed in November 1966, was labeled "Phase A/Phase B," and involved the suspension of U.S. bombing of the North. In return, but after a pause whose length would have to be agreed upon, Hanoi would respond by reducing troop infiltration to the South and the United States might cut back on its own troop reinforcements. But by January 1967 Westmoreland's massive search and destroy operations, with their favorable "body count" of the enemy, made Washington more confident of a military victory than it had been a few months earlier and its terms consequently hardened. "The prospect of winning the war complicated the effort to end it by negotiations in 1967," one official told historian Allan Goodman. "It meant we had to prove to LBJ that what we could get at the conference table was better than what we could get on the battlefield."[13]

Instead of negotiating a beginning to the talks and winning himself a major place in the history of mediation, Harold Wilson found himself completely embarrassed as the terms he had confidently communicated to Kosygin turned out not to be at all the terms Washington was ready to offer. On the contrary, as Johnson said in a letter addressed directly to Ho Chi Minh and dispatched on February 10 even as Kosygin and Wilson continued to discuss possible terms for the opening of negotiations, talks would begin only after Johnson was assured that "infiltration into South Vietnam by land and by sea has stopped." Chester Cooper, who had been working with the British to delay the resumption of bombing, concluded that Washington had never been really serious about the Wilson initiative, and by mid-February peace efforts "ended in another pall of smoke over Hanoi."[14]

The measure of Washington's interest in peace talks can be taken in the response Harry Ashmore and William Baggs received after returning from a nine-day trip to Hanoi in January 1967. Ashmore had been executive editor of the *Arkansas Gazette,* Baggs was the editor of the *Miami News,* and both were associated with the Center for the Study of Democratic Institutions in Santa Barbara, California. They had gone to Hanoi with the help of the State Department and returned bearing, they thought, important news which Ashmore later detailed to Merle Miller:

> We brought back from Ho Chi Minh the basic proposition that they would not hold a meeting as long as the bombing continued, but they would discuss the terms of a meeting in some fashion on the assumption that if there was agreement the bombing would stop, that beyond that anything was open for discussion . . . the separation of the country could continue for quite a long time as far as the North was concerned. They would insist that the NLF, which at that time was literally doing most of the fighting . . . had to be recognized and had to be part of some kind of coalition government. Beyond that, they were fairly flexible as to how long the American withdrawal would take, et cetera.

A month passed and nothing happened. Ashmore, puzzled and anxious, got Senator Fulbright to speak to Johnson and, at a cocktail party, Fulbright did so: "Lyndon, what did you think of what Ashmore and Baggs had to say about Ho Chi Minh and Vietnam?" But Johnson had no opinion: "they talked to some fellows over there at the State Department. . . . You know, Bill," the president pointed out, "I can't see everybody that goes over there and talks to Ho Chi Minh." Afterwards, Johnson was concerned about the impression this casual dismissal might have made on the powerful chairman of the Senate Foreign Relations Committee and he called a meeting with Undersecretary of State Nicholas Katzenbach, Averell Harriman, William Bundy, Bundy's Vietnam "experts," and Fulbright. Fulbright was furious: "All you guys are committed to a military settlement. You don't want to negotiate; you're not going to negotiate. You're bombing that little piss-ant country up there, and you think you can blow them up. . . . It's a bunch of crap about wanting to negotiate." The group hastened to reassure Fulbright and the editors that negotiations were what everyone wanted. The State Department drafted a conciliatory letter to Ho Chi Minh for Ashmore and Baggs to sign. In it they expressed their personal confidence in the commitment of the United States to finding a peaceful solution. Later, when Hanoi released the entire correspondence, Ashmore and Baggs discovered that their letter was overshadowed by the one Johnson had sent on February 10, "one that was designed," Ashmore commented, "to be rejected. I think that's the only way you could read it. It meant that they—Johnson—didn't want to talk for whatever reason."[15] On February 15, as the brief New Year's cease-fire came to an end, Ho Chi Minh responded to Johnson's letter. Hanoi would talk only after an unconditional end to American bombing of the North. The American answer was to increase the ferocity of the air war.

From the start of the air war in 1964, the Joint Chiefs of Staff had pushed against the limits to bombing set by the civilian managers of the war. Every target had to be approved and the geographical limits of bombing contained so as not to send the wrong message to China or, in Taylor's phrase, "kill the hostage." For a time the city centers of Hanoi and Haiphong and a strip along the Chinese border were off-limits. Still, the planes were busy: by the end of June 1965, 55,000 sorties (each sortie one round-trip mission by one plane) had been flown against the North. One year later, the figure rose to 148,000 and the tonnage increased from 33,000 to 128,000.[16] Costs were also rising: 318 planes were shot down in 1966 and the CIA estimated the "direct operational cost" of the air war (not counting air base or logistical support) at $1,247 million in 1966.[17] But as the air war failed to produce the expected results (decreased infiltration north to south, collapse of Hanoi's will, increase in Saigon's will), the pressure grew to bomb more targets more heavily.

Despite some disenchantment with the bombing policy in the office of the secretary of defense, Robert Gallucci describes, on the civilian side, "a process of submission to the military rather than an exercise in control over the military." On the whole, civilians were less ready than the Joint Chiefs to risk bombing targets that might provoke a Chinese or Soviet reaction and showed some reluctance to conduct an all-out war against the North Vietnamese civilian population. In a position paper written early in 1966, John McNaughton, the assistant secretary of defense, argued that striking at "population targets" would not only create "a counterproductive wave of revulsion abroad and at home, but greatly . . . increase the risk of enlarging the war with China and the Soviet Union." McNaughton had his own proposal, however. Destroying North Vietnam's system of dams and dikes, "if handled right—might . . . offer promise. . . . Such destruction does not kill or drown people. By shallow-flooding the rice, it leads after a time to widespread starvation (more than a million?) unless food is provided—which we could offer to do 'at the conference table.' "[18]

The advocates of airpower measured their effort not in numbers of bombs dropped and targets hit but in terms of what they were not allowed to drop. For this reason, an atmosphere of constraint surrounded the bombing policy, although 70 percent of North Vietnam's petroleum, oil, and lubricant (POL) storage facilities had been destroyed by the summer of 1966, and by the spring of 1967, as General Wheeler observed, the bombing campaign was "reaching the point where we will have struck all worthwhile fixed targets except the ports." There were no other "major military targets" left.[19]

In Saigon, the political middle ground, a narrow strip at most, began to disappear altogether. In 1966 as earlier, George Kahin argues, "American objectives remained incompatible with any assertion of the actual balance of indigenous political forces."[20] The Buddhist movement had offered the United States a political way out of the war, and one, moreover, that would have fulfilled a declared American commitment to non-Communist nationalism and self-determination. Having once again rejected that possibility, the way forward was through an ever-larger war, but one that still required a Vietnamese front. The suppression of the Buddhist movement in the spring of 1966 meant that national elections could now be held without undue fear of the results. Still, departing ambassador Henry Cabot Lodge advised caution. The elections must not be too free; Saigon "should not be discouraged from taking moderate measures to prevent [the] elections from being used as a vehicle for Communist takeover."[21] Generals Thieu and Ky sorted things out between them and, in September 1967, Thieu became president and Ky vice president.

Even in these heavily stage-managed elections, the Thieu/Ky ticket received only 34.8 percent of the vote, while a surprising 17 percent of the electorate voted for Truong Dinh Dzu, a prominent Saigon lawyer, president of the Rotary Club, member of the right-wing Moral Rearmament Association, and *persona non grata* with the new American ambassador, Ellsworth Bunker. Dzu boldly ran on a peace ticket that called for a bombing halt, talks among all the principals, with separate discussions to be held with the NLF, and a reconvened Geneva Conference. Phan Khac Suu and Phan Quang Dan, two leading anti-Communist nationalists, received 10.8 percent of the vote; their platform was less explicit but in its call for a civilian government of "national reconciliation" implied the possibility of NLF political participation. Both Dzu and Suu de-

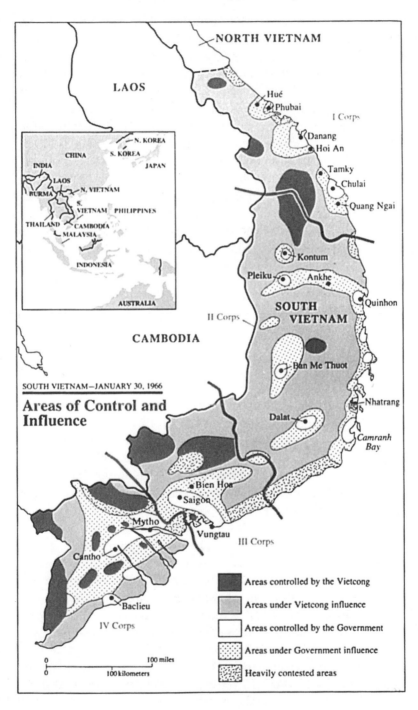

NORTH VIETNAM

LAOS

Hué
Phubai

I Corps

Danang
Hoi An

Tamky
Chulai

Quang Ngai

Kontum

Pleiku
Ankhe

Quinhon

SOUTH
VIETNAM

II Corps

CAMBODIA

Ban Me Thuot

Nhatrang

SOUTH VIETNAM—JANUARY 30, 1966

**Areas of Control and
Influence**

Dalat

Camranh
Bay

Bien Hoa
Saigon

Mytho
Vungtau   III Corps

Cantho

Baclieu

IV Corps

0   100 miles
0   100 kilometers

Areas controlled by the Vietcong

Areas under Vietcong influence

Areas controlled by the Government

Areas under Government influence

Heavily contested areas

nounced the election results as fraudulent. "I consider this government illegal and incompetent," Dzu told the press, "and I do not accept the results of this election." Legally, Thieu's election would have to be ratified by the Provisional Legislative Assembly, whose election committee had voted against validation by 16–2. "I thought I had the necessary majority in the Assembly to invalidate the elections," Dzu said later, "but I don't know now because Ambassador Bunker spent the afternoon with . . . Ky . . . and the same evening Ky invited 58 deputies to have lunch with him. . . ." Shortly thereafter, the Assembly validated the election by a vote of 58 to 43. Dzu himself, who had been arrested and briefly held on an old charge of financial irregularity, protested his arrest and was rearrested for "defamation of the judicial system."[22]

From the perspective of MACV and the embassy, the battlefield picture seemed satisfactory. The war would not be over soon, as Westmoreland had warned Johnson when he took command of U.S. troops from the inveterately optimistic General Paul Harkins. A war of attrition was bound to take time. But the daily body count was looking good and the "kill-ratio" (of U.S. to enemy casualties) was excellent. Westmoreland was pleased with the results of several large sweep operations: Operation ATTLEBORO, in April 1966, had pounded War Zone C (known to Vietnamese as Tay Ninh Province), achieving a kill-ratio of 1:15 and capturing large stocks of weapons and material; January 1967 was the month of CEDAR FALLS, and the leveling operation in the Iron Triangle; in February 1967, Operation JUNCTION CITY returned to War Zone C with twenty-two American and four ARVN battalions in an effort to surround and capture COSVN, the "Viet Cong Pentagon." COSVN was never located, but once more the kill-ratio was excellent, with three thousand enemy dead and many captured weapons, supplies, and documents.

Yet despite the immense firepower expended, in the end, as William Turley points out, "ATTLEBORO, CEDAR FALLS and JUNCTION CITY failed to deny War Zone C and the Iron Triangle to the Communists." In addition to these big sweeps, Westmoreland ordered a quantum increase in the number of small units patrolling the countryside around Saigon. From the rooftop bar of the Hotel Caravelle, foreigners could drink the local beer and watch as the thick foliage across the Saigon River exploded in spectacular fireworks of artillery shells, napalm drops, bombing runs. But the strategic initiative remained in the hands of the NLF, and a summary report by the National Security Council observed that throughout 1966 and 1967, 75 percent of all battles were "the enemy's choice of time, place, type and duration." According to the CIA, less than 1 percent of almost 2 million small-unit operations involved contact with the enemy; for the ARVN, the percentage dropped to one tenth of 1 percent.[23]

The body count was not an entirely satisfactory measure of success. Its logic seemed to have no conclusion short of the progressive elimination of the population of the South; for, as reporters sometimes noted, the bodies were not always readily identifiable as soldiers. A pacification adviser in Quang Ngai Province described a typical operation in which the response to a sniper attack on a U.S. convoy was for the heavily armored personnel carriers to fire into the village and then call in "helicopter gunships which flew down the axis of the hamlet, strafing the most densely populated portion." When the battle was over, "there were no VC bodies available for counting but 58 houses had been destroyed, 10 villagers killed and 12 wounded."[24]

The enemy was routinely reported as "NVA/VC," which obscured their point of origin. Were larger numbers of North Vietnamese being infiltrated down the constantly bombed Ho Chi Minh Trail or was the NLF still able to recruit fresh forces, despite all the searches, all the destruction? And how was either possible? For not only did the bombing fail to halt the flow of men and supplies, both figures actually increased in 1966–67.

During the war and in its aftermath, bombing advocates remained convinced that the air war could have succeeded if instead of a gradual escalation North Vietnam had been bombed harder, and without pause, from the start. While it is certainly true that more people could have been killed, the continued flow of supplies and the fact that society in the North did not collapse cannot be attributed to American restraint. To keep supplies moving south, some 300,000 people worked full time (another 200,000 farmers joined them on a spare-time basis) to repair the Ho Chi Minh Trail and expand it, so that what began as a network of small trails was at war's end an enormous all-weather highway system, looping and backtracking to provide alternative routes to bombed-out sections for 9,600 miles. Chinese engineers and Russian earth-moving equipment helped, but it was mainly people on bicycles or bearing carrying poles who moved the earth, filled in the craters with shovels, constructed and maneuvered pontoon bridges by hand, and camouflaged not only trucks but the road itself. Over ten thousand people are known to have died maintaining the Trail; the bodies of thousands more were never recovered.

Meanwhile, those who could be spared—the very young and the very old—were evacuated from Hanoi and other major cities. In the countryside, where three quarters of the population lived, village arsenals, deep air-raid shelters, storehouses for food were built and two million people recruited into the militia, ready to help defend the country in case of a ground attack. The economy was dispersed as well, and textile mills, machine shops, and small factories were moved into the mountains. Production fell, of course, but small cottage industries helped to meet basic consumer needs. The most heavily bombed provinces were just north of the DMZ: here a deep tunnel system allowed life to continue, though underground and with great hardship. "Yet people seemed more willing to sacrifice the more they were bombed," William Turley observed.[25] The CIA computed the costs of such mobilization to the United States: by 1966 it took the United States $9.6 to inflict $1 worth of damage. Experts estimated that 23,000 to 24,000 people had been killed—80 percent civilian—but "the numbers remained small relative to the 18 million population." By May 1967, McNamara was ready to admit that, "with respect to interdiction of men and materiel, it now appears that no combination of actions against the North short of destruction of the regime or occupation of North Vietnamese territory will physically reduce the flow of men and materiel below the relatively small amount needed by enemy forces to continue the war in the South."[26]

RAND social scientists continued to study the enemy in the South, trying to answer how the NLF was able to recruit and maintain its coherence in the face of what the body count indicated was the steady decimation of its ranks. In a detailed account of one Delta province for the years 1966–67, David Elliott and his colleagues analyzed the organizational system of the NLF in immense detail, listing its vulnerabilities, demonstrating how it was able to function even in the dire circumstances of Westmoreland's war of attrition. Political and military efforts were always in balance and the "system as a whole" was "stronger than the sum of its parts." Any approach to the defeat that was not itself both political and military could only fail. Central to the system were the civilian and military cadres, the women and men who served the Front in a variety of local leadership roles, from village officials to assistant squad leaders. Elliott found that despite "difficulties, hardships, defections and desertions, the VC cadre structure has remained strong and largely impervious to evidence of declining strength and prospects. . . ." Those who defected to the government side did so, almost without exception, "more for personal motives than for ideological reasons."[27]

For all that, Westmoreland's tactics were certainly taking a toll. In some areas the bombing made it extremely difficult to call village meetings, to mobilize voluntary labor, to tax without causing grave hardship. Increasingly it became hard to keep people in the villages at all, for "when they began to be harassed by bombs and bullets and the fear of death, nothing could deter them from leaving."[28] Sometimes, the cadres could not persuade people of the "necessity of the tasks entrusted to them. When the people refused to perform these tasks, the cadres screamed at them, but in so doing, they behaved exactly like the mandarins, and this attitude, in turn, isolated them further from the people." Since, as every interview RAND conducted testified, the relationship between the people of the villages and the NLF was at the heart of NLF strength, such alienation was very dangerous. "In the cadres' eyes," one defector told his interrogator, "the loss of the people's support is always the worst thing, because all of them know well that every cadre had to rely on the people's support for his own security. . . . They are convinced that they could never accomplish their assignments if they cannot get the people's support." And a prisoner of war, worried about the flow of refugees out of the countryside, agreed: "The present war . . . is a people's war. The people are considered its main power. If all the people flee, the NLF armed forces can have nobody to support and strengthen them."[29]

To deal with the crisis, organizers returned to an early stage of the struggle, mobilizing people by house. As David Hunt has summarized the picture presented by the RAND accounts for this period, the NLF was able to maintain a presence in contested villages even in the worst of times, giving reality to their claim of ultimate victory. One nineteen-year-old woman prisoner, who had been badly tortured before her interview, tried to explain why she had joined the NLF and why, despite all the hardship, she would go right back into their ranks if she were released from prison. Her "belief," the Vietnamese RAND interviewer noted, "was so big she can't distinguish what is wrong." She had met Front cadres in her village, attended a funeral they organized for four men killed by the ARVN, and been persuaded to join, against her family's wishes, by the head of the Village Liberation Women's Committee. The Front members she met were "living embodiments of heroes of our legends; they are those who stand up to fight the evil in order to protect the people."[30]

Another study of these same years, 1966–67, addressed itself not to potential vulnerabilities, as Elliott had, but to "elements of cohesion in the enemy camp." Drawing on 219 interrogations conducted from early 1966 to August 1967, Konrad Kellen found that the "fish's water may have become shallower, but it still sustains him. . . . We cannot even discern a 'weakest link.' In fact, what we see is really not comparable to a chain at all. It appears rather to be an organism, in which all parts not only interact but are equally important." The enemy was sustained by a sense of mission, by the trust of the rank and file in the leadership, by the relationship of the soldiers to the villagers, and by the "nonexpectation of defeat." Kellen was convinced that while villagers in contested areas often had negative feelings toward both the Saigon government and the NLF, those feelings differed significantly: "rejection of VC troops by villagers, where it occurs . . . seems to be the result of actual damage incurred by bombings in response to the VC presence, taxation, draft and, occasionally, disappointment with a lack of a VC victory, whereas negative villager feelings towards the GVN seems to be a more basic hostility resulting from GVN aims and behavior. . . . Villagers apparently reject the VC 'in sorrow rather than in anger.' "

Kellen's account of life in the PLAF, drawn from interviews, was almost lyrical: "Reading the interviews one often feels transported into a group of people who are principally concerned with treating each other with care and respect. . . . This helps, it appears, to alleviate hardships, dissolve dark thoughts of death and defeat, ban doubts concerning the cause or its ultimate success, and maintain confidence and trust." One man who had defected to the government side was asked how long he thought the war would continue. "How can I guess that," he answered. "If I knew when the war would be over, I would have tried to remain in the Front to fight until the end." Kellen ended his report with a chilling reflection. Was it possible that the NLF was simply incapable of "collapse, surrender or disintegration short of being ground up altogether. . . ."? If that was the case, "the enemy could conceivably force us not only to accept increasing losses of our own, but also to kill more of him (and his civilian population) than can be in our national interest."[31]

There was no lack of methods of annhilation, though one 1967 study argued that some approaches were counterproductive. A RAND study of the crop defoliation program noted that it had failed to deny food to NLF soldiers, however devastating its impact on civilian farmers in NLF and contested areas. Prisoners and defectors spoke of "increased support for the VC resulting from such operations." "The feeling that the US/GVN is at best minimally concerned with the peasant's welfare," the authors pointed out, "tends to exacerbate the feelings engendered by the act of spraying itself. There is an almost total absence of indications in our data of efforts . . . to educate people about herbicide spraying, to warn them of attack, or to assist those who have been affected." The report's major recommendation underscores the problem U.S. methods of war created: an effort should be made to "communicate to the peasants, in VC as well as GVN areas, its concern for their welfare as Vietnamese citizens. It would be valuable to communicate to the farmers in a believable manner that this program is undertaken reluctantly for the welfare of the country. . . ." The military rejected the RAND study, insisting that defoliation *did* deny food to the enemy and made search and destroy operations easier. The program was expanded and 1,570,114 acres were destroyed in 1967.[32]

For the U.S. military, Vietnam became a laboratory in which weapons and "weapons systems" could be battlefield-tested. New varieties of cluster bombs were developed, releasing up to 180,000 fiberglass fleshettes; the "daisy cutter," dropped by slow-flying cargo planes, weighed 15,000 pounds, of which 12,600 were high explosive. Detonating just above ground level, daisy cutters cleared a zone 300 feet in diameter to create helicopter landing zones; they were also used against enemy troops. Great ingenuity was expended on the development of land mines, some as small as an aspirin tablet, some, like the Claymore, spraying an enormous area with steel pellets just above ground level.[33] B-52s were now in constant use north and south, each plane capable of delivering 150 tons of bombs in a fraction of a second. DC-3 planes were specially equipped with rapid-fire machine guns and magnesium flares to illuminate the target. They were called "Puff the Magic Dragon," in ironic reference to a popular song. Infra-red photography was widely employed to identify presumed Viet Cong campfires, though of course there was no way to be certain just who it was down there, cooking their evening meal. Heat-sensitive, urine-sniffing devices were developed to pinpoint and destroy the enemy—though he might be a water buffalo or a child; a lightweight battery-powered blower was distributed for raising the temperature inside an enemy tunnel network to 1,000 degrees. Weather alteration, reflectors that could literally end the night—the unfair friend of the guerrilla—over all of Vietnam were considered. Varieties of poisonous gas, crop defoliants, and herbicides were "improved" and employed. There seems to have been at least one experiment with germ warfare, when CIA analysts thought an influenza outbreak might have beneficial military effects.[34] The genius of American applied science flourished in the exploration of new ways to kill or inflict injury. New helicopter assault tactics, portable grenade launchers, the benefits of both saturation and surgical bombing could all be tested. In the North, such testing could be costly, as Soviet and Chinese aid made anti-aircraft defenses more effective. In the South, there was no such danger.

CHAPTER TEN

The War in America
(1965–1967)

What do the peasants think as we ally ourselves with the
landlords and as we refuse to put any action into our many
words concerning land reform? What do they think as we test
our latest weapons on them, just as the Germans tested out
new medicine and new tortures in the concentration camps of
Europe? Where are the roots of the independent Vietnam we
claim to be building? . . . We must find new ways to speak for
peace in Vietnam and justice throughout the developing world.
. . . If we do not act we shall surely be dragged down the long,
dark and shameful corridors of time reserved for those who
possess power without compassion, might without morality, and
strength without sight.

MARTIN LUTHER KING, JR.,
"DECLARATION OF INDEPENDENCE
FROM THE WAR IN VIETNAM,"
APRIL 4, 1967

DESPITE UPBEAT battlefield reports from Westmoreland, skep-
ticism about the war was growing even among those who
normally supported the establishment. Harrison Salisbury's
report of his trip to Hanoi in December 1966 scrutinized military claims
for the surgical precision of the bombing with a new independence.
Salisbury, a Pulitzer Prize-winning *New York Times* reporter, wrote his
account two weeks after the Defense Department had denied bombing
civilian areas or, indeed, any part of the city of Hanoi at all. Salisbury,
however, reported heavy concentrations of population outside the

"heavy-lined city boundaries" on official U.S. maps. Moreover, "inspections of several damaged sites and talks with witnesses make it clear that Hanoi residents certainly believed they were bombed by United States planes, that they certainly observed United States planes overhead and that damage certainly occurred right in the center of town."[1] Salisbury went on to report the destruction of the city of Nam Dinh, which had suffered fifty-one raids between June 1965 and December 1966, causing hundreds of civilian casualties and eighty-nine deaths. Assistant Secretary of Defense Arthur Sylvester protested that Salisbury's statistics were suspiciously close to those published by the North Vietnamese, a coincidence Salisbury readily admitted. Who else would know how many civilians died?

As important as the information Salisbury's dispatches provided, perhaps more important, was the way in which they reported Hanoi as a real place, whose government handouts were therefore no less worthy of note than those of other capitals. In his history of the media and the war, Daniel Hallin observed that Salisbury summarized the views of the North Vietnamese government the way Washington reporters summarize U.S. official views, thus drawing Hanoi into what Hallin calls the "Sphere of Legitimate Controversy." In this Salisbury represented a minority; most of the press and virtually all the television reporting "painted an almost one-dimensional image of the Vietnamese and Vietcong as cruel, ruthless, and fanatical," inhabitants of the "Sphere of Deviance."[2]

Yet even journalists who had little doubt as to the legitimacy of American war aims sometimes found themselves at odds with their initial convictions as they reported what they saw. An aviation analyst named Frank Harvey went to Vietnam in 1966 to report on the air war for the magazine *Flying*. His troubled book *Air War—Vietnam* was widely distributed in a Bantam paperback in the summer of 1967. Harvey spent time with pilots bombing both South and North Vietnam, and learned that maiden runs over the South gave young pilots their first taste of combat. The pilot was guided by a small spotter plane "over a flat country in bright sunshine where nobody was shooting back with high-powered ack-ack. He learns how it feels to drop bombs on human beings and watch huts go up in . . . orange flame when his aluminum napalm tanks tumble into them. He gets hardened to pressing the firing button and cutting people down like little dummies, as they sprint frantically under him. He gets his sword bloodied for the rougher things to come." The experience was very different in the North, where serious ground defenses made bombing raids "real hell."

At a hospital in Can Tho, Harvey saw and vividly described the victims of the bombing in the South, taking pictures so horrible no one would look at them, in an angry effort to document what he had seen and to make it more difficult for anyone to say: " 'I'm sorry it's necessary to fight this kind of war, where civilians are bound to get hurt, but there's no way out of it. Civilians have always been hurt in wars and they probably always will be.' " Harvey flew with the FAC—the low-flying single-engine planes that served as spotters (he called them the "death bringers") over a peaceful agrarian scene south of Can Tho City. No one shot at them; there was no movement on the ground at all. A few miles into the flight, with the scene beneath them unchanged, the pilot checked his map coordinates for the "VC hooches" ("hooch" was the American term for a Vietnamese house) an informer had said should be there and called in long-range artillery and a jet napalm strike. How did the pilot know they were VC? "You can just tell."

The fierce simplicity of Harvey's reporting demythologized the war even as it was being fought. At the same time readers could glean from it signs of passive resistance among the American military. In a bar in Can Tho, for example, he met a FAC pilot who had been ordered to direct artillery against a village because three VC had been reported there that morning. Flying over the target, the pilot saw neither hooches nor VC, but people—women, children, men going about their daily business. Radioing this information back to base, he was ordered to go ahead and he dutifully called in the air strikes. Were many people killed, Harvey asked. The pilot laughed. Not at all—he had directed the fire at empty paddy fields.[3]

The spring 1965 teach-ins had been dominated by academics, with only American government officials speaking from direct and personal experience in Vietnam. By the summer of 1965, however, alternative sources of direct information were available, as anti-war activists met with both North Vietnamese and NLF officials. In the summer of 1965, a delegation of Women Strike for Peace (a group organized in the late 1950s to protest nuclear testing and the arms race) met with North and South Vietnamese women in Indonesia, and that winter Herbert Aptheker, Tom Hayden, and Staughton Lynd traveled to Hanoi during the Christmas bombing pause. Lynd and Aptheker were both American historians, of New Left and Old Left political persuasions, respectively; and Hayden was one of the founders of Students for a Democratic Society. The three Americans brought back personal accounts of the brutality of the war, the high number of non-combatant casualties, and the readiness of the NLF and Hanoi to negotiate a just peace. It was perhaps to be expected that the vision they projected of the other side's virtue was

the reverse of the evil for which they judged the United States responsible. Any qualifications they might have made they submerged in their
sense of the dire immediacy of the war.[4]

No American journalist reported from the NLF side in the South
but, like Harvey, some reported critically from the American side. Along
with the testimony of disaffected American soldiers, these accounts contradicted official reports of a war fought on behalf of the people of South
Vietnam. In September 1965, Master Sergeant Donald Duncan, a much-
decorated Green Beret who had served in Vietnam for eighteen months,
turned down a field commission to the rank of captain, left Vietnam and
the Army, and in February 1966 published a powerful indictment of the
war in *Ramparts* magazine. "The whole thing was a lie!" Duncan announced in the title of his essay. A militant anti-Communist when he
arrived in Vietnam, Duncan had become convinced that the majority of
people in South Vietnam were "either anti-Saigon or pro-Viet Cong or
both." His first-hand description of the war and its injustice was a call for
American withdrawal. It did not romanticize the NLF or Hanoi.

> The world is not just good guys and bad guys. Anti-communism is a
> lousy substitute for democracy. I know now that there are many types
> of communism but there are none that appeal to me. In the long run,
> I don't think Vietnam will be better off under Ho's brand of commu-
> nism. But it's not for me or my government to decide. That decision
> is for the Vietnamese.

Sometimes local newspapers would publish a soldier's letter home,
as the Akron *Beacon Journal* did on March 27, 1967:

> Today a buddy of mine called . . . into a hut and an old man came
> out of the bomb shelter. My buddy told the old man to get away from
> the hut and since we have to move quickly on a sweep, just threw a
> hand grenade into the shelter. As he pulled the pin the old man got
> excited and started jabbering and running toward my buddy and the
> hut. A GI, not understanding, stopped the old man with a football
> tackle just as my buddy threw the hand grenade into the shelter.
> . . . [Then] we all heard a baby crying from inside the shelter! There
> was nothing we could do. After the explosion we found the mother,
> two children . . . and an almost newborn baby. That is what the old
> man was trying to tell us! . . . We looked at each other and burned
> the hut. . . . The old man was just whimpering in disbelief outside the
> burning hut. We walked away and left him there.[5]

The accounts of reporters traveling with American troops made it
increasingly difficult for Americans to escape the reality of what the war

was doing to Vietnam. Eight pages of an appeal by Howard Zinn for complete U.S. withdrawal, written late in 1966, consisted of excerpts from the mainstream press. Jack Langguth in *The New York Times,* June 5, 1965, reporting the saturation bombing of Quang Ngai: "Many Vietnamese—one estimate is as high as 500—were killed by the strikes. The American contention is that they were Vietcong soldiers. But three out of four patients seeking treatment in a Vietnamese hospital afterward for burns from napalm . . . were village women." Charles Mohr, also in the *Times,* September 5, 1965, reported this horror: "In [a] delta province there is a woman who has both arms burned off by napalm and her eyelids so badly burned that she cannot close them. When it is time for her to sleep her family puts a blanket over her head. The woman had two of her children killed in the air strike that maimed her." But he also drew the moral: "Few Americans appreciate what their nation is doing to South Vietnam with airpower . . . this is strategic bombing in a friendly allied country . . . innocent civilians are dying every day in South Vietnam." A *Herald Tribune* report in September 1965: "United States Air Force B-52 jet bombers . . . dropped hundreds of tons of high explosives on the hamlet of Phuong X Tay. . . . The raid had been ordered after intelligence experts concluded the hamlet to be a large Communist communications center. But . . . what aerial photoanalysis thought were sandbagged bunkers appeared to be an ancient wall. What had appeared to be fortified trenches turned out to be seldom-used oxcart trails." Neil Sheehan in February 1966: "within three hamlets, about 1000 peasant homes have been blasted apart by bombs and shells or incinerated by napalm." UPI, August 1966: "30 civilians were killed and 30 others wounded last week when jet planes strafed a river barge convoy near Saigon . . . mistakenly identifying [it] as Viet Cong-operated vessels." The news items, Zinn wrote, were "not exceptions but examples . . . a tiny *known* part of an enormous pattern of devastation. . . ."[6]

The New Yorker ran a series of essays by Jonathan Schell which described the destruction of Quang Ngai and Quang Tin, two provinces in South, not North Vietnam, which he witnessed in the summer of 1967. Schell insisted he only "set down" what he had seen, but it was difficult for readers not to draw moral lessons from his account:

> . . . the peculiar character of this war tended to be defined for me by how the men in our armed forces reacted to the various special conditions of the war: the immense disparity in size and power between the two adversaries, the fact that the Americans are fighting ten thousand miles from home, the fact that the Vietnamese are an

Asian and non-industrialized people . . . the fact that it is often impossible for our men to distinguish between the enemy and friendly or neutral civilians, the anomalousness and the corruption of the Saigon government, the secondary role played by the South Vietnamese Army we are supposedly assisting, the fact that the enemy is fighting a guerrilla war while we are fighting a mechanized war, and, finally, the overriding, fantastic fact that we are destroying, seemingly by inadvertence, the very country we are supposedly protecting.[7]

Thus living in America increasingly meant having guilty knowledge of the war and of the government's lies about it. By 1967, a complex national anti-war movement to resist the war had developed. The movement was never uniform in its ideology, its composition, or its tactics. But at its lowest common denominator—the demand to bring the troops home now—it sounded like the voice of the people. Out of the 1965 teach-ins a number of local committees had formed to organize ongoing demonstrations of protest (in Berkeley, the Vietnam Day Committee; in New York, the Fifth Avenue Parade Committee), and by the fall of 1965 tens of thousands of people had joined local marches calling for an end to U.S. intervention. In 1966 the radical pacifist A. J. Muste was able to draw a large number of peace and civil rights groups together in a broad-based coalition, the Spring Mobilization Committee, which led a New York City demonstration on April 15, 1967 of between 125,000 and 400,000 protesters (depending on who was counting, but in either case the largest anti-war demonstration in New York City history). On the same day, 75,000 people marched in San Francisco.

One feature of the New York march was a public draft card burning, part of a national movement that began in Boston in May 1964. By 1967 it had achieved national prominence as a way of resisting the war, and it involved not just draft-age young men but women and older men who encouraged, aided, and abetted these acts of resistance, daring the government to retaliate. To make their complicity unmistakably clear, a "Call to Resist Illegitimate Authority" was circulated and published in the fall of 1967 by a group of anti-war activists who invited the "young men of America" to refuse to serve in an illegal, immoral, unconstitutional war.

In mid-1965, there were already 380 prosecutions for induction refusal; three years later, the number was 3,305. Draft resistance in the South, which drew its strength and its logic from the civil rights movement, began in McComb, Mississippi, in July 1965 when a group of young people who had taken part in voter registration campaigns gathered to consider the death of a classmate, John D. Shaw, in Vietnam. There were "five reasons why Negroes should not be in any war fighting for America," the group's leaflet declared:

> No Mississippi Negroes should be fighting in Viet Nam for the White Man's freedom, until all the Negro People are free in Mississippi. . . .
>   No one has a right to ask us to risk our lives and kill other Colored People in Santo Domingo and Viet Nam, so that the White American can get richer. . . .
>   . . . We can write and ask our sons if they know what they are fighting for. If he answers Freedom, tell him that's what we are fighting for here in Mississippi. And if he says Democracy, tell him the truth—we don't know anything about Communism, Socialism, and all that, but we do know that Negroes have caught hell here under this *American Democracy*. [8]

Moderate civil rights groups condemned the leaflet; but in 1966 the Student Non-Violent Coordinating Committee (SNCC), one of the major civil rights organizations in the South, declared its support for "the men in this country who are unwilling to respond to the military draft which would compel them to contribute their lives to U.S. aggression in the name of the 'freedom' we find so false in this country." When the recently elected Georgia state representative Julian Bond refused to repudiate the statement, he was expelled from his elected office, thus drawing the moral of the SNCC statement. There were daily demonstrations against the Atlanta induction center and many arrests. In May 1967, as part of a "We Won't Go" campaign, Cleveland Sellers, SNCC program secretary, refused induction on the grounds that the draft boards in South Carolina, Georgia, Alabama, Mississippi, and Louisiana employed only six blacks out of their 1,691 members. By the summer of 1967, seventeen staff members of SNCC had refused induction and were under indictment.[9]

Reverend Martin Luther King, Jr., recent winner of the Nobel Peace Prize, marched in the April 1967 New York demonstration. King had spoken against the war on strictly pacifist grounds for several years. But in the spring of 1967 he began to oppose the war on more politically specific grounds. A week and a half before the march, King delivered a sermon at New York's Riverside Church that went far beyond his standard appeal to the principles of non-violence. For the first time, King linked the civil rights movement to the anti-war movement and Johnson's war against poverty to his war against Vietnam. The poverty program, King said, had offered hope.

Then came the build-up in Vietnam, and I watched the program broken and eviscerated as if it were some idle political plaything of a society gone mad on war, and I knew that America would never invest the necessary funds or energies in rehabilitation of its poor so long as Vietnam continued to draw men and skills and money like some demonic, destructive suction tube. So I was increasingly compelled to see the war as an enemy of the poor and to attack it as such.

King went on to make other, even more telling connections:

. . . it became clear to me that the war was doing far more than devastating the hopes of the poor at home. It was sending their sons and their brothers and their husbands to fight and to die in extraordinary high proportions relative to the rest of the population. We were taking the young black men who had been crippled by our society and sending them 8000 miles away to guarantee liberties in Southeast Asia which they had not found in Southwest Georgia and East Harlem. So we have been repeatedly faced with the cruel irony of watching Negro and white boys on TV screens as they kill and die together for a nation that has been unable to seat them together in the same schools. So we watch them in brutal solidarity burning the huts of a poor village. . . . I could not be silent in the face of such cruel manipulation of the poor.

King was speaking in the spring of 1967, in the afterlight of three summers in which the ghettos of the country had literally burned with rebellion. Armed young men had challenged his appeal for non-violent action:

But, they asked, what about Vietnam? . . . Their questions hit home, and I knew that I could never again raise my voice against the violence of the oppressed in the ghettoes without having first spoken clearly to the greatest purveyor of violence in the world today—my own government.

Vietnam was damning the soul of America, King insisted, and would continue to do so for as long as the United States "destroys the deepest hopes of men the world over."

The major importance of King's speech lay in its movement from a generalized moral denunciation of the violence of the war to a specific indictment of U.S. policy in Vietnam, and from an indictment of policy in Vietnam to a denunciation of the American alliance with counterrevolution in Latin America and Africa. Finally, King outlined a plan for extrication and redemption: end the bombing of North and South Vietnam; declare a unilateral cease-fire; accept the NLF as a legitimate force in South Vietnam; set a date for withdrawal of troops in accordance with the 1954 Geneva Accords. Most damaging to the government case and to the war effort was King's invitation to ministers of all faiths to counsel young men to seek conscientious objector status. For an Army whose combat troops were disproportionately poor and black, King's speech, along with the draft resistance movement sponsored by SNCC, was a genuine threat.[10]

To support draft resistance was, of course, itself against the law. Nevertheless, in New York, Boston, San Francisco, the number of demonstrations at induction centers increased geometrically. At 6:00 A.M., the writer Grace Paley remembers, "we would walk up and down before the Whitehall Street Induction Center wearing signs that said 'I Support Draft Refusal.' " In two or three hours inductees would climb into vans to be transported to boot camp. "At 9:30 on one of those mornings, about twenty women sat down all across the street to prevent the death wagons from moving. They sat for about thirty minutes. Then a plainclothesman approached an older gray-haired women. 'Missus, you don't want to get arrested.' 'I have to,' she said. 'My grandson's in Vietnam.' Gently they removed her. Then with billy clubs, a dozen uniformed men moved up and down that line of young women, dragging them away, by their arms, their hair, beating them, I remember . . . mostly in the breast."[11]

In the fall of 1967, plans for a national draft card turn-in merged with the call for a march against the Pentagon planned by A. J. Muste's group, now called the National Mobilization Against the War. On the West Coast, organizers planned a Stop the Draft Week focusing on the Oakland draft board. Both events involved direct confrontation with the police reminiscent of the Southern civil rights battles. In California, three thousand protesters surrounded the induction center at dawn on October 16, 1967. The police ordered them to leave and when they stayed, attacked the crowd with nightsticks, injuring twenty and clearing the area in time for the first busloads of inductees. The demonstrators returned the next day and ninety-seven of them were arrested. On the third day, ten thousand demonstrators appeared, many wearing makeshift protective garb. This time when the police attacked, the protesters retreated in a more orderly way, successfully blocking streets as they went, breaking into small groups and scattering as the police gave chase, tasting and later celebrating the heady if ambiguous pleasures of defying the armed and violent authority of their own state.

In Washington, D.C., about 100,000 people arrived for a protest that would combine what by this time was being called a "traditional" demonstration with more militant acts of civil disobedience. After a rally in the Mall, the march proceeded across the Arlington Memorial Bridge to the Pentagon itself, where a smaller contingent were determined to commit civil disobedience by sitting down in front of the Pentagon in defiance of a ban on demonstrations at this site, which both sides saw as the headquarters of sanctioned violence. Over a thousand sat down in front of a line of specially deputized marshals supported by troops with fixed bayonets, and settled in for a long cold night. When it got dark, small flames appeared as "dozens of draft cards began to burn, held aloft, amid increasing cheers and applause."[12]

Throughout the night, as they did on other marches, demonstrators appealed to the armed young men who faced them to join the protest, insisting that they were not protesting against them but against the warmakers who had pitted demonstrators and soldiers against each other. Reports that individual soldiers had expressed sympathy for the marchers and opposition to the war spread through the crowd in front of the Pentagon, creating rushes of power and fellowship. In the middle of the night, orders came to clear the steps of the Pentagon, and this was done with a brutality that was still surprising, though in time it came to feel routine. "They were eager with their clubs," Thomas Powers says of the marshals and soldiers, "and the worst victims, according to every witness, were women. The scene at times was one of pure horror, women beaten senseless and dragged off into the dark with bloody, broken faces. No one moved or got up to leave despite the violence, and the marshals and soldiers slowly worked their way through the crowd."[13] Later accounts, perhaps more hopeful than accurate, insisted that while the MPs had been brutal, the soldiers themselves were not. The next day, two thousand demonstrators returned to the scene, remaining through the evening until, this time without violence, the police began arresting them at midnight.

The Washington and Oakland protests differed radically in style—the one a model of non-violent civil disobedience, the other an exercise in political street fighting. Between them they established the limits within which citizens would attempt to stop their government from making war. Among the protesters were figures difficult to ignore or dismiss. Benjamin Spock, Dr. Spock to millions of American children and their parents, was arrested and tried on charges stemming from his circulation of the "Call to Resist Illegitimate Authority." Muhammed Ali, heavyweight champion of the world, refused to serve in this "white man's war" and was deprived of his championship by the World Boxing Association. Besides laws, the rules of gentility were regularly broken by those who had seemed to define American culture. Arthur Miller, America's preeminent playwright, refused to attend a White House function, as did the poet Robert Lowell; the singer Eartha Kitt denounced the war at a White House reception (Johnson complained that some artists insulted him by staying away from his receptions, others by attending them). Writers walked out on Vice President Hubert Humphrey at a National Book Award ceremony in New York City, while in Hong Kong a group of young American scholars of China, invited to lunch with McGeorge Bundy, refused to "break bread with a war criminal."

By 1968, to point the direction of the movement, symbolic protests merged with practical harassment of the war effort. In Baltimore a priest, Philip Berrigan, joined three Catholic friends to deface draft records with pig's blood. A few months later, in May 1968, Philip and his brother Daniel, a Jesuit priest, along with seven others destroyed records of the draft board in Catonsville, Maryland, with napalm made at home from a recipe they found in the *Special Forces Handbook*. Daniel Berrigan explained the action of the "Catonsville 9" at his trial: "Our apologies, good friends, for the fracture of good order, the burning of paper instead of children, the angering of the orderlies in the front parlor of the charnel house." Throughout 1968, 1969, and 1970, raids against draft boards multiplied: the "Boston Two" poured black paint over hundreds of records; the "Milwaukee Fourteen" burned ten thousand files; the "Pasadena Three," the "Silver Springs Three," the "Chicago Fifteen," "Women Against Daddy Warbucks," the "New York Eight," the "Akron Two," the "Beaver Fifty-five," the "Boston Eight," and the "East Coast Conspiracy to Save Lives," all attacked draft files in their cities and towns.[14]

These actions were more than disruptions; they were acts of resistance that extended from the moment of the action itself through the education and legal defense work of committees formed to support the protesters, to the trial itself where defendants sought to turn the indictments around so that it was the government that stood accused. And over time more and more defendants received light sentences or were acquitted. The last draft board protest was that of the "Camden [New Jersey] Twenty-eight" in the late summer of 1971. After the trial two years later where they were acquitted, they received a letter of congratulations from one of the jurors, a fifty-three-year-old black Army veteran: "To you . . . I say, well done. Well done for trying to heal the sick irresponsible men, men who were chosen by the people to govern and lead them."[15]

ROTC, the Reserve Officers Training Program, which supplied half of the officers on duty in Vietnam, became a direct target of student protest. In 1966, 191,749 college students enrolled in ROTC; by 1973, there were fewer than half, 72,459. War-related activities—the secret defense research that had made post-World War II universities and their scientific faculties rich in laboratories, grants, and fees—came under repeated attack and many universities distanced themselves from such facilities (without, however, entirely severing their connections).

Beyond this, the war opened up for debate not only the principles that had governed American foreign policy since the end of World War II, but the larger structure of the nation and its political procedures. Democracy, the noun that traditionally named American society, acquired the modifying adjective of "capitalist." "Imperialism," hitherto applicable only to the British in India or the French in Indochina, was applied to the United States by Americans trying to understand how the United States had come to fight in Vietnam. The nature of human society and its optimal organization, whether this was socialist or capitalist, was reemerging as a topic of discussion after what had appeared to be a state of permanent suspension since the McCarthy era of the 1950s.

Alternative media, journals, news services, radio networks announced the demonstrations, reported on them, and served as theatres of lively political debate. Inside the professional organizations of historians, sociologists, political scientists, literary critics, economists, doctors, and health workers, radical caucuses formed not only to protest the war but also to reexamine their respective disciplines as to how they might have contributed to the American war machine. The momentum was astonishing.

The movement was certainly not limited to college campuses. On the contrary, from the start, opposition to the war was strongest among poorer and less-educated Americans, those who would have to fight and die. In 1966, according to a survey conducted by the University of Michigan, only 27 percent of those with college educations favored withdrawal from Vietnam as opposed to 41 percent of those with an eighth-grade education. President Johnson, who had been accustomed to walking around the White House with the latest poll results in his pocket, eager to show them to any doubting reporters, dropped that habit toward the end of 1967.

Draft resistance and civilian dissent were deeply troubling; but for actually carrying on the war, the most serious problem Washington faced was rebellion within the military itself, which now increased in direct response to the escalating violence of the war. In 1965, a young Army officer, Richard Steinke, refused to follow an order in Vietnam, declaring that the war was "not worth a single American life." He was court-martialed and dishonorably discharged from the service. One year later, in the summer of 1966, three Army privates refused orders to leave for Vietnam, denouncing the war as criminal and unjust. Although there had been earlier cases of such resistance, the "Fort Hood Three" were the first to ask the peace movement for help, and their case brought wide publicity to the anti-war movement within the military.[16]

In the summer of 1967, Howard Levy, an Army doctor, refused to train Special Forces soldiers, calling them "murderers of women and children." To train them would be to violate the Hippocratic Oath he swore when he became a doctor. He was court-martialed and jailed. At a press conference called by anti-war GIs at Fort Sill, Oklahoma, in June 1967, a private named Richard Perrin, then eighteen, explained how he had come to oppose the war. Sitting in a base cafeteria, he overheard two sergeants reminiscing about their recent war experience. "One described how he had gotten a confession from a captured Vietnamese by pushing the naked prisoner against a very hot engine of a tank so his genitals would burn. The sergeant was talking in a very normal voice, not as if he was telling a secret." "I realized I was being trained to support these atrocities," his statement read. "At this point I decided to find out for myself whether there was any justification for the war. Everyone said there was, but they couldn't tell me what it was." Shortly after the press conference, Perrin was arrested for a minor infraction of the rules and demanded a court-martial. Instead, the Army sent him to West Germany where he promptly joined RITA—"Resist Inside the Army"—and deserted.[17]

The number of deserters mounted steadily, and they were often public, political deserters. Between July 1, 1966, and December 31, 1973, the Department of Defense counted 503,926 "incidents of desertion"; although not all of them can have been the result of opposition to the war, there were enough to establish an underground network of deserters in Western Europe. In 1965 a Japanese anti-war group, *Beheiren* (Citizens' Federation for Peace in Vietnam), was organized and, among many other activities, encouraged American troops in Japan for "rest and recreation" or on their way to Vietnam to desert. Four sailors from the U.S.S. *Intrepid* were among many who responded.[18] Anti-war "coffee houses" opened near bases everywhere, and GIs began publishing anti-war newspapers both at home and overseas.

A sanctuary movement, in which a local community kept vigil with a deserter in danger of arrest, represented desertion as a moral act when it was inspired by principled dissent. The deserter, traditionally an outcast, became a moral force for an increasingly alienated community.

*   *   *

In Congress, disaffection from the war was expressed in a series of hearings by the Senate and later the House Foreign Relations Committee, the first of which took place in January 1966. Senator William Fulbright, angered by what he now saw as Johnson's lies and manipulations at the time of Tonkin, conducted what was effectively a full-scale debate on the war and the underlying principles of postwar American foreign policy; NBC televised the hearings live. Fulbright disputed every administration argument. Vietnam was not a test of American power, it was not even a legitimate area in which the United States should operate. "After all," Fulbright instructed Dean Rusk when the secretary of state faced him in the hearing room, "Vietnam is their country. We do not even have the right the French did. We have no historical right. We are obviously intruders from their point of view. We represent the old Western imperialism in their eyes." Fulbright did not go so far as to question American motives ("I think our motives are very good"), but he left almost no other aspect of the policy unquestioned.

Senator Frank Church raised even broader considerations:

> The question that I think faces this country is how we can best cope with the likelihood of revolt in the underdeveloped world in the years ahead, and I have very serious doubts that American military intervention will often be the proper decision. I think too much intervention on our part may well spread communism through the ex-colonial world rather than thwart it.

Despite such powerful criticism, Congress continued to fund the war. And although many testified before the Fulbright Committee that Vietnam served no vital American interest and that unilateral withdrawal would do the United States no permanent damage ("it would be a six months' sensation, but I dare say we would survive it in the end," George Kennan said), remarkably, not one critic advised immediate and unilateral withdrawal. Church interrupted his questioning of one witness to make sure neither he nor the Committee was being misunderstood: "I do not know anyone around this table, certainly no members of the Foreign Relations Committee, that has advocated withdrawal . . . under the present circumstances . . . in Vietnam."[19]

For the "respectable opposition," novelist and journalist Mary McCarthy wrote in 1967, "unilateral withdrawal has become steadily more unthinkable as United States intervention has widened." Kennan, Fulbright, Church, all retained a "sympathy for American power," in

McCarthy's telling phrase, that prevented their advocacy of immediate and unilateral withdrawal. Indeed, she thought that the more they talked, the clearer it became that at some level they did not really oppose the war, "or not enough to stop thinking of it in terms of 'solutions,' all of which imply continuing the war by slightly different means. . . ."[20]

Nonetheless, and despite still optimistic reports from Westmoreland and the Saigon Embassy, the intensity of public opposition to the war seriously worried some senior officials. "A feeling is widely and strongly held," John McNaughton, assistant secretary of defense, wrote McNamara in a May 6 memorandum, "that 'the Establishment' is out of its mind. . . . Related to this feeling is the increased polarization that is taking place in the United States with seeds of the worst split in our people in more than a century."[21]

McNaughton wanted the president to repudiate the National Security Action Memorandum (NSAM-288) he had himself drafted in March 1964 and which had served as the explanation and justification of the American war. "We seek an independent non-Communist South Vietnam," that earlier memorandum read. "Unless we can achieve this objective in South Vietnam, almost all of Southeast Asia will probably fall under Communist dominance . . . " for the "South Vietnam conflict is regarded as a test case of U.S. capacity to help a nation meet a Communist 'war of national liberation.' " Now McNaughton urged a clarification of U.S. war aims that cast them in the most limited terms, and McNamara was in full agreement. The draft presidential memorandum prepared for Johnson and submitted to him on May 19 stated the U.S. commitment as "only to see that the people of South Vietnam are permitted to determine their own future." However, even this commitment ceases "if the country ceases to help itself." Moreover,

> our *commitment* is *not:*
>   to expel from South Vietnam regroupees, who are South Vietnamese (though we do not like them),
>   to ensure that a particular person or group remains in power, nor that the power runs to every corner of the land (though we prefer certain types and we hope their writ will run throughout South Vietnam),
>   to guarantee that the self-chosen government is non-Communist (though we believe and strongly hope it will be) and
>   to insist that the independent South Vietnam remain seperate from North Vietnam (though in the short-run, we would prefer it that way).[22]

The memorandum continued to place the United States and Hanoi in equivalent positions with respect to South Vietnam, but for the first time acknowledged that Hanoi had a legitimate role:

> We *are* committed to stopping or offsetting the effect of North Vietnam's application of force in the South. . . . Even here, however, the line is hard to draw. Propaganda and political advice by Hanoi (or by Washington) is presumably not barred; nor is economic aid or economic advisors. Less clear is the rule to apply to military advisors and war material supplied to the contesting factions.

Above all, the memorandum insisted, "the importance of nailing down and understanding the implications of our limited objectives cannot be overemphasized." This was ultimately the position the United States would take as it signed the Paris Peace Accords after five more years of war.

McNamara was convinced that Hanoi would not negotiate until after the 1968 elections; meanwhile bombing North Vietnam should be confined to the area south of the 20th parallel, a cap should be placed on the increase in U.S. ground troops in South Vietnam (Westmoreland had just requested an additional 200,000), and finally, vigorous prosecution of U.S. military and pacification programs in the South and an improvement in South Vietnamese military performance were essential.

The Joint Chiefs of Staff repudiated McNamara's memorandum with considerable passion, reaffirming NSAM-288 in every particular and demanding an escalation of the bombing. The memorandum failed to "appreciate the full implications for the Free World of failure to achieve a successful resolution of the conflict in Southeast Asia." Even worse, "modification of present US objectives, as called for in the DPM [Draft Presidential Memorandum] would undermine and no longer provide a complete rationale for our presence in South Vietnam or much of our effort over the past two years." Victory was the sole objective; escalation of war the means to achieve it. Johnson sought Rostow's advice, with predictable results. There were "dangerously strong feelings in your official family," Rostow warned. The way to "hold our family together" would be to launch a final attack on the Hanoi power plants (located about a mile from the center of the city) and then ease off on the Hanoi-Haiphong area. After a month, both sides could re-present their case.[23]

In August 1967, congressional advocates of an increased air war against the North called for hearings to learn why a particular set of targets remained unbombed. In the course of these hearings before the

Stennis Subcommittee of the Senate Armed Services Committee, the growing division between the civilians and the military in the Defense Department became starkly apparent. Robert McNamara, secretary of defense and architect of ROLLING THUNDER, in effect testified to its failure. No matter which targets were selected, the air war against the North would never do more than "continue to put a high price tag on North Vietnam's continued aggression." His testimony repeated what had become a litany of the loyal critics: Bombing would not bring Hanoi to the negotiating table. It would not halt the infiltration of troops to the South. Closing the harbor at Haiphong would reduce but not entirely stop the flow of aid from China and the Soviet Union. Damage to Hanoi's industrial plant had limited meaning in a country whose total power output *before* the bombing had been one fifth that of a single plant in Alexandria, Virginia. The import of McNamara's testimony before the Stennis Committee was that the strategy of bombing the North in order to achieve a political settlement in the South was bankrupt.[24]

Johnson was furious; McNamara had gone "dovish" on him. To a staff member he complained that he was like a "man trying to sell his house, while one of the sons of the family went to the prospective buyer to point out that there were leaks in the basement."[25] Three months later, in November 1967, the president surprised the secretary of defense and the country by announcing the appointment of Bob Mc-Namara to the World Bank. The disloyal son had been shown the door. But Johnson faced more and more questioning sons.

At the end of a cabinet meeting early in the new year, the president wound up the proceedings with a standard question: "Does anyone have anything to bring up?" "Yes, I have, Mr. President," Wilbur Cohen, the new secretary of health, education and welfare, said. As he recalled the scene for Merle Miller years later,

> There was a deathly silence among the cabinet. Here was the most junior guy opening up. I said, "My fourteen-year old son and a lot of young men were over at my house the other night, and they asked me, 'Why are we in Vietnam?' I discussed it but my answer was not satisfactory to all these young boys who might have to serve. If you were asked that question, Mr. President, how would you answer it."
> ... The president took half an hour to answer, and the answer didn't make any sense whatsoever. I can't remember the words now, but it was very shocking to me. If he had given that answer publicly, he would have been laughed out of court.[26]

In the confines of the cabinet meeting, no little boy arose to point to the emperor's nakedness. Still, as anti-war protests deepened and expanded, there were fewer and fewer places outside of military bases in which the president might parade safe from embarrassment. The president, Mary McCarthy wrote, "acts as if he had a mournful obligation to go on with the war unless and until somebody finds him an honorable exit from it. There is no honorable exit from a shameful course of action," she insisted, "though there may be a lucky escape."[27]

CHAPTER ELEVEN

The "Cross-Over Point" (1967–1968)

It is significant that the enemy has not won a major battle in more than a year. In general, he can fight his large forces only at the edges of his sanctuaries. . . . His guerrilla force is declining at a steady rate.

—GENERAL WILLIAM WESTMORELAND,
NATIONAL PRESS CLUB,
NOVEMBER 21, 1967.

To a large extent the VC now control the countryside. Most of the 54 battalions formerly providing security for pacification are now defending district or province towns. MACV estimates that US forces will be required in a number of places to assist and encourage the Vietnamese Army to leave the cities and towns and reenter the country. This is especially true in the Delta.

—REPORT TO THE PRESIDENT BY
GENERAL EARLE G. WHEELER,
CHAIRMAN, JOINT CHIEFS OF STAFF,
FEBRUARY 27, 1968

ALTHOUGH Lyndon Baines Johnson remained uninterested in either honorable exits or lucky escapes, the cost of remaining in the war was becoming prohibitive. By the middle of 1967, Vietnam was costing $20 billion per year, and in August a 10 percent surcharge on individual and corporate taxes ended the illusion that the economy could painlessly supply both guns and butter. The tax increase

210

was immediately reflected in Gallup and Harris Poll results; for the first time, those who said the war was a "mistake" outnumbered those who felt it wasn't (46 percent to 44 percent).

In the summer and early fall of 1967 there were renewed contacts with Hanoi and a new American formula for starting talks. Rather than insist that all infiltration stop before a bombing halt was instituted, a more conciliatory proposal, made public on September 29, 1967, proclaimed that the United States "is willing to stop all . . . bombardment of North Vietnam when this will lead promptly to productive discussions." The offer was conditional and reciprocal: "We, of course, assume that while discussions proceed, North Vietnam would not take advantage of the bombing cessation." The fate of this "San Antonio formula" (named for the city in which Johnson announced it) is best expressed in the laconic language of the official historian responsible for this section of the Pentagon Papers:

> The unfortunate coincidence of heavy bombing attacks on Hanoi on August 21–23, just prior to the transmission of the message, coupled with the fact that the Hanoi suspension [an announced temporary halt within a 10-mile perimeter of Hanoi] was to be of limited duration must have left the DRV [Democratic Republic of Vietnam] with the strong impression they were being squeezed by Johnsonian pressure tactics and presented with an ultimatum.[1]

Apparently so concluding, Hanoi rejected the overture.

Wilbur Cohen and his son had worried about why the United States was in Vietnam. It was not a question that had seriously troubled cabinet officials so long as they believed the war was going well, and going well at an acceptable cost. It was the apparent endlessness of the task, the expense of lives and treasure without clear issue, that had begun to bother the sorts of people Johnson could not ignore—Democratic congressmen, his own secretary of defense, loyal newspaper editors. They were questioning not the enterprise itself but the cost of the enterprise, the more so as the stability of the dollar in European markets wavered disturbingly.

McNamara, who in August 1967 had embarrassingly defected from the bombing policy at the Stennis hearings, had been troubled enough to instruct an aide, Leslie Gelb, to coordinate a study of U.S. policy toward Vietnam from the 1940s to the present. According to David Halberstam, as McNamara began reading the ensuing report, he told a friend: "You know they could hang people for what's in here." Which may account for government efforts to keep the study, dubbed the Pentagon Papers when it became public property in 1971, top secret.[2]

Still, official reports from high officials in Saigon remained upbeat. Ellsworth Bunker dismissed the pessimistic estimates made by his own staff; General Westmoreland's stolid confidence never wavered; Robert Komer, head of CORDS (Civilian Operations and Revolutionary Development Support), told reporters at Saigon dinner parties that "he had assured the President that the war would not be an election issue in 1968."[3]

Komer's confidence was based on his own reorganization of pacification in the countryside. Civilian and military pacification efforts had multiplied over the years into a management nightmare appalling to a former Ford executive like Robert McNamara. Starting in late 1966 and culminating in 1967, civilian and military pacification programs were combined in CORDS, which would operate under the military but be directed by a civilian with the rank of ambassador and direct access to Westmoreland. Working closely with people he judged particularly knowledgeable about the Vietnamese countryside, such as John Vann and Daniel Ellsberg, Komer concentrated on the development of a program intended to contest NLF control in hamlets and villages throughout South Vietnam by using the techniques and tactics of the NLF itself. The Revolutionary Development Cadres program would match the organizational efforts of the NLF.[4]

The program recalled John Vann's call for an American-supervised "revolution" in South Vietnam. Revolutionary development teams combining civic action and security cadres would establish a presence in every hamlet in the country, remaining in place for six months while they worked at a variety of welfare projects; secondly, rural paramilitary forces—the Regional and Popular Forces known to the Americans as "Ruff-Puffs"—would be greatly expanded (to 500,000 by 1970), trained, and better equipped. Finally, all intelligence agencies working in South Vietnam would pool their information so as to better target and eliminate the "Viet Cong infrastructure (VCI)," that organic network of people, soldiers, and political cadres David Elliott and other RAND analysts had studied so closely. This program had its origins in the CT (counterterror) organization the CIA had initiated in 1965 under William Colby. It too was expanded in 1967 (as Provincial Reconnaissance Units) and in 1968 emerged as "Phung Hoang," the Phoenix program, once more directed by Colby, this time in his capacity as Komer's deputy. The teams operating under Phoenix were Vietnamese with American advisers.[5]

Komer set a quota of three thousand VCI to be "neutralized" each month, and the figures were not unsatisfactory. From 1968 to mid-1971, 28,000 VCI were captured, 20,000 assassinated, 17,000 persuaded to defect (though whether all these people were in fact VCI is doubtful, since Phoenix early on became an extortionist's paradise, with payoffs as available for denunciation as for protection). "People who were just complicit were good for ten thousand or more piasters on the presentation of a head or an ID card or an ear to identify them," K. Barton Osborne recalled in an interview after the war. "It was a very wild kind of program. There were an awful lot of vendettas being carried out with Phoenix license." Moreover, the "process of bringing these people in and interrogating them, the process of even considering legal recourses, was just too overpowering, considering the mania of the body count and the quotas assigned for V.C.I. and neutralization. So quite often it was a matter of expediency just to eliminate a person in the field rather than deal with the paperwork. . . ."[6]

Osborne, a military intelligence officer in South Vietnam from September 1967 through December 1968, testified before Congress as to what happened when the interrogation was undertaken, as for example, by Marine Counterintelligence: "The use of the insertion of the 6-inch dowel into the canal of one of my detainee's ears and the tapping through the brain until he died. The starving to death [in a cage] of a Vietnamese woman who was suspected of being a part of the local political education cadre in one of the local villages . . . the use of electronic gear such as sealed telephones attached to . . . both the women's vagina and the men's testicles [to] shock them into submission." Corrupt and brutal, despite being frequently mistaken in its targets, over time Phoenix took a heavy toll on local NLF cadres.[7]

But what gave Komer a special sense of security were the results of the Hamlet Evaluation Survey, a system by which every hamlet in the country could be graded for both "security" and "development." The figure for fall 1967 was gratifying: 75 percent of the South Vietnamese population was pacified. The figure, William Gibson points out, was obtained by adding the number of refugees (4 million) to the number of Vietnamese who worked for the United States in one capacity or another (1 million) plus the ARVN military and police (another million) and the 2.4 million who lived in and around Saigon, combined with 4 million in hamlets graded A ("everything going right"), B (24-hour security, adequate development), and C (relatively secure day and night) for a round 12 million.[8]

Johnson invited the optimists home to counter critics in the halls of Congress, college campuses, and the streets. At the National Press Club,

Westmoreland outlined a plan for victory and assured the audience that "we have reached an important point when the end begins to come into view." He promised "some light at the end of the tunnel," though "mopping up the enemy" could well take another two years.[9]

Westmoreland's confidence derived from an earlier statistical calculation that at last the "cross-over point" had been reached: U.S. and ARVN troops were killing the enemy faster than they could be replaced. And that calculation was based on a major dispute within the bureaucracy in the spring of 1967 which itself turned on an unacknowledged—indeed, unacknowledgeable—political disagreement. According to Westmoreland's figures, there were a total of 285,000 NLF and North Vietnamese troops fighting in the South. It was on the basis of this figure that he was able to claim progress. Attrition worked. But the CIA counted almost twice as many in the enemy "order of battle"—between 500,000 and 600,000. That meant not only that there had been no significant "progress" but that in the face of the American war machine operating at full tilt, the NLF had been able to recruit new members, for neither the military nor the CIA claimed that the extra 300,000 were infiltrated from the North. They were local and southern; the efforts of the United States to create a government in Saigon capable of attracting the allegiance of the rural population had failed. (The number of "free world forces"—American, South Vietnamese, Korean, Thai, Filipino, and Australian—stood at a combined 1,300,000.)

Notified of the discrepancy, the head of the Joint Chiefs of Staff, General Wheeler, warned Westmoreland that the higher figure was simply unacceptable. "If these figures should reach the public domain," Wheeler wrote Westmoreland, "they would, literally, blow the lid off Washington. Please do whatever is necessary to insure that these figures are not repeat not released to news media. . . ." Westmoreland, in turn, informed subordinates that high estimates of enemy strength would cause grave political difficulty. In the fall, over the strong protests of the CIA analyst in the field, Sam Adams, Richard Helms, then head of the CIA, agreed to the lower figure. At issue was who was to be counted as the enemy. The military, and some civilian officials like Robert Komer, insisted that only main force NLF and North Vietnamese troops should be included. The additional hundreds of thousands that Adams wished to count were merely local self-defense forces, "low-grade, part-time . . . mostly weaponless" in Komer's words.

This was more than an argument about numbers, it was a disagreement about the nature of the war in which the United States was engaged. Counting "low-grade, part-time" people involved a recognition that in fighting the NLF, one fought the ordinary villagers of the country.

It even made sense of the GI "mere gook" rule: if it's dead and Vietnamese, it's VC. At its furthest logical extension, to agree to the higher figure meant that the United States, not North Vietnam, had invaded the South, was an aggressor against its people, and should withdraw.

On the other hand, to number as the enemy only those who were well-armed, full-time soldiers, who moved from province to province rather than remaining at home for local self-defense, meant one fought a subversive army, aided by uniformed infiltrators from another country (the North), who used neighboring countries as sanctuaries (Cambodia and Laos) and were aided by powerful allies (the Soviet Union and China). By this arithmetic, which was of course the logic of the entire war, the United States and North Vietnam were in structurally equivalent positions. The United States helped the legitimate government in Saigon; Hanoi helped an insurgent army seeking to overthrow that government. Washington's demand for reciprocity in the peace talks was fair and reasonable; Hanoi was testing America's will, and it was essential not to be found wanting.

Every Tuesday, lunch at the White House was the time for selecting the weekly bombing targets in North Vietnam. Monday lunches were more political than military. With Walt Rostow chairing, a Psychological Strategy Committee met to review all the speeches made, newspaper stories written, letters to the editor that dealt with the war. Pessimism must be instantly combated. "If a government report to the White House reported little or no 'progress,' " Dan Oberdorfer has written,

> Rostow wanted to know what was the problem or—another way of looking at it—*who* was the problem. Convinced that the central military fact in Vietnam was the rapid erosion of the Communist base, he expected reports which buttressed this position. When one official balked at changing reports to suit him, Rostow complained, "I'm sorry you won't support your President."[10]

In the Johnson White House, loyalty was a key issue. "I don't want loyalty," the president had told an aide early in his administration, "I want *loyalty.* I want him to kiss my ass in Macy's window at high noon and tell me it smells like roses. I want his pecker in my pocket." Vice President Hubert Humphrey was loyal. Though he was attending a reception at the Independence Palace in central Saigon when it was shelled, Humphrey returned from Vietnam to tell reporters, "We are beginning to win this struggle. We are on the offensive. Territory is being gained. We are making steady progress."[11]

In Saigon, reporters were summoned to briefings in which it was confidently announced that Communist military strength had fallen, that 67 percent of the South Vietnamese population lived in secure areas, that, as General Bruce Palmer put it, "the war—the military war—in Vietnam is nearly won. The Viet Cong has been defeated from Danang all the way down in the populated areas. He can't get food and he can't recruit."[12] Lower down in the military hierarchy, they sometimes told a different story. In March 1967, the senior U.S. military adviser for Long An Province confessed to a Reuters reporter that despite years of effort and ever-increasing sums of money, "in reality, we can control only a very small area. . . . I would say that we control only four percent in the daytime and only one percent in the night."[13]

In January 1968, a Vietnamese acquaintance with an unexpected sense of humor gave General Westmoreland a statuette of the eighteenth-century Vietnamese hero Nguyen Hue, whose surprise attack against a Chinese occupying army on Tet 1789 had driven the Chinese across the Red River back into their own country. "Fight to let [the Chinese] know the heroic southern country is its own master," Nguyen Hue's troops had sung on their way to battle. As the series of cease-fires in honor of Christmas and of Tet, the Vietnamese lunar New Year, began, Ambassador Bunker threw a New Year's Eve party, inviting everyone to come "see the light at the end of the tunnel." But the light at the end of the tunnel, as Robert Lowell once observed, may be the light of the oncoming train. Had Westmoreland known more Vietnamese history he might have suggested rewording the invitations; for two hundred years after Nguyen Hue, in a surprise move that consciously recalled the heroic past, NLF and North Vietnamese troops launched a series of coordinated attacks throughout the country. The Tet Offensive had begun.

The most important objectives of Tet, the historian Ngo Vinh Long has written, "were to force the United States to de-escalate the war against the North and to go to the negotiating table." The war had reached a stalemate; the hope was that through a stunning series of attacks which would display the strength of the NLF position in the South, the war would be forcibly moved to a new phase, one that would lead to U.S. withdrawal. Southern troops would carry the main burden of the fighting, with the regular North Vietnamese Army working to create diversions, as they were to do at Khe Sanh, or serving as a reserve force, as in the battle over Hue. There were hopes, but not expectations of a "decisive" victory: the collapse of the Saigon government, followed by popular demands for a coalition government that would include the NLF, and the consequent withdrawal of the United States. That did not occur, but the more modest hope, that a successful offensive would halt and perhaps even reverse the steady escalation of the American war machine, was fulfilled.

For the first time, the war was brought directly to the cities. Five of the six largest cities in the country, thirty-six of forty-four provincial capitals, about one quarter of the two hundred and forty-two district towns, Cholon, the sprawling Chinese section of Saigon, the heavily fortified American embassy, the imperial city of Hue, places that should have been absolutely secure, all were engulfed in battle. The fighting was astonishingly fierce. In Saigon a force of one thousand NLF troops fought eleven thousand combined American and ARVN troops to a standstill; it took three weeks to subdue them. Hue was swiftly occupied, and a coalition municipal government drawn from those who had been active in the 1966 Buddhist Struggle Movement administered the city. A French correspondent described teams of NLF supporters moving through the city in groups of ten, distributing leaflets and pamphlets. As for the soldiers: "Joking and laughing, the soldiers walk in the streets and gardens without showing any fear. . . . They give an impression of discipline and good training. . . . Numerous civilians brought them great quantities of food. It didn't seem that these residents were being coerced in any way."[14] For almost a month the NLF flag flew from the Citadel, until the Marines, bombing and strafing from the air, fighting street by street and house by house, retook the city. "Nothing I saw during the Korean War, or in the Vietnam War so far," Robert Shaplen wrote as he toured the remains of the city, "has been as terrible, in terms of destruction and despair, as what I saw in Hue." Of Hue's 17,134 houses, 9,776 were completely destroyed; 3,169 seriously damaged. (The figure was almost as high in the rest of Thua Thien Province.)[15]

In the rubble of Hue and its outskirts, shallow mass graves of civilians, many with their hands bound, were discovered. The official U.S. figures vary from a low of 2,800 to 5,700. Supporters of the war seized on the "Hue massacre" as yet an additional justification for the war: Hue was only the foretaste of the inevitable bloodbath of a Communist victory.

The most careful estimate of the death toll, made at the time by free-lance journalist Len Ackland, puts the figure between three hundred and four hundred. Most of the victims seemed to have had some connection with the government of South Vietnam or the Americans. There is little question that there were executions in Hue, both in the initial stages of the occupation and in the last days of the battle there. And it is unseemly, even obscene, to argue about the numbers. Neverthe-

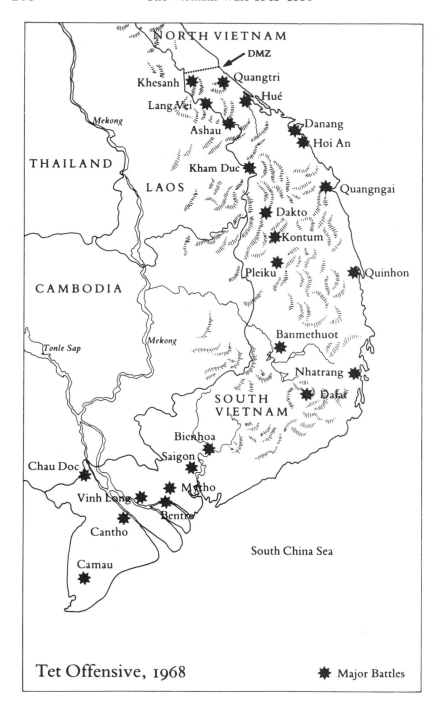

Tet Offensive, 1968   ✸ Major Battles

less, an effort to understand what happened is essential if we are to be able to grasp the war and its aftermath. The task of the NLF in Hue was not only to destroy the government administration of the city, but to establish, in its place, a "revolutionary administration." The disposition of those who had controlled the city until its takeover was carefully laid out: there were lists of those in the Saigon government police apparatus at all levels (to be rounded up and held outside the city); lists of high civilian and military officials (the same; both to await study of their individual cases); lists of ordinary civil servants (those "working for the enemy because of their livelihood and who do not oppose the revolution" who were destined for reeducation and possible later employment); lists of those low-level civil servants who had at some point been involved in paramilitary activities (to be held for reeducation, but not employed). In the early days of the occupation, there were indeed summary executions.

But in his detailed study of the event, the political scientist Gareth Porter, argues that "the official story of an indiscriminate slaughter of those who were considered to be unsympathetic to the NLF is a complete fabrication." The thousands of civilians who died in Hue, the photojournalist Philip Jones Griffiths wrote, "were killed by the most hysterical use of American firepower ever seen." At the same time, in the last days of the NLF occupation of Hue, teams of Saigon government assassins fanned out through the city with their own list of targets, underground NLF supporters who had revealed themselves in the course of occupying the city. And as the occupation ended in the firestorm of artillery and aerial bombardment, retreating NLF troops executed many of those they held in custody (rather than either releasing them or keeping them prisoner), not in the numbers Saigon and Washington charged, but certainly enough to have posed troubling questions for the people of Hue who survived, as Richard Falk has recently suggested: "The subsequent history of Vietnam makes one wonder whether the shadow cast by Tet did not add significantly to the fear and hostility of Southerners towards the North, to the mass exodus after liberation, and to the phenomenon of the boat people, which undercut the basic claim of national liberation and reunification." However, all the accounts agree that NLF rather than North Vietnamese units were responsible for the executions. Beyond those speculations, one thing seems certain: what the history of Tet in the city of Hue reveals is the extraordinary harshness and brutality of a struggle that had been going on for over twenty years.[16]

The cities and towns captured in the Tet Offensive were ultimately retaken by Saigon and the Americans, but at a Pyrrhic price. "We had to destroy the town to save it," the commanding officer in charge of recapturing the provincial capital of Ben Tre told reporters. The same could have been said of Hue, Cholon, My Tho, and Vinh Long. It would take ten U.S. battalions to restore "security" to the Saigon area; according to Saigon government figures, 6,300 civilians died, 11,000 were wounded, 206,000 became refugees, and 19,000 homes were destroyed. Throughout the country the official, and probably low, figure for civilians was 14,300 dead, 24,000 wounded, 627,000 made homeless.

Part of the shock of Tet was the contrast between recent official optimism and the reality illuminated by the Tet attacks. Dan Oberdorfer's account is full of such moments. In the Mekong Delta, for example, the head of the U.S. advisory team, Brigadier General William Desobry, who had just completed a tour of eighteen months' duration, told reporters that the local Viet Cong were "poorly motivated, poorly trained" and that the ARVN "has the upper hand completely." "At the time he spoke," Oberdorfer writes, "Viet Cong units were closing their grip on important roads, canals and routes of approach to provincial and district capitals throughout the region." The people of the Delta knew, of course. But not the Americans. "In the opening hours of the Tet Offensive, Viet Cong troops attacked thirteen of the sixteen provincial capitals of the Mekong delta and many of the district capitals. There was no alarm, in many cases, until enemy troops began firing in the middle of town."[17]

The Iron Triangle, as we have seen, had been repeatedly burned over, bombed, swept, and destroyed. In October 1965, the commanding officer of the 173rd Airborne Brigade declared with confidence: "The Iron Triangle was thoroughly searched and investigated, and all enemy troops and installations were destroyed." The following year, Operation CEDAR FALLS came back to make sure. "The enemy turned the land into a desert," one guerrilla told a reporter after the war; "there was not a tree left." This the U.S. Army could see, and it was the basis of its confidence. "But," the guerrilla continued, "I could still count on over 200 men to fight beside me. . . ."[18] That the U.S. Army could not see.

The next year, Tet 1968, the attack against Saigon some 22 miles away was launched from the tunnel complex inside the Iron Triangle. Arms that had been stored in preparation were transported to Saigon in carts carrying vegetables to market; four thousand guerrillas moved into the city, mingling easily with the crowds visiting relatives for the Tet holiday, hiding in the homes of sympathizers. The Americans knew nothing of this; if any ARVN troops knew, they didn't tell.

There were many signs of the coming offensive. But the only one Westmoreland took seriously was a North Vietnamese Army attack on

Khe Sanh, a base in the northwest mountains close to the DMZ and the Lao border. The French had had a base there, too. This was the war that fit American theory: North Vietnamese troops attacking targets in the South with regular army troops. And it was the war American troops were best equipped to fight, a war not against peasants who might or might not be guerrillas, but against a regular, heavily armed uniformed enemy. There was even room for feeling smug. The Vietnamese had done this once before, against the French at Dienbienphu. But they would see that America was not France.

Earlier probes by the North Vietnamese led Westmoreland to reinforce the base, so that when the attack that began the siege finally came, on January 21, 1968, there were six thousand U.S. and ARVN troops facing two North Vietnamese divisions (some twenty thousand soldiers). Eventually Westmoreland concentrated yet more troops, so that at its height some fifty thousand American soldiers were tied down at Khe Sanh, making things considerably easier for attacking NLF troops to the south. The Americans denuded the mountainside with 60,000 tons of napalm, 40,000 tons of regular ordinance. The siege ended in early March, not broken by the Americans but broken off by the North Vietnamese, its diversionary function fulfilled.

To have taken other signs of the coming offensive seriously—captured documents, rumors, warnings given American civilians by Vietnamese friends—would have meant revising the view of the war to which Americans, civilian as well as military, were firmly wedded. To believe the signs, the American command would have had to acknowledge that the NLF was the popular revolutionary force it claimed to be; that probably a majority of the population of the South saw the United States as the lineal descendant of French colonialism and the Saigon government as no more than a pliant, corrupt clique; that the United States and the Vietnamese military it had trained were the enemy of the people of the South rather than their friend and protector. Such a set of propositions was clearly unacceptable.

The least disheartening interpretation of events, therefore, was that Tet was a desperate last-ditch attempt by the North Vietnamese (the NLF was given little or no credit for either the planning or execution of the attacks, though it had been NLF troops that bore the brunt of the fighting) to drive the Americans into the sea. The effort had failed, obviously. The Americans remained and were in the process of punishing the enemy for its temerity.

The February offensive received the most publicity in the United States, but there were two further phases. The one beginning in May lasted until early June: 119 cities, towns, and bases were attacked on the single night of May 4. The third, final phase opened on August 17 and lasted for the next six weeks. Losses at each stage of the campaign were high, and as the U.S. military kept score (by counting the dead) all three phases of Tet represented defeats for the NLF and Hanoi. Westmoreland was certain his strategy of attrition was working; Hanoi could not continue to sustain such high losses.

The changes the Tet Offensive brought were decisive. Before Tet, Robert Komer remembers, Washington couldn't do enough for him—"I was one of the lesser lions of the hour." After Tet, "it was all the other way." Everyone was too busy to see him. ". . . I knew in one day that whatever had happened out there, Tet had changed absolutely everything in Washington."[19] Beyond that there is little agreement. Interpreting Tet involves political judgments now as it did when it was happening. Those Americans who insist that Westmoreland and Bunker were right, that the United States was winning the war, still see the reporting of Tet, rather than the event itself, as the crucial factor. Because Tet was reported as an American defeat, they claim, politicians lost heart, rejected making an increased effort, and took the first steps on the slippery slope toward withdrawal and admitted defeat.

There are several problems with this interpretation. Tet was in fact not reported as an NLF victory; and the U.S. military effort did not slacken in its aftermath. The press accepted official statements that Tet had been a major military defeat for Hanoi and the NLF. What it did not accept, however, was that the defeat spelled victory in the war for the United States and Saigon. As Daniel Hallin has summarized the reporting: "journalists seem to have interpreted Tet, without consciously making the distinction, for what it *said* rather than what it *did*—as proof, regardless of who won or lost it, that the war was not under control."[20] And the notion that the war slackened after Tet is wholly misleading. To be sure, as we shall see, President Johnson declared a bombing halt north of the 20th parallel in North Vietnam; but there was no reduction in tonnage dropped, only a shift southward. Moreover, such a partial bombing halt had been discussed within the administration for several years as a relatively risk-free way to improve America's image. B-52 raids in the South, especially in the populous Mekong Delta, increased after Tet, with devastating results. And an "accelerated pacification program" lived up to its name, with consequences for the inhabitants of a village named My Lai, whose population was massacred by U.S. troops in March 1968. During the first six months of 1969, the U.S. 9th Infantry Division conducted a "pacification" effort in one Delta province that yielded an official body count of 11,000 with only 748 captured weapons. The issue, *Newsweek* reporter Kevin Buckley wrote, was not the "indiscriminate" use of American firepower but its "quite discriminating use—as a matter of policy, in populated areas."[21]

The cost to the NLF, especially of the second and third phase of the offensive, was enormous. In the countryside, the absence of so many main force units had left hamlets and villages exposed to the ravages of U.S. firepower and ARVN depradations. "Looting and other misconduct by the Republic of Vietnam Armed troops toward the civilian populace have undermined the confidence of the people in RVNAF [Republic of Vietnam Armed Forces]," the CIA reported after Tet. But by the same token, the inability of the NLF to protect the villagers, the efficiency with which members of the NLF who had surfaced during Tet were captured and executed, and the sheer weight of those dead in the attacks against the cities, encouraged passivity, a longing for peace. Revolutionary warfare depends upon active commitment. It was this commitment that had enabled the NLF to recruit new members in the face of massed U.S. and ARVN technology and firepower. It was this commitment that enabled the Tet Offensive to be launched in the first place. But the magnitude of the NLF's losses was deeply felt.

In Long An Province, for example, local guerrillas taking part in the May–June offensive had been divided into several sections. Only 775 out of 2,018 in one section survived; another lost all but 640 out of 1,430. The province itself was subjected to what one historian has called a "My Lai from the sky"—non-stop B-52 bombing. (By the end of the war, the province itself, whose total population was 350,000, had lost over 84,000 combatants. On average, each village had lost 500 combatants.) NLF leaders before Tet and after questioned the wisdom of a three-phase offensive, preferring to retreat to the countryside in the aftermath of initial attacks. And while the air war against the North may have been partially limited after Tet, in the South *all* forms of warfare intensified.

To many southern revolutionary fighters, Ngo Vinh Long writes, "it now seems . . . that an important factor that contributed to the ability of the US to carry out that massacre [in the countryside] was the mistake of carrying out the third phase (and even perhaps the second phase) of the Tet offensive rather than protecting their rural base after the tremendous success of the first phase." General Tran Van Tra, a chief planner of the offensive, has retrospectively criticized the extent to which "we did not correctly assess the concrete balance of forces between ourselves and the enemy . . . had we considered things more carefully . . . our victory would have been even greater, our cadres, troops and people would have spilled less blood, and the subsequent development of the revolution would have been much different."[22] Rebuilding hamlet and village organization after Tet was slow, hard work, all undertaken in the face of intensified U.S. military activity. One NLF military commander, Madame Nguyen Thi Dinh, has spoken of the "especially difficult time" revolutionary forces experienced after Tet.

Near Hue, in the village of My Thuy Phuong, for example, the 101st Airborne (the "Screaming Eagles") established a camp toward the end of January 1968. During the first phase of the Tet Offensive, the Saigon government presence, both civilian and military, simply disappeared. "I think everyone respected the Communist side more because so many of the guerrillas died in the attacks," one peasant recalled years later. "The important thing about Tet . . . is that the Communists made the Government very weak." Despite the retreat from Hue, one student said, "it was a very strong victory. It showed the people that the Americans could be defeated." An American historian of the village concluded that the 80 to 85 percent of the people of My Thuy Phuong who supported the NLF had "proud memories of the boldest strikes yet against the Government and its ally."[23]

By late February, however, the Americans were back and Camp Eagle expanded. At times there were more Americans than Vietnamese in the village—some 10,000 to the normal village population, including children, of about 7,600. Families were relocated, graves bulldozed, garden plots taken over, and the village transformed by helicopter landing pads, new roads, barracks, barbed wire, and constant military traffic as men and supplies for fire bases throughout the area shuttled in and out of Camp Eagle. "Incidents" between villagers and soldiers were frequent. The village history records a night in 1969 when a squad of soldiers patrolling the hamlet closest to the camp "entered a peasant house. . . . One soldier remained in front and another moved behind it to stand guard." After a hasty search, which revealed nothing, the mother of the family remembers, "they pushed us around and attacked my daughters. They pushed them to the ground, and raped them again and again." More significant for the people of the province, however, were the daily patrols throughout Thua Thien Province for a 288-day period in 1968–69. The effect on local NLF strength was dramatic. Support decreased to 50 percent of the people of My Thuy Phuong, only 30 percent of whom were really active in local guerrilla networks; government supporters, both passive and active, increased from 5 to 10 or even 15 percent. As in provinces further south, military pressure between 1968 and 1970 increased rather than decreased. In My Thu Phuong, over half of the village guerrilla force was killed or captured in these years and the new leadership was young and untested. But some level of Front activity was maintained throughout the period: "the insurgents made tactical changes, kept up their military pressure, and continued to circulate word of their struggle. In effect, the Front adjusted to the Eagle."

The adjustment that the NLF in My Thu Phuong made to Camp Eagle was repeated by NLF cadres and guerrillas throughout the South as the impact of Tet was learned from and absorbed. By conventional measures of military success, Tet might be judged an NLF defeat. But the war in Vietnam was not a conventional war.

Henry Kissinger thought Tet "brought to a head the compounded weaknesses—or, as the North Vietnamese say, the internal contradictions—of the American position." Tet may have been a military victory for the American side, but it was "a political defeat in the countryside for Saigon and the United States." Henceforth, "the prevalent strategy could no longer achieve its objectives within a period or with force levels politically acceptable to the American people."[24] Whatever the body count, the intensity and scope of the attacks (carried out by an estimated one quarter of the available NLF and North Vietnamese troop strength), the revelation that no place in South Vietnam, not even the grounds of the American Embassy, was safe, the inescapable conclusion that this vast coordinated effort could only have taken place with the cooperation of the people of the South, forced a reevaluation of policy. "I am much affected by my belief," McGeorge Bundy told the president, "that the sentiment in the country on the war has shifted very heavily since the Tet offensive. This is not because our people are quitters. . . . What has happened is that a great many people—even very determined and loyal people—have begun to think that Vietnam really is a bottomless pit."[25]

One of the most lasting images of the war has been a single moment of the Tet Offensive in Saigon, when both television and still cameras caught General Nguyen Ngoc Loan, notorious head of the South Vietnamese National Police, as he shot an unarmed, handcuffed prisoner in the head. Although the television footage was edited for family viewing, the pictures captured what was most disturbing about the war to many Americans: the disparity between the barefooted bound prisoner and the general, with his flak jacket, his heavy American pistol, the callous indifference to constituted rules of war; the terror of death meted out in America's name, with American means, by men like Loan. Rusk, catching this footage on the nightly news, angrily asked newsmen which side they were on.

Walter Cronkite, dean of TV news commentators, whose reassuring, impeccably non-partisan voice marked the safe passage of another day for millions of Americans, was one of them. It was time, he said later, "to go out there and just do some pieces on what it looks like and try to give some guidance." In an unusual personal statement on February 27, 1968, Cronkite informed the nation that "we are mired in stalemate" in Vietnam. "To say that we are closer to victory today is to believe, in the face of the evidence, the optimists who have been wrong in the past." Listening to the broadcast, Johnson is said to have concluded that "Cronkite was it"—there was no stopping the tide against the war.[26]

The latest Gallup Poll illustrated the difference Tet had made: in November 1967, after Westmoreland's optimistic predictions, 50 percent of those polled believed the United States was making progress in the war; after Tet, the figure dropped to 33 percent, and an astonishing 49 percent believed the United States should never have intervened in Vietnam to begin with. After that it seems the blows kept falling. The administration had hardly caught its breath after Cronkite's defection when on March 10 a *New York Times* story revealed to the public that Westmoreland was requesting an additional 206,000 troops, which would require mobilizing the reserves. If the United States was winning the war, even the 33 percent of the country who believed in its progress might reasonably wonder, why this new request? The story, Rostow told a historian bitterly, "churned up the whole eastern establishment and created a false issue. It caused an unnecessary crisis and distorted things. It overrode the hopeful news and had quite substantial effects on public opinion."[27] News of the troop request, which appeared the day before Secretary of State Rusk was due to testify before the Senate Foreign Relations Committee and three days before the New Hampshire Democratic primary, had a dramatic impact. On live TV, for a total of six and a half hours over a two-day period, Rusk was cross-examined. And while he was able to avoid any specific discussion of troop levels or future strategy, he nevertheless received a stern warning from Senator Fulbright that any escalation in the war had better be cleared with Congress first.

Then, on March 12, 1968, the results of the New Hampshire presidential primary were announced. Johnson had declined to enter, on the high-minded ground of his total engagement with the problems of the nation. But neither he nor any member of his political team imagined that the quixotic peace candidacy of Senator Eugene McCarthy of Minnesota (announced in November 1967) posed a serious challenge. "The Democratic Party in 1964 promised 'no wider war,' " McCarthy's basic campaign speech declared. "Yet the war is getting wider every month. Only a few months ago we were told that 65 percent of the population was secure. Now we know that even the American embassy is not secure." McCarthy's campaign, fueled by an immensely enthusiastic crew of young volunteers, received an improbable 42.2 percent of the popular vote and twenty of the state's twenty-four convention delegates. When the write-in votes were counted during the week following the election, McCarthy was within 230 votes of a majority.[28] Even more damaging than McCarthy's near win, however, was the likelihood that the New Hampshire vote would encourage the candidacy of a far more threatening political figure, Robert Kennedy.

For a time Johnson's post-Tet response was to make a series of militant speeches, declaring the determination of the United States to "win the peace on the battlefield by supporting our men who are doing that job there now." But should that support include sending over 200,000 more of their fellows to join in the job? Clark Clifford, the new secretary of defense, urged the president that it was time to call a meeting of senior advisers. On March 25, there gathered to assess the situation those David Halberstam has called the "great names of the Cold War," among them Arthur Dean (who had helped to negotiate an end to the Korean War), Douglas Dillon (former secretary of the treasury), Cyrus Vance (former undersecretary of defense), Dean Acheson (with Averell Harriman the most senior American statesman), Generals Omar Bradley, Maxwell Taylor, and Matthew Ridgway (all former chairmen of the JCS), Robert Murphy (a high State Department officer), former ambassador Henry Cabot Lodge, and George Ball. Others long associated with Vietnam policy were also present, including McGeorge Bundy, now head of the Ford Foundation, as well as Walt Rostow, among other current Johnson advisers.

For his part, the president wanted to grant the troop request. One scholar, Paul Joseph, argues that after Tet, Johnson was more determined than ever to pursue the war and had himself encouraged the military to make the request for increased troops in the first place. Gabriel Kolko suggests that it was General Wheeler, head of the Joint Chiefs of Staff, who tried to use the occasion to get more troops to build up the much-weakened strategic manpower reserves. On January 23, the North Korean government had seized a Navy intelligence ship, the U.S.S. *Pueblo*, creating fear of renewed conflict on the Korean peninsula. Moreover, the South Korean government insisted it would need to withdraw 46,000 of its 70,000 soldiers from the "allied" effort in Vietnam. How would they be replaced? Two days later, 14,000 U.S. reserve units were mobilized.

What the Pentagon wanted now was a much larger mobilization, one that could meet not only the needs it foresaw in Vietnam, but those elsewhere in the world, including domestic needs. The nation, a Department of Defense estimate warned, must be assured that it "still had the resources left for the ghetto fight."[29]

On earlier occasions the senior advisory group—the Wise Men, as they seemed to enjoy being called by the press—had on the whole approved Johnson's handling of the war, with the expected exception of George Ball. This time things were different. After a briefing by the military and the CIA, the discussion began. The military claimed that the enemy had lost 45,000 dead in the February Tet Offensive. UN Ambassador Arthur Goldberg wanted to know what was enemy troop strength at the start of Tet. The answer: between 160,000 and 175,000. And the ratio of killed to wounded? Estimated at three and a half to one, answered the officer. "Well, if that's true," Goldberg calculated quickly, "then they have no effective forces left in the field." This certainly made additional American forces seem redundant.

Arthur Dean felt that "time was running out" and there was no sense of a "military conclusion in sight." Dillon was also persuaded of the impossibility of military victory; instead, the United States should "head toward an eventual disengagement." Public opposition to the war dominated much of the discussion. The United States could not succeed "in the time we have left," Dean Acheson said; "time is limited by reactions in this country." "Unless we do something quick," Cyrus Vance joined in, "the mood in this country may lead us to withdrawal." George Ball also pointed to the "sharp division of opinion in the United States," not to speak of the rest of the world where "we look very badly because of the bombing. That is the central defect in our position. . . . As long as we continue to bomb, we alienate ourselves from the civilized world. . . . A bombing halt would quieten the situation here at home."[30]

Perhaps the most complete admission of defeat came from Henry Cabot Lodge. He recommended an end to search and destroy operations in the South and instead the use of American troops as a "shield to permit the South Vietnamese society to develop as well as North Vietnamese society has been able to do." But it had been to provide such a shield that the United States had intervened some eight years earlier; and was it not odd for Lodge to take Hanoi as the measure of success?

Not all the Wise Men thought deescalation a good thing. Robert Murphy believed the CIA should try assassinating Ho Chi Minh. Maxwell Taylor urged a call-up of the reserves to demonstrate "to our friends and allies alike that we meant business and did not consider turning back." But the majority argued for deescalation, either unilaterally or through a renewed effort at negotiations with Hanoi. Acheson, speaking for this majority, declared that the United States "could no longer do the job we set out to do in the time we have left and we must begin to disengage."

The president, Clifford recalled, "could hardly believe his ears . . . he said that 'somebody had poisoned the well.' He tried to find out who had done so." Maybe it was the report by the CIA man, George Carver, or General DePuy's briefing. "He was so shocked by the change in attitude of the Wise Men that he wanted to hear the briefings they had received. The meeting with the Wise Men served the purpose that I hoped it would. It really shook the president." He may have been only jostled. A few days after the Wise Men adjourned, Clifford, Rusk, Rostow, and William Bundy were helping Harry McPherson, the President's speechwriter, with the draft of a major speech Johnson was to deliver on March 31. A version written before the senior advisory group met had called for renewed American resolve, a draft call of fifty thousand, and a war tax surcharge. According to McPherson, the speech that Johnson eventually delivered, with its emphasis on peace and declaration of a partial bombing halt, was the result of Clifford's unrelenting pressure. "Now I make it a practice," Clifford told his colleagues,

> to keep in touch with friends in business and law across the land. I ask them their views about various matters. Until a few months ago, they were generally supportive of the war. They were a little disturbed about the overheating of the economy and the flight of gold, but they assumed that these things would be brought under control; and in any event they thought it was important to stop the Communists in Vietnam.
>
> Now all that has changed. . . . The idea of going deeper into the bog strikes them as mad. They want to see us get out of it.
>
> These are leaders of opinion in their communities. . . . It would be very difficult—I believe it would be impossible—for the president to maintain public support for the war without the support of these men.

As Gabriel Kolko has pointed out, Johnson was being asked to assume the burden "not simply of his own political errors in Vietnam but also of the failure of an entire class in pursuing the war and the hegemonic goals of American foreign policy, a class that was now abandoning escalation. . . ."[31] Indeed, they abandoned the president himself. On March 31, Johnson announced a unilateral partial bombing halt and his own resignation in the only form this can take in America: he would not run for office in 1968.

One should not overstate the concessions Johnson was making. The bombing halt, which was generally understood to end all bombing except, as the speech said, "in the area north of the demilitarized zone where the continued enemy build-up directly threatens allied forward positions," was in fact a very meager offering to peace. Bombing was to be halted north of the 20th parallel—but within that area lived some 25 percent of the North Vietnamese population, not the 10 percent Johnson claimed in his speech. Such a move had been suggested over a year earlier, in April 1967, by Chester Cooper and likeminded aides in the State and Defense Departments. "The arguments," Cooper wrote, "were based on the casualties we had been sustaining as a result of the concentration of anti-aircraft weapons in the area of Hanoi and Haiphong and on the lack of profitable, suitable targets still remaining in north and central North Vietnam."[32] Moreover, the number of sorties, over the more restricted area, actually *increased* after March 31. And since Hanoi was not expected to respond positively to the speech, the possibility of new escalation remained open. The partial halt, one American official said, "would extend the lease on public support for the war." On March 30, a cable was sent to all American ambassadors advising them of the impending announcement and suggesting that "Hanoi is most likely to denounce the project and thus free our hand after a short period." Instead, Hanoi responded positively, creating increased pressure on the president to declare a complete bombing halt.[33]

The larger significance of Johnson's speech, beyond the specific concession, was its acknowledgment that a limit to the American commitment had been reached. For the first time since the Marine landing in Danang in June 1965, the number of American troops was capped at 543,000—a move McNamara had urged before he left office the preceding November. The policy of "Vietnamization," which Richard Nixon would announce with much fanfare the following year, was already under way.

Martin Luther King, Jr., also spoke on the last day of March 1968. A year earlier he had warned that the war in Vietnam was poisoning the soul of America. Now, preaching in the National Cathedral in Washington, King warned that if nothing were done to "raise ghetto hope," the coming summer would be "not only as bad but worse than last time." Four days later, King was dead, shot down as he stood on the balcony of a motel in Memphis, Tennessee. The popular response to his death was an explosion: in one hundred cities across the country, Americans took to the streets in a rage of grief. "By the dawn of April 6," a British reporter has written, "a pall of black smoke [from ghetto and downtown fires] hung over the national monuments. The capital of the United States was under military occupation."[34]. In Vietnam, Michael Herr wrote, King's assassination "intruded on the war in a way that no other outside event had ever done."[35] One black veteran remembers thinking: "If they kill a preacher, what are they going to do to us, even though we're over here fighting for them?"

Two months after King's death, Robert Kennedy, who had entered the Democratic presidential primaries as a peace candidate in the wake of Eugene McCarthy's successful New Hampshire campaign, was assassinated at a celebration marking his tremendous success in the California primary.

In August, at the Democratic National Convention in Chicago, a police riot turned the city into a battlefield as the world watched on television. Establishment journalists were shocked. "Miraculously," *Newsweek* reported, "no one was killed by Chicago Mayor Richard Daley's beefy cops, who went on a sustained rampage...." Stewart Alsop feared that he might be witnessing the coming of "some form of American fascism."[36]

"The War," the poet Denise Levertov wrote, "comes home to us . . ."

CHAPTER TWELVE

Bloodbaths
(1968–1971)

People talk a lot of trash about Charlie. Well, let me tell you
something about him. He's bad. But we're badder. They say
that's his country out there. But it's our country too. We go
any GOD damn where we please, and they ain't nothing in
this world Charlie can do about it.

—WILLIAM E. MERRITT,
"IN-COUNTRY TRAINING," FROM
Where the Rivers Ran Backward

*Our rivers, our mountains, our
people will always be;
The American aggressors defeated,
we will build a country
ten times more beautiful.*
—HO CHI MINH, "TESTAMENT,"
MAY 10, 1969

MACBETH complained about the weary course of bloodletting
in which he was engaged: "I am in blood/Stepp'd in so far
that, should I wade no more,/Returning were as tedious as
go o'er." Johnson, angry at his advisers, cursing the "establishment bas-
tards" who had "bailed out," authorized the increased pace of both air
and ground wars in Indochina, and then, after all, slowly and reluctantly
began the tedious route back. It would prove as bloody as the way in; nor
was the direction always certain. In Paris, Hanoi's positive response to
the partial bombing halt led to the opening of peace talks on May 13,

1968, which moved at once into a deadlock that lasted until the following October.

By fall 1968, concerned Democrats, hoping to aid Hubert H. Humphrey's flagging campaign, urged some dramatic progress toward peace, and Johnson reluctantly agreed to a complete bombing halt over North Vietnam. In implicit exchange, Hanoi agreed to the terms the American negotiators, Cyrus Vance and Averell Harriman, had worked out months earlier (a halt to rocket attacks on the cities; respect for the DMZ) with one addition, the participation of Saigon in the talks in accordance with an elaborate formula devised by Harriman that would, as well, provide for NLF participation. The talks were scheduled to begin November 6, one day after the U.S. election. American public response was immediate: with the announcement that serious negotiations were about to begin, Humphrey's standing in the polls rose to within two percentage points of Nixon, who until then had held an 8 percent lead. Peace in hand seemed worth more than the promise held out by Nixon's campaign assurance that he had a "secret plan" for peace.

And then, a foretaste of the Nixon style, the talks were sabotaged only three days before election day. Working secretly through Henry Kissinger, who kept the Nixon staff up to date on the progress of the talks in Paris, and Anna Chennault, an old friend of Chiang Kai-shek and other Asian and American right-wing politicians, and chairwoman of the Republican Women for Nixon, word of Harriman's efforts in Paris was passed on to Thieu, who was explicitly encouraged to "hold on." In the last week of the campaign, John Mitchell, Nixon's campaign manager, called Chennault daily, urging her to keep Thieu from agreeing to the peace talks.[1]

Thieu was entirely willing to cooperate with Nixon. Even better, he would deliberately mislead Johnson into believing all was well. In conversations with Vietnamese politicians over phones he knew to be tapped by the CIA, Thieu expressed his readiness to participate in the Paris talks, while for his part, Nixon magnanimously refrained from comment on Johnson's peace efforts, except to express hope for their progress. Then on November 1, in a speech before the South Vietnamese National Assembly, Thieu declared his implacable opposition to the peace talks; his government would never agree to sit down with the Viet Cong. And so the talks were stalled dramatically, the blow all the heavier for the hopes the promise of talks had held out. Although it is impossible to calculate the precise impact of their collapse on the final close presidential vote, the incident is revealing. Secrecy, duplicity, and a ruthless attention to immediate political advantage regardless of larger moral issues marked Nixon's approach to Vietnam during the campaign; election to the presidency did not change him. (Indeed, among his first acts as president was an angry inquiry into the failure of the Washington police and Secret Service to prevent anti-war demonstrations during the inaugural parade. Why had arrests not been made before the demonstrations even began? In the margin of the memo informing him that the demonstrators had permits, Nixon wrote: "I question the advisability of permits. They seem to aggravate the situation by making it lawful and easier to congregate."[2] Nixon's aides believed he would have lost the election if it had been held only a few days earlier, before Thieu's sabotage; even so, the vote was very close, 43.40 percent to Humphrey's 42.70 percent.

Johnson could have pressed ahead in Paris without Thieu, as Harriman and even Rusk urged him to do. But he refused. Nor can it be said with any certainty that the talks would have yielded peace even if Thieu had not protested. For the basic negotiating stance of both sides remained unchanged. Peace could only come, Hanoi insisted, with the withdrawal of all foreign forces and the formation of a new government in the South that included the NLF. In due course the people of North and South would discuss together the manner and timing of their reunification. Peace could only come, Johnson instructed his delegation, with the end of direct and indirect aggression by North Vietnam against the South. A separate anti-Communist South Vietnam remained the goal. In time, the American negotiating posture would moderate to allow for a non-Communist rather than an anti-Communist possibility; but the demand for a separate country in the South did not waver.

Although he had been persuaded to extend the bombing halt to all of North Vietnam, Johnson at the same time approved a dramatic increase in the air war against Laos. Indeed, if histories had musical scores, events in Cambodia and Laos would have accompanied this account of the war in Vietnam as a leitmotif running through all of the preceding chapters. To the people of Cambodia and Laos, of course, there was nothing peripheral about their engulfment in the American war against Vietnam.

"This is the end of nowhere," an American official had observed in Laos in 1960. "We can do anything we want here because Washington doesn't seem to know it exists."[3] The "secret" bombing of Laos, which began, as we have seen, shortly before the Tonkin Gulf incident, may have established the existence of Laos in Washington, but the constraints on U.S. actions were if anything even lighter than before. By 1967, Americans had essentially replaced Lao civil and military authorities.

William Sullivan, now the American ambassador in Vientiane, ran the air war. Targets were "developed" by the CIA, the U.S. Air Force, and consulting members of the Royal Lao armed forces, and then checked out at the embassy for "political criteria." The check was part of Sullivan's effort to reduce, though he could hardly eliminate, the amount of non-combatant suffering the bombings caused. Sullivan, convinced no good could come of it, managed to fend off Pentagon plans for a ground invasion of Laos, relying instead on the air war to achieve American goals.[4]

In late 1967 and 1968, however, as the fighting in Vietnam escalated, so too did the level of violence in Laos. Although Sullivan denied it to Senate subcommittees investigating the fighting in Laos two years later, increasingly towns and villages were targeted and destroyed. The Plain of Jars, a prosperous region in northeastern Laos whose fifty thousand people had lived under the Pathet Lao since 1964, became a prime object of American bombing. "By 1968," Georges Chapelier, a Belgian working with the United Nations reported, "the intensity of the bombing was such that no organized life was possible in the villages."

With Nixon's electoral victory, William Sullivan became deputy assistant secretary of state. Replacing him as ambassador in Vientiane was George McMurtrie Godley, whose experience in the Congo in 1964–66 had given him a taste for executive action. In Indochina, Godley earned the nickname "air marshal." All bombing restrictions, including those on B-52s, were removed. Chapelier reported that "villagers moved to the outskirts and then deeper and deeper into the forests as the bombing climax reached its peak in 1969 when jet planes came daily and destroyed all stationary structures. Nothing was left standing. . . . In the last phase, bombings were aimed at the systematic destruction of the material basis of the civilian society." Between 74,000 and 150,000 tons of bombs were dropped on the Plain of Jars from 1964 to 1969. By September, an observer has written, "after a recorded history of seven hundred years, the Plain of Jars disappeared."

Over a quarter of the population of Laos was now officially classed as refugee—the number had doubled in less than a year. In 1970, a Senate staff report described the goal of the air war as the destruction of "the social and economic infrastructure of Pathet Lao held areas." Translated from the bureaucratic jargon, this meant the destruction of Lao society in such areas, and in this the policy did indeed succeed. "My village stood on the edge of the road from Xieng Khouang to the Plain of Jars," a thirteen-year-old refugee told an American.

There were rice fields next to the road. At first, the airplanes bombed the road, but not my village. At that time my life was filled with great happiness, for the mountains and forests were beautiful; land, water, and climate were suitable for us. And there were many homes in our little village. But that did not last long, because the airplanes came bombing my ricefield until the bomb craters made farming impossible. And the village was hit and burned. And some relatives working in the fields came running out to the road to return to the village but the airplanes saw them and shot them. . . ."[5]

In mid-September 1969, Senator John Sherman Cooper of Kentucky, concerned that Laos might become a new area for U.S. troop engagement despite Nixon's promise to begin troop withdrawal, offered an amendment to the Military Procurement Authorization Bill that "prohibited combat involvement by U.S. forces in support of local forces in either Laos or Thailand." (Unfortunately, Cooper did not have the foresight to include Cambodia.) In modified form, the amendment passed both Houses of Congress in December 1969. Under its provisions, Congress would vote no funds for the introduction of American ground troops into Thailand or Laos. Nothing was said about the air war; nothing about the continued support for the Meo army or the Royal Lao armed forces; nothing about the possible use of South Vietnamese troops in Laos. Although a clear sign of congressional disaffection from the war in Vietnam and an announcement of limits on future action, the Cooper Amendment left the White House free to pursue its own course in Laos, Cambodia, and Vietnam.

Cambodia was the last of the three Indochinese states to be consumed by the war, and perhaps for that reason the most deeply damaged. American bombing in Indochina was like an insane game of musical chairs. As a region was removed from the list of acceptable targets, the total tonnage was simply shifted to the remaining allowable areas. (Occasionally the policy created bizarre problems for those charged with its implementation. After Cambodia had been opened up for bombing, a "targeteer" in the American Embassy in Phnom Penh was faced with a serious problem when the Air Force insisted on flying a set number of B-52 sorties daily despite the lack of targets "suitable" for such raids. After the accidental destruction of a Royal Cambodian naval base, he began to submit phony "underwater storage areas" as targets.)[6]

Aware of this deadly arithmetic, Prince Norodom Sihanouk worked with desperate energy to keep the war at a distance. As part of an early understanding with Hanoi, Sihanouk agreed to ignore the sanctuaries established by the NLF on the Vietnam-Cambodian border. In exchange Hanoi agreed to ignore the small Cambodian Communist movement, the Khmer Rouge. However unhappy this made both the United States and Khmer insurgents, it seems to have served the majority of Cambodians very well. Despite numerous close calls, Sihanouk walked a tightrope across the inferno of the war.

What forever changed the world for the Cambodians was Richard Nixon's conviction that the way to end the war in Vietnam was to expand it. As he was fond of telling friends and confidantes, he had learned how to end wars against Communists from the master, Dwight David Eisenhower. "How do you bring a war to a conclusion?" he asked one group of delegates to the Republican Convention in 1968. "I'll tell you how Korea was ended. . . . Eisenhower let the word go out . . . to the Chinese and the North Koreans that we would not tolerate this war of attrition. And within a matter of months, they negotiated." It was all a poker game, he assured his listeners, "we've got to . . . walk softly and carry a big stick." In conversation with White House aide Bob Haldeman, Nixon was more explicit:

> "I call it the madman theory, Bob. . . . I want the North Vietnamese to believe I've reached the point where I might do anything to stop the war. We'll just slip the word to them that, "for God's sake, you know Nixon is obsessed about Communists. We can't restrain him when he's angry—and he has his hand on the nuclear button,"—and Ho Chi Minh himself will be in Paris in two days begging for peace.[7]

In March 1969, Nixon decided to send Hanoi this message by agreeing to a longstanding request from the Pentagon to conduct B-52 raids on Vietnamese base camps close to the Cambodian border. For Johnson, Vietnam seemed to have been all about sex, seduction, submission, if need be, rape. Nixon cast Cambodia as food, a country to be consumed. The first raids were code-named BREAKFAST. Later raids deeper into Cambodia were called LUNCH and were intended to send a message not only to Hanoi but also to North Korea, which had recently shot down an American spy plane.[8] Eventually there were raids enough to have DINNER, SNACKS and DESSERT; MENU was the overall codename. BREAKFAST was to be followed by lightning Special Forces raids on what the Pentagon still assured the president was the main command headquarters (COSVN) for all enemy troops fighting in South Vietnam. Some of the B-52 raids were very damaging to the base camps, although follow-up ground attacks by Special Forces units met stiff and on several occasions overwhelming resistance. In general the Vietnamese response was to move deeper into Cambodia, away from the border; the B-52s followed them.

Fearing a public outcry over what most people would take as blows against rather than for peace, the decision was made to keep the raids entirely secret from Congress and the American public. Through an elaborate system of double reporting, even the *secret* records of B-52 bombing targets were falsified so that nowhere was it recorded that the raids had ever taken place. At the first hint of a leak to the press, a story by *New York Times* reporter William Beecher (which was answered by routine White House denials and aroused almost no interest in Congress), the White House exploded (behind closed doors) with anxiety and anger. An ever-expanding network of illegal wire taps was put in place to trace the leaks. Indeed, the first tendrils of the Watergate conspiracy, and the beginning of Nixon's downfall, can be seen here, not in the actual bombing of a neutral country but in keeping it secret. Over a fourteen-month period ending in April 1970, Operation MENU conducted 3,630 B-52 raids on Cambodia, dropping 110,000 tons of bombs. The effect on the war in Vietnam was nil; the effect on Cambodia was devastating.

Whatever messages Nixon might choose to send in future, Ho Chi Minh himself would not receive them. On September 2, 1969, exactly twenty-four years after he had proclaimed the independence of Vietnam in the words of the American Declaration of Independence, Ho Chi Minh died. (His death was announced as occurring on September 3, perhaps because the government in Hanoi was reluctant to make its National Day a day of mourning.) The previous May, his health already failing, Ho had written a Testament that was now released. He was seventy-nine years old, convinced that "total victory" was certain but not that he would survive to see it. "Our compatriots in the North and in the South shall be reunited under the same roof," Ho wrote. "We, a small nation, will have earned the unique honor of defeating, through a heroic struggle, two big imperialisms—the French and the American—and making a worthy contribution to the national liberation movement." There must be no grand funerals upon his death, and no waste of people's time or money. To "the whole people, the whole Party, the whole army, to my nephews and nieces, the youth and children, I leave my boundless love."

Omitted from the version published at the time was a promise that post-war rural taxes would be reduced and Ho's very specific wish with respect to his burial: "I request that my corpse be cremated. My ashes should be divided into three parts and put into three boxes, one for the

North, one for the South, and one for the Center." Then the people of each area must choose a beautiful mountain and bury the ashes. There must be no tombstone, nor statue, but instead "a large, airy, simple house that visitors can enjoy." Provisions would be made so that trees could be planted around the mountain. "Everyone who comes to visit the tomb can plant a tree. In time, there will be a jungle, and a beautiful landscape, to the profit of the people. Let the senior citizens take care of the mountain." Instead, Ho's carefully embalmed body was laid to rest in a marble mausoleum which, though large, was neither airy nor simple nor enjoyable. As an architectural form, the weight and mass of the mausoleum would echo the form that reunification finally took some six years later: not the promised elections of the Geneva Accords in 1954, nor the ratification of the successful insurgency of the 1960s, but rather the rumble of tanks through the streets of Saigon in 1975.

Le Duan, Pham Van Dong, and Vo Nguyen Giap, whose lifetimes, like Ho's, had been spent entirely in the cause of the Vietnamese revolution, pledged themselves to continue "until there is not a single aggressor in the country."[10]

"You are to start without any preconceptions at all," Henry Kissinger told his National Security Council staff in August 1969. "It shall be the assignment of this group to examine the option of a savage, decisive blow against North Vietnam." Including nuclear weapons? Not directly against North Vietnam, Kissinger replied, but "you are not to exclude the possibility of a nuclear device being used for purposes of a blockade in the pass to China. . . ." "I refuse to believe," Kissinger explained, "that a little fourth-rate power like North Vietnam does not have a breaking point."

"Duck Hook," the code name given to Kissinger's plans for forcing Hanoi to its knees, nevertheless explored a range of new options, including a land invasion of the North, the systematic bombing of its dikes so as to destroy the food supply, and the saturation bombing of Hanoi and Haiphong. A North Vietnamese diplomat who negotiated with Kissinger in Paris explained to an American reporter after the war that Kissinger had the notion that "it is a good thing to make a false threat that the enemy believes is a true threat. It is a bad thing if we are threatening an enemy with a true threat and the enemy believes it is a false threat." "I told Kissinger," Nguyen Co Thac remembered, that "there must be a third category—for those who don't care whether the threat is true or false."[11]

Kissinger's failure to understand the Vietnamese was matched by his failure to understand the American anti-war movement. In an interview with *Look* magazine in his first year at the White House, Kissinger expressed sympathy for a younger generation he saw as without "great purposes in the world." But he profoundly disapproved of those members of the student generation who refused to fight in Vietnam. "Conscientious objection," he warned, "must be reserved only for the greatest moral issues, and Vietnam is not of this magnitude."[12]

Only part of Nixon's strategy called for persuading Hanoi that he was mad; the remainder rested on U.S. troop withdrawal and "Vietnamization." Articulated in July 1969 as the "Nixon Doctrine," it expressed a determination by the administration to limit the role of U.S. ground troops in Asian wars. Secretary of Defense Melvin Laird explained that the new policy would rely on "indigenous manpower organized into properly equipped and well-trained armed forces with the help of materiel, training, technology and specialized military skills furnished by the United States."[13] In effect, a mercenary army on the ground combined with American airpower. That same month the President announced that twenty-five thousand American troops would be withdrawn by the end of the summer; thereafter, troops were ordered home in ever larger increments. Three programs supplemented troop withdrawal: the intensified air war; the "accelerated pacification" program, to which the Phoenix program was central; and increased training, support, and equipment for an expanded ARVN. All three programs proceeded under the shadow of the ongoing peace talks, for a premature peace would endanger American goals. A *Wall Street Journal* reporter, Peter R. Kann, drew some of the connections: "The year-old Phoenix campaign," Kann wrote in March 1969, "obviously is related to the Paris negotiations. When peace comes, South Vietnam's claims to control the countryside will be strongest where the VCI cadre are fewest."

Kann accompanied troops on one operation 50 miles southwest of Saigon, a village that informers insisted was solidly NLF. Rather than the "sophisticated and productive affairs" Phoenix was reputed to run, the raid on Vinh Hoa in March 1969 was a "largely fruitless interrogation of fearful, tight-lipped villagers, calculated brutality applied to suspected Vietcong, the execution of one suspect, looting of homes by Vietnamese troops, systematic destruction of village installations [including a medical clinic] and a largely unproductive hunt for Vietcong officials who apparently had fled by sampan long before. . . ." The village had been NLF, one of the American advisers on the operation mused, for ten or maybe twenty years. "How are you going to change that? We come here on an operation, and what does it prove? We've got some crook sitting in Don

Nhon picking up a salary every month because he claims to be the government village chief here. . . . The VC will be back in control here tonight. . . ."[14] Still, the operation had used a minimum of U.S. troops, killed a total of eight people, forced the NLF village administration to withdraw, and sown doubt about the loyalty of those who had been detained, then released. Combined with the air war and a constantly supplied ARVN, Vietnamization raised the possibility of perpetual war at an acceptable cost.

In Vietnam, the Nixon Doctrine strove for the high level that had already been achieved in Laos and would later be reached in Cambodia ("The most perfect embodiment of the Nixon Doctrine," Sihanouk called it in 1989): "a new way of fighting a war," a Foreign Service officer told an interested historian in 1971; a way of "maintaining a level of violence so as to keep from losing. . . ."[15] Captured North Vietnamese documents indicate that Hanoi understood American tactics very well: the plan, one such document read, is to *"de-Americanize and de-escalate the war step by step, to preserve their manpower and material . . . especially to preserve U.S. troops. . . ."* The objective, the astute analysts in Hanoi went on, was to create a *" 'neutral' South Vietnam whose real nature is pro-America. . . ."* (italics in the original).[16]

Leaders of the anti-war movement were equally astute. Rejecting Kissinger's blandishments to have patience and wait for the White House to reveal its secret plan for peace, a national committee worked through the summer of 1969 planning a new protest effort for the fall. October 15 was designated the first Vietnam Moratorium Day—a day on which "business as usual" would cease and Americans everywhere would gather to protest the war and petition the government to end it. In Boston, 100,000 people gathered on the Common; in New York, Mayor John Lindsay declared a day of mourning and flew the flags at half-mast, while protest rallies attracted tens of thousands in sites around the city; Coretta King led 30,000 people in a silent candlelight parade past the White House. The big-city response was predictable; more significant perhaps were the rallies in smaller cities and towns and on non-elite college campuses like the president's alma mater, Whittier College.

Nixon's response was Vice President Spiro Agnew. In a series of blistering speeches, Agnew rebuked the students, the press, and "eunuch" politicians who opposed the war. On November 3, Nixon himself sought to defuse the peace movement in a solemn address to the nation that denounced the demonstrators as a noisome minority, promised reduced draft calls, reduced casualties, and an early "Vietnamization" of the war. Nixon appealed to the "silent majority" to remain steadfast: "North Vietnam cannot defeat or humiliate the United States," Nixon said. "Only Americans can do that." In this much, at least, the anti-war movement and the president were in agreement.

The White House watched the rising tide of demonstrations with immense anxiety. At least one account of the Nixon White House argues that the October Vietnam Moratorium might well have deterred implementation of "Duck Hook," the Kissinger-Nixon "madman" plan.[17] Certainly the White House prepared for the November Moratorium as if for battle. Nixon was advised to advertise his calm by announcing that he would be watching football that day. But he also ordered three hundred airborne troops flown to Washington and had them hide in strategic locations inside the White House and the Executive Office Building. In an underground bomb shelter deep beneath the East Wing of the White House, John Erlichman, one of Nixon's closest advisers, supervised a 24-hour crisis control center.

The November Moratorium began with a March Against Death that set out from the gates of Arlington National Cemetery just as night fell on a bitter cold November 13. In their history of the anti-war movement, Nancy Zaroulis and Gerald Sullivan have described the scene:

> Twelve hundred marchers crossed the Arlington Memorial Bridge every hour as they began their nearly four-mile walk, each carrying a name placard and, in the hours of darkness, a lighted candle. . . . Hour by hour they silently came, forty-five thousand marchers, through two nights and into Saturday morning, through rain and thunderstorms, wind and biting cold, in what may have been the longest "parade" in American history.

As each marcher passed the White House, they called out the name of the dead soldier whose memorial placard they carried—for Judy Droz, the twenty-three-year-old woman at the head of the march, it was her husband's name—then kept on marching until they reached the steps of the Capitol where the placard was placed in a coffin. On Saturday, November 15, there was a mass demonstration on the Mall in front of the Washington Monument. Hundreds of thousands arrived by bus, train, and car throughout the day, as many as 800,000 by some estimates (as few as 250,000 according to the White House). The White House itself, like a campsite in an old Western, was completely surrounded by a protective circle of buses parked bumper to bumper.[18]

The White House was not alone in feeling besieged. Although

The NLF answer to the Saigon government's *chieu hoi* program: an explicit appeal to black GIs. (Photograph by Dana Stone; UPI/Bettmann Archive)

U.S. NEGR ARMYMEN !

YOU ARE COMMITTING THE SAME IGNOMINIOUS CRIMES IN SOUTH VIETNAM AS THAT THE KKK CLIQUE IS PERPETRATING AGAINST YOUR FAMILY AT HOME

NLF soldiers reading *Life* magazine in a secure area south of Loc Ninh. The picture was taken in 1973. (UPI/Bettmann Archive)

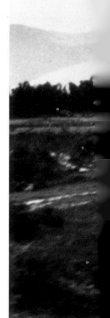

From 1964 to 1969 between 74,000 and 150,000 tons of bombs were dropped on the Plain of Jars in Laos, destroying all possibility of continued settlement. Over a quarter of the Lao population became refugees. Here villagers have drawn the American attacks as they experienced them.

THE INTENSIFICATION OF THE WAR

Cratered landscape north of Hue, 1967. (Photo by Len Ackland)

The face of war. An American soldier, Hue, 1968. (Photo by Donald
McCullin. Magnum Photos)

During a "sweep" through villages north of Qui Nhon, the lack of young men was taken as evidence of NLF "infiltration." Here a marine guards villagers rounded up on an operation in September, 1965. (Photograph by Martin Stuart Fox; UPI/Bettmann Archive)

Villagers flee after an accidental napalm raid twenty-six miles southwest of Saigon. (UPI/Bettmann Archive)

The following three photographs are all by Philip Jones Griffiths; the captions are his, excerpted from his book *Vietnam Inc*. (Macmillan, 1972). Wounded VietCong . . . GIs often show a compassion for the enemy that springs from admiration of their dedication and bravery. This VC had a three-day-old stomach wound. He'd picked up his intestines and put them in an enamel cooking bowl (borrowed from a surprised farmer's wife) and strapped it around his middle. [When he indicated that he was thirsty, the Vietnamese interpreter said he could drink from the rice paddy.] With real anger a GI told him to keep quiet, then mumbled, "Any soldier who can fight for three days with his insides out can drink from my canteen any time!" (Magnum Photos)

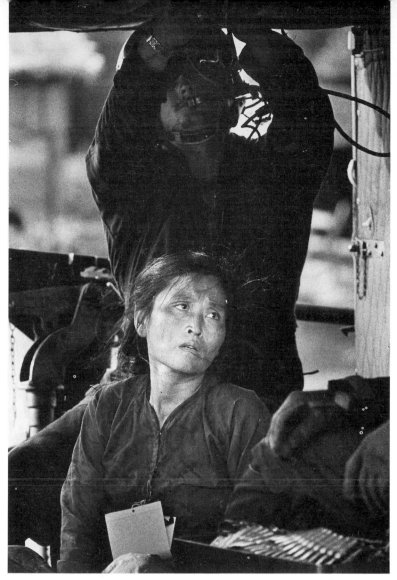

Captured VietCong. The woman was the sole survivor of a communications squad caught in the open. Wounded in the spine, she was forced to crouch all day with her hands tied behind her back before being taken off by helicopter. When reproached, a US officer replied, "What's the hurry? When the GVN boys have interrogated her, she'll only be raped and killed anyway." (Magnum Photos)

Mother and child, shortly before being killed. A unit of the American division operating in Quang Ngai Province six months before My Lai. . . . This woman's husband, together with the ten other men left in the village, had been killed a few moments earlier because he was hiding in a tunnel. After blowing up all tunnels and bunkers where people could take refuge, GIs withdrew and called in artillery fire on the defenseless inhabitants. (Magnum Photos)

Sergeant P.L. Thompson posing on the throne of the Emperor Tu Duc after the capture of the Citadel, Hue, February 24, 1968. (Courtesy U.S. Department of the Army)

Downtown Nam Dinh before and after, April 1972. (Courtesy Ngo Vinh Long Collection)

Sometimes protests ended peacefully, as here on the steps of the Capitol. Washington, DC, May 1971. (UPI/Bettmann Archive)

DEMONSTRATIONS IN

VIETNAM AND THE

UNITED STATES

Sometimes violently: Jackson State College dormitory riddled by police bullets. (Photograph by David Doggett)

Kent State, May 4, 1970. (Left: Photograph by Kent State News Service; right: Photograph by John A. Darnell, Jr.)

Students burn Thieu election posters, September 1971. (Photograph by Tran Dai Minh; UPI/Bettmann Archive)

Dewey Canyon III, April 1971. Rusty Sachs, one of the organizers of the demonstration, returns his medal in the name of friends who have died in Vietnam. (Photo by Bernard Edelman)

A march in San Francisco. (Photo by Flax Hermes. Courtesy of Pathfinder Press)

AND THE WAR GOES ON...

North Vietnam bombed military targets in New York City today, in an attempt to force the U. S. to seriously negotiate.
—Imaginary News Item

Tony Auth cartoon describes U.S. negotiating position. (Universal Press Syndicate)

A North Vietnamese cartoon. Nixon pulls U.S. troops out, as the bombs continue to fall—the hat is labeled THE NIXON DOCTRINE.

North Vietnamese tanks in front of the Saigon Presidential Palace, April 1975. (Courtesy Ngo Vinh Long Collection)

THE END

North Vietnamese troops in Danang, 1975.

After the Khmer Rouge: a display of skulls. (Courtesy Ngo Vinh Long Collection)

THE WAR AFTER THE WAR

War games: Graffiti on the side of a house in a village just outside of Hanoi, 1988. (Photo by Hugh Swift)

Vietnamese memorials: *Mother Courage* outside of Danang. Swords into sculpture—the statue was fashioned from artillery shells. (Photo by Hugh Swift)

John L. Steer places a rose at the Vietnam Veterans Memorial.
(Photograph by Ron Bennett; UPI/Bettmann Archive)

Nixon hardly spoke for a silent majority, there was a feeling of intense division within the country. The consensus around major issues of foreign and domestic policy that had marked American politics while masking American realities since 1945 had been definitively broken by the Vietnam War and by the multiple social movements in its wake. Earlier, poverty and racism had been understood as discrete problems, confined to specific regions of the country and more or less easily remediable. Prosperity and the chance to move up the scale of wealth and power were the birthright of every American, guaranteed by the extraordinary wealth of the country's resources and the rectitude of its social system. Nuclear readiness and the occasional resort to limited war were sad necessities forced on the United States by the nature of its nuclear-armed and ubiquitous Cold War enemy.

But now racism and poverty were being explained as endemic, the social system seen as inherently unfair to minority groups; natural resources were described as depleted and limited, and the Cold War as at least as much an American as a Soviet creation. Now Europe and Japan prospered, while in the United States, economic decline had become a fearful possibility. Moreover, fundamental moral values connected to family, sex, and work that had only rarely been challenged in the past were held up to public scrutiny, even scorn.

On November 13, as the March of Death slowly crossed Arlington Bridge, the questions raised by the war were given sharper focus by the first reports of an American atrocity in South Vietnam, the massacre of the inhabitants of the village of My Lai. The slaughter at My Lai had occurred almost a full year earlier, in March 1968, one part of the U.S. response to the Tet Offensive; some soldiers would later testify that it was not unique but commonplace to the way America fought the war. My Lai was a real massacre, the sort of thing Americans were used to seeing in old war movies about the Nazis or the Japanese. It was also the sort of thing the United States claimed the Viet Cong might do. Indeed, the United States justified staying in Vietnam to prevent bloodbaths, not to commit them. Yet in a series of news reports by Seymour Hersh in *The New York Times* it became clear that not only had a platoon of soldiers cold-bloodedly killed virtually the entire population of a village (raping many of the women before murdering them), and a village from which not a single shot had been fired, but that the Army had systematically covered the whole thing up.

Some Americans, incapable of believing that the United States could commit atrocities, argued that either My Lai had not happened at all, or that if it had, there was probably a good reason for it. But for most people, My Lai was an event the more terrifying because it seemed inexplicable. Indeed, the comfortable paradigm of the nation's history—as taught in school, celebrated on holidays, so fully embraced it felt natural rather than learned—had no more room for My Lai than it had for the genocide of the American Indians, for slavery, for the conquest of the Philippines, or the persistence of poverty and inequality. Used to thinking of their country as America the Good, Americans were shocked to see the streets filled with angry young people who insisted it was America the Bad. The massacre at My Lai, they accused, was neither impossible nor aberrational.

The values a majority of people had thought made America great—hard work, individualism, family morality, and discipline—were being criticized as rationalizations for exploitation and oppression. Some critics put it differently: the values which had made America strong and prosperous were the very values which would destroy the world, either through nuclear war or massive ecological damage. It was time to stop mastering nature and live in harmony with it. Parents watched in dismay as their children—repelled by the world the parents had built, by the values the parents cherished, by the ambitions the parents nourished for them—dropped out of school to join a working class their parents had striven to leave, or returned to the land for a life of subsistence farming and voluntary poverty, or lost themselves in drug-altered states of consciousness. The young people who stayed in school joined movements to change the institutions in which they studied, protesting what they saw as the hypocrisy of administrations that claimed to serve the interests of all but in fact reproduced class, race, and gender privilege. Some joined revolutionary sects whose desire for change "by any means necessary" inspired rituals of violence which shattered the windows of banks and ROTC buildings in a self-conscious assault on private property and governmental authority.

At Harvard, a law school student named Meldon Levine addressed an audience of parents and alumni:

> The streets of our country are in turmoil. The universities are filled with students rebelling and rioting. Communists are seeking to destroy our country. Russia is threatening us with her might. And the republic is in danger. Yes! danger from within and without. We need law and order! Without law and order our nation cannot survive.

When the thunderous applause with which his audience responded had died down, Levine informed the audience that the words were not his: "These words were spoken in 1932 by Adolf Hitler."[20]

* * *

In March 1970, Prince Norodom Sihanouk's tightrope finally snapped. While the prince was in Europe, Prime Minister Lon Nol overthrew him in a coup that Washington welcomed, having perhaps aided in bringing it about. Among Lon Nol's first acts was an invitation to Saigon to join his own army in expelling NLF and Vietnamese troops from Cambodia. One month later, to Lon Nol's surprise and reported distress, Nixon announced that U.S. troops would join in the enterprise, reserving for themselves the task of locating and eliminating COSVN, which had become the Holy Grail of the American war.

Nixon's decision to invade Cambodia, announced to the world on April 30, 1970, came as an immense shock to the American public. The desire to end the war fueled the general eagerness to believe that it was indeed winding down, that at last they had succeeded in electing a "peace president." As promised, the president seemed to be turning the war over to the Vietnamese. Only ten days before the U.S. invasion of Cambodia, another 150,000 combat troops were ordered to come home. And the war was disappearing from the nightly news, surely a sign that it was nearly over. Yet while the absolute number of American combat troops declined, direct U.S. participation in the war did not. And the disappearance of combat footage from the news did not mean it was not being filmed in Indochina, only that producers in New York had reached a conscious decision not to air it. The executive producer of the Huntley-Brinkley NBC News program later told the British journalist Godfrey Hodgson that "we got tired of combat footage and we said, 'Let's get some pacification footage,' and that was soft stuff so it went at the tail end of the show. So straightaway people got the impression the war was less important." Combat footage had been featured three or four times a week; now, with the same amount of film coming in from the field, it was shown only three times in two months. ABC News came to a similar decision in March 1969. Av Westin, the executive producer, advised the Vietnam staff "to alter the focus of their coverage from combat pieces to interpretative ones, pegged to the eventual pullout of American forces. This point must be stressed for all hands." The Saigon bureau received an emphatic telex from Westin: "I think the time has come to shift some of our focus from the battlefield . . . to themes and stories under the general heading: We Are on Our Way Out of Vietnam." By the spring of 1969, Hodgson concluded, "the war was over, because you didn't see it on the tube any more."[21]

Then came the "incursion" into Cambodia. Not peace then, whatever the President's promises, but indefinite war. In Washington, State Department East Asian specialists had urged the president to reject persistent requests from the military to expand its operations in Cambodia from air attacks on NLF and North Vietnamese sanctuaries to a ground invasion. Direct American military involvement, they warned, would delay negotiations and endanger Vietnamization. Characteristically, those who expressed any level of disagreement with the policy, including Defense Secretary Melvin Laird and Secretary of State William Rogers, were not consulted. The military, however, were full of advice. Admiral John D. McCain, Jr., father of one of the first U.S. pilots to be taken prisoner in North Vietnam, Commander-in-Chief of U.S. Forces in the Pacific (CINCPAC), known to his colleagues as the "Big Red Arrow Man" because of his enthusiastic use of large-scale maps whose sweeping arrows illustrated the latest Communist advance, met with Nixon in mid-April and strongly urged an American invasion of Cambodia so as to protect troop withdrawal from Vietnam. Stated this way, as it often was, the logic of the argument was vague and made little sense. Protect U.S. troops from whom? For years spokespeople for Hanoi and the NLF had assured Washington they would provide an escort for American troops, ushering them to their ships and planes with full military honors, garlands of flowers, and a band.

What the proposed invasion really intended, however, made a different, more ominous sense. Damaging the NLF and North Vietnamese in Cambodia would protect U.S. troops in South Vietnam because it would permit them to return home without having to forfeit the policy goal that had sent them into combat in the first place: the creation and maintenance of a separate state in the southern part of Vietnam. The notion was that crippling blows to the enemy in Cambodia would bring Saigon that much closer to being able to defend itself without American ground forces. The goal of U.S. policy had hardly changed since the days of Ngo Dinh Diem. Nixon's secret peace plan was turning out to be just another way to continue fighting the war.

Despite the alarm of several members of his staff, who thought the invasion would delay rather than promote Vietnamization, Kissinger seemed calm, convinced that whatever its effect on Vietnamization, the invasion would increase America's overall bargaining power with Hanoi and the Soviet Union. In any event he was not about to risk his growing power by opposing the President. Nixon, furious at earlier congressional rejection of his two Supreme Court nominees, raged not only at foreign but domestic enemies: "Those senators think they can push Nixon around. . . . Well, I'll show them who's tough." Mixing metaphors with wild abandon, Nixon explained his decision to Nelson Rockefeller in the same language of belligerent defiance, possibly enhanced by the heavy drinking he seems to have been doing throughout this period:

> I sat right here with two cabinet officers and my security adviser and I asked what we needed to do. The recommendation of the Department of Defense was the most pusillanimous little nit-picker I ever saw. . . . If you are going to take the heat [Nixon said, rejecting suggestions of a smaller operation] go for all the marbles. . . . I have made some bad decisions, but a good one was this: when you bite the bullet, bite it hard—go for the big play.[22]

Two of Kissinger's principal aides, Roger Morris and Anthony Lake, thought the invasion was not only useless but wrong, and resigned the day before Nixon's speech. Out of loyalty to Kissinger, they did so quietly. Later, Morris told Seymour Hersh that the decision not to call a news conference at the time of the resignation was "the biggest failure of my life. We didn't do so on the single calculation that it would destroy Henry. I knew the administration was squalid, but there still was this enormous illusion about Henry. I clung to the delusion that the man was still rational and that even his own strong sense of self-survival would keep him out of real trouble. In effect, it was my theory of the limits of the ruthlessness of Henry Kissinger; in truth, there were no limits."[23]

On April 30, 1970, in an eerie echo of the Hitler speech Meldon Levine had quoted to Harvard parents and alumni, Richard M. Nixon warned his fellow countrymen that they were living in an "age of anarchy." He had written the speech himself, rejecting proferred revisions from Kissinger and finishing it at four-fifteen in the morning of the day he delivered it, voice slightly slurred, to the nation. The speech was full of lies, some outright, such as the assertion of consistent respect for Cambodian neutrality, some the product of self-delusion, such as the notion that this time COSVN would be located and eliminated. Yet whatever its inaccuracies about Cambodia, the address starkly revealed Nixon's understanding of the world. It was a world full of danger:

> We see mindless attacks on all the great institutions which have been created by free civilization in the last five hundred years. Even here in the United States, great universities are being systematically destroyed. Small nations all over the world find themselves under attack from within and from without.

It was a world whose most powerful country, the United States, could be reduced to a "pitiful, helpless giant." In Cambodia, not America's power but its "will and character" were being tested. Indeed, what was at issue was not Cambodia at all: "If we fail to meet this challenge, all other nations will be on notice that despite its overwhelming power the United States, when a real crisis comes, will be found wanting." Joseph Heller's satire of this mad logic in his novel *Good As Gold* did not exaggerate: "If we are willing to go to war everytime our vital interests are at stake, then I say we must go to war every time our vital interests are NOT at stake, to make sure friend and foe alike understand we will."

Even Lon Nol was shocked. He had not been informed of Nixon's decision and learned about it from the American chargé d'affaires, who had himself heard the news only as he listened to Nixon's speech over Voice of America.

The reaction to Nixon's speech was a rush of protest that swept college campuses, professional circles, Congress, government agencies, even the cabinet. Over one third of all the colleges and universities in the country simply shut down as faculty and students joined in protest; two hundred and fifty employees of the State Department, including fifty Foreign Service officers, signed a letter of protest to Secretary of State William Rogers; the commissioner of education dissociated himself from Nixon's war policies; and the secretaries of the interior and of health, education, and welfare defended student protest. On the other side, resistance to this wave of dissent matched it in passion. A furious Nixon denounced the demonstrators as "bums . . . blowin' up the campuses." Vice President Agnew and the governor of Ohio, James Rhodes, both compared the protesters to Nazi Stormtroopers, Brown Shirts, Communists, and the KKK. Governor Rhodes swore that in his state they would not "treat the symptoms" but "eradicate the problem."[24]

The National Guard unit Rhodes ordered onto the campus of Kent State University on May 4, 1970, was as good as his word, firing on a group of fifteen students and killing four. Two days later, two protesting students were killed at Jackson State College in Mississippi. "What are we going to do to get more respect for the police from our young people?" Nixon asked the president of Jackson State. Secretary of the Interior Warren Hickel was fired; Rogers was instructed to hand over the names of the two hundred and fifty dissenting State Department employees (he refused); and when a group of construction workers in New York City violently attacked a peaceful protest, the White House proclaimed the hard hat a symbol of high patriotism. Kissinger thought the President's speech a bit "self-pitying" and "vainglorious"; nonetheless the "merits of the case were overwhelming."

In his speech, televised from the Oval Office of the White House,

Nixon had compared the order to invade Cambodia to other "great decisions" taken by his predecessors: "In this room, Woodrow Wilson made the great decisions which led to victory in World War I, Franklin Roosevelt made the decisions which led to our victory in World War II. . . ." Yet in an attempt to still the uproar his decision had engendered, Nixon promised the rapid withdrawal of the invading force, which made nonsense of the military arguments he had used to explain the action. At a news conference on May 8, he announced that most U.S. troops would leave Cambodia by the second week in June, and by July 1 the entire force would be withdrawn. He insisted that "at the same time we are cleaning out the enemy sanctuaries in Cambodia, we will pursue the path of peace at the negotiating table [in Paris]. . . ."

That night, as demonstrators gathered from all over the country to protest the Cambodian invasion and the killings at Kent State and Jackson State, Nixon had trouble sleeping. He returned telephone calls until around two-fifteen in the morning, slept until sometime after 4:00 A.M., wandered into the Lincoln Sitting Room to listen to a Rachmaninoff concerto, and then, looking out of the window, saw the protesters beginning to gather on the Mall. Have you ever seen the Lincoln Memorial at night? Nixon asked his valet, Manolo Sanchez, who had come to ask if the president wanted coffee or hot chocolate. Sanchez, a newly naturalized citizen, had not. So, accompanied only by the Secret Service, Nixon and Manolo went out into the night.

Reading Nixon's eight-page memorandum on the event written several days later, it is clear the president saw himself as the heroic figure in an epic of transcendent significance. The president of the world's most powerful democracy would visit the memorial of his great predecessor, accompanied by his manservant, with whom he was in easy, democratic accord, and speak to the people directly. At the Lincoln Memorial, Nixon pointed out the major inscriptions to Manolo and then walked over to a group of young anti-war demonstrators. He, the president; they, citizens of the Great Republic. He knew that most of his staff wouldn't understand: "to their credit, [they] are enormously interested in material things . . . but . . . very few seem to have any interest and, therefore, have no ability to communicate on those matters that are infinitely more important—qualities of spirit, emotion, of the depth and mystery of life which this whole visit really was all about." He could have just debated policy with the students, but that wasn't the point. The major contribution he could make to them "was to try to lift them a bit out of the miserable intellectual wasteland in which they now wander aimlessly around." And so Nixon, like Virgil in one of the circles of Hell, approached the students:

> They were not unfriendly. As a matter of fact, they seemed somewhat
> overawed. . . . To get the conversation going I asked them how old
> they were, what they were studying, the usual questions. I asked how
> many of them had been to Washington before. . . . I told them that
> it was a beautiful city, that I hoped they enjoyed their visit there, that
> I wanted them, of course, to attend the anti-war demonstration, to
> listen to all the speakers; that I hoped that they had the time to take
> a tour of the city and see some of the historical monuments.

Nixon explained that he shared the protesters' goals, "to stop the killing and end the war to bring peace. Our goal was not to get into Cambodia by what we were doing but to get out of Vietnam." The students kept their own counsel. No, really, Nixon explained; he did. Probably they all thought he was an "S.O.B. but I want you to know that I understand just how you feel." He himself had thought Chamberlain a great hero after Munich. The students were still silent so Nixon tried to "move the conversation into areas where I could draw them out." Travel, he advised the group, travel was the thing. The United States first, but then Mexico, Central America, Asia. Everyone else would tell them to go to Europe and that was okay. "Europe was fine, but it's really an older version of America."

And on he went, "touching lightly on places like Malaysia," urging environmental issues, suggesting India as a good place to visit and praising the people of Haiti who were poor but had great "dignity and grace which was very moving." Manolo kept trying to get him back to the limousine, but Nixon continued until "dawn was upon us, the first rays of the sun began to show and they began to climb up over the Washington Monument. . . ." After having his picture taken with a "bearded fellow from Detroit," Nixon proceeded to the Capitol, where he gave Manolo a brief tour and told him to sit in the Speaker's Chair. After which the expanded party (Nixon's personal physician, press secretary Ron Ziegler, White House aide Bud Krogh) went to the Mayflower Hotel restaurant for breakfast (corned beef hash and poached egg for the president), and so home to the White House.[25]

The scene is hallucinogenic. How could those students and that president occupy the same historical moment? Students who had traveled through the night to protest the policies of a murderous president; the president himself, avuncular, welcoming them to the capital, hoping they'd take in a few of the sights before they left. It should have been played against a curtain painted by Bosch or Goya, bombs falling, people grievously wounded, the dead. The president before dawn in earnest dialogue with the students is a vision not so much of the banality of evil as of the evil of banality, for Nixon believed his homilies about the broadening effect of travel, the grace of native peoples, the magnificence of America. In his sentimental embrace of Lincoln, of the students, of the newly naturalized Manolo, lay the justification, indeed the mandate, for the destruction of Vietnam, Cambodia, and Laos.

Neither at his May 8 news conference nor in his early morning talk with the students did Nixon mention his initiation of an elaborate, and illegal, domestic surveillance plan, to be supervised by a former Army Intelligence Officer named Tom Charles Huston. Nor did he announce his order to resume the bombing of North Vietnam. "As soon as the President finishes his press conference," the poet Robert Bly wrote, "black wings carry off the words,/ bits of flesh still clinging to them."

In the middle of the month of May 1970, as the anger and agitation over the Cambodian invasion continued to swirl around the White House, Nixon distributed Purple Hearts handsewn by the girlfriend of his old friend and drinking buddy, Bebe Rebozo. "For all the wounds you have sustained in the line of duty over the past few weeks," Nixon explained, as he handed them out to Haldeman, Erlichman, and Kissinger.[26]

Nixon's "madman" strategy, designed to frighten foreigners, succeeded as well in scaring Americans, especially those who sat in Congress. Increasingly the issue was not only the war and its conduct but the system of checks and balances, of separation of powers that were presumed to safeguard the country from tyranny, as sixth-grade civics teachers had dutifully taught their students since at least the Civil War. The legitimacy of congressional concern is reflected in Nixon's post-Watergate response to an interviewer's question about the patently illegal tactics of domestic surveillance, infiltration, and harassment of opposition groups and individuals he had authorized Tom Huston to explore in May 1970. How could Nixon justify his approval? "Well," the ex-president answered, "when the President does it, that means it is not illegal."[27]

To constrain the acts of a president with so imperial an understanding of his powers was extremely difficult, given the narrow parameters within which most congressmen felt it was safe to operate. Congress attached riders to military appropriation bills which were intended to limit the acts of war Nixon could take; the president's supporters in Congress lobbied to incorporate loopholes which, in essence, allowed

Nixon to do anything that was not specifically prohibited. Nevertheless, immediately after the invasion of Cambodia, Senators Frank Church and John Sherman Cooper proposed an amendment to the Foreign Military Sales Act that in forthright language sought to bar all forms of direct military action or assistance to the government of Lon Nol. U.S. troops were to leave Cambodia by June 30; there was to be no U.S. combat support for Cambodian military operations, nor U.S. advisers to Cambodian troops, nor the hiring of other nationals to advise those troops. Which would seem to have covered the situation.

The Nixon administration worked for months to modify the impact of the Cooper-Church proposal; by the time the amendment finally passed Congress, on the last day of December 1970, it contained a saving loophole allowing the president to act so as to "protect the lives of United States armed forces wherever deployed." Thus every military appropriation bill from 1970 on, P. Edward Haley notes, "prohibited direct American combat support of the Lon Nol government unless such support was coincidental with action taken to protect the withdrawal of U.S. forces from Indochina and the return of all prisoners of war."[28] The military quickly discovered that the world was full of just such coincidences.

In the course of the compromise and concession that surrounded passage of the Cooper-Church Amendment, the specific ban on combat air support to Cambodian troops was dropped. Indeed, close air support missions increased after the amendment passed Congress; as did military aid to Lon Nol's army; as did Cambodian and American casualties. Nixon was free to bomb Cambodia, P. Edward Haley concludes, not because Congress approved it, but because it had not explicitly prohibited it. For the next three years, until the passage of the War Powers Act in 1973, Congress and the executive would fight repeated guerrilla skirmishes over amendments to appropriations bills, as Nixon sought to maintain the widest possible latitude for the continued use of force and Congress attempted, slowly and clumsily, sometimes ambivalently, to shut the war machine down.

Meanwhile, under the code name FREEDOM DEAL, tactical fighter bombers flew eight thousand missions over Cambodia between July 1970 and February 1971. By the summer of 1970, much of Cambodia had become a free fire zone. Yet the net impact of the invasion on the policy it was allegedly undertaken to support was minor. "The South Vietnamese are wandering all over Cambodia protecting the [Lon Nol] government," Secretary of Defense Melvin Laird complained, "while we, in turn, are in South Vietnam protecting the South Vietnamese."[29]

If the invasion of Cambodia was intended to protect the process of

"Vietnamization"—the return of the conduct of the war to the South Vietnamese government and army—the invasion of Laos by ARVN troops in February 1971 was intended to demonstrate that the ARVN were capable of handling the task. The plan called for Saigon troops fighting on their own (albeit with full American air support) to attack the Lao sector of the Ho Chi Minh Trail, search for and destroy known concentrations of North Vietnamese and NLF troops and supplies, and thoroughly disrupt any plans they may have had for a dry season offensive in 1971 or 1972. Standard American distrust for its military ally deepened in the course of this operation, as it became clear that full intelligence of the operation, down to the location of the helicopter landing zones, had been leaked to the NLF by its agents inside the Saigon government and military. The ARVN was ambushed, its offensive smashed, and its army sent headlong into disorderly retreat.

Intense U.S. air attacks (48,000 tons of bombs were dropped) and evacuation procedures probably kept casualties down, though still they amounted to 45 percent of the attacking force (1,146 killed; 4,236 wounded; 246 missing; out of the 659 U.S. helicopters used to airlift ARVN troops into battle, 453 were damaged and 90 lost). American news media had been barred from the initial assault, but they were present in full for the retreat, recording desperate soldiers clinging to the skids of evacuation helicopters (sometimes causing them to crash, so that American crews took to coating the skids with grease) and pushing wounded comrades out of the way in their scramble to escape. The Laos invasion, Kissinger wrote years later, "was a splendid project on paper. Its chief drawback, as events showed, was that it in no way accorded with Vietnamese realities."

Still, the Nixon White House had learned a bit more about American realities. There were no U.S. ground forces involved (thanks to Cooper-Church prohibitions); nor were there any major anti-war demonstrations. And the president avoided making any dramatic speeches. Instead, he chose February 8, the opening day of the invasion, to release a position paper on improving the environment. Nixon introduced his proposals with a quotation from T. S. Eliot's play, *Murder in the Cathedral:* "Clean the air! Clean the sky! Wash the wind!" Perhaps the choice arose from the murky depths of Nixon's unconscious, or perhaps a dovish speechwriter intended the curious reader to look up the rest of the speech: "The land is foul, the water is foul, our/beasts and ourselves defiled with blood./A rain of blood has blinded my eyes."[30]

CHAPTER THIRTEEN

"A Savage Retreat" (1971–1973)[1]

... one Province Senior Advisor began his review of the security situation with a series of colored charts indicating changes in the security situation in the province since 1968. When asked what the corresponding situation had been in 1966 or earlier, he replied that he did not know. Another American present, whose knowledge of the province dated back to the early 1960s, then noted that the districts which the advisor had described as the most insecure today, and in which government search and destroy operations were then being planned, were the very districts that had constituted the province's most serious security problems 10 years ago.

—VIETNAM: MAY 1972. STAFF
REPORT FOR THE SENATE FOREIGN
RELATIONS COMMITTEE

We are to be blamed for not doing in 1969 what we did in 1972. . . . That's the lesson I am learning from it. . . . You do not have the choice to lose with moderation. If you use power, you must prevail.

—HENRY KISSINGER IN *The Wall
Street Journal,* FEBRUARY 14, 1985

THE Cambodian invasion had forcibly reminded Americans that despite some troop withdrawals, the war continued; and despite the lowered draft calls there was an ongoing deposit of fresh young American soldiers in Vietnam.* In December 1970, one such

*Nixon ended all student and occupational deferments in favor of a lottery in 1971; the draft itself ended in January 1972.

254

recent arrival wrote his parents a series of reassuring letters but was more honest with a friend:

> I'm so embittered I don't believe it—but there is nothing you can do. . . . And it seems no one gives a damn besides us grunts in the bush. You people in the world don't know what's happening because the Army won't let you know and the goddamn lifers . . . could care less—as long as the [American] death count is reasonable—say under 40 a week.

Private Kingsley had watched a medivac operation that was accidentally hit by "friendly fire," injuring everyone and killing four; Vietnamese children spat at him and "there's a bitter hatred between us and the South Vietnamese troops because . . . we do all the goddamn fighting while they sit on their asses all the time." Waiting to be attacked, fearing death and injury, "how do you blow off steam?" My Lai, Kingsley wrote his friend, was one answer, but other soldiers "take it out on the Army; in Nam they average two frags a week (fragging is where a man simply pulls the pin on a hand grenade and tosses it at a lifer)."[2] For obvious reasons the precise number of fraggings is difficult to determine, though official Army figures list a minimum of 788 incidents (with 86 deaths) for the period 1969–72, more than enough to worry the Pentagon.

Nor could those who came home always leave the war behind them; it stuck, psychic napalm, burning their imaginations. Abruptly shipped home from the battlefield as if where they had been and what they had done was nothing out of the ordinary, met with inappropriate congratulations or hostility they did not feel they deserved, veterans were perhaps most disturbed by the overwhelming indifference they encountered. People seemed not to know they had even been away, or what had happened to them on the other side of the world. Some veterans found themselves able to talk only with others who had been there, while the traditional veterans' organizations, the VFW or the American Legion, whose members seemed to have fought in quite other sorts of wars, were irrelevant or worse.

In 1967, a group of young men who had fought in Vietnam organized Vietnam Veterans Against the War (VVAW). For them, struggling to end the war was the only way to make sense of the 365 days they had spent fighting it. Until 1971, members of VVAW participated in peace events organized, in the main, by others. Then in January and February of 1971, in deliberate counterpoint to the trial of a young lieutenant, William L. Calley, whom the Army had decided to hold primarily responsible for the massacre of civilians at My Lai, the VVAW invited veterans to conduct an investigation of the conduct of the war in general. Al Hubbard, executive secretary of VVAW, said their purpose was to show that "My Lai was not an isolated incident" but "only a minor step beyond the standard official United States policy in Indochina." For three days, over one hundred veterans and sixteen civilians described their acts of war in a downtown Detroit Howard Johnson motel. The "Winter Soldier Investigation" took its name from Tom Paine, invoking his contempt for the "summer soldier and the sunshine patriot."

The witnesses, whose testimony sometimes sounded like a confession, described acts they had witnessed, acts they had performed: rape, torture, petty brutalities, the routine killing of non-combatants. Sergeant Jamie Henry, after recounting the execution of nineteen women and children during his tour (which he had reported, without effect), explained: "you are trained 'gook, gook, gook' and once the military has got the idea implanted in you that these people are not humans . . . it makes it a little bit easier to kill 'em." Racism and dehumanization, Henry elaborated, accounted for the ease with which atrocities took place. There was one further element: "It doesn't take very long for an infantryman in the field to realize that he is fighting for nobody's freedom. You can ask any of the men here. They may have thought they were fighting to protect their mother when they got there, but they sure didn't believe that very long. . . . You're just getting your asses shot up and all you want to do is go home."[3]

In June 1971, Marine Colonel Robert Heinl wrote an article for the *Armed Forces Journal* detailing what he called the "collapse" of the armed forces. By every indicator, Heinl insisted, "our army that now remains in Vietnam is in a state approaching collapse, with individual units avoiding or having refused combat, murdering their officers and noncommissioned officers, drug-ridden, and dispirited where not near-mutinous." To this daunting list, Heinl added race war, sedition (he pointed to 144 underground newspapers, 14 GI dissent organizations, off-base coffeehouses, symbolic peace fasts by active-duty soldiers, and the "booing and cursing of officers and even of hapless entertainers such as Bob Hope"), and startlingly high desertion rates in all services, expressing the "lowest state of military morale in the history of the country."[4] Given the disintegration of the American military in the field, it is clear that Vietnamization was a matter not of choice but of necessity. The ARVN had better fight their war, because the U.S. Army would have difficulty doing it for very much longer.

In one respect, Vietnam had become a society of abundance: hard and soft drugs, in quantities and quality unimaginable on the city streets of "the world" (the GIs' name for the United States) were readily available to American soldiers and supplied by high-ranking Saigon military officers, including, it was rumored, Vice-President Nguyen Cao Ky. Americans profited as well. In 1970, the command pilot for the American ambassador was caught with $8 million worth of heroin in his plane. By 1973, a conservative Pentagon estimate reluctantly admitted that 35 percent of all enlisted men in the Army were known to have tried heroin; 20 percent became addicted during their tour of duty in Vietnam. Perhaps hoping to distract potential addicts, the military began allowing prostitutes to work in the barracks on some major bases.

Military authorities liked to think of all this as a technical problem. "Morale" had to be built, cultivated; its decay halted, turned around. The American fighting man, the best in the world, had only to be properly "motivated." Private Kingsley, for one, was immune: "I'll tell you, man, if I ever get back there and hear someone say Viet Nam was worthwhile or it was our obligation—I'll hit him right in the face," he wrote to his friend. "Because this is nothing but a shame. . . ." After seeing an ad for Vietnam Veterans Against the War in *Playboy* magazine, Kingsley and a friend "got the whole squad together and joined in each sending a contribution. We also all signed a petition stating our feelings and gave it to the CO." One month later, Kingsley was dead. "He was on a military mission," the Army telegram read, "when an automatic explosive device placed by a friendly force detonated."[5]

Had Kingsley lived and gotten home in time, he might have participated in one of the most compelling anti-war demonstrations of the entire conflict. In February 1969, the 3rd Marine Division had been sent into Laos in an operation code-named DEWEY CANYON I. DEWEY CANYON II was the American name for the ARVN invasion of Laos in February 1971. Now there was DEWEY CANYON III: for five days in April 1971, from the 19th to the 23rd, those who had fought the war demonstrated against it in Washington, D.C., throwing their medals, their campaign ribbons, their insignia of rank over a high wood and wire barrier erected to separate them from the government that had sent them to Vietnam. The organizers, Vietnam Veterans Against the War, called it a "limited incursion into the country of Congress." Gloria Emerson has described it best:

> They started to come on a Friday, an eccentric, a strange-looking army, wearing fatigues and field jackets, helmets and their old boonie hats, the same boots they had worn in Vietnam. Some brought bed-

rolls and all slept outdoors on a camping site on a small quadrangle of the Mall. . . . All came with their discharge papers so their bitterest critics could not accuse them of being imposters, although some did anyway. There were a few men who did not have two legs, a few who could not rise from wheelchairs, but they were in good spirits and among their own.

They marched from the Lincoln Memorial to Arlington Cemetery, where they were refused entrance. They lobbied Congress and listened to hearings on the war. They returned to Arlington with a contingent of Gold Star mothers and were allowed to enter. They conducted a sit-in on the steps of the Supreme Court protesting the unconstitutionality of the war.

A middle-aged man from Russell, Pennsylvania, wearing the fatigue jacket of his dead son, blew taps before the medals went back. Sometimes, after a man hurled a bit of a ribbon or a Bronze Star or a Purple Heart . . . he would break down and be hugged by other men. . . . Some threw in fury, others in sorrow, but nearly all made faces as they did it.

John Kerry, one of the organizers, spoke before the Senate Foreign Relations Committee. He had undertaken, he said, this one last mission,

to search out and destroy the last vestige of this barbaric war, to pacify our own hearts, to conquer the hate and the fear that have driven this country these last ten years and more, so when thirty years from now our brothers go down the street without a leg, without an arm, or a face, and small boys ask why, we will be able to say "Vietnam" and not mean a desert, not a filthy obscene memory, but mean instead the place where America finally turned and where soldiers like us helped in the turning.[6]

DEWEY CANYON III ended on April 23. On April 24, over 500,000 demonstrators arrived in Washington to protest the war, and for days thereafter, anti-war and welfare activists lobbied Congress insisting upon the link between poverty in the United States and war abroad. Increasingly Washington looked like a city under military occupation. On May 3, 30,000 demonstrators, promising to "stop the government" if the government refused to stop the war, faced 5,100 Washington police, 1,500 National Guardsmen, 500 National Park Police, 10,000 federal troops, and wave upon wave of tear gas. As demonstrators moved to block cars coming to work early that Monday morning, the arrests began, hundreds and hundreds, mostly without benefit of due process. On May 4, over one thousand four hundred people were arrested on the steps of Congress, while four representatives—Bella Abzug, Ronald Dellums, Charles Rangel, and Parren Mitchell—who had come to listen to the grievances of their constituents protested in vain.

Among those who tried to block traffic on May 4 was Henry Kissinger's onetime adviser, Daniel Ellsberg. An ex-Marine and former Pentagon staff aide, Ellsberg had publicly, if politely, protested Nixon's war policy in mid-1969 in a letter to the president co-signed by five colleagues at RAND. In May 1970, six years after he had served as a government spokesman at the very first anti-war teach-in, Ellsberg changed sides at an anti-war rally at Georgetown University. He was convinced that the Nixon White House would continue to pursue the war; he was appalled at the "madman" theory, and frustrated at the resistance he encountered in the press when he explained it. And then what Ellsberg believed to be one more lie, a small one, by Secretary of the Army Stanley R. Resor about who had ordered the dismissal of charges against six Special Forces men accused of an assassination, pushed him into more direct action. "This is a system that I had served for fifteen years," Ellsberg told Seymour Hersh. "It is a system that lies automatically from top to bottom to protect a cover-up murder. I've got a safe full of documents that are full of lies."

The documents were the heart of the history of the war Ellsberg and his colleagues had worked on for Secretary of Defense Robert McNamara in 1967–68. In 1969, with the help of a fellow RAND employee, Anthony Russo, Ellsberg started to photocopy the contents of his safe.[7] He had given the papers first to Senator Fulbright, in November 1969, hoping the Committee on Foreign Relations would hold public hearings on their contents. But the Committee delayed, uncertain what to do with the documents handed to them, especially after Secretary of Defense Laird refused to declassify any of them.[8] Finally, Ellsberg decided to go to the press.

In late March 1971, after reading a book review by Neil Sheehan in the Sunday *New York Times,* Ellsberg contacted him. This was a logical choice. Ellsberg had known Sheehan in Vietnam; both shared a complex admiration for John Paul Vann and, it was now apparent, a deep abhorrence for the war. For in Sheehan's compendium review of thirty-three books on the war, he had asked the question, should the United States have a war crimes trial? And answered it: "if you credit as factual only a fraction of the information assembled here about what happened in Vietnam, and if you apply the laws of war to American conduct there, then the leaders of the United States for the past six years at least, including the incumbent President, Richard Milhous Nixon, may well be guilty of war crimes." The documents in Ellsberg's possession, soon to become public property as the Pentagon Papers, were material for the prosecution, as McNamara himself had remarked when the study was first presented to him in 1968. On June 13, in a deliberately low-key fashion, *The New York Times* began publishing excerpts from Ellsberg's documents.

It was hardly the first time secret documents had been published in a daily newspaper. Indeed, leaking documents to the press was a standard practice of bureaucratic warfare. But these secret documents were different, leaked not by an official in pursuit of some official gain but by a dissident in pursuit of a reversal of government policy. The Papers "chronicled a major breakdown of democratic government," Jonathan Schell wrote, "for the overall effect of the Johnson war policy had been deception of the public on the most important issue facing the country at the moment it was choosing its President."[9]

To the Nixon White House, as guilty as Johnson of treating "what it said and what it did as two separate matters," the publication of the Papers was a complicated business. On the one hand, insofar as they supplied documents critical of two Democratic administrations, they could be useful politically. On the other, an administration as deeply engaged in covert activities as the Nixon White House could hardly take the unauthorized disclosure of government documents lightly. Nixon's first action was to punish the *Times.* In a memo to Haldeman on June 15, Nixon ordered that "under *no circumstances* is anyone connected with the White House to give any interview to a member of the staff of the *New York Times* without my express permission. I want you to enforce this. . . ." And in case Haldeman didn't understand, Nixon repeated it: "Under absolutely no circumstances is anyone on the White House staff on *any subject* to respond to an inquiry from the *New York Times* unless and until I give express permission (and I do not expect to give such permission in the foreseeable future)." The decision was taken "because of the national interest" and "is not subject to appeal or further discussion unless I bring it up myself."[10]

A court injunction against the *Times* stopped the presses for a while; and a discussion of how further to punish those responsible consumed Nixon's inner circle. It was important, Nixon aides agreed, to separate possession and publication of the Papers from their contents. Ellsberg had stolen government documents and the *Times* had published them. Both must be dealt with. On the other hand, the "Kennedy/Johnson Papers," as the White House called them, could be useful. Kissinger, in an effort to distance himself as far as possible from Ellsberg, did not hesitate to describe him in lurid language. "We were told," Erlichman remembered, that Ellsberg "was a fanatic, known to be a drug abuser and in knowledge of very critical defense secrets of current validity, such as nuclear deterrent targeting." In other meetings Kissinger described Ellsberg as a sexual pervert, a murderer of Vietnamese civilians, a man who " 'must be stopped at all costs.' "[11]

The cost included the expansion of illegal wiretaps and the organization of what one memo called a "nonlegal team" to investigate all possible sources of leaks and deal with them. These "White House plumbers" included former CIA and FBI operatives E. Howard Hunt and G. Gordon Liddy, as well as staff members from the State Department, the Defense Department, the Attorney General's Office, the National Security Council, and offices of close presidential advisers like John Erlichman, H. R. Haldeman, and Charles Colson. This high-powered underground team took Daniel Ellsberg as its first project. Ellsberg had been indicted under the Espionage Act at the end of June. But legal prosecution was the least of their plans for him. As the 1972 elections approached, the secret team developed "scenarios" that would discredit Ellsberg and "destroy his public image," and through him the Democratic Party. In pursuit of the first end, plans were made to burglarize the office of Ellsberg's psychiatrist.

More broadly, Haldeman decided, the Papers should be used to "poison the Democratic well."[12] This process took two forms. First, anyone suspected of involvement in their release was to be wiretapped and publicly pilloried. At the same time, the Papers were to be closely studied for "politically damaging material involving the Democratic hierarchy." Perhaps it would be good tactics to defend Johnson, Colson suggested, which would make those who now attacked him look bad. "We could of course plant and try to prove the thesis that Bobby Kennedy was behind the preparation of these papers because he planned to use them to overthrow Lyndon Johnson. . . ." And then, yielding to the great temptation of any fantasist to believe in his own inventions, Colson added parenthetically: "(I suspect there may be more truth than fantasy to this)."[13] If the Papers themselves did not say quite what the White House wished them to say, forge them. Ellsberg was to be prosecuted for releasing the actual documents; E. Howard Hunt was set the task of forging cables that would directly tie John F. Kennedy to the murder of Diem.[14]

Kissinger had remarked on the perfection of the plans to invade Laos, which were marred only by their failure to conform to the reality of the situation. The Nixon White House solution to this dilemma was simple, even elegant: reality was what people believed to be the case. If you could not change the situation itself, change what people believed about the situation. Forged documents, persuasive lies, cooperative newsmen, opponents discredited by stolen medical records, planted stories, or the activities of agents provocateurs were all the "reality" necessary. In a sense, this was no more than the Kennedy doctrine of credibility extended, expanded, and domesticated. It would now receive its most difficult test: was it possible to make war look like peace? This was the burden of the 1972 election campaign.

Sometimes Richard Milhous Nixon found the constraints of the American system of government intolerably frustrating. His authorization of illegal taps, searches, surveillance, infiltration of enemy organizations—including the Democratic Party—"dirty tricks," and disinformation probably stemmed from his impatience with more stately political procedures. During the demonstrations in May 1971 he had welcomed a suggestion by Haldeman that the White House call on the Teamsters for help. Nixon was enthusiastic: "They, they've got guys who'll go in and knock their heads off. . . . Murderers. . . . They're gonna beat the shit out of these people."[15] But having demonstrators beaten up, however pleasant a prospect, was of limited utility. Far more important was Nixon's effort to obscure what it was they protested. As far as possible, the war's ongoing reality had to be kept at a distance from the American public.

"The American voter is willing to vote for Nixon now," one television news executive told a British journalist, "because the voter, who is also the viewer, thinks that Nixon has ended the war. And he has ended the war, because you don't see the war on the tube any more. So the war has ended, though we are bombing the hell out of those poor people, more than ever."[16] And if the war was over, what were all those people doing demonstrating in the streets? Nixon's answer and the campaign strategy that flowed from it were simple: the protesters themselves were the issue—their denigration of American values, their ingratitude to the system that nurtured them, their whining complaints about a war Nixon was clearly ending.

Around the renewed bombing of North Vietnam, and the ongoing pounding of South Vietnam, Laos, and Cambodia, a cloak of invisibility was drawn under whose cover the air war against Indochina might go on forever, a perpetual-motion machine. Few reporters asked questions about it, and those who did had trouble learning anything useful. Tom Oliphant, for example, found it difficult to get statistics on how many bombs were being dropped and where. Oliphant was convinced that if the air war got the same newspaper coverage the ground war had received, the public would respond with equal anger. It was precisely to avoid this consequence that the actual extent of the ongoing war was obscured by the Nixon administration.[17] Part of the reason too was the nature of the air war in 1971 and 1972. "The 'use it or lose it' imperative began to govern the employment of . . . air resources," Major Earl H. Tilford, Jr., has written. "For example, a fixed number of B-52 sorties was available every day throughout Southeast Asia. . . . It seemed that every one of these sorties had to be targeted somewhere, even if the targets justifying a B-52 strike were not available."[18] In the case of North Vietnam, the bombing was disguised as "protective reaction strikes" against anti-aircraft installations which had allegedly fired at unarmed U.S. reconnaissance planes. In fact they hadn't, except in the deliberately falsified reports Air Force General John D. Lavelle submitted for the record.

Briefly, in the summer of 1971, the possibility of peace surfaced, only to be buried once more. In June, Hanoi and the Provisional Revolutionary Government (PRG), the governmental form the NLF had adopted in 1969, responded positively to the first sign of a shift in the U.S. negotiating stance. In late May, Kissinger offered to set a specific date for the complete withdrawal of U.S. troops in return for a cease-fire and the return of all U.S. prisoners of war. For the first time there was no demand for "mutual withdrawal"; North Vietnamese troops in the South were simply not mentioned one way or the other. The secret peace talks in Paris, stalled for months, resumed as for the first time both sides seemed to yield ground on issues that had until then remained unnegotiable. The insistence of both the DRV and the PRG that Nguyen Van Thieu would have to be removed before serious negotiations could take place gave way to a demand that the United States simply stop "supporting" his regime. What made the plan especially feasible was the upcoming presidential election in Saigon. If the United States refrained from interfering in the electoral process, there was a better than even chance that Thieu would be voted out of office. With Thieu defeated, there was real hope for a Saigon government ready to negotiate a political settlement with the PRG. Fair elections in Saigon in October 1971 could fulfill Nixon's expressed wish for peace with honor.

In July, Hanoi and the PRG announced a new seven-point proposal for peace, which spelled out the steps toward the organization of a coalition government in Saigon, the withdrawal of U.S. troops, and the return of all U.S. prisoners of war. Since Hanoi had made the peace proposal public, the administration could not, as Tom Oliphant had found to be its wont, "bury a fact" by not announcing it. Instead, it did the next best thing by systematically distorting the contents. Hanoi, Kissinger insisted, demanded the "overthrow" of Thieu as a precondition for peace, and this obviously dishonorable course was entirely unacceptable. But for Hanoi, as George Kahin learned when he spoke with the leadership in August 1971, the key to peace was to "permit reasonably free elections in South Vietnam—elections that would permit its inhabitants to replace Thieu; that was the *essential* foundation of the proposal that the PRG and Hanoi were offering."[19]

And that was the problem for the United States. "A reasonably" free election would no doubt produce a government anxious to negotiate a neutral solution and, as one of Kissinger's aides told a reporter later, the United States "distrusts neutral solutions, because we would lose control."[20] In his memoirs, Kissinger took ironic note of how troublesome the electoral system, imposed by the United States in 1967, had proven; it was a source of nothing but "turmoil and anxiety." Most distressing was the new policy of the NLF, which focused on getting out the vote instead of boycotting the entire proceedings as in the past.

For a short time it looked as if there might be a three-way electoral contest which Duong Van Minh, who had briefly headed the junta that overthrew Diem in 1963, would most likely win. The only other candidate was Thieu's longtime rival and sometime collaborator, Nguyen Cao Ky. Embassy analysts worried that Ky would split Thieu's usually safe constituency in the military and the bureaucracy, leaving a clear field for Minh, and the likelihood of an opening to the NLF after he took office.

Instead, with the help of the CIA and the embassy, Thieu spent the summer and early fall rigging the election. In addition to mobilizing the secret police to sweep through the countryside making sure people knew for whom they should vote, he realized it would be an altogether easier election if he were the only serious contender. Thieu decided to eliminate Ky as a rival, confident that his control over the state apparatus would be sufficient to contain Minh. Rather than dip into his private funds, Thieu used CIA money to bribe legislators first to pass legislation requiring candidates to obtain the signatures of forty assemblymen in order to qualify for candidacy in the election and then bribing them not to give Ky their signatures. The Supreme Court upheld the procedure and Ky was eliminated. Minh, observing these tactics, contemplated withdrawing, but he was reassured by the American Embassy (anxious to avoid the embarrassment of a one-person "race") that it would force Thieu to conduct a relatively open election.

While Thieu plotted, Minh's strength as a candidate grew. Powerful

Buddhist and Catholic leaders favored his election. As one influential Catholic told George Kahin, Minh was clearly preferable to either Ky or Thieu. "[Minh] could be expected to make one small step in the direction of negotiating with the [NLF] and the NLF, recognizing his character and the sentiments of the Vietnamese backing him, will probably be realistic and clever enough to take two steps towards meeting him half-way."[21] But they were not to get the opportunity. In August, Minh obtained a copy of a secret memorandum to province chiefs throughout Vietnam in which Thieu instructed them in the fine points of electoral fraud. In addition, the Phoenix program was being used to target and eliminate Minh supporters in the countryside. Minh sought an audience with Ambassador Ellsworth Bunker, asking once again for some guarantee of fair elections. The United States, he was told, did not interfere in the internal affairs of another country. Rather than lend legitimacy to the election, Minh politely withdrew from the contest; not even an American offer of $3 million tax-free, proffered to avoid the absurdity of the single presidential slate, could persuade him to run. At Ambassador Bunker's urging, Thieu ordered the Supreme Court to reverse the ruling against Ky's candidacy, but Ky declined the honor.

One group of Americans who had worked in South Vietnam for years took the elections very seriously. The Vietnam Elections Project spent the summer lobbying Congress to support honest elections. At one point the group was able to discuss the situation in Saigon with Kissinger, to whom they complained about the way in which the embassy was helping to rig the elections for Thieu. Kissinger was unmoved. Publicly, the United States insisted that it was maintaining perfect neutrality toward the elections; privately, everyone knew the fix was in. Thieu ran alone, garnering 94.3 percent of the vote. Genuine U.S. neutrality in the 1971 elections would have indicated a readiness to allow the participation of the NLF in the politics of the South. Instead, as one of the negotiators in Paris observed after the war, it was clear that Nixon's goal remained "the maintenance of the Saigon government and not the sharing of power with the PRG. We [saw] that they would like to have all the cake."

Kissinger's memory of the election is different. In his memoir, he recalls only a storm successfully weathered. "It would be preposterous to maintain that Hanoi lamented the absence of a fair election in Saigon. What bothered it was our refusal to use the election as a pretext to decapitate the leadership of the non-Communist political structure in South Vietnam." So long as Washington considered an open political process in the South tantamount to the decapitation of what it termed the "leadership of the . . . political structure in South Vietnam," the war would continue.[22] The week after Thieu's reelection, Kissinger put forward a new peace proposal in Paris which offered the possibility of fair elections in the near future. But it was too late. Le Duc Tho had already left Paris, and Hanoi's response came five months later in the shape of a massive new offensive.

Yet perpetual war was not Nixon's goal, but rather victory. Fearless of contradiction and undaunted by inconsistency, to gain victory Nixon looked for help toward the Soviet Union and the People's Republic of China. Eisenhower had intervened in the affairs of Indochina in order to prevent a world in which China controlled the countries on its periphery. The success of communism in Vietnam was often explained by Washington, against all historical knowledge of the region, as a Chinese triumph. Yet now Nixon sought to persuade the Chinese to assume just the sort of regional hegemonic power it had recently been fundamental U.S. policy to oppose. How else to pressure Hanoi to negotiate on terms acceptable to Washington?

Nixon's approach to China was breathtakingly bold. He had first come to political notice through rich invective against the Democrats who had "lost" China; he had visibly relished threatening China with nuclear attack at the end of the Korean War and then again during the crisis involving Quemoy and Matsu, two Nationalist-held islands close to the Chinese coast. But as early as 1960, Nixon also saw the possible value of a breakthrough in U.S.-China relations, and by 1968 he was in a position to act. "You're not going to believe this," an aide told Roger Morris that year, "but Nixon wants to recognize China." Indeed, until it was actually announced in July 1971, it *was* impossible to believe, for nothing in Nixon's past behavior nor in the nation's current situation—as American soldiers continued to kill and die fighting "Asian communism"—would seem to permit, let alone predict, it.

Rapprochement with China would bring Nixon's foreign policy immense gains. In the midst of war it allowed Nixon to present himself as preeminently a man of peace, an image reinforced in October when he announced that he would follow his journey to Beijing with one to Moscow. Secondly, these summits were bound to exacerbate tension and suspicion between the Soviet Union and China. A third benefit lay in the possibility that the Chinese, with some additional inducements, might now be persuaded to reduce their aid to Hanoi. Finally, any move toward peace was certain to contribute to electoral victory in 1972.

On February 17, 1972, Richard Nixon traveled to China, the first serving American president ever to do so. For the next ten days, Nixon in China dominated the television news. Flanked by TV camera people, he looked upon the Great Wall and pronounced it "very great," and compared his trip to Beijing with the first moon landing. To the pleasure of the entire party, it was discovered that the fine art of Chinese cuisine had not disappeared even during the dark night of Communist rule. Rarely in the history of international tension has an enmity so long sustained disappeared so quickly, almost without trace. Loyal friends of Chiang Kai-shek protested, of course, but the majority of Americans abandoned what politicians had for decades insisted was an ingrained fear and loathing for "Red" China with remarkable ease. Public response to Nixon's trip was puzzled enthusiasm. Anything that brought the world closer to peace, it would seem, was welcome.

Yet despite the best efforts of the Comintern, or its successor, the Cominform, there had never been a monolithic, expansionist world Communist system dominated by Moscow and/or Beijing, although every U.S. president since Harry S Truman claimed to be fighting it. In 1965, Nixon himself had described the Vietnam war as a "confrontation—not fundamentally between Vietnam and the Vietcong or between the United States and the Vietcong—but between the United States and Communist China." The question facing the nation then, in Nixon's judgment, had been: "Do we stop Chinese Communist aggression in Vietnam now or wait until the odds and the risks are much greater?"[23] Now Kissinger and Nixon were definitively taking the beast apart, and it was unclear what they could offer to take its place. Even more unclear was what could justify the war in Vietnam outside of the perpetual-motion machine of American credibility combined with the reasoning of a bully, albeit in Kissinger's case apparently, a reluctant one: "The North Vietnamese were cocksure; it was our duty to prove them wrong. I myself pursued the ambiguities of our complex policy with a heavy heart and not a little foreboding. But there was no acceptable alternative. We had the duty to see it through in a manner that best served its chances for success—because a defeat would not affect our destiny alone: the future of other people depended on their confidence in America."[24]

Engaged in what he thought of as a fundamental redefinition of the world body politic, Kissinger was impatient with crude and anachronistic rhetoric. Yet the task of redefining the world and the proper role of the United States could not go forward until the war in Vietnam was either won or resolved without undue cost to U.S. prestige.

The Nixon summit meetings with the Chinese in February 1972 and the Soviets in October 1972 were intended to bring increased pressure on Hanoi to settle the war on U.S. terms. The Soviets in particular were advised of the operation of "linkage," a Kissinger strategy whereby Soviet action in one sphere (positive or negative) would be rewarded or punished in another, whether or not there was in fact any link between the two events. But the talks in Paris remained deadlocked; if Hanoi's allies would not or could not push it into a peace acceptable to the United States, it was difficult to see how such a peace could be gained. There was, of course, an alternative: direct dealing with the Vietnamese for peace on terms acceptable to them. So long as Nixon and Kissinger interpreted this alternative as defeat, the war would continue.

Nixon's friendly dinners in Beijing, his cheerful exchange of toasts in Moscow were accompanied by an intensification of the air war against North Vietnam. Hanoi had hoped for a healing of the Sino-Soviet split in the light of Vietnam's wartime needs. Instead, it watched its allies compete to be gracious toward its enemy while the bombs continued to fall. To reassure Hanoi, both China and the Soviet Union significantly increased their military aid; but at the same time the Chinese had begun to suggest that Hanoi consider stepping down the war in the South, settling in for long-term guerrilla warfare rather than looking toward victory in the near future. It was clear that in the future Hanoi could expect growing pressure from both allies for major compromises with the United States.

If Hanoi felt under pressure from Beijing to settle on terms it considered unacceptable, Nixon and Kissinger faced a different but no less compelling force: the U.S. Congress. If they did not succeed in ending the war in Vietnam soon, Congress would end it through the simple mechanism of cutting off funds. To avoid this, as well as to sabotage the Democrats, Kissinger released the text of the last secret peace proposal to the press in January 1972, shortly before Nixon's scheduled visit to China. It appeared remarkably generous: an electoral commission that included the NLF, Thieu's resignation one month before new elections, a cease-fire throughout Indochina, the return of U.S. prisoners in return for a withdrawal of American troops. But, unnoticed by most, the terms had actually hardened: troop withdrawal, once more, would have to be "mutual."

It was a brilliant ploy. Many congressional critics now praised Nixon as a serious peacemaker; even more important, those who persisted in criticizing him could be readily portrayed as either interfering with the peace process, urging U.S. surrender, or both. The instructions to the president's speechwriters were explicit: "Now [the president's] proposal has been made and has so clearly shown that the United States has offered everything that any honorable government could offer, [his critics] are consciously giving aid and comfort to the enemy. They want the United States to surrender." When Democratic presidential hopeful Senator Edmund Muskie proposed an alternative peace plan, one in fact much closer to what Hanoi would have accepted, he was silenced by the unanswerable charge that he was sabotaging ongoing negotiations, for the Vietnamese had not yet formally rejected Kissinger's proposal. As a way of negotiating peace, the administration's publication of its last offer left much to be desired; as a means of disarming opposition at home, it was perfect.[25]

At dawn on March 30, 1972, tanks and troops of the People's Army of North Vietnam rolled across the demilitarized zone in the first of a three-pronged offensive whose force and power should have been, but were not, expected. Preparations for the offensive had been as bold and open as Nixon's trips to China. In the mountains where the Laos, Cambodian, and Vietnamese borders meet, American advisers on advanced fire bases could hear the bulldozers of the North Vietnamese engineer corps widening old roads and building new ones. Using tanks and heavy artillery, a combined force totaling 200,000 (of which only 35,000 to 40,000 were North Vietnamese regulars) swept aside ARVN defenses, challenging the premise as well as the substance of Vietnamization. For Hanoi, this was the main point of the entire effort: to demonstrate to Nixon that Vietnamization would not work, that his administration would have to sit down to serious negotiations or look forward to an endless war in Vietnam.

At its maximum, the leadership hoped, the offensive might actually cause the collapse of the Saigon government; at the very least, it promised a victory over the ARVN as visible and significant for the policy of Vietnamization as its defeat of Lam Son 719 (the ARVN invasion of Laos) had been a year earlier. Despite American airpower, ARVN troops steadily retreated; by April, the Saigon government had lost control of the area north of Quang Tri City; on May 1, the NLF flag flew over the entire province and the road to Hue lay open as the ARVN fled, abandoning equipment as they went.

The advance was so rapid it took Hanoi by surprise, and instead of going on to seize Hue, the offensive hesitated and stalled. The villagers in places like My Thuy Phuong, southwest of Hue, had the impression less of victory for the Front and Hanoi than of government defeat. "We saw the Third Division [AVRN] soldiers coming through here," one student told an American. "Some of them walked, some of them came by buses, trucks, or motorcycles they stole. It was very frightening, because those soldiers completely lacked discipline. It made us think that the Government was losing the war."[26]

General Creighton Abrams seems to have thought so, too. On the day Quang Tri City fell, he cabled Washington that he felt "it was quite possible that the South Vietnamese have lost their will to fight, or to hang together, and that the whole thing may well be lost." Even where the offensive failed to take territory, it changed the local balance of forces. As the ARVN 2nd Division was drawn out of Quang Ngai Province to defend Hue, local NLF forces moved rapidly to recover territory recently lost to the process of pacification as practiced by the Phoenix program. In the Delta, too, Communist control was reestablished as the ARVN retreated and local guerrilla forces were once more able to move freely.[27]

Binh Dinh Province on the Central Coast, where pacification was supposed to have entirely eliminated the NLF, turned out to be remarkably hostile. "Friendly troops may bug out at any time," an American adviser to the government troops advised his superiors. "Request guidance. If friendlies bug out before guidance arrives, will bug out with them." And he did, while around him ARVN soldiers "were reverting to instant peasants, tossing away M-16s rifles and helmets and combat web gear and stripping off boots and uniforms to run across the paddies in bare feet and undershorts." There were refinements on the messy retreat from Laos as ARVN MPs sold seats on evacuation helicopters to the highest bidder while the wounded lay waiting and often dying nearby.

In the highlands, the attackers came close to taking it all. One analyst argues that a lack of a "tradition of pursuit" alone explains the failure of the North Vietnamese to move on the strategic town of Kontum. "If Kontum had fallen in 1972," Neil Sheehan writes, "the panic that was always just waiting beneath the surface on the Saigon side would have burst forth in an uncontrollable contagion in II Corps. The Highlands would have been lost, and much of the Central Coast would have become untenable." Instead, as after the capture of Quang Tri, the North Vietnamese paused, giving the Saigon government troops time to regroup and dig in for the defense of the city. In direct if unofficial command of the ARVN army was an American, John Paul Vann, who pulled every available ARVN unit into the battle.

What turned the tide, however, was not his leadership but American firepower. In one three-week period, Vann ordered three hundred B-52 strikes in and around Kontum, then circled the huge craters they left, firing his M-16 at survivors, or ordering Cobra gunships in to do the job. Having earlier argued passionately against big-unit warfare, insisting there was no need to use a rifle where a rapier would do, Vann was now as passionate in his admiration of the B-52, telling a reporter during the battle for Kontum: "Anytime the wind is blowing from the north where the B-52 strikes are turning the terrain into a moonscape, you can tell from the battlefield stench that the strikes are effective. Outside Kontum, wherever you dropped bombs, you scattered bodies."[28]

Bodies were scattered also around An Loc on the Cambodian border, and in much of the Mekong Delta, which was subject to the heaviest B-52 bombing of the entire war in this period. Quang Tri Province was bombed daily by forty specially assigned B-52s, each carrying 30 tons of bombs. Flying in cells of three, the B-52s flattened a "box" two miles long, one-half mile wide. In the southeastern quadrant of the province, 98 to 99 percent of the buildings had been destroyed. The capital city was simply obliterated by the fighting, which included a six-day non-stop attack by two hundred fighter bombers. When it was finally recaptured, a reporter who was present described it as "no longer a city but a lake of masonry. Even the thick citadel walls were so thoroughly smashed one could no longer see where they had stood."[29]

North Vietnam received the same treatment. There were seven hundred B-52 raids in April, including a sustained forty-eight-hour attack on Hanoi and Haiphong. On May 8, Nixon ordered a major escalation of the bombing of all military targets in the North and the mining of Haiphong Harbor. It should be noted that in this spring and early summer of 1972, the skies over Cambodia were temporarily free of B-52s for the first time in many months.*

Nevertheless, Hanoi's minimal goals had been achieved: the series of highly visible victories would convince any observer that the policy of Vietnamization was, if not completely forfeit, certainly very vulnerable. ARVN desertions were up to 20,000 men each month and its losses in killed and wounded were estimated at 150,000 men. One million more people were now refugees, and the yearning for peace, even at the cost of Communist rule, was being openly expressed to American correspondents in Saigon. Moreover, NLF and North Vietnamese forces continued to control northern Quang Tri Province, and by all reports there had been a considerable recovery of guerrilla strength in the Delta and along the Central Coast. Still, the cost had been high, pressure was mounting

*When the 1973 peace agreement in Paris ended the bombing of Vietnam and Laos, the bombers returned to Cambodia. Indeed, to the distress of Secretary of the Air Force Robert Seamans, Nixon demanded an additional one hundred B-52s sent over. "This was appalling. You couldn't even figure out where you were going to put them all, you know. How were you going to base them?"[30]

from China and the Soviet Union for the DRV to modify its negotiating position, and in any event the main objective was to convince the Americans to negotiate on acceptable terms. This now seemed possible.

In Washington, domestic resistance to further military moves rose in the face of the spring offensive. There were renewed threats by Congress to cut off all funding for the war, and Secretary of Defense Laird quietly increased the pace of troop withdrawals for fear that Nixon would halt them during the crisis, so that by June, only 47,000 U.S. ground troops remained in Vietnam. Some of this decrease was deceptive, as the number of Americans involved in fighting the war was actually rising. However, they were fighting not on the ground but in the air, and not inside South Vietnam but from bases in Thailand, Guam, or from the decks of an enhanced carrier fleet. In fact a whole series of Nixon gambles had paid off fairly well. Renewing the air war against North Vietnam, even bombing its dikes, had not disrupted détente with either the Soviet Union or the People's Republic of China. "At last," a Kissinger aide recalled, "we had a free hand to use all our force to end the war."[31] And however bloody the policy of all-out bombing of both South and North Vietnam, the successful change in (as George McGovern put it) the color of the corpses made large-scale peace demonstrations more difficult to mobilize. In the White House there was some question as to whether a peace treaty before the November election would enlarge or reduce Nixon's margin of victory. However, by the late summer of 1972, Kissinger, his eyes fixed on his ascension to the office of secretary of state in Nixon's anticipated landslide second term, had become convinced that an acceptable peace could and should be negotiated before the elections. He seemed oblivious to any hesitancy on the part of the White House.

President Thieu saw no reason to cooperate. In August, he reiterated his undying dedication to a policy of "Four No's"—no recognition of the enemy, no neutralization of South Vietnam, no coalition government, no surrender of territory. Hanoi and the PRG paid close attention to Thieu's pronouncements; not so Kissinger. As the secret peace talks resumed in May 1972, the possible reactions in Saigon seemed of no interest to the United States. Kissinger held all Vietnamese in contempt. He considered the North Vietnamese "nothing but shits" who made even the Russians look good, but he had no choice but to deal with them. The South Vietnamese he felt he could afford to dismiss entirely. "When he lied," one Saigon government official told an American reporter, "it was so obvious that it was humiliating to us—even a child wouldn't believe him. Too obvious lies do not make you angry, but humiliate you."[32]

Through much of August and September, Kissinger and the principal negotiator for the North Vietnamese, Le Duc Tho, met regularly in negotiating sessions. Kissinger had indicated U.S. readiness to set a definite timetable for total troop withdrawal and to acquiesce in the continued presence of North Vietnamese troops in the South, but he was adamantly opposed to any formula for a coalition government. On October 8, Tho presented Kissinger with a nine-point draft proposal that broke the deadlock. Gone was the insistence that Thieu step down in advance of a settlement; gone was the demand for a full-scale coalition government; gone too was the refusal to consider a military cease-fire in advance of a full political settlement. (Ho Chi Minh had been forced to accept a military settlement at Geneva and wait two years before nationwide elections were to resolve the political situation.) The proposal provided for a cease-fire in place; withdrawal of all foreign troops within sixty days of the cease-fire; and the exchange of prisoners of war in the same time period. Military aid was restricted to replacement of used or worn-out supplies. Politically, the Thieu government would be one of two recognized "administrative entities," the other being the PRG. After a cease-fire, Premier Pham Van Dong explained later in an interview with a *Newsweek* reporter, there would be "two armies and two administrations in the south." Then the Thieu government, the PRG, and a third group made up of representatives belonging to neither would negotiate to form a National Council of Concord and Reconciliation. In the words of Pham Van Dong, "they [Saigon and the PRG] will have to work out their own arrangements for a three-sided coalition [including the third force] of transition." The National Council would arrange for democratic elections; reunification would take place at an indefinite date in the future through "peaceful means."

Despite Kissinger's efforts to have them included, Cambodia and Laos remained outside of the agreement. With minor modifications, Kissinger accepted the draft and arranged an efficient schedule for the final signing. At no time did Kissinger present Saigon's approval as a necessary precondition.

When trouble developed inside Kissinger's negotiating team over the nuances of the Vietnamese-language version of Tho's plan (which seemed to lend to the Council of Concord and Reconciliation a quasi-governmental authority the English-language version avoided), Kissinger stormed at them: " 'You don't understand,' he shouted. 'I want to meet their terms; I want to reach an agreement; I want to end this war before the elections. It can and it will be done.' " Kissinger took it for granted Hanoi would cheat; but then so would the United States. "The question," Kissinger wrote, "is how to set up communications, intelligence and command arrangements," so that the United States could continue to aid the Saigon military after a complete troop withdrawal. The great point was to get a peace agreement in place before the elections so that Nixon, and of course Kissinger (who could not then be denied the office of secretary of state), would appear before the American public as architects of an extraordinary series of foreign policy achievements: recognition of China, the strategic arms limitation initiative with the Soviet Union, and peace in Vietnam. Gareth Porter suggests that Nixon was beginning to reach the opposite conclusion: the United States would have greater leverage with both Saigon and Hanoi *after* the election. The best tactic was to delay the agreement.[34]

Meanwhile, Kissinger made plans to fly to Hanoi to initial the agreement on October 22. The following week, Secretary of State Rogers would sign the formal treaty and then the cease-fire would begin. Two issues—the status of political prisoners in Saigon jails, and the allowable schedule of military resupply to Saigon armed forces—remained unsettled, but neither side expected peace to be delayed on this account. Describing himself later as more elated than he had ever been in his life of public service, Kissinger took off first for Washington, then back to Paris for a final touch-up of the draft agreement, and then at last to Saigon.

As Hanoi interpreted the agreement, Vietnam's foreign minister explained to Seymour Hersh in 1979, it would mean that the Saigon government would no longer be *"uniquely* lawful . . . there is to be no lawful Saigon government. There are to be two lawful governments and not only one." The Kissinger team, on the other hand, hoped to persuade Thieu that the agreement "permitted him to remain in power and allowed for the continuation of military and economic assistance to the GVN [Saigon government]." Thieu's understanding was closer to Hanoi's. To admit the participation of the PRG in a National Council of Concord and Reconciliation was to grant it the legitimacy for which it had been fighting.[35]

The agreement fell short of what Hanoi and the PRG might have expected to win. Millions of refugees, hundreds of thousands dead, uncounted wounded, the devastation of the countryside north and south, the atomization of rural social structures in the South, the destruction of the infant industrialization in the North, the corruption of the urban South, and the prostitution of tens of thousands of Vietnamese women were a heavy price to pay for the right of the NLF to political participation in the life of South Vietnam. Still, the American effort to create an anti-Communist state south of the 17th parallel had been deferred; perhaps defeated.

None of the precise terms of the agreement had been communicated to the Thieu government over the summer, but Kissinger advised Ambassador Bunker to urge ARVN military commanders to secure as much territory as they could in the coming weeks in the light of a possible cease-fire. At about the same time a resupply operation code-named ENHANCE was renamed, rather like a detergent or deodorant, ENHANCE PLUS. Under the provisions of ENHANCE PLUS, Saigon was treated to an airlift of 105 mm and 155 mm howitzers, helicopters, fighter aircraft (making its air force the fourth largest in the world), armored personnel carriers, tanks, trucks, and naval artillery. "If we had been giving this aid to the North Vietnamese," an American general joked, "they could have fought us for the rest of the century."[36]

Kissinger thought that the conclusion of a peace agreement would garner the most votes for the Republicans in the November election (and the most honor for himself). The President and his closest advisers were not entirely persuaded. It could work the other way, freeing "Nixon Democrats," whose reason for supporting the president was the hope he would bring peace, to return to their party of origin. Indeed, one of Nixon's private pollsters, Otto Sindlinger, strongly advised against a peace treaty before the first Tuesday in November. Monitoring the polls was one worry; but another, greater anxiety was the connection some ambitious reporters on *The Washington Post* had begun to make between the mid-June break-in at Democratic Party headquarters in the Watergate complex in Washington and persons very close to the president.

On October 19, Kissinger received word that Hanoi had yielded on the two issues still outstanding and that evening he cabled back over Nixon's signature: "The text of the agreement is considered complete." However, Nixon had also asked for several points to be clarified and for the bombing halt, the initialing, and signing to be postponed by a day or two. A complete bombing halt, intended to herald Kissinger's trip to Hanoi twenty-four hours later, was now set for October 23, Kissinger's trip for the 24th, and formal signing on the last day of the month. Hanoi agreed to the changes and, for the second time, the United States accepted the agreement. A secret U.S. communications unit monitoring Hanoi transmissions listened in as plans were made to celebrate the coming peace. While Kissinger was cabling the glad tidings to Hanoi, several of Thieu's close aides reviewed the English text of the agreement—the only one they had been given—listing objections as they went. When they were done, they handed Kissinger a list of sixty-nine objections.

Years later Thieu still fumed: "What happened Mr. Kissinger have negotiated over our head with the Communist and try to impose on us a peace that he has agreed with the Communist [sic]." Two provisions especially enraged Thieu: that North Vietnamese troops would remain in the South, and that a form of coalition government had been agreed upon. These two points were the heart of Thieu's frequently repeated "Four No's." "Now for years I say never, never, never a coalition, never accept a coalition. . . . I say that the life of South Vietnam rely on those two main points."[37]

Despite Kissinger's earnest reassurances that any violation of the agreement would lead to instant and terrible U.S. retaliation, Thieu was adamant. Worried that his handiwork might be destroyed by the intransigence of people he thoroughly despised, Kissinger flew back to Washington to urge that Nixon threaten to cut all aid to Thieu if he continued to refuse to sign. En route he postponed his trip to Hanoi, without spelling out the reasons but reassuring Hanoi that the United States "reaffirms its commitment to the substance and basic principles of the draft agreement."[38]

Once home he realized that no one in the Nixon White House was as anxious as he to sign the agreement. While ready to push Thieu up to a point, Nixon was not prepared to sign a separate peace. Moreover, a general agreement had emerged that Nixon would win the upcoming election by a larger margin without an agreement than with one. Kissinger found himself without strong allies in the increasingly byzantine inner politics of the White House. General Alexander Haig, Kissinger's chief aide, seemed to be rising in popularity as Kissinger's own stock fell. On October 23, Kissinger cabled Hanoi that instead of a bombing halt there would be a continuation of the bombing—albeit only south of the 20th parallel, sparing Hanoi and Haiphong while implicitly reserving them for a later day of punishment. Nor would Kissinger visit Hanoi in the near future. And it was all Hanoi's fault: it had pushed too hard too fast; Pham Van Dong's interview in *Newsweek* jeopardized the agreement; and there was the ongoing problem—which Hanoi thought had been solved—of the presence of northern troops in the South. In response to the disintegration of the agreement they had assumed was forthcoming, on October 26 Hanoi began publishing a complete history of the secret talks as well as the text of the agreement which Nixon had explicitly accepted.

It is impossible to know what Kissinger felt as he faced the press twelve hours later. The text Hanoi had published was accurate. It was indeed the case that the United States had agreed no less than three times to set a date for signing the agreement. Hanoi had acceded to each postponement, each change in the wording of the text itself. At no time had acceptance by the Saigon government been a precondition to the agreement. If Hanoi had been double-crossed, so had Kissinger, who had negotiated in good faith. But ambition—for he still hoped to be secretary of state—triumphed over principle.

Another man, or perhaps the same man in another country, might have resigned his office. Instead, Kissinger told the press that yes, the text as published by Hanoi was essentially correct. "Now, what is it, then, that prevents the completion of the agreement?" Kissinger asked the hundreds of reporters facing him, pencils poised, cameras rolling. "The principal reason is that in a negotiation that was stalemated for five years, and which did not really make a breakthrough until October 8, many of the general principles were clearly understood before the breakthrough, but as one elaborated the text, many of the nuances on which the implementation will ultimately depend became more and more apparent." In case this did not entirely clarify the matter, Kissinger went on to more specific items: there were ambiguities of language, there were technical problems. Then there were the problems arising from "a last effort to seize as much territory as possible" (though he had himself instructed Bunker to urge this on Thieu). The problems, Kissinger insisted, were not very great. As earnest of goodwill, bombing north of the 20th parallel had been halted. Peace, ladies and gentlemen, was at hand.[39]

Another country's press corps might have asked tougher questions, and pressed Kissinger on why negotiations, which had been completed with an agreed text and date for exchange of signatures, were now to be reopened. Instead, the American press basically accepted Kissinger's account of the history of the talks and dismissed Hanoi's claim to have been double-crossed as propaganda. The Nixon administration had it both ways: the illusion of peace, the reality of ongoing war.

On November 14, Nixon sent Thieu a reassuring message promising to try to renegotiate the agreements in accordance with Saigon's objections. But he also told him not to worry overmuch about the language of the agreement. More important than what it said was what it promised the United States would do "in the event the enemy renews its aggression. You have my absolute assurance that if Hanoi fails to abide by the terms of this agreement it is my intention to take swift and severe retaliatory action."[40]

Meanwhile in Saigon Thieu was taking care of himself. Grateful for the respite, he acted swiftly to secure his position in the face of a likely future peace. Tens of thousands of dissidents and suspected NLF sympathizers were arrested in all areas under Saigon government control. On November 25 a new law extended the scope of the repression: detention without trial would be legal in times of cease-fire, as it had been in time of war. At the same time, thousands of political prisoners were reclassified as common criminals to make certain they would not fall under any future exchange of prisoners agreement.

On November 19, Kissinger returned to Paris bearing the list of sixty-nine Saigon government objections (which he himself characterized in his memoirs as "preposterous") and some gifts for the North Vietnamese delegation, including a coffee-table book of Harvard Yard photographs. Hanoi at first insisted on the original nine-point proposal, but soon agreed to renegotiate minor points. But when Kissinger tried to reopen major issues settled a month earlier (the withdrawal of some portion of North Vietnamese troops from the South; a reduction in the status of the National Council; elimination of references to the PRG in the preamble to the agreement; rewording the agreement on the demilitarized zone so as to imply South Vietnamese sovereignty over it), Le Duc Tho refused. Kissinger threatened "savage" bombing if the new demands were not met. Sensing the future, the government of the DRV evacuated children and old people from Hanoi and once more readied the air-raid shelters.[41]

What was needed was something that would demonstrate, unambiguously, the solidity of an ongoing American commitment to South Vietnam. Shortly before his landslide reelection, Nixon had called his private pollster to check something out for him. Despite Sindlinger's sometimes misguided predictions (he had insisted that Kissinger's "peace is at hand" announcement would lose Nixon the election when, by all indications, the prospects of peace increased Nixon's margin of victory), Nixon trusted him. "He asked me what would be the public reaction if we bombed Hanoi?" Sindlinger requested ten days to do the research and then called back saying the reaction would be entirely positive. Thus reassured, and quite indifferent to Kissinger's advice that he should explain his actions to the public first, Nixon authorized the renewed mining of Haiphong Harbor and the saturation bombing of Hanoi and Haiphong. On December 17, two hundred B-52s began their round-the-clock bombing of Hanoi and Haiphong. On that first day, two planes were shot down. In all, Hanoi claimed to have shot down thirty-four B-52s; although official military statistics listed only fifteen, privately the Pentagon admitted to a much higher number and let Nixon know the Air Force could not sustain such losses for long.[42]

Confuting Sindlinger's prediction, public reaction was overwhelmingly negative, both at home and abroad. Nixon named the operation LINEBACKER after his favorite sport. But to everyone else it was the "Christmas bombing," the very name a reproach. Protest spread to the Air Force itself, where the same communication unit that had already monitored Hanoi's plans to celebrate the cease-fire in October now was required to guide the B-52s past the city's anti-aircraft defenses. There were work stoppages: ". . . it was like we were putting them [the B-52s] up there. A lot of guys felt the same way. It was a funny feeling: like what the B-52s were doing wasn't right. Rather than working, guys were refusing."[43] In Congress, the action the White House had long dreaded seemed imminent. On January 2 and 4, 1973, the House and Senate Democratic caucuses voted by large margins to cut off all funding for the war as soon as U.S. troop withdrawal and the repatriation of prisoners of war could be arranged.

Thus three months later than originally planned, on January 23, the nine-point proposal Le Duc Tho had handed Kissinger on October 8 was signed. In a secret protocol, the United States promised to "contribute to the postwar reconstruction in North Vietnam without any political conditions." A sum of $3.25 billion was proposed, though Kissinger pointed out appropriations could only be made if Congress agreed. Secret too, of course, were Nixon's promises to Thieu that the United States would "meet all contingencies in case the agreement is grossly violated."[44]

Although Nixon, Kissinger, the press, and a surprising number of historians insist that Hanoi was bombed back to the bargaining table, the text of the agreement speaks for itself. Nothing of substance changed between October and January. But in a reverse sense, as Gareth Porter points out, it is true: "by its political and military failure, the bombing of Hanoi and Haiphong made the Paris Agreement possible. For it forced Nixon and Kissinger to accept the very terms which they had rejected in October, November, and December." Or as John Negroponte, one of Kissinger's aides, put it, "We bombed the North Vietnamese into accepting our concessions."[45]

Nor was Thieu's recalcitrance any longer tolerable. Sign by January 21, Nixon warned him, or the United States will sign without you. Perhaps satisfied that the United States would keep its word to reintervene, Thieu accepted what Arnold Isaacs has called this "farewell gift of destruction," and signed. The next day he issued clear orders on how the cease-fire was to be observed. If "Communists come into your village, you should immediately shoot them in the head." Those who "begin talking in a Communist tone . . . should be immediately killed."[46]

The air war against North Vietnam had finally ended; the air war against the South would henceforth be carried out by U.S.-serviced South Vietnamese fighter bombers. The B-52s rested and then resumed their bombing. From February to August 1973, they dropped 250,000 tons of bombs on Cambodia, whose Calvary was now begun. Between 1969 and 1972, as Nixon made war in the name of peace, 15,315 Americans, 107,504 Saigon government troops, and an estimated 400,000+ DRV/NLF soldiers died in combat. There are no reliable statistics on civilian dead and wounded, though one source estimated 165,000 civilian casualties in South Vietnam for each year of Nixon's presidency.[47]

CHAPTER FOURTEEN

"Their War"
(1973–1975)

It's their country, their weather, their insects. They [the ARVN] can speak to anyone they meet. Anything the VC can do, they can do. If they thought it was their war, then they would fight it.

—PFC. FRANCIS MCCARTEN

I N JULY AND AUGUST 1973, while the bombs pulverizing Cambodia continued to fall, the Armed Services Committee of the Senate held hearings on those dropped there years earlier. On August 8, former Air Force Captain Gerald J. Greven, who had served as a forward air controller in 1969, added to the evidence given by previous witnesses his personal knowledge of B-52 raids as early as May 1969. But the interesting part of his testimony lay elsewhere than in this date, which earlier witnesses had already established. Greven described the secret raids and other illegal acts of war, among them the routine torture of suspected guerrillas (in this instance two teen-aged boys and their mother), the execution of prisoners of war, the mutilation of enemy bodies, and the bombing of enemy hospitals. The Air Force immediately issued a fierce denial of the last charge and noted that Greven had been "admonished for reporting that one of his strikes had been on a hospital." Not exactly, Greven said. "I deny that I was admonished for making an attempt to strike a hospital. . . . I was admonished for using the terminology 'hospital' both in a briefing room and on the air with the fighters. . . . It was not for the nature of the target but for using the terminology. . . ."[1]

It was not the stated policy of the U.S. Air Force to bomb hospitals,

Greven told the Committee, but it was Air Force practice. The distinction Greven drew can be applied very broadly to American policy in Indochina under Richard Nixon. It was not the stated policy of the United States to annihilate Cambodia, but by 1973 it was American practice. When the bombing began in 1969, the administration argued, it was essential to the protection of U.S. troops in Vietnam. Moreover, it had to be done in secret so as not to embarrass Prince Norodom Sihanouk, whom the administration always represented as welcoming the bombing, no matter how often he denied it. But by 1973 both Sihanouk and the American troops were gone; only the bombing remained.

Secretary of State Rogers explained to a dubious Congress that the bombing continued in order to encourage Hanoi to fulfill the twentieth article of the Paris Peace Accords, which looked toward a cease-fire in Laos and Cambodia.[2] Finding this explanation less than satisfactory, in June Congress voted to end its funding of the air war against Cambodia. But Nixon vetoed this effort on the grounds that the bombing was central to his search for a cease-fire. A compromise amendment relieved the deadlock, allowing Nixon six more weeks of bombing, which was now scheduled to end definitively on August 15, 1973.

No one bothered to justify these last six weeks of death. The targets of the bombs were densely populated villages, but the main audience was elsewhere. For each bomb was intended to reassure Thieu that Nixon's promise to reenter the war in force if Hanoi "violated the Peace Accords" was solid. The bombs were meant to announce, in the only language the White House believed the world understood (increasingly the only language it seemed able to speak), that the United States remained a formidable enemy and a reliable ally. At the same time the bombing sustained the foundering government of Lon Nol, whose corruption, incompetence, and demoralization it would be difficult to overstate.

Rather than create the conditions for a cease-fire, the bombing made one almost impossible, while real opportunities for peace in Cambodia were systematically rejected. The only hope for a cease-fire rested on an immediate end to the bombing and direct communication with Sihanouk, who had thrown in his lot with his former enemies, the Khmer Rouge. Both the Chinese and the Vietnamese sought to arrange negotiations in which Sihanouk would play the leading role, but Kissinger adamantly refused even to see the prince. Nor is it difficult to understand why. A genuine coalition government in Cambodia, such as Sihanouk might still have been able to construct, would surely have raised questions about Thieu's refusal to honor the political protocols of the Paris Accords. If Sihanouk and elements of the Khmer Rouge could share power in Phnom Penh, by what right could the PRG be excluded from power in Saigon? And more: if the United States could abandon Lon Nol just because his government was illegitimate, how good were Nixon's guarantees to Thieu?

In any event, the shelf life of the "Sihanouk solution" was severely limited. An increasingly powerful faction in the Cambodian insurgency, led by Pol Pot, distrusted Sihanouk and despised Hanoi, convinced that Vietnam had bought peace for itself at the expense of Cambodia. The longer the bombing continued, the stronger Pol Pot's faction grew, until the space left for a more moderate leftist coalition disappeared entirely. A genteel Congress had expected the intensity of the bombing to decrease in its final weeks; instead, the number of sorties increased: "On Air Force maps of Cambodia thousands of square miles of densely populated, fertile areas are marked black from the inundation." As William Colby, head of the CIA, explained to Congress when asked to justify the ferocity of the bombing, "Cambodia was then the only game in town," and it was about to close down. By the end of 1973, 2 million of Cambodia's 7 million people were refugees, although the United States, an AID report observed, "assumed no responsibility for the generation of refugees in Cambodia." Thus, only $2.5 million had been made available for humanitarian aid while economic and military aid amounted to $1.85 billion. It cost another $7 billion to bomb the place.[3]

Sidney Schanberg, whose friend Dith Pran would later describe to him the post-1975 "killing fields" of Cambodia, reported on some of the fields plowed by America in 1973. On August 6, the town of Neak Lung was accidentally hit by a single B-52 plane. "All my family is dead!" a survivor screamed at him. "Take my picture! Take my picture! Let the Americans see me." The American ambassador apologized for the error, observing sadly that "in war one learns to suffer, but it is especially disheartening to receive death and destruction from your friends."[4]

On August 15, 1973, as Congress had decreed, the bombs at last stopped falling; Cambodians continued to kill each other but with only limited help from the United States. Yet the shape of the eventual Khmer Rouge victory was to a considerable degree determined by the bombing campaign of 1973. Ben Kiernan, in his account of how Pol Pot came to power, concludes that the bombing campaign "sowed a whirlwind which the CPK Centre [Pol Pot's group] was ready to reap. Not only did it harden the base of the movement, but it also prevented what would otherwise have been an inevitable insurgent victory in 1973, at a time when the Centre's domestic and foreign policy extremism was far from generally accepted. . . ."[5] Bombing had been the "sacrosanct absolute" of American policy in Cambodia. It should not be surprising then that the nightmare Pol Pot made of the final victory of the Khmer Rouge was marked by a violence as absolute, though technologically less sophisticated.

Surveying the American destruction of Cambodia, William Shawcross concludes that Cambodia was "not a mistake; it was a crime." It was a view shared by many of the men who participated in its commission. One, Air Force pilot Donald Dawson, was finally unable any longer to deny what he knew to be the impact of the B-52 missions he flew. His request for conscientious objector status was refused and instead he was ordered to get back in his plane and resume bombing. When Dawson disobeyed this direct order, he was court-martialed. In response, he turned to the courts, on the grounds that the war against Cambodia was itself illegal.

On July 15, 1973, Judge Orin Judd in the Federal District Court of New York issued an injunction against the bombing as constitutionally illegal since the grounds that had initially served to justify it, the protection of American lives, were no longer valid. The administration immediately appealed the decision, which automatically suspended Judd's injunction. After considerable delays the case went to the Supreme Court, which did not rule on it until early in 1974; by that time the bombing was over, but a retrospective ruling on its legality might have been a major victory in the struggle against what many Americans now saw as a criminal executive. Instead, the government dropped the court-martial charges against Dawson; by this stroke he ceased to have plaintiff standing and the Court dismissed the case.

At about the same time that the Dawson case appeared in the New York court, July 1973, Congress itself began to investigate just what sort of crime Cambodia constituted. One of the first acts of Nixon's presidency had been the initiation of the "secret" bombing of Cambodia. When a few accounts appeared in the press, as we have seen, despite the fact that no one noticed, Nixon and Kissinger instituted a wide array of illegal wiretaps of reporters and White House aides. And each illegal act, from the burglary of the office of Daniel Ellsberg's psychiatrist to that of Democratic headquarters during the 1972 election campaign, had to be covered up. These acts of covering up and deception constituted the heart of the congressional bill of impeachment against Richard Nixon in 1974. But the actual bombing of Cambodia in 1969, an unconstitutional act of war against a neutral country taken in deepest secrecy by the president without the knowledge or approval of Congress, was dropped from the indictment. "It's kind of hard to live with yourself," Congressman William Hungate of Missouri reflected, "when you impeach a guy for tapping telephones and not for making war without authorization."[6] There are some crimes, after all, it seemed best to classify as mistakes. For if the 1969 bombing of Cambodia was an impeachable offense, what of the entire Vietnam enterprise? Who would escape indictment?

Nevertheless, Nixon's open defiance of a clear congressional wish to disengage from Indochina, combined with the unraveling of the administration as the Watergate investigation proceeded, contributed to that constitutional rarity, the overturn of a presidential veto. On November 6, 1973, over Nixon's veto, Congress passed the War Powers Act, which restored a modicum of its constitutional power over warmaking by limiting the time period in which the executive could deploy U.S. troops without congressional approval. Equally significant was the passage the following week of an amendment to the Military Procurement Authorization bill that banned the funding of any U.S. military action in any part of Indochina.

Nixon had repeatedly promised Thieu the United States would come to his rescue if necessary. It was now difficult to see how this could occur without open defiance of the will of Congress. Thieu, whose weak grasp of the U.S. Constitution was perhaps forgivable, seemed unperturbed. More ominous was the lack of apparent concern on the part of Nixon or his new secretary of state, Henry Kissinger.

In Vietnam itself, those elements of the cease-fire agreement which involved the health and well-being of the American armed forces were readily fulfilled. The release of the remaining American prisoners of war was timed to coincide with the departure of the last GI, and arrangements had been made for search teams to continue to look for those still missing in action. On the sixtieth day after the truce, the Military Assistance Command Vietnam (MACV) officially closed down, declaring its mission accomplished. When the last GIs had left Camp Alpha, the processing barracks at Tan Son Nhut air base in Saigon, it was systematically dismantled by Vietnamese soldiers and civilians, and what could not be carted off for sale or use was smashed. On the grounds of the base, a set of small stuffy barracks had been set aside to house the North Vietnamese and PRG delegations to the Four Party Joint Military Commission. They were subject to constant harassment by the Saigon government, which controlled their access to water, electricity, telephones, and the Western press corps, and regularly cut one or another of these services in retaliation for real or imagined violations of the peace agreement.

The last American troops in Vietnam left on March 29, 1973. (One of the very last, Master Sergeant Max Beilke, was the surprised recipient of a straw-mat painting of a Hanoi street scene as a kind of door prize from the North Vietnamese.) The peculiarities of the cease-fire agreement now emerged in high relief. The two zones to which the agreement was supposed to apply had never been precisely defined. Indeed, Thieu denied there was such a thing as a PRG zone at all. Instead, he reiterated his "Four No's": no recognition of the enemy, no neutralization of South Vietnam, no coalition government, no surrender of territory. Neither Kissinger nor any other American diplomat pointed out to Thieu the contradiction between the "Four No's" and what his government and the United States had agreed to in Paris. When Joint Military Commission teams moved into the countryside to begin to map respective zones, as required by the agreement, Thieu ordered his air force to bomb them.[7]

Just as it was in Thieu's interest to dismiss the agreement, it was, up to a point, in the interest of Hanoi and the PRG to attempt to force its implementation. The experience of Geneva 1954 informed the behavior of commanders on both sides in the South, as it did the policy debate taking place in Hanoi and Saigon. And in both cities the possibility of future American reintervention was a crucial component of the calculation.

For Saigon, congressional reluctance to continue to fund the war at the level Thieu and his government had come to expect was becoming a major issue. Would Congress be more generous if it thought the Saigon army was strong and successful, or weak and on the ropes? Thieu tried it both ways, launching offensives against long-term PRG zones in open contravention of the cease-fire agreement as a demonstration of strength. But if his army was strong and capable, did it really need much more in the way of military aid? So Thieu also tried it the other way, secretly evacuating a base 55 miles northwest of Saigon and claiming it had been overrun by the enemy in a massive ground attack, leaving no survivors. In retaliation for this alleged violation of the Paris Agreement, Thieu ordered the isolation of the PRG delegation at Tan Son Nhut, cutting their phone lines, canceling their weekly press conferences and the liaison flights to PRG headquarters in Binh Long Province. The American Embassy, unlike the press, was fully informed of the facts. John Markham, on the other hand, duly reported the "fall" of the outpost as well as Saigon's protest at this supposed violation of the Paris Agreement in *The New York Times*. "I don't know what these guys were thinking," one CIA agent remarked of the American press corps in Saigon, "but I do know that a lot of the stuff we handed out showed up pretty much unfiltered in the press."[8]

In Thieu's view, the continued presence of troops from the North relieved him of any obligation to honor the cease-fire agreements. Some of Thieu's colleagues urged a less stringent stance, one that could have acknowledged a zone of PRG control and a consolidation of those areas held by the ARVN. But Thieu was adamant in defining the struggle as control over all of South Vietnam. He was convinced that if he could hold on to it, the Americans would help him to defend it should the enemy grow too threatening. Otherwise, piece by piece, the Communists would take over, their triumph signaled by his own departure from the Presidential Palace and the installation of a coalition government.

For a long time, the American Embassy, the head of the CIA station in Saigon, and the Nixon White House stood squarely behind him, and all three assured Thieu they could fulfill earlier promises of sufficient military and economic aid to see him through any crisis. But the Nixon White House itself came under siege in 1973 as the Select Committee on Presidential Campaign Activities opened its investigation into campaign abuses in 1972, including the Watergate break-in; and Congress had no intention of fulfilling promises of massive aid made to Thieu by Nixon without its consent.

The debates in Hanoi and within the PRG mirrored those in Saigon. How strong were the ARVN forces? What would the Americans do? Would they reenter the war with troops or bombs? Would the Americans be more likely to reenter the war if the forces of the PRG were strong or if they were weak?[9] "Was not history repeating itself?" Lieutenant General Tran Van Tra asked in his personal history of the war, written in 1982. A southerner, Tra had fought against the French in the 1930s, been arrested by them and fought against them again from 1945 to 1954. Regrouped to the North after the Geneva Accords, he returned to the South in the 1960s as commander of the southeastern region, carrying with him a gift from Ho Chi Minh, a box of Cuban cigars. "I have only this gift—sent to me by comrade Fidel," Ho told him. "Take it with you and pass them out among the cadres in the south."

In 1973 Tra was appointed to head the military delegation of the PRG, part of the Joint Military Commission that was supposed to supervise the cease-fire. "I had been away from [Saigon] for decades, and was now returning in full view of the people and my comrades," he wrote, "and within the thick encirclement of the enemy.

"The French," Tra reflected, "had been heavily defeated and had to sign the Geneva Agreements in 1954, after which the Americans endeavored to prevent the agreements from being implemented." Now Saigon and the Americans seemed to be repeating history not as farce (as

Marx had predicted) but a second time as tragedy. This time, however, "we were people who were experienced." Tra described two possibilities, one in which Thieu and the United States would implement the peace agreements and the second in which the agreements would be sabotaged by them. It was up to the enemy, Tra insisted. "We were attempting to bring about the first contingency, but we were prepared to cope with the second one." Tra was thus not surprised when ARVN forces bombed and strafed the agreed-upon meeting place for transporting him to Saigon. Instead, he protested and arranged for a new pick-up, this one in Loc Ninh, which had been captured during the 1972 offensive and was now, in Tra's words, "a highly populated, prosperous town" in the Central Highlands, which not incidentally was heavily fortified as well.

On February 1, 1973, Tra and his aides were taken to Saigon by a fleet of U.S. helicopters, but not before the Americans, "who tried to appear civilized and stood looking on in silence," were treated to a revolutionary festival: "There was a forest of gold-starred red flags, mixed with half-blue, half-red flags and countless banners and slogans applauding the victory of the Paris Agreements. . . . A quick, seething, and spirited rally was held beside the waiting American helicopters." How did the Americans and the Saigon soldiers feel, Tra wondered, to look down on the people waving up at them as they flew off, people working in rice paddies or traveling on the road, waving at the helicopters which had "caused much death and separation for countless families"? "Suddenly," Tra records, "the American major turned toward me and half jokingly, half seriously said, 'You have won the war!' " But Tra knew that was not yet the case. The two approaches he described were in fact two sides of an ongoing debate in the Politburo. In April 1973, Tra managed to inveigle an American C-130 into flying him back to Hanoi for a major meeting. It was the first time he had flown over the entire length of his country, though he had walked its jungle paths often enough: "I felt disturbed and moved. . . . It was very beautiful, that homeland of ours. . . . I was very grateful for my ancestors."

Perhaps, some argued at the meeting, now was the time for rebuilding in the North, hopefully with the reconstruction funds Nixon had agreed to deliver. In the South, the tasks should be defensive and focused on mobilizing the population to demand the enforcement of the ceasefire. The troops in the South were exhausted and short of supplies; they badly needed time to recuperate. An effort should be made to "clarify zones of control," but in general troops should withdraw from contested areas and avoid offensive actions. Local commanders in the South protested. To withdraw from contested areas would mean that the "area under our control would gradually become a contested area. . . ." Consolidation could only mean retreat and eventual collapse; contested areas must remain contested.

The Politburo decision was to resist challenging Saigon's offensive strategy with one of their own. To match Thieu's "Four No's," the military forces of Hanoi and the PRG in the South labored under the "Five Forbids": they were forbidden to attack the enemy; to attack enemy troops carrying out land grab operations; to surround outposts; to shell outposts; to build combat villages. A related issue was whether or not to consolidate their forces in one clear zone or retain the "leopard spot" pattern that was the result of the cease-fire in place. The advantage of dispersed control was how effectively it tied down Saigon's troops. The disadvantage was the necessity to constantly defend and even extend the spots against Saigon's insistent offensive without so open a violation of the agreements as to invite American retaliation. And over every decision was the shadow of Geneva and the ghosts of thousands of Viet Minh slaughtered by Diem between 1954 and 1959. At that time, as General Tra recalled, there had been only one army, "that of Diem—holding sway on the battlefield, like a martial arts performer demonstrating his skills in a ring without an opponent." But now there were two in the ring; to abandon contested areas, to give up the "leopard spots" in expectation that the Paris Agreements would be honored, would be to repeat the "naïveté" of the 1950s.

Some local commanders, Tra wrote long after the war was over, ignored Hanoi's orders to withdraw their forces. In their view, nothing had changed, there were no agreements that made any difference, and the overriding necessity was to just keep on fighting. And they did. "This was an incorrect understanding of the Paris Agreement and the new strategic phase," Tra observed. "But it was correct in that it correctly evaluated the obstinacy and perfidy of the enemy, just like during the Geneva Agreements period, and resolutely retained the revolutionary gains that had been made." Fortunately, Tra concluded, this defiance occured on a "distant battlefield, so upper-echelon politics were often slow in reaching it and the rectification of mistakes was not prompt."

In the main, however, Hanoi's approach prevailed for almost a year after the agreements were signed. Rather than engage Thieu's army, thirty thousand troops and support workers constructed a highway network 1,000 kilometers long running from the demilitarized zone to a base camp north of Saigon. With its connecting side routes, Corridor 613 comprised some 20,000 kilometers of communications and supply lines and cut the time it took to send reinforcements south to a mere twenty-five days; slower than the C-130s which supplied Saigon, to be sure, but a full one third faster than previously. By early 1975 the new roadway was capable of carrying ten thousand trucks and fueling them by means of a 5,000-kilometer pipeline. A few months later, Corridor 613 became obsolete, as excellent French and American-built highways were abandoned by the ARVN forces and the armies of Hanoi and the PRG rolled south fully accommodated by their enemies.

The "cease-fire war" claimed 26,500 ARVN dead in 1973, and almost 30,000 in 1974. Pentagon statistics listed 39,000 and 61,000 PRG/DRV dead for the same time period. Fifteen thousand civilians died, 70,000 were wounded, over 800,000 became refugees. Throughout the war it had always been true that most of the corpses were Vietnamese; now virtually all were. Although Thieu and the American Embassy complained bitterly of a lack of supplies, a General Accounting Office audit reported large quantities of unused military equipment and some $200 million worth of items gone missing, including 143 small warships, a couple of million dollars worth of ammunition, and $10 million in small arms. And while the word was out to cut down on the amount of ammunition regularly expended by ARVN troops on the grounds that America's deadly cornucopia was shutting down, ARVN forces continued to expend far more ammunition than their enemy, as much as 56 tons to every 1 used by the PLAF.[10]

Saigon's main problems, however, were not on the battlefields but in the cities themselves. From 1966 to 1972, the United States had pumped $2 billion into the local economy, employed, directly or indirectly, some 300,000 people, and, through the workings of the Commercial Import Program, more or less controlled inflation. Now all of that was gone almost overnight. Combined with the global economic downturn of 1973, inflation rates in the South began to climb precipitously; urban unemployment reached 40 percent of the workforce, and there were severe food shortages.

"Last evening at 6 o'clock," David Shipler reported from Saigon in the spring of 1974, "as the streets were choked with rush hour traffic, Vo Van Nam said good-by to his five children, walked into a green, wooded park across from Saigon's main cathedral and set himself on fire." Not in political protest, Shipler explained, but from the "despair of one man who was without the means to feed his family, which is a deepening preoccupation in South Vietnam's deteriorating economy." Demobilized from the army, Nam had driven a pedicab and sold his blood to support his family. One day while he was giving blood, someone had stolen his pedicab and he complained to his wife that "it was as if the money from his blood had been in a way, stolen." Nam sold his watch and with the proceeds treated his children to a farewell movie. Then he bought matches and gasoline and told his children to behave themselves. The children tried to stop him and appealed to passers-by to help but, his daughter said, "nobody cared, nobody paid attention." By the time someone responded, "my father was already burning like a torch."

Rice was so expensive, Michael Parks reported in the *Baltimore Sun,* that it consumed almost the entire paycheck of most workers; the urban poor (a majority of the city population) could no longer afford to buy cooking fuel and had taken to burning tree bark instead. "The government confesses it has no solutions beyond austerity, seeking American assistance and hoping that foreign investment will increase."[11]

The government preached austerity, of course; but it was difficult to persuade people of its sincerity, given the corruption at every level of government and society. In September 1974, a leader of a right-wing Catholic group in Saigon, Father Tran Huu Thanh, issued an itemized manifesto which denounced members of Thieu's inner circle, including his family, for their involvement in everything from rice and fertilizer speculation to the opium trade. Three hundred priests signed his indictment. Although Thieu confiscated the Vietnamese newspapers which printed the story, he could not do much about the American press.[12]

Growing poverty affected the Saigon armed forces in many different ways. As the price of rice rose, allotments to soldiers were converted into cash which, given inflation, could not possibly buy enough to feed their families. Two hundred thousand men deserted the ARVN in 1974; those who stayed began to charge for everything, from a round of artillery fire in support of ground action to medical evacuation from the battlefield.

In the face of this mounting crisis, President Thieu, the White House, and the American Embassy had one response: pressure Congress for larger and larger amounts of aid. But by the spring of 1974, the struggle over aid had become almost entirely symbolic. Refusal to grant it would lay the blame for the "loss" of Vietnam on the doorstep of Congress, granting the money would or could mean the possibility of American reintervention. In April 1974, Congress refused an increase in aid; in August, it reduced military appropriations from a requested $1 billion to $700 million. Nixon's resignation in August did not affect executive strategy. President Gerald Ford renewed Nixon's promise of "adequate" aid to Thieu and pressured Congress for increased aid.

On paper, the hysteria over increased aid hardly seemed justified.

ARVN forces outnumbered their opponents by two to one; they possessed one thousand four hundred artillery pieces as against four hundred on the other side and twice as many tanks. The Air Force, equipped to the point of excess, was efficiently maintained by Americans on civilian contract to the Department of Defense. Yet on the battlefield, as Hanoi and the PRG moved to take the offensive in early 1975, the disparity in equipment had little meaning.

Hanoi's debate over tactics had been resolved by late 1973. Efforts to enforce the Paris Agreements might still have propaganda value, but no one any longer believed they would ever be seriously implemented. Timing remained a question, as more cautious voices resisted the pleas of southern-based commanders for more troops, more artillery, more of everything necessary to launch an all-out campaign in 1975. A string of local victories gave those in favor of a bolder strategy an edge at a Politburo meeting in December 1974, and a two-stage, two-year plan was drawn up. Attacks in 1975 would be constant, though without the expectation of victory until 1976 or even 1977. And the first focus would be on the Central Highlands, where ARVN forces were overextended and the newly built Corridor 613 could readily bring tanks and artillery to bear. But these plans were modified in the face of the impassioned advocacy of southern-based commanders confident that a move further to the south would have a devastating effect on ARVN morale and could be achieved by providing sufficiently heavy artillery to local forces. On January 7, 1975, the confidence of these commanders was fully justified as the city of Phuoc Binh fell and the entire province of Phuoc Long came under PRG control. Now the question of timing and focus began to disappear in the dust of retreating ARVN forces. In February, General Van Tien Dung, who had served as chief of staff to Vo Nguyen Giap at Dienbienphu, arrived in the South to lead what was to be the final offensive.

In March, an attack was launched on the key highland city of Ban Me Thuout, which fell on March 11; and General Dung's forces, as one military historian describes it, "could barely keep up with their enemy's collapse."[13] At this point Thieu took the major tactical decision he had been avoiding for the past two years: sacrificing territory for time, he pulled major ARVN forces back toward Saigon, hoping to construct an impregnable enclave in that part of Vietnam the French had always regarded most highly—the Mekong Delta, with its 10 million people and rich resources. Thieu ordered the commanding general in charge of ARVN forces in the key highland bases of Pleiku and Kontum to withdraw at his discretion and in secret—neither the Americans nor the

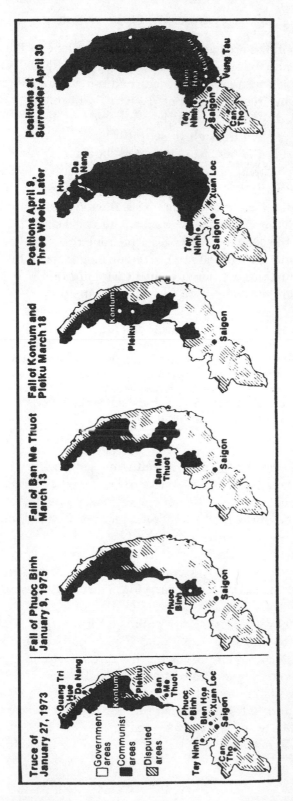

The speed at which Saigon forces collapsed is reflected in this *New York Times* map of the first four months of 1975.

regional forces in the area were to be informed. General Phu gathered a few close friends and simply took off, leaving subordinates in charge of the retreat, which by March 15 had turned into a panicky rout. "Why, it's like a goddam circus parade gone haywire!" CIA station chief Thomas Polgar grumbled. "The elephants have moved out in front and everybody else is stumbling through their shit."[14]

In contrast to the hesitation they had shown in the 1972 offensive, this time North Vietnamese and PRG forces maintained the pressure. On March 22, the battle for Hue began, and three days later ended. On March 28, the tenth anniversary almost to the day of the landing of U.S. Marines, the city of Danang was attacked, and on March 29 the flags of the PRG and the DRV were raised. The rout that had begun in the Central Highlands now threatened to engulf Saigon itself. In a summary report of the situation written on March 25, CIA analyst Frank Snepp noted the rapid deterioration of the military situation:

> Eight provinces have been lost in the past three weeks, four more are in imminent danger, and over a million people have been left homeless. . . . The strategic withdrawals . . . have been so precipitous and haphazard they are unlikely to yield any benefits. Huge stocks of ammunition and hardware have been abandoned. The surviving units from Kontum and Pleiku are still pinned down at a river crossing twenty miles inland and are unlikely to reach the coast intact. . . .

That same day, Earl Martin, a Mennonite aid worker who had been working in Quang Ngai for several years, watched as a large group of farmers marched into town. "From our vantage point atop an empty oil drum at the side of the road," he wrote, "it appeared as though a river of conical hats was moving across the bridge. A white-shirted youth, perhaps a student, near the front of the crowd, carried a large Liberation flag. . . . The group was virtually unarmed except for long bamboo staves, which many of the farmers were carrying. The crowd was raucous with laughter and chants in praise of the liberation of Quang Ngai." An old man told him they were from longstanding NLF villages: "We have lived with this war too long. Our villages have been bombed and shelled too long. Now all Quang Ngai province is liberated, including Quang Ngai city, so we are coming into the city to celebrate."[15]

A few days later, invited by some Vietnamese friends to leave the city for the countryside to "see what the war really meant to the people of Vietnam," Martin passed a refugee camp where a man was smashing in the mud walls of his house, a last act before going home to the village from which he had been forcibly removed some ten years earlier. About to board a ferry in an area where the dikes had been bombed so that three thousand to four thousand acres of rice land were destroyed by salt-water floods, Martin was stopped by a ferryman who shouted out to the crowd: "American! American! Grab him! Watch him! He's running loose! Get him!" The ferryman was only barely appeased by the insistence of Martin's companions that this American had opposed the war, not fought in it: " . . . he shouldn't just be walking around loose like that," the ferryman responded. "After all, just look at what the Americans have done around here. Look at this dike, look at our houses, look at our fields—Open your eyes, I say, and see what the Americans did to our village."[16]

Martin had personal grounds to be deeply impressed by the discipline of the ordinary foot soldiers *(bo doi)* of the DRV/PRG forces; their behavior was in stark contrast to that of the retreating ARVN forces. There have been many descriptions of the havoc the fleeing ARVN soldiers left in their wake, but one can stand for the others. Working around the limitations of the War Powers Act, the U.S. Navy had put a number of military and civilian ships under contract to the Defense Department at the disposal of the ARVN in order to evacuate them to other war zones. Ron Howard, a CIA logistics officer at Danang, escaped the city at a penultimate moment and made his way to an American cargo ship, the *Pioneer Contender,* which was picking up military and civilian refugees. As he climbed on deck he saw some one thousand five hundred "South Vietnamese troops sprawled, lounging, fighting among themselves on the main decks and the bridge and practicing their *aim* at the hapless Vietnamese civilians in their midst. Less than thirty yards away an ARVN trooper was in the process of raping a Vietnamese woman while another soldier held her male companion at gunpoint" (italics in the original).[17]

In Thieu's hour of crisis, some devoted Americans moved back into place, convinced the situation could still be saved. General Frederick Weyand, the last commander-in-chief of MACV, returned to Saigon and drafted a new strategic plan, then flew back to the United States to lobby for more aid to carry it out. For its part, and despite its dominant military position, the PRG offered to negotiate peace provided the Thieu government was replaced by one that would implement the terms of the Paris Agreement. "We understand that General Minh is ready to negotiate peace," the PRG foreign minister, Madam Nguyen Thi Binh, said on April 2, "and we are ready to talk with him." Instead, Thieu made defiant speeches ("We will never accept a coalition with the Communists") while

President Ford requested $722 million in military aid. In 1964, the possibility of a peace negotiated by Duong Van Minh had been rejected by the United States; eleven years later, the United States continued to reject peace in favor of pursuing the war to its last bitter drop.[18]

By mid-April, Saigon was beginning to look like a city under siege. Frank Snepp's diary entry for April 15 described the way the beggars were "out en masse now, and increasingly aggressive, tearing at your pockets or your car windows," while the rest of the population sold everything "too large to fit into a suitcase." Vietnamese friends, foreseeing the end, told Snepp they didn't hate the Communists but "They fear them. They've lived so long with the French and the Americans and with Thieu's loose autocracy, they can't imagine any other way. Change may be all right for the peasants in the countryside. But what will happen to them?" The embassy meanwhile churned out endless atrocity fantasies: " 'They're tearing out women's fingernails. . . .' " one embassy staff aide "gleefully" told Frank Snepp. " 'That should turn some heads in Congress.' "[19]

On April 20, with great reluctance, Ambassador Martin finally asked Thieu if he would resign for the good of the country; Thieu agreed. There was still time, however, for one last burst of American-sponsored death. Hours after Thieu's resignation, the military commander of the Saigon region, General Nguyen Van Toan, long a favorite of the Americans because of his height and "aggressive look" (Toan had been in charge of the My Lai area at the time of the massacre and had considerately not embarrassed the Americans about it), asked the defense attaché if the United States would please conduct a B-52 raid. This was refused but instead he was offered a CBU-55, among the most lethal of all nonnuclear weapons, which until now had never been used in Vietnam. Technicians in the office of the defense attaché rigged up a special bomb rack, and a C-130 dropped it on the troops which had just captured one of the few remaining government outposts. The CBU-55, as Frank Snepp has described it, is essentially a giant aeresol can which, when detonated, produces a cloud of fuel 50 feet in diameter and 8 feet thick. Once ignited, the cloud "itself generates a down-pressure of about three hundred pounds per square inch, sufficient to crush anything in its field. Anyone who survives the initial blast quickly suffocates in the post-explosion vacuum." The casualties were enormous. In addition, Toan was given large numbers of "daisy cutters," the monstrous 15,000-pound bombs originally developed to clear landing zones in the jungle; and, as a special gesture, an American air strike was flown against a convoy of North Vietnamese mobile missiles.[20]

On April 21, a special curfew in Saigon ensured that all its citizens in possession of a radio or TV set would hear their president's farewell address. Thieu spoke for three hours, berating the United States for its perfidy while praising his own steadfastness. How did the Americans expect him to win when they had failed to do so "with half a million powerful troops and skilled commanders and with nearly $300 billion in expenditures over six long years"? At the heart of Thieu's indictment, as it would be for many American revisionist historians in the years to come, was the Paris Agreement. "Kissinger didn't see that the agreement led the South Vietnamese people to death. Everyone else sees it, but Kissinger does not see it. . . . I said at the time, we must fight. No coalition! If there is a coalition, South Vietnam cannot stand." His listeners might have reflected that his army had indeed fought, the agreement notwithstanding, there had been no coalition, and still his government could not stand.[21] Five days later, Thieu loaded a U.S. transport plane with 15 tons of baggage and flew to exile in Taiwan.

Thieu's successor quickly passed power on to Duong Van Minh, whose reputation for being ready to reach an accommodation with the NLF was well known, though the Americans had never allowed it to be tested. It was hoped that, in this penultimate moment, Minh could reach some such accommodation now, avoiding the ignominy of total defeat. But, as General Van Tien Dung notes in his history of *Our Great Spring Victory*, Saigon was already completely encircled. "The Duong Van Minh card which they had played far too late, proved useless." On the morning of April 30, Minh ordered a general cease-fire. "In a final extraordinary irony," James Harrison writes, "the man who transmitted Big Minh's cease-fire order, a one-star general named Nguyen Huu Hanh, was . . . a longtime Communist agent. . . ."[22]

After the broadcast, Minh waited with a small entourage in Thieu's old office in the Presidential Palace. A startled *bo doi* (the Liberation forces equivalent of the American "grunt"), who had just hung the PRG flag from the balcony, found the group there and ran off in search of a senior officer. "We have been waiting for you," Minh told the man when he arrived, "so that we could turn over the government." "You have nothing left to turn over," he was told.

James Fenton, a British freelance journalist, had hitched a ride on the back of the first tank to reach the Presidential Palace. Now he watched as other tanks rolled onto the grounds, firing a salute as they drew up in a semicircle in front of the palace. "Their vehicles and helmets were covered in leaves, their uniforms were green. A great wave of greenery swept over the city. It blended into the grass and the trees of the avenue. Only the red armbands and the red tags on the guns stood out. Everything had changed in a trice."[23]

Still some distance from Saigon, Lieutenant General Tran Van Tra, General Van Tien Dung, Le Duc Tho, and Pham Hung, head of the Central Committee Directorate for South Vietnam (COSVN), followed the progress of the troops on a large map of the city. "Suddenly," Tra later wrote, "a cadre gleefully brought in a tape recorder and placed it on the table: it was the voice of Duong Van Minh announcing his unconditional surrender over the radio. . . . Everyone gathered around, listening silently." And then with Minh's order that his troops lay their weapons down:

> Everyone jumped with joy. Le Duc Tho, Pham Hung and Van Tien Dung . . . hugged and kissed one another and firmly shook hands. There are few moments in life when one is so happy that they want to cry. I suddenly felt as if my soul was translucent and light, as if everything had sunk to the bottom.

"This historic and sacred, intoxicating and completely satisfying moment," Van Tien Dung writes in his account of the day,

> was one that comes once in a generation, once in many generations. Our generation had known many victorious mornings, but there had been no morning so fresh and beautiful, so radiant, so clear and cool, so sweet-scented as this morning of total victory, a morning which made babes older than their years and made old men young again. . . .

Driving into town, Dung was impressed by the main road, "built by the enemy . . . to serve their operations. All of the enemy bases and storage depots were vast. The banks, the American billets, the hotels, many stories tall, were imposing advertisements for neocolonialism, implying that it would stand firm here, that it would stand for time without end."

Once in Saigon, Tra drove around to old haunts, visiting the streets in which he had fought the French in 1945 and the neighborhoods in which friends had died in the battles of Tet, 1968, proud of the complete orderliness of the takeover, the absence of the bloodbath the United States had for so long predicted. "Thank heavens you *bo doi* came in time to save us from the Communists," a Saigon market woman is said to have exclaimed. "The Communists were threatening to shell the city and kill off all the people."[24]

Van Tien Dung found that the headquarters of the Saigon General Staff and the national police had been abandoned rather than evacuated, but the "modern computer with its famous memory containing bio-data on each officer and soldier in their million-plus army was still running." The Vietnam War was over.

In the wake of the war, the government in Hanoi, impatient and distrustful, facing enemies real and anticipated, moved decisively in the South, appointing officials, re-organizing society, indifferent to local sensibilities or ambitions. For thirty years North and South had been separated, developing along sharply different lines, joined by wars differently experienced. In the South, in contrast to the North, the war had been both a civil war and a war of resistance against outside aggressors and it had been fought on home ground. With peace came the realization of how different the two societies had become: the centralized party state of the North a stark contrast to the South, still swollen with all the Americans had left behind, including hundreds of thousands of disoriented refugees. Now the North, secure in its power, went about the task of bringing order and coherence without paying undue attention to the mobilization of popular support. Thousands of former government officials and military officers were sent to re-education camps for periods which, families were assured, would last only a few months but could stretch to years of imprisonment. Economic transformation was pursued dogmatically. Many of those who had welcomed the outcome of the war, including some who had fought to bring the revolution to power in the South, felt cheated, even betrayed. The necessities of war had justified the people's immense sacrifices; the necessities of peace, more difficult to determine, could prove harder to accept.

CHAPTER FIFTEEN

After the War
(1975–1990)

In the night rain, my dreams are cast to the trembling
glimmer of the lamp.
After the war, the people you meet differ so from former
times.

—NGUYEN TRAI,
FIFTEENTH-CENTURY VIETNAMESE
POET

After the war, with such Cheshire cats grinning in our trees,
will the ancient tales still tell us new truths?
Will the myriad world surrender new metaphor?
After our war, how will love speak?

—JOHN BALABAN,
TWENTIETH-CENTURY AMERICAN
POET

AFTER OUR WAR . . . ," John Balaban wrote, "the dismembered bits/—all those . . . eyes, ear slivers/jaw splinters, gouged lips, odd tibias, skin flaps, and toes—/came squinting, wobbling, jabbering back." For a short time, President Gerald Ford kept them all at bay by giving the war a brief reprise. Early in May 1975, an American merchant ship, the *Mayaguez,* was detained by local Cambodian forces. Only minimal diplomatic efforts were made to recover the crew of the *Mayaguez* before the Marines were ordered to attack the island where the crew had first been held. A Cambodian announcement that the seamen were to be released did not deter a massive bombing attack against the port of Kompong Son and a nearby naval base. Forty-one Marines died, forty-nine were wounded (there is no word on Cambodian casualties), in order to recover forty Americans who had already been released. "The genitals, of course," Balaban's poem continues, "were the most bizarre,/inching along roads like glowworms and slugs./ The living wanted them back but good as new./The dead, of course, had no use for them." "It was wonderful," Senator Barry Goldwater said of Ford's quick reaction to the capture of the *Mayaguez*, "it shows we've still got balls in this country."[1]

For their part, in the first flush of victory the triumphant Vietnamese seem to have expected that the promise of reconstruction aid, made by President Nixon in the secret protocol to the 1973 Peace Agreement, would be fulfilled, that the United States would accept responsibility for the damage wrought and help to repair it. The government welcomed foreign investment, and the giant oil companies, which had begun to explore offshore deposits during the war, were specifically invited to continue their work. Foreign aid was essential for rebuilding and development; when it came from the West, it was also the best way to avoid overdependence on either China or the Soviet Union.

"At festive occasions in Vietnam we have wrestling games; at the end we embrace," a Vietnamese official said in November 1975. "Vietnam is ready, but Ford is not."[2] But at Vietnamese festivals, the winners and losers are both Vietnamese; American customs are different. Much as Thieu had assumed President Ford would honor the secret commitment Nixon made to reenter the war should this become necessary, so the new Vietnamese government confidently imagined Ford would see to the necessary appropriation of the promised economic aid. Instead of the embrace of aid, however, the embargo that had governed trade relations with North Vietnam during the war was extended to all of Vietnam and Cambodia. The United States froze $150 million of Vietnamese assets and vetoed Vietnamese membership in the United Nations. As if to underline all of the above, Congress, whose restrictions on aid to South Vietnam during the war had made executive prosecution of the war somewhat more difficult, now declared a plague on all Indochinese houses: a congressional amendment to the Foreign Assistance Appropriation Act of 1976 explicitly barred any aid whatsoever for Vietnam, Cambodia, or Laos.

Vietnam's need for aid was extreme: in the South, 9,000 out of 15,000 hamlets, 25 million acres of farmland, 12 million acres of forest were destroyed, and 1.5 million farm animals had been killed; there were an estimated 200,000 prostitutes, 879,000 orphans, 181,000 disabled people, and 1 million widows; all six of the industrial cities in the North had been badly damaged, as were provincial and district towns, and 4,000 out of 5,800 agricultural communes. North and south the land was cratered and planted with tons of unexploded ordnance, so that long after the war farmers and their families suffered serious injuries as they attempted to bring the fields back into cultivation. Nineteen million tons of herbicide had been sprayed on the South during the war, and while the long-term effects were unknown in 1975 (and are not clear now), severe birth defects and multiple miscarriages were apparent early on.[3]

President Jimmy Carter, seeking to heal domestic wounds and launch a new foreign policy, moved cautiously away from the punitive policy of the Ford administration. Ford had insisted that normalization must await a full accounting of the Americans still listed as missing in action (MIA). But even before he left office, a House report acknowledged that it was impossible to trace every last American missing in action. The way seemed cleared for the resumption of relations between Vietnam and the United States. Carter declared that the war had been a tragedy in which "the destruction was mutual." Despite his dubious bookkeeping, Hanoi immediately welcomed Carter's readiness to normalize relations.

In March 1977, the first official U.S. delegation to visit Vietnam since the end of the war set off for Hanoi. Led by Leonard Woodcock, former head of the United Auto Workers, the group's task was to clear the way for normalization by reaching an agreement on searching for the remaining MIAs. The Vietnamese insisted that the 1973 agreements be fulfilled on both sides, meaning that they would cooperate in the search for the MIAs only if the United States paid the stipulated reparations. The Americans found this formula unacceptable and the talks almost ended before they began. But Woodcock had taken an early morning walk around Hanoi and, moved by the scars of war he had observed, appealed to Phan Hien, the deputy foreign minister, not to pass up this opportunity for normalization; in an emotional reversal, the talks resumed. The Woodcock delegation left for Washington with the remains of twelve MIAs and a promise that a special office would be established to continue the search. In return, Woodcock had projected the possibility of humanitarian aid, a classification that might outflank the congressional ban on direct aid to Indochina.

Carter was careful to separate the issues of aid, of the MIAs, and of normalization: the Vietnamese had a moral obligation to search for the MIAs, but the United States did not *owe* Vietnam anything at all. Aid might, probably would, follow normalization, but it could not be linked to either MIAs or normalization. However, as a gesture of goodwill, travel restrictions to Vietnam were eased, and while the trade embargo continued, permits were granted for $5 million in private humanitarian aid. As further evidence of goodwill, the United States dropped its veto of Vietnam's admission to the United Nations. And delegations from the International Monetary Fund and the World Bank arrived for talks in December 1976 and January 1977.

But progress on normalization came to a full stop when the Vietnamese once more raised the issue of Nixon's promise during the next scheduled meetings in Paris, in May 1977. The American position was firm: there were to be no preconditions for mutual recognition, no advance assurances of reconstruction aid, no fulfillment of Nixon's promise. In short, nothing that in any way implied a debt, moral or otherwise. One does not pay reparations for mistakes, even tragic ones. The United States considered that it had intervened in Vietnam with excellent motives which had then gone bad. This did not make America a wrongdoer like Germany and Japan, who not only paid for the damage each had done but were forced to accept international constraints against recidivism. None of that, Carter made plain, could have anything to do with the United States. Drop the aid precondition, the State Department negotiator, Richard Holbrooke, advised Ambassador Hien. "Let us go outside and jointly declare to the press that we have decided to normalize relations."[4] Hien refused. Need and a sense of entitlement probably combined to keep alive the hope that the Americans could yet be persuaded to do the right thing.

Wire service reports from Paris that Phan Hien was insisting that the United States had an obligation to Vietnam caused an explosion of anger in Congress. The supporters of the war had not disappeared; indeed, the armistice freed them to be vociferously patriotic without fear of the consequences. By a vote of 266 to 131 Congress voted to forbid the State Department to negotiate "reparations, aid, or any other form of payment" to Vietnam. On May 19, 1977, the Vietnamese released the text of Nixon's secret letter to Pham Van Dong, dated February 1, 1973, in which he promised aid "without any preconditions." But Nixon was discredited and the peace agreement long buried under the rubble of the 1975 offensive. In June 1977, an amendment to a foreign aid bill explicitly renounced Nixon's promise of aid. Worse still, direct and indirect funding to any of the Indochinese states was prohibited, which meant Vietnam was cut off from any international lending agencies to which the United States contributed.

By the next set of Paris meetings, held in December 1977, the Vietnamese were desperate. Hoping for a more congenial atmosphere, they had earlier released new findings about MIAs. "You just whisper in my ear the amount you'll offer and that is enough," Hien told Holbrooke. But Holbrooke was silent, and the talks broke, scheduled to reconvene in February 1978.[5]

The February meetings never took place. Instead, all movement toward normalization ended in a flurry of espionage indictments involving a low-level USIA employee and passage of information to the Vietnamese Embassy in Paris and the United Nations mission in New York. The USIA employee seems to have had limited access to secret information: among the documents introduced at the trial was the Air France schedule of flights between Bangkok and Saigon.[6] The case "just froze everything," an assistant to Richard Holbrooke told Nayan Chanda. The Vietnamese might have found the sequence of events suspicious, but there was nothing they could do about it.

The refusal of the United States to end the embargo, fulfill Nixon's aid commitment, extend loans, or open diplomatic relations greatly exacerbated the economic crisis in Vietnam. It had been expected that unification of the North and South and the complex task of integrating the two economies would take place over several years. But the breakdown of the Paris Peace Agreements, the collapse of the South Vietnamese Army, and the subsequent rapid unification of the country through force of arms made economic integration an immediate necessity. There had been no preparation for the urgent questions that now arose. What should be the pace of "socialist transformation" of the economy of the South? What sorts of controls should be established over the flourishing commercial enterprises run by ethnic Chinese in Saigon? Should agricultural collectivization occur now or later? What sort of aid could Vietnam expect from its socialist allies, and what would these allies require in return?

"We are a poor country," the agricultural editor of the newspaper *Nhan Dan* explained to Christine Pelzer White, an American research scholar, "and the problems of distribution can even arise within a family at the most basic level." "Imagine," he went on,

> a family with only one fish for a meal. One son is the only fulltime worker in the family; another was wounded in the war and cannot work. The family income is dependent on the strength of the former, but it is the latter who has made the greatest sacrifice for the independence of his country. How should the fish be divided? All our prob-

lems lie in the question. . . . The war lasted thirty years, but it will take another twenty years before we will be able to overcome the legacy of the problems it has left.[7]

But things were worse still, for the Vietnamese discovered almost immediately that there was to be no respite from war after all. As the principal combatant against the French and the Americans, Vietnam claimed a "special relationship" to Laos and Cambodia, acknowledging Vietnamese leadership, however loosely. For its part, China sought a "special relationship" with Vietnam, one that would firmly tie it to the People's Republic in open opposition to China's main international enemy, the Soviet Union.

For the Cambodians with respect to Vietnam, as for Vietnam with respect to China, such special relationships were obstacles to full independence. Neither the historical past nor present political rivalries encouraged mutual trust. Gareth Porter explains it succinctly:

> The cultural and national identity of the Vietnamese people was forged largely in the process of resisting Chinese efforts to sinify Vietnamese, giving Vietnamese leaders an extreme sensitivity to any Chinese effort to force Vietnam to follow China's lead. . . . The first hint of postwar Chinese pressure on Vietnam to conform to its international line thus provoked an almost instinctive Vietnamese determination to resist.

The Chinese, however, recalling the sacrifices they had been called on to make in order to supply Vietnam with military and economic aid through the long years of the war, thought it time for a show of gratitude. And there was as well the matter of the Spratly and Paracel Islands in the South China Sea to which both China and Vietnam laid claim, an issue of sovereignty made urgent by the possibility of substantial offshore oil deposits. Not to speak of Hanoi's persistent refusal to choose between Moscow and Beijing.[8]

On their side, the Khmer reacted with equal passion to a history of Vietnamese encroachments on their territory beginning in the seventeenth century and culminating in the nineteenth century with actual occupation. Some members of the Khmer Rouge talked of recovering Kampuchea Krom (the lower Mekong Delta) and Prey Nokor (otherwise known as Saigon). The leadership, more modest, demanded only the unilateral right to define the border as compensation for the lost territories. For their part, the Vietnamese considered that their role in "creating, nourishing and defending the Kampuchean revolution" implied that

"Kampuchea under a Communist regime would regard Vietnam as its closest ally."[9]

Between 1975 and 1978, tension among the three countries increased as each saw the others endangering their most vital interests. The Chinese found their expectation of postwar predominance in Southeast Asia thwarted by Vietnam's independent stance and felt their security threatened by Vietnam's close ties with the Soviet Union. The Vietnamese saw Chinese aid to Cambodia encouraging Pol Pot to escalate the border war (with its persistent irrendentist implications) and foretelling a direct effort by the Chinese to subordinate Vietnam. Pol Pot was convinced the Vietnamese and their sympathizers inside his own party plotted his overthrow and the subordination of Cambodia to Vietnam. In a short time the fears of each had become self-fulfilling prophecy.[10]

A million and a half ethnic Chinese (Hoa) became hostage to these tensions. Amidst rumors of an imminent Sino-Vietnamese conflict, ethnic Chinese in the North were pressured by the government to evacuate border areas, and large numbers (133,000 by mid-June 1978) began to leave the country altogether, crossing the land border into China. The momentum of the flight from the North, as well as the nationalization of thirty thousand Chinese businesses (a move toward socialism made more imperative, the Vietnamese argued, by the fear that China would use overseas Chinese to control the Vietnamese economy) encouraged numbers of families in the South to seek exit visas. China retaliated by cutting a score of aid programs in Vietnam, claiming a need for funds to care for these refugees. When the Chinese, in May 1978, charged the Vietnamese with deliberate persecution of overseas Chinese and sent a few symbolic ships to Vietnam to "rescue" them, the Vietnamese response was swift and punitive, amounting to outright expulsion of the overseas Chinese population, for a hefty fee. Over 250,000 ethnic Chinese bought their way out of Vietnam, setting off in ill-equipped boats, and between 30,000 and 40,000 died at sea. In a move reminiscent of the Soviet treatment of China in 1960, the Chinese then canceled all remaining aid projects in Vietnam and withdrew some five thousand to eight thousand technical advisers. The following month, June 1978, Vietnam, with no prospect of a Western alternative, yielded to three years of Soviet pressure and joined COMECON.[11]

Meanwhile, in the eastern zone of Cambodia, which borders on Vietnam, Pol Pot unleashed a massacre of Cambodians alleged to be sympathetic to Vietnam that left 100,000 dead. Vietnam, convinced that only the overthrow of Pol Pot would end the border war with Cambodia and the larger threat posed by his ambitions, strengthened by Chinese

military and economic support, began to gather a nucleus of Khmer
Rouge refugees to replace him.[12] Now, as Nayan Chanda observes,

> all the gears of a large conflict merged. Viewed from Peking, the
> Vietnamese treatment of the ethnic Chinese was neither part of
> Socialist transformation nor simple racial discrimination, but an inte-
> gral part of Moscow's policy of encircling China. Vietnam's conflict
> with Cambodia was increasingly seen as part of a Soviet drive against
> Peking's regional leadership by using . . . Vietnam. The Vietnamese
> saw the orgy of violence inside Cambodia and the Khmer Rouge
> attacks on Vietnam as part of a well-laid Chinese plan to crush Viet-
> nam.[13]

It is impossible to know what might have happened in the region
had normalization between Vietnam and the United States occurred in
1977. Insofar as Vietnamese treatment of overseas Chinese was a serious
source of tension with China (and it is unclear that it did more than serve
to express those tensions), long-term loans and aid might have modified
Vietnam's domestic economic programs and eased pressure on overseas
Chinese businesses. Vietnam's ability to maintain its distance from the
Soviet Union would certainly have been enhanced by normalization,
calming Chinese fears and perhaps rendering the leadership less interested in backing Pol Pot militarily. In the absence of such support, it
seems likely that the status of ethnic Chinese in Vietnam could have been
resolved. American support for Vietnam, even in the minimal form of
recognition, would have made it difficult for China to play its "American
card" against the Soviets and discouraged Chinese military action against
Vietnam. And without Chinese backing, it is conceivable that Pol Pot
would have moderated his attacks against Vietnam.

But perhaps not. The defeat of the American war against Indochina
had released new configurations of power in Southeast Asia, not readily
susceptible to control from outside. In Phnom Penh, as in Hanoi and
Beijing, there were bitter rivalries older than the entire history of the
United States as a country, however exacerbated they might have been
by twentieth-century American foreign policy. Henceforth, the history
of the region would be made by the countries occupying it. Nobody said
this history had to be peaceful. Indeed, as Grant Evans and Kelvin Rowley explain,

> In Asia, Communism was rooted in nationalism from the start. And
> since nationalism means above all the political mobilization of the
> masses for purposes of state, it is not surprising that the triumph of

nationalism has added a further element of popular passion to clashes between states. In this context, there is no good reason to expect that Communist states would be basically different from non-Communist ones.[14]

In the fall of 1978 the Vietnamese decided to strike against Cambodia during the forthcoming dry season, which began in December. And by the summer of 1978, the Chinese Politburo had decided that the "ungrateful and arrogant" Vietnamese must be taught "a lesson." Publicly, Deng Xiaoping denounced the Vietnamese as "hooligans"; privately, he called them "dogs."[15]

The campaign against Cambodia would require, the Vietnamese knew, a closer military relationship with the Soviet Union, including negotiation of a treaty of mutual friendship. Strong nations speak positively about a balance of power because they see themselves as controlling the fulcrum. Weak nations seek only to balance powers against one another, leaving a small space in which to practice a degree of independence. To balance the weight of the Soviet Union, Hanoi sought once more to open negotiations for normalization with the United States, this time with no preconditions. For the Chinese, normalization would mean an end to American military support for Taiwan and thus the possibility of a final conclusion to China's own civil war. Troops that had been tied down for three decades guarding the coastline could now be released for duty on the Soviet border or the southern border with Vietnam.

To their distress, the Vietnamese found the climate for talks with the United States had changed since the 1977 Paris meetings due to the growing influence of Zbigniew Brzezinski, Carter's National Security adviser, on the White House. The initial foreign policy strategy of Secretary of State Cyrus Vance encompassed normalization with both China and Vietnam, a second strategic arms limitation treaty with the Soviet Union, a general deescalation of the Cold War, and an insistence on respect for "human rights" everywhere. Carter's campaign for human rights was both a useful propaganda weapon against the Soviet Union and Eastern-bloc countries and the expression of a genuine desire for a measure of reform in some of the more unsavory governments sustained by U.S. economic and military aid. Vance resisted the notion of "playing the China card," which he considered a dangerous ploy. For Vance, normalization was not a matter of geopolitical poker but a recognition that "China constituted a political, economic, and cultural weight in the world that the United States could not ignore."[16]

Brzezinski, whose obsession with the Soviet Union ran directly counter to the foreign policy approach of the State Department, was Vance's rival ideologically and bureaucratically. "Brzezinski," Vance observed, "looked at normalization largely in the light of the impact it would have on the U.S.-Soviet geopolitical competition." For months Brzezinski had quietly solicited the Chinese for an invitation to visit, and in May 1978, over Vance's objections, Carter approved the trip. Brzezinski was in his element in the heady anti-Soviet atmosphere of Beijing. On the obligatory visit to the Great Wall, an occasion which always seems to inspire great silliness in American officials, Brzezinski challenged his Chinese interpreter to a race: "Whoever gets to the top [of the Great Wall] first gets to fight the Russians in Ethiopia," he shouted as he outstripped the competition. In Deng Xiaoping, he had found a kindred soul. "Zbig [sic] . . . back from China," Carter noted in his diary on May 16, 1978. "He was overwhelmed with the Chinese. I told him he had been seduced."[17]

Brzezinski and his China staff aide, Michel Oksenberg, shared a contempt for Vietnam ("the cesspool of civilization," according to Oksenberg) and a conviction that an alliance with China would best serve U.S. interests. Moreover, in contrast to Vance, Brzezinski was delighted with the way the Chinese played cards. Like John Foster Dulles, who in the 1950s sought to split the Chinese and Russians by driving them ever closer together, Deng argued that the way to "remove the Soviet threat from Vietnam was to push them into closer cooperation, which would lead to eventual friction between the two and put an end to the Soviet presence." Brzezinski, who saw the Vietnamese as despicable Soviet puppets, was in complete agreement.[18]

Throughout the summer of 1978, Brzezinski lobbied Carter against normalizing relations with Vietnam, insisting that it would "only be an irritant to expanding our understanding with China." At the same time, the State Department, still interested in normalization with both countries, had responded to renewed Vietnamese appeals to reopen talks. In September, Holbrooke met with Foreign Minister Nguyen Co Thach at the Vietnamese UN mission, an apartment in an anonymous highrise in New York. Thach raised the subject of aid, but it was clearly *pro forma*. "Okay," he said finally, "I'll tell you what you want to hear. We will defer other problems until later. Let's normalize our relations without preconditions."[19] In 1977, when Holbrooke had invited Phan Hien to step outside and announce the restoration of relations, the Vietnamese, hoping to secure reconstruction funds, refused. Wiser now and in even greater need, Thach suggested to Holbrooke that a memorandum be signed at once. Holbrooke was delighted, but refused to make any official announcement until after he had consulted with the president. Planning for the opening of an embassy went forward in the meanwhile and the Vietnamese put a fresh coat of paint on the old U.S. consulate building in Hanoi.

Normalization with Vietnam would not have seriously interfered with the establishment of diplomatic relations with China, but it might have interfered with Brzezinski's desire to develop a "strategic relationship" with China, one useful in the world of permanent Cold War he strove to maintain. In September 1977 Carter had approved the State Department policy of simultaneous normalization but, as Brzezinski proudly told Nayan Chanda, "I shot it down."[20]

At first it seemed to be simply a matter of delaying recognition until after normalization with the Chinese. But by the end of October 1978, Vietnam was presented with a set of preconditions it could not possibly meet in the current situation. Recognition would not occur until three problems had been resolved to the satisfaction of the United States: the near war between Vietnam and Cambodia; the close ties between Vietnam and the Soviet Union; and the continued flood of refugees from Vietnam. Within three months, all three had been exacerbated rather than resolved: the near war became outright war, as Vietnamese tanks rolled across the border into Cambodia. In the expectation of war, a treaty of mutual friendship had been signed with the Soviet Union. The economic impact of the U.S. trade embargo, the denial of international loans and credits, and the war itself led to an ever-increasing number of "boat people."

Normalization was forfeit. On December 25, 1978, the invasion of Cambodia began. To the surprise of the Vietnamese, Khmer Rouge resistance gave way almost at once; after only two weeks of fighting, Phnom Penh fell on January 7, 1979. The Vietnamese installed a new Cambodian government, and its 120,000-man army settled in for what looked to be a long period of occupation.

Now, the isolation of Vietnam intensified. On December 15, normalization of U.S. relations with China was announced. One month later, a beaming Deng Xiaoping arrived in Washington to confirm a new era of Sino-American friendship, a friendship Deng hoped would be sealed by American "moral support" for the forthcoming Chinese punitive war against Vietnam. Carter overrode the objections of Secretary of State Vance and gave Deng and the triumphant Brzezinski what they wanted. Later, Brzezinski described how moved he had been, listening to Deng's invasion plans, "the single most impressive demonstration of raw power politics" he had experienced since coming to the White House. Deng was "tough, even brutal," and Brzezinski fervently wished his "cold and even ruthless appreciation of the uses of power" would rub off an American policymakers.[21]

In February 1979, with the blessing of the United States, China launched its invasion of Vietnam, laying waste an area of the countryside that had been relatively untouched by the United States during the war for fear of provoking Chinese intervention. After sixteen days of fighting, the Chinese withdrew, publicly expressing satisfaction that they had taught the Vietnamese a lesson, although it was clear that the cost had been very high and Chinese armed might less than overwhelming. Only one main force unit of the Vietnamese Army had been engaged; for the rest, some 100,000 Vietnamese regional and local militia troops had contained twice as many regular Chinese units. Casualty figures were of course disputed; at a minimum, China suffered twenty thousand casualties and claimed fifty thousand Vietnamese; parts of four Vietnamese border provinces were devastated, and Vietnam's fragile economy further weakened.

Brzezinski was well satisfied: the conflict had imposed "major costs on [the Vietnamese], produced a great deal of devastation, and, above all, showed the limits of their reliance on the Soviets." The terms in which Brzezinski interpreted the results of China's war against Vietnam are curious:

> The invasion revealed some limits to Soviet power by demonstrating that an ally of the Soviet Union could be molested with relative impunity. This was a lesson bound not to be lost on a number of observers, notably those potentially threatened by the Soviet Union. I also felt that a steadfast U.S. position would convince the Chinese that we were not a "paper tiger" and that the relationship with us had certain longer-range and reciprocal security benefits.[22]

It is not entirely clear how passive acquiescence in China's invasion proved the United States to be a real rather than a paper tiger. Perhaps the distinction lay in a real predator's readiness to encourage others to kill one another without endangering itself, though the better animal analogy here would be the vulture. But the most significant part of Brzezinski's statement is its direct articulation of the meaning of "credibility," the *sanctum sanctorum* that the administrations of Kennedy, Johnson, and Nixon had all sought to protect in Vietnam. Credibility is the capacity to molest a rival's allies with "relative impunity." In this way (and without running the danger of war between the principals) the limits on Soviet power, and conversely the unlimited power of the United States, could be demonstrated, to the edification of a watching world. In the zero-sum politics of Brzezinski's world, as in its economics, power is the ability to control client states.

Brzezinski's policy toward Vietnam forced the country into the embrace of the Soviet Union, thus justifying America's ongoing economic war against Vietnam and drawing harsh lessons for other nationalist aspirants. American support for Chinese policy in Cambodia salvaged the defeated remnants of Pol Pot's forces and put them back into the field against the Vietnamese army of occupation so as to "bleed Vietnam." "It is wise for China to force the Vietnamese to stay in Kampuchea," Deng Xiaoping reflected, "because that way they will suffer more and more. . . ."* American policymakers agreed, adding a double-bind of their own: until Vietnam withdrew from Cambodia, it would remain an international outlaw, unfit for recognition, trade, or aid.

Whatever their feelings about the Vietnamese army of occupation, the majority of Cambodians have consistently expressed their preference for the Hun Sen government it installed to the return of Pol Pot. No one knows how many Cambodians died in satisfaction of the Khmer Rouge vision of perfect sovereignty and revolutionary purity. The estimates range from 700,000 to 2 million.[24] Nor is there much doubt that the guerrilla war Pol Pot launched in the aftermath of his defeat could not have lasted for very long without military and financial support from the United States and China. Ostensibly U.S. aid has gone only to Pol Pot's "non-Communist" allies, in a coalition led by Prince Sihanouk. But Sihanouk is a captive of the Khmer Rouge, which totally dominates the coalition (nor are the Khmer Rouge especially Communist, having explicitly rejected Marx and Lenin in favor of an ideology of Cambodian nationalism).

Indifferent to the suffering its policies cause, the United States has helped to keep Cambodia at war for over a decade, deliberately impoverishing both Vietnam and Cambodia in the process. It has been an inexpensive way to punish Vietnam and pursue a "strategic alliance" with China at the same time. Internationally, the United States has consistently supported Pol Pot's right to represent Cambodia in the UN. When the issue first arose, in the Carter administration, it caused Vance and Holbrooke some discomfort, as Holbrooke explained in an interview:

---

*The last U.S. ambassador to Cambodia must have had this outcome in mind. "I assume," John Gunther Dean cabled Washington in March 1975, "we would prefer that the successor regime in Cambodia be oriented toward Peking rather than Hanoi."[23]

"...nothing I did, nothing Cy Vance did, was ever designed to...restore the Khmer Rouge to power in Phnom Penh. But once Hanoi was in control of Phnom Penh we decided that what the Vietnamese had done was not a precedent we wished to accept. And on that narrow ground we voted ... for the Cambodian seat in the UN to go to [Pol Pot] and not to the ... Vietnamese-backed regime." The decision troubled Holbrooke, but he was at pains to point out to a reporter that the vote did not represent support for the Khmer Rouge but rather a desire not to "legitimize the Vietnamese invasion."[25]

The niceties of the distinction mattered little to Pol Pot, who over the past decade has benefited from the UN seat in a variety of ways. Like the king in a nightmare fairy tale, the United States has set Vietnam task after task as the price of normalization and aid. As each one is fulfilled, a new one is proferred: another glass mountain must be scaled, another heap of grain counted. When Vietnam fulfilled one of the longstanding demands, the withdrawal of all troops from Cambodia, the United States, in conjunction with the Chinese, introduced a new condition, the admission of the Khmer Rouge into a coalition government. Nor is normalization the only issue. Although officials of both the World Bank and the IMF agree that recent Vietnamese efforts to stabilize the economy are "exemplary," the United States still blocks the aid they would like to grant.[26]

In a statement that projected a whole Orwellian world, Richard H. Solomon, assistant secretary of state for East Asian and Pacific affairs, declared that the "integrity of the international system" rested on rejection of any regime "imposed and sustained by foreign force of arms." The commitment of the United States in Cambodia was to a "political process that permits national self-determination for the Cambodian people." On these grounds, the administration Solomon served would continue to support the Khmer Rouge coalition as "the political center of a process of national reconciliation." Solomon spoke in September 1989, in the waning months of a decade-long American effort to overthrow the government of Nicaragua and only a few weeks before a Bush administration-sponsored coup against the government of Panama.[27]

Looking at the policies Brzezinski and his Republican successors have pursued in Indochina, or noting direct U.S. military interventions (Lebanon, Libya, Grenada, Panama) and indirect military interventions (El Salvador, Nicaragua, Angola), it is possible to conclude that not much has changed since the Vietnam War.[28] Yet the course of the Vietnam War challenged all the axioms of the post-World War II world, and the ideological conviction the United States needs to pursue its global domination has yet to be recovered, if it ever can be. The Vietnam War remains today and is likely to remain for the foreseeable future a zone of contested meaning; and the struggle over its interpretation is central to contemporary American politics, foreign and domestic, and of American culture as well.

A fundamental axiom of U.S. foreign policy had been that this nation is always on the side of freedom and justice. "When I got to Saigon I was twenty-two," Richard Holbrooke remembered, "and I believed everything I had been told by the United States government. I believed that the commitment was correct—freedom of choice, self-determination, save the country from Communism—and that we were doing the right thing because the U.S. government *did* the right thing. In those days you didn't question it."[29] Vietnam seriously weakened that automatic response for Holbrooke and for much of his generation; many Americans born during the decade of the war grew up not believing *anything* their government told them.

If axiomatic American goodness was brought into question by the war, so too was the axiomatic evil of the government's designated enemies. Everything that had been used to characterize the enemy—his indifference to human life, his duplicity, his ruthlessness—had at various times during the war been seen to characterize the United States as well. And while this might have been a surmountable problem in the name of a cause fervently embraced by a majority of Americans, it had become a very serious problem in the absence of such a cause.

Nor have American policymakers been able to appeal to the experience of Munich quite as confidently as in the past, although the Bush administration repeatedly did so during the Iraq crisis. For the post–World War II generation of voters, Vietnam has replaced Munich as their foreign policy paradigm.

Popular revulsion from the Vietnam War has been a sufficiently serious constraint on foreign policy to merit special designation by pro-war publicists and politicians: "the Vietnam syndrome." Thus pathologized, its symptoms—grave reluctance to send American troops abroad, close questioning of administration interventionist appeals, consistent poll results indicating that an overwhelming majority judge the Vietnam War to have been not simply a mistake but fundamentally wrong—require a cure, a pacification program. As in Vietnam itself, pacification is both military and civilian. Reagan's 1983 invasion of the tiny island of Grenada—in which 6,000 elite troops won 8,700 medals in the course of an exceedingly brief war against the Grenadian militia and a small group of Cuban advisers—was designed to make Americans "stand tall" again, confident in their capacity to exercise force when their government deems it necessary. Similarly, in 1986 Reagan met the problem of international terrorism by terror-bombing Muammar el-Qadaffi's headquarters in Libya. And in 1989, the Bush administration invaded Panama to remove a former ally who had fallen out of favor. In the summer of 1990, President Bush's rapid military buildup in Saudi Arabia seemed directed not only at Iraq but also at a war-phobic American public.

Militarists, both civilian and in the armed forces, took comfort from the positive response of the public to these actions. But Pentagon analysts were also quick to note the speed and secrecy with which these interventions were launched and, more to the point, terminated. Reagan administration efforts to enlist popular support for American armed intervention in Nicaragua, on the other hand, received little encouragement.

On the civilian front, postwar pacification addresses itself to the restoration of the belief in the essential benevolence of U.S. actions, or, if not always its actions, then certainly its intentions. Jimmy Carter's human rights policy was an effort to achieve the restoration of America's good name, to give the world, in Brzezinski's words, "greater respect for the moral meaning of America . . . and for the President himself as the personal expression of the fundamentally spiritual message of America." The policy required certification of good behavior before congressional appropriations could be approved for regimes whose human rights violations had reached a sufficient level of abuse to come to general international attention. The policy was more rhetorical than real, for whenever serious policy choices had to be made, human rights invariably took second place. In El Salvador in 1979 and 1980, for example, tens of thousands of citizens were being killed by U.S.-trained and -funded military death squads (30,000 between 1979 and 1981; double that number by 1985). Shortly before his assassination, in February 1980, Archbishop Oscar Romero appealed to Carter to end military aid to El Salvador, and he was ignored.

Ronald Reagan jettisoned Carter's human rights policy and set out on a more direct and less expensive approach to healing spiritual wounds: he renamed them. The United States invasion of Vietnam was a "noble cause," the American-paid mercenaries in Nicaragua were "freedom fighters." In one press conference, he rewrote the history of Vietnam itself, informing reporters that it had always been two countries that France had liberated after World War II and whose possible reunification was disrupted by Ho Chi Minh's refusal to participate in elections.[30]

Another postwar necessity has been the development of a satisfactory approach to popular insurgencies or governments in the Third World, a task both complicated and made urgent by the ongoing impact of Vietnam on the United States: "Our failure in Vietnam still casts a shadow over U.S. intervention anywhere," a Reagan administration report warned. Unless the pessimism engendered by Vietnam is overcome and an interventionist policy restored, "America's ability to defend its interest in the most vital regions, in the Persian Gulf, the Mediterranean and the Western Pacific" will be undermined.[31] In this area too there has been renaming, from the "counterinsurgency" of the 1960s to "low intensity conflict."

The phrase "low intensity conflict" may do more than rename, however. As Michael Klare has pointed out, "for U.S. policymakers and war planners . . . low-intensity conflict . . . represents a strategic reorientation of the U.S. military establishment, and a renewed commitment to employ force in a global crusade against Third World revolutionary movements and governments."[32] It is a "broad concept that spans the spectrum of conflict from relative peace to conventional war." Perhaps this is the major departure from the past: low-intensity conflict frankly embraces a policy of permanent war.

The Reagan report identified a monolithic Third World forever poised on the brink of change as the permanent enemy in this permanent war. Communist-led or not, change uncontrolled by the United States endangers its interests. In the report, all the countries of the Third World look alike, all peasants are either passive or terrorized into support for guerrilla movements, and all guerrillas are the same: outsiders supported by the Soviet Union or its regional surrogates. On the other side, all legitimate governments are also alike: modernizing elites, prevented from achieving reasonable reforms by the need to first defeat Communist-inspired popular movements from below, while all revolutionary governments are also the same: totalitarian minorities kept in power by force and Soviet support.

None of the above was true. But acting as if it were sometimes made it so, or effectively so—self-fulfilling prophecies, which exacted a terrible cost on the countries involved. Nicaragua, Angola, Mozambique, have each been blocked from exploring the larger possibilities of their revolutions in order to defend their countries against U.S.-funded mercenary armies. In this way, insurgencies were punished, their example tarnished, and American interests, as recent administrations have defined them, safeguarded.

As this is written, moreover, the notion that communism has to be contained at all costs, dealt a body blow by Nixon's trip to China, may have permanently collapsed. The United States is said to have "won" the Cold War. Why then are there still battlefronts as in El Salvador, where the United States continues to fund a murderous civil war and advise an army whose elite units slaughter civilians with impunity; or in Peru, where the Bush administration will spend $35 million to build a U.S. military base and train the Peruvian Army to fight Shining Path guerrillas under cover of the drug war (rather than respond to repeated requests to fund the transformation of agriculture so as to eliminate peasant reliance on the coca crop)? Perhaps it is because, as in Vietnam, change not sponsored or sanctioned by the United States or its agents is still a threat.

Bertolt Brecht wrote with bitter irony of those people who go around "saying someday the war will end. I say you can't be sure war will *ever* end. Of course it may have to pause occasionally. . . ." Nothing was perfect, Brecht mused; a war *could* come to a "sudden halt—from unforeseen causes—you can't think of everything—a little oversight, and the war's in the hole, and someone's got to pull it out again!" Without irony, Jeane Kirkpatrick, former ambassador to the United Nations, complained about America and its "whole world view and view of history [which] predisposes us to believe that peace is a norm and that war and violence are abnormal."[33]

Epilogue

History is a source of strength for us.
—PHAM HUY THONG TO AN
AMERICAN STUDENT, HANOI,
JANUARY 1973

. . . we have always been people who dropped the past and then could not remember where it had been put.
—GLORIA EMERSON, Winners and
Losers (1976)

Many of us have some of the war still inside us. This creates difficulties in lives.
—LE LUU, VIETNAMESE VETERAN
AND NOVELIST

OVER 26 million American men came of draft age during the Vietnam War; 2.15 million of them went to Vietnam, 1.6 million were in combat. Those who fought the war and died in it were disproportionately poor, badly educated, and black. (A high school dropout who enlisted had a 70 percent chance of being sent to Vietnam, a college graduate only 42 percent; until 1971, student deferments protected the majority of students from the draft altogether.)[1] It was also a teen-aged army—over 60 percent of those who died in Vietnam were between the ages of seventeen and twenty-one, and the average age of those who served was nineteen, five to seven years younger than in other American wars.

Between 1966 and 1972, a special Great Society program—Project 100,000—scooped up over 300,000 young men previously considered ineligible for the military because of their low test scores. Project 100,000, Secretary of Defense Robert McNamara declared, was the "world's largest education of skilled men." With lower admissions scores, the "subterranean poor" would have an opportunity to serve their country in Vietnam; simultaneously, the program had the advantage of avoiding the politically unpleasant alternative of requiring students or reservists to do the same. The benefits, especially to young black men, were said to be especially striking. As Daniel Patrick Moynihan pointed out, the military was "an utterly masculine world. Given the strains of disordered and matrifocal family life in which so many Negro youth come of age, the armed forces are a dramatic and desperately needed change, a world away from women, a world run by strong men and unquestioned authority, where discipline, if harsh, is nonetheless orderly and predictable, and where rewards, if limited, are granted on the basis of performance." In its first two years of operation, 41 percent of those brought into the military through Project 100,000 were black, 80 percent had dropped out of high school, 40 percent could read at less than sixth-grade level, and 37 percent were put directly into combat. Court-martialed at double the usual rate, over eighty thousand of these veterans left the military without the skills and opportunities McNamara assured them would be theirs, and many of them with service records that would make civilian life far more difficult than if they had never served at all.[2]

Each young man who went to war had an individual tour of duty, 365 days, and then home, on his own, with no effort on anyone's part to prepare for the shock of return, to help make the transition from war to peace, from the privileging of violence to its prohibition, from the sharp edge death brings to the life of a soldier to the ordinary daily life of a civilian, which denies death altogether. They had spoken always of coming back "to the world," counting each day "in country" which brought them closer to the end of their tour. But the homecoming was harder than any of them had expected. Later, many veterans would tell stories of having been spat upon by anti-war protesters, or having heard of veterans who were spat on.[3] It doesn't matter how often this happened or whether it happened at all. Veterans *felt* spat upon, stigmatized, contaminated. In television dramas, veterans were not heroes welcomed back into the bosom of loving families, admiring neighborhoods, and the arms of girls who loved uniforms; they were psychotic killers, crazies with automatic weapons. It was as if the country assumed that anyone coming back from Vietnam would, even should, feel a murderous rage against the society that had sent him there. The actual veteran—tired, confused, jet-propelled from combat to domestic airport—disappeared. Or rather, he became a kind of living hologram, an image projected by conflicting interpretations of the war: a victim or an executioner, a soldier who had lost a war, a killer who should never have fought it at all.

Of course there were also just the daily bread-and-butter problems of finding work in an economy far less open than it had been when the war was young. Today, from one quarter to one third of the homeless (between one quarter and three quarters of a million men) are Vietnam-era veterans. Without training or skills, without any public sense that the country owed them anything at all, many Vietnam veterans found themselves not only unrewarded but even disadvantaged by their service records. The war had begun to unravel even as it was being fought, so that by 1971 dissent and disobedience within the armed forces were endemic. The result was a tremendous increase in the number of less than honorable discharges—"bad paper"—which have followed the 500,000 to 750,000 men who received them ever since, making it difficult for them to get and keep jobs, and depriving them of educational and even medical benefits.

The lack of skills, the bad service records, the war wounds, have been only part of the difficulty many veterans face. At first, the widespread appearance of psychological problems was named "postwar trauma" and assimilated to the literature on the problems of veterans of other wars. It soon became clear, however, that Vietnam veterans were not like veterans of other wars. As early as 1970, Vietnam Veterans Against the War organized "rap sessions," sometimes attended by sympathetic psychiatrists, to help returning soldiers deal with their experiences. Even the Veterans Administration, obviously reluctant to single out Vietnam veterans as having any particular difficulties (especially in the light of the meager benefits accorded them), reported a "greater distrust of institutions" and a "bitterness, disgust and suspicion of those in positions of authority and responsibility."

More disturbing was the persistence—or sudden onset ten or even fifteen years after the war—of symptoms of acute distress, accompanied by flashbacks, severe sleep problems, depression, and rage. "Postwar trauma" was renamed "post-traumatic stress disorder" and assimilated not to battle fatigue or shell shock but to what people experience as survivors of floods or earthquakes. A V.A. doctor estimates that as many as 700,000 veterans suffer from some form of "post-traumatic stress disorder" (or PTSD). A massive study of Vietnam-era veterans revealed that those who had been "exposed to significant amounts of combat and/or witnessed or were participants in abusive violence [against prisoners, civilians, etc.] demonstrate long term problems" with disabling memories of the war.[4]

Veterans of other American wars, Robert Jay Lifton argued in his book *Home from the War,* had come to terms with the absurdity and evil of war by believing that *their* war "had purpose and significance beyond the immediate horrors [they] witnessed." But "the central fact" of the Vietnam War," Lifton wrote in 1973 while it was still going on, "is that no one really believes in it."[5] Although it is possible to challenge Lifton and demonstrate that soldiers in World War II also had difficulty discerning significance beyond the immediate horror of their situation, it is nevertheless true that when they got home, the purpose and significance of what they had done was universally affirmed and most were able to accept it. This was not the situation of Vietnam veterans, for even those who came home to families or communities who approved of the war were aware of those who protested against it. Moreover, the announced goals of the war—to repel an outside invader, to give the people of South Vietnam the chance to choose their own government—were daily contradicted by the soldier's sense that in fact he was himself the invader, and that "the government he had come to defend [was] hated by the people and that he [was] hated most of all."[6]

"What kind of a war is it?" Larry Rottman, poet and veteran, asked in a poem written during the war,

> where you can be pinned down
> all day in a muddy rice paddy
> while your buddies are being shot
> and a close-support Phantom jet
> who has been napalming the enemy
> wraps itself around a tree and explodes
> and you cheer inside.[7]

"To have been in a war does not mean you understand the memories of it," Gloria Emerson has written. In published and unpublished novels, memoirs, poems, Vietnam veterans have tried to understand their memories.

For women veterans the problem was compounded by the initial inability of anyone, including themselves, to acknowledge that they too were combat veterans. No one seems to have kept close count of their numbers. The Department of Defense says 7,500 women were on active military service in Vietnam during the war; the Veterans Administration lists 11,000 women as having served there. Together with civilians working for the Red Cross or other voluntary services, the general estimate is that a total of between 33,000 and 55,000 women worked in Vietnam during the war.[8] Like the young men who fought the war, the young women who nursed their wounds, or tried to "take their minds off the war," were confused, often defensive, almost always pained by their memories. "Our job was to look them [wounded soldiers] in the eye and convince them that everything was all right." It took practice, but "you finally built up a facade and could literally look at somebody dying and smile like Miss America or whatever we personified to them." The war gave many women responsibilities and a sense of power usually denied them in civilian life. But this new status too was confusing and even distressing in that there was no way to extricate it from the death and dehumanization that were its occasion. One nurse resisted having to treat wounded Vietnamese until one day she was forced to take care of an infant and broke down: "How, I wondered, could I ever come to believe I hated a baby?"[9]

Lynda Van Devanter tried to join a VVAW demonstration when she returned from Vietnam, but was told, "This demonstration is only for vets." "I am a vet," she explained. "I was in Pleiku and Qui Nhon. . . ." "I . . . don't think you're supposed to march," came the answer. "But you told me it was for vets." "It is. . . . But you're not a vet."[10]

In 1982, the Veterans Administration acknowledged that women were truly Vietnam vets: for the first time groups were established for women suffering from post-traumatic stress disorder. "She is afraid to trust again," Marilyn McMahon says in her poem "Wounds of War":

> Her days are haunted
>   by the texture of blood
>   the odor of burns
>   the face of senseless death;
> friends known and loved
>   vanished
>   abandoned.
> She sits alone in the darkened room
>   scotch her only hope.[11]

"The war is never over," one homeless man explained to a reporter in 1987. "You drink one too many beers and it pops up. . . . Sometimes, I hope to settle down somewhere where I won't be reminded of what I've seen. But I really don't see a future for myself." Being unable to imagine a future often precludes having one. More veterans have committed suicide since the war than died in it—at least sixty thousand. Nor is the connection between their war experience and their death at all obscure. Steven L. Anderson's parents, for example, found this note next to the body of their dead son: "When I was in Vietnam, we came across a North Vietnamese soldier with a man, a woman and a three- or four-year old girl. We had to shoot them all. I can't get the little girl's face out of my mind. I hope that God will forgive me."[12]

In May 1971, Medal of Honor winner Dwight W. Johnson was shot dead by the owner of a store he was attempting to rob. In Vietnam, Johnson killed "five to 20 enemy soldiers, nobody knows for sure," when the tank crew he was trying to rescue blew up in front of his eyes. "When he ran out of ammunition," his obituary continues, "he killed one with the stock of his machine gun." Unskilled and jobless in Detroit, Skip Johnson's fortunes turned when he was awarded the Medal of Honor for his heroism that day. Civic notables showered him with gifts and the Army persuaded him to return to the service as a recruiter in Detroit's predominantly black high schools. But his wife noticed some changes in him, as she had in other veterans she knew: "They get quiet. It's like they don't have too much to say about what it was like over there. Maybe it's because they've killed people and they don't really know why they've killed them."

Eventually Skip Johnson went AWOL from his recruiter's job and ended up in Valley Forge VA Hospital, where the head psychiatrist reached a preliminary diagnosis: "Depression caused by post-Vietnam adjustment problem." Later, the doctor observed Johnson's guilt over having survived the tank ambush and over "winning a high honor for the one time in his life when he lost complete control of himself. He asked: 'What would happen if I lost control of myself in Detroit and behaved like I did in Vietnam?' The prospect of such an event apparently was deeply disturbing to him." The psychiatrist refrained from answering Johnson's question; but a store manager in the western end of Detroit was more forthcoming: " 'I first hit him with two bullets,' the manager . . . said later. 'But he just stood there, with the gun in his hand, and said, "I'm going to kill you. . . ."' 'I kept pulling the trigger until my gun was empty.' "

Johnson's mother, thinking about her son's life and death after he was buried at Arlington National Cemetery with full military honors, wondered whether he had simply "tired of this life and needed someone else to pull the trigger."[13]

And many of those who have not tired of their lives, nor suffered from "post-traumatic stress disorder," who have homes, jobs, families, ambitions, nevertheless find the war somehow remains central to their lives. George Swiers tried to explain this at a conference called "Vietnam Reconsidered: Lessons from a War," which was held in Los Angeles in 1983. In 1970 he had flown direct from the battlefield to San Francisco airport, a survivor of an "honest-to-god magical mystery tour."

> And so, with a bravado inspired by two hours' worth of drugs and alcohol, and his uniform disheveled beyond embarrassment, he set out to speak to his Fellow Americans. To share with them his hideous secrets, to tell them what went on daily *in their names.*

No one listened; no one would engage his eyes. When Swiers completely lost control, a security officer gently led him away, advising him to "have a drink, you'll feel better."

> This week, exactly thirteen years have passed since I was last in California. I return to a place [the conference] where Vietnam is all that is spoken of. And there is some measure of comfort in that. But if I have learned anything in these thirteen years, it is this: I'm not *supposed* to feel better.

"My friend Patrick Finnegan," Swiers went on,

> a fellow activist and former grunt, often marvels at the government's willingness to permit any Vietnam veteran reaccess to America. For we brought with us the awful, suffocating truth of the war: that lies, though they be cleverly camouflaged, neatly packed and endorsed by presidents are still lies. And that no lie clicked out in a military press release could bury deep enough the death, dishonor, and defecation that was Vietnam.[14]

For thousands of soldiers exposed to Agent Orange, Vietnam is a daily scourge, suffered in migraines, ulcerated skin rashes, liver problems, cancer. Worse, they find themselves passing on the horrors of Vietnam to another generation. "When I came home," one veteran tried to explain to a student interviewing him for a class project,

> "I hated that I had anything to do with the war. But I knew that it was over. I got my life together and went on with it. I had a few nightmares, but it was a lot less than some of my friends had. I got married, had Billy and Johnny and I was doing well. . . . Then Billy grew up and that GOD DAMN pesticide shit they dropped on us came

back to haunt me and my kid. He has five Mother Fuckin scars on his body from cancer. . . . My own government that I was fighting a war for is making my son suffer for their mistakes, and I have to live with the guilt, not them!!. . . . I don't want to talk about this anymore."

"This is the first war that reached into our maternity wards," Tom Valelly, a veteran and Massachusetts state representative told Myra MacPherson. "The Vietnam experience does not belong to the past. The warfare we saw in Vietnam is the warfare of the future. Vietnam was a *laboratory.* Our own men were the guinea pigs."[15] But then, as visitors to the main Saigon maternity hospital report, so were the hundreds of thousands of Vietnamese exposed to a decade of spraying.

The soldier-poets of the war have said it powerfully. Bruce Weigl sings of napalm as he and his wife stand quietly in the doorway gazing out on a green field after a heavy rain:

> But still the branches are wire
> And thunder is the pounding mortar,
> Still I close my eyes and see the girl
> Running from her village, napalm
> Stuck to her dress like jelly,
> Her hands reaching for the no one
> Who waits in waves of heat before her.
>
> So I can keep on living,
> So I can stay here beside you,
> I try to imagine she runs down the road and wings
> Beat inside her until she rises
> Above the stinking jungle and her pain
> Eases, and your pain, and mine.

But Weigl, braver and more honest than any of those who sent him to Vietnam, knows that it is a lie which "swings back again."

> The lie works only as long as it takes to speak
> And the girl runs only as far
> As the napalm allows
> Until her burning tendons and crackling
> Muscles draw her up
> Into that final position
> Burning bodies so perfectly assume. Nothing
> Can change that; she is burned behind my eyes
> And not your good love and not the rain-swept air

And not the jungle green
Pasture unfolding before us can deny it.[16]

William Ehrhart returned to Vietnam in 1985, as many veterans
have begun to do recently, perhaps to find an answer to a poem he wrote
during the war.

Do they think of me now
in those strange Asian villages
where nothing ever seemed
quite human
but myself
and my few grim friends
moving through them
hunched in lines?

When they tell stories to their children
of the evil
that awaits misbehavior,
is it me they conjure?

A Vietnamese poet, after listening to Ehrhart's poem, offered one of his
own:

When there are no more bombs,
Shall you let me go up on earth again?
Why do you keep asking, little one . . .
I want to see the uncles and aunts I loved,
Are they still fighting, Mama?
I want to see the Yankee,
Mama, does it look like a human being?

Meeting the man against whose troops he had fought seventeen
years earlier, Ehrhart, rather disarmingly, asked the Vietnamese general
what he had thought of the Americans, as fighters, as warriors. "You
were—brave," the general answered. Pressed for a more specific answer,
the general lists American errors: fixed positions, dependency on air
support; ignorance of the land. "Would it have mattered if we had done
things differently?" Ehrhart asked. " 'No,' he replies after a pause. "Probably not. History was not on your side. We were fighting for our homeland. What were you fighting for?' " Remembering himself at seventeen,
the "inflexible certainty of my decision, and the terrible collective igno-

rance of the small town that buried half a dozen of my high school classmates," Ehrhart answers: " 'Nothing that really mattered.' "[17]

After the Korean War, the poet Thomas McGrath memorialized the American war dead—"brave: ignorant: amazed: Dead in the rice paddies, dead on the nameless hills."[18] In November 1982, the brave, ignorant, amazed dead of Vietnam were remembered at the dedication of a Vietnam Veterans Memorial. Money for the memorial had been raised by the veterans themselves; the winning design, by Maya Ying Lin, provided for two black granite walls bearing the names of the Americans who died in Vietnam. There was a protest by those who deemed the design insufficiently patriotic, and so a life-size statue of three GIs, two white, one black, was added to the original conception. Maya Ying Lin protested that it was like "drawing a moustache" on her design, but in the event, the statues have a different impact, as unpredictable as that of the wall itself.

Unlike the commemoration of the flag raising at Iwo Jima, these soldiers are flagless and exhausted. They seem to be waiting for something, but the only thing visible in the direction in which they look are the giant slabs with the names of their dead comrades. At first Bruce Weigl wondered why he had come to the dedication ceremony in Washington on Veterans Day, 1982. "I think we came," he wrote later,

> without really knowing it, to make the memorial our wailing wall. We came to find the names of those we lost in the war, as if by tracing the letters cut into the granite we could find what was left of ourselves. It turns out that, beyond all the petty debates over the monument, no veteran could turn his back on the terrible grace of Maya Lin's wall and the names of the 57,939 who died or disappeared in Vietnam from July 1959 to May 1975: America's longest most vicious sin.[19]

What militarists deplore as the Vietnam syndrome can better be understood as a relatively unique event in American history: an inability to forget, a resistance to the everyday workings of historical amnesia, despite the serious and coordinated efforts of the government and much of the press to "heal the wounds" of the war by encouraging such forgetting, or what comes to the same thing, firm instructions on *how* to remember. At the dedication of the Vietnam Memorial, President Reagan announced that the time had come to move on, "in unity and with resolve, with the resolve to always stand for freedom, as those who fought did, and to always try to protect and preserve the peace." Harry Haines, a Vietnam veteran, terms Reagan's call the "administrative version of

Vietnam memory." According to Reagan, in Vietnam Americans stood for freedom "as Americans have always stood—*and still do.*" The Vietnam War, Haines observes, is thus "normalized, the deaths are made rational, and the veterans are whole once again, stronger for their expiated burden."

To Harry Haines, the design of the memorial is ambiguous, able to contain Weigl's meaning but also that of a veteran who shouted at a group that attempted to hold a vigil for peace at the memorial: "No, not here. . . . These people died fighting against communism and for freedom. Those people [the vigil group] have no right. It's the same thing that went on with Vietnam, saying we don't belong in El Salvador." How the memorial is interpreted is part of an *ongoing* political struggle. Its meaning, Haines insists, lies "not so much in how the dead are remembered by those of us who survived Vietnam at home or abroad, but in how that remembrance is used by power to explain—to justify—sacrifices in future Vietnams."[20]

What distinguishes many Vietnam veterans from those who fought in other U.S. wars, Peter Marin has written, is their exceptional "moral seriousness," emerging from a "direct confrontation not only with the capacity of others for violence and brutality but also with their own culpability, their sense of their own capacity for error and excess." When a friend asked Marin, as those faced with the morally serious so often do, "Well, what is it [the veterans] really want?" Marin found himself answering spontaneously, " 'Justice.' That is what they want, but it is not justice for themselves—though they would like that too. They simply want justice to *exist* for there to be justice in the world. . . ." Which is why, perhaps, Tim O'Brien insists that a "true war story is never moral. It does not instruct, nor encourage virtue, nor suggest models of proper human behavior. . . . If a story seems moral do not believe it. If at the end of a war story you feel uplifted, or if you feel that some small bit of rectitude has been salvaged from the larger waste, then you have been made the victim of a very old and terrible lie. There is no rectitude whatsoever. There is no virtue."[21]

Michael Herr, a reporter who breathed the war in as deeply as any combat soldier, wrote that it "took the war to teach it, that you were as responsible for everything you saw as you were for everything you did. The problem was that you didn't always know what you were seeing until later, maybe years later, that a lot of it never made it in at all, it just stayed stored there in your eyes."[22] Vietnam has remained stored in the eyes of America; very slowly it is becoming possible to know what we have seen. To figure out what it might mean, to accept responsibility for it, will take much longer.

Notes

Chapter 1

1. Quoted in Michael Gillen, "Sailing into War: The American Troopship Movement to Vietnam in 1945," paper given at MidSouth Sociological Association Convention, Birmingham, Ala., October 28, 1983.

2. "The Path Which Led Me to Leninism," reprinted in *Vietnam and America: A Documented History*, edited by Marvin E. Gettleman, Jane Franklin, Bruce Franklin and Marilyn Young (New York: Grove Press, 1985), pp. 20–22.

3. The best account is Huynh Kim Khanh, *Vietnamese Communism, 1925–1945* (Ithaca, N.Y.: Cornell University Press, 1982). See especially pp. 125–133; the attack on Ho is discussed on pp. 182–186. The text of the February platform is reprinted in Gettleman, et al., eds., *Vietnam and America*, pp. 22–24.

4. See Huynh Kim Khanh, *Vietnamese Communism*, pp. 179–180; Jean Lacouture, *Ho Chi Minh: A Political Biography* (New York: Random House, 1968), pp. 62–69.

5. Huynh Kim Khanh, *Vietnamese Communism*, p. 254 and n. 49, pp. 254–255.

6. Huynh Kim Khanh, *Vietnamese Communism*, p. 261; James P. Harrison, *The Endless War: Fifty Years of Struggle in Vietnam* (New York: Free Press, 1982), p. 84.

7. The text (written across the border in a small Chinese town) is reprinted in Gettleman, et al., eds., *Vietnam and America*, pp. 37–38. In 1942, seeking aid for the Viet Minh, Ho crossed into China once more; this time he was arrested by the Kuomintang and jailed for over a year. Both the French and the Japanese attempted to manipulate "traditional Vietnamese patriotism" in order to undermine each other, a process that ultimately redounded to the benefit of the Communist-led national liberation movement. See Huynh Kim Khanh, *Vietnamese Communism*, pp. 240–245.

8. *Reminiscences on the Army for National Salvation: Memoir of General Chu Van Tan,* translated by Mai Elliott, Data Paper No. 97, Southeast Asia Program, Cornell University, September 1974, p. 27. The memoir is enhanced by Mai Elliott's excellent and instructive historical introduction.

331

9. Alexander B. Woodside, *Community and Revolution in Modern Vietnam* (Boston: Houghton Mifflin, 1976), pp. 225–234; David Marr, "Vietnam: Harnessing the Whirlwind," in Robin Jeffrey, ed., *Asia—The Winning of Independence* (New York: St. Martin's Press, 1981).

10. See Memorandum of Conversation with Roosevelt by Charles Taussig, March 15, 1945, in *Vietnam: A History in Documents*, edited by Gareth Porter (New York: New American Library, 1981), pp. 11–12.

11. Ho's code name was "Lucius." See Harrison, *Endless War*, p. 91. Two accounts of Ho's career as an agent (and more broadly, the relationship between the OSS and the Viet Minh) are Charles Fenn, *Ho Chi Minh: A Biographical Introduction* (New York: Charles Scribner's Sons, 1973), pp. 72–84, and Archimedes Patti, *Why Vietnam? Prelude to America's Albatross* (Berkeley, Calif.: University of California Press, 1980), pp. 43–136.

12. The text of the Declaration of Independence is reprinted in Gettleman, et al., eds., *Vietnam and America*, pp. 40–42.

13. Vo Nguyen Giap, *Unforgettable Months and Years*, translated by Mai Elliott, Data Paper No. 99, Southeast Asia Program, Cornell University, May 1975, pp. 26, 53.

14. Nehru quoted in *The History of the Joint Chiefs of Staff: The Joint Chiefs of Staff and the War in Vietnam; History of the Indochina Incident, 1940–1954*, Vol. 1, Prepared by the Historical Division of the Joint Secretariat (Wilmington, Del.: Michael Glazier, 1982), pp. 86, 87–88, n.22. The account notes that Japanese sympathy lay with the Viet Minh: "There was little doubt that they would have preferred to see the Vietnamese victorious in a struggle between 'white imperialism' and 'Asiatic nationalism.' " Some Japanese actually joined the Vietnamese in fighting against occupation troops. For a vivid description of the coup in Saigon, see Patti, *Why Vietnam?* pp. 315ff.

15. Porter, ed., *A History in Documents*, pp. 38, 39.

16. Report by Arthur Hale on a thirteen-day stay in Hanoi, October 15–October 28, 1945. Appendix I, *The United States and Vietnam: 1944–1947*, A Staff Study based on the Pentagon Papers, prepared for the Committee on Foreign Relations, United States Senate, Study No. 2 (April 3, 1972), p. 23–36.

17. Ellen J. Hammer, *The Struggle for Indochina* (Stanford, Calif.: Stanford University Press, 1954), p. 143.

18. Text in Robert M. Blum, "Ho Chi Minh and the United States: 1944–1946," in *The United States and Vietnam, 1944–1947*, Staff Study No. 2, p. 10.

19. The Viet Minh Committee of the South had made similar arguments in September 1945 in the weeks before the British arrived. The Trotskyists had urged immediate resistance and accused the Communists of treason when, instead, the instructions were to cooperate with Gracey for as long as possible. In turn, the Communists moved with speed and brutality against the Trotskyist leadership, executing six, including the head of the Party.

20. Description of Giap from Lacouture, *Ho Chi Minh*, p. 136. Philippe Devillers's *Histoire du Viet-Nam de 1940 à 1952* (Paris: Editions du Seuil, 1952) gives as vivid an eyewitness account of events in the North as Patti does for the South. Giap compared the agreement to the treaty the Russians had signed with the Germans at Brest-Litovsk in 1918. For the March 7 meeting, see pp. 227ff.

Devillers includes French translations of the text of speeches by Giap, Ho, and others.

21. Marr, "Harnessing the Whirlwind," p. 207; Porter, ed., *A History in Documents*, p. 45.

22. Truong Nhu Tang, *A Viet Cong Memoir: An Inside Account of the Vietnam War and Its Aftermath* (New York: Vintage Books, 1986), pp. 12, 13.

23. Lacouture, *Ho Chi Minh*, pp. 126, 124; Harrison, *Endless War*, p. 112.

24. Lacouture, *Ho Chi Minh*, p. 154; Porter, ed., *A History in Documents*, p. 51. See also Devillers, *Histoire*, pp. 289ff.

25. See the interesting argument on French policy of this period made by Stein Tonnesson, "A French Decision for War: French and Vietnamese Decision-making Before the Outbreak of War in Indochina, December, 1946," *Vietnam Forum*, 12 (Summer–Fall 1988), pp. 112–135.

26. Quoted in *ibid.*, p. 130.

27. Devillers's translation into French, *Histoire du Viet-Nam*, p. 357, n. 6, has Ho concluding: "Long live Democracy."

Chapter 2

1. Porter, ed., *A History in Documents*, pp. 54, 56, 65 (italics in original).

2. Quoted in Lloyd Gardner, *Approaching Vietnam: From World War II Through Dienbienphu, 1941–1954* (New York: W.W. Norton, 1988), p. 58.

3. In November 1945, Ho wrote to Secretary of State Brynes inquiring as to the possibility of sending fifty Vietnamese students to the United States for study. Abbot Low Moffat was asked if the United States would not like to establish a naval base at Cam Ranh Bay. Appendix II, *The United States and Vietnam: 1944–1947*, Staff Study No. 2 (April 3, 1972), p. 42.

4. Quoted in Blum, "French Indochina and the United States in the early postwar period," in *Ibid.*, p. 21. Blum's short essay is an excellent summary of policy in this period.

5. The text of Acheson's May 20 telegram is in *Department of State, Foreign Relations of the United States* (hereinafter cited as FRUS), 1949, 7, part 1, p. 29. The Acheson cable was a direct response to one from the consul in Hanoi, who reported that non-Communist Vietnamese of his acquaintance were worried that an article in *Newsweek* magazine stressing Ho Chi Minh's independent nationalism reflected official U.S. thinking. The article, published on April 25, 1949, was by Harold Isaacs, whose attempts to interview Ho were blocked by the French. Instead, Isaacs talked to Ho by radio phone and concluded that "Ho Chi Minh is more of a Vietnamese nationalist right now than a Moscow stooge."

6. See John Lewis Gaddis's essay, "Drawing Lines: The Defensive Perimeter Strategy in East Asia, 1947–1953," in *The Long Peace: Inquiries into the History of the Cold War* (New York: Oxford University Press, 1987), pp. 72–103, and Thomas McCormick, Introduction, in *America in Vietnam: A Documentary History*, edited, with commentaries, by William Appleman Williams, Thomas McCormick, Lloyd Gardner, and Walter LaFeber (New York: Doubleday, 1985), pp. 45–60.

7. For the full text, see *FRUS*, 1950, 1, pp. 234ff.

8. McCormick, Introduction, p. 49.

9. Gaddis, "Drawing Lines," p. 114.

10. The application of this notion of weakened links or falling dominos to Indochina made an early appearance in NSC-64, February 1950, which argued that Thailand, Burma, the Philippines, Indonesia, and Malaya would all be in "grave hazard" if Indochina fell to communism—*FRUS*, 1950, VI, p. 747. Discussed by McCormick, Introduction, p. 51.

11. See Gaddis, "Drawing Lines."

12. See Joseph Buttinger, *Vietnam at War*, Vol. II of *Vietnam: A Dragon Embattled*, (London: Pall Mall Press, 1967), pp. 761, 1071 (n. 2).

13. For the role of land reform in the war against the French, see Gabriel Kolko, *Anatomy of a War, Vietnam, the United States and the Modern Historical Experience* (New York: Pantheon Books, 1986), pp. 57–61, and Christine Pelzer White, "The Peasants and the Party in the Vietnamese Revolution," in *Peasants and Politics: Grass Roots Reaction to Change in Asia*, edited by D. M. Miller (Melbourne, Australia: Edward Arnold, 1978), pp. 32–34.

14. The press conference is reprinted in Williams, et al., eds., *America in Vietnam*, pp. 156–157.

15. Dienbienphu is the subject of many books, among the most interesting of which are Jules Roy, *The Battle of Dienbienphu* (New York: Harper & Row, 1965), and Bernard Fall, *Hell in a Very Small Place: The Siege of Dien Bien Phu* (Philadelphia: J. B. Lippincott, 1967). For a Vietnamese perspective, see Vo Nguyen Giap, *People's War, People's Army* (Hanoi: Foreign Languages Press, 1961).

16. Quotes are from Fall, *Hell in a Very Small Place*, p. 137.

17. Quoted in Gardner, *Approaching Vietnam*, p. 202. See also McGeorge Bundy, *Danger and Survival: Choices About the Bomb in the First Fifty Years* (New York: Vintage Books, 1990), pp. 260–270.

18. The most recent account of Eisenhower's policy in these months is Melanie Billings-Yun, *Decision Against War: Eisenhower and Dien Bien Phu, 1954* (New York: Columbia University Press, 1988). See also John Prados, *The Sky Would Fall: Operation Vulture, the U.S. Bombing Mission in Indochina, 1954* (New York: Dial Press, 1983). Quote is from *The U.S. Government and the Vietnam War: Executive and Legislative Roles and Relationships, Part I, 1945–1961*, Prepared for the Committee on Foreign Relations, U.S. Senate, April 1984, by William Conrad Gibbons (hereinafter cited as Gibbons, *The U.S. Government and the Vietnam War*), p. 190. See also George C. Herring and Richard H. Immerman, "Eisenhower, Dulles and Dienbienphu: 'The Day We Didn't Go to War,' Revisited," *Journal of American History*, 71:2 (September 1984), pp. 343–363.

19. Gibbons, *The U.S. Government and the Vietnam War*, I, pp. 215, 241.

20. Roy, *The Battle of Dienbienphu*, pp. 268ff. There were many levels of irony, given the large number of former SS men fighting in the French ranks. Ten years after the defeat, Bigeard told Bernard Fall: "If you had given me 10,000 S.S. troopers we'd have held out."

21. Lucien Bodard, *The Quicksand War: Prelude to Vietnam* (Boston: Little, Brown, 1967), p. 3.

22. For a hostile discussion of Giap's tactics, see Phillip B. Davidson, *Vietnam at War: The History: 1946–1975* (Novato, Calif.: Presidio, 1988), pp. 25–31.

23. Quoted in Buttinger, *Vietnam at War*, p. 795.

24. General Vo Nguyen Giap, *People's War, People's Army* (New York: Frederick Praeger, 1962), p. 187. This is a facsimile edition of the Hanoi Foreign Languages Press edition. A later, expanded version of Giap's essays on the subject was published in English by the Foreign Languages Press in 1964. What is especially interesting about the Praeger edition, however, is its American subtitle: "The Viet Cong Insurrection Manual for Underdeveloped Countries," and the Introduction by Roger Hilsman, an aide to President Kennedy.

25. Roy, *The Battle of Dienbienphu*, pp. 230, 231, 295–296; Hilsman Introduction to Giap, *People's War*, p. viii.

Chapter 3

1. For an account of the United States at Geneva, see Gardner, *Approaching Vietnam*. See also James Cable, *The Geneva Conference of 1954 on Indochina* (New York: St. Martin's Press, 1986), which credits the British for the "limited agreement" reached there. François Joyant's *La Chine et le réglement du premier conflit d'Indochine* (Paris: Publications de la Sorbonne, 1979) is the most comprehensive account of China's role.

2. See George McT. Kahin, *Intervention: How America Became Involved in Vietnam.* (Garden City, N.Y.: Doubleday, 1987), p. 60.

3. Report by Ho Chi Minh to the Sixth Plenum of the Party Central Committee, July 15, 1954, in Porter, ed., *A History in Documents*, pp. 156–157.

4. In the event, the Chinese were actually helpful to France on Laos and Cambodia. So long as no U.S. military bases were established in either place, Zhou Enlai was ready to ignore the claims of local Viet Minh-backed insurgents. See Kahin, *Intervention*, p. 58. For the text of the agreements, see Porter, ed., *A History in Documents*, pp. 159–160, or Gettleman, et al., eds., *Vietnam and America*, pp. 70–84.

5. Quoted in Gibbons, *The U.S. Government and the Vietnam War*, I, p. 91.

6. Quoted in D. Michael Shafer, *Deadly Paradigms: The Failure of U.S. Counterinsurgency Policy* (Princeton, N.J.: Princeton University Press, 1988), p. 217; Dulles quote in Gibbons, *The U.S. Government and the Vietnam War*, I, p. 260, n. 105. Shafer explores the problems with the Philippine model with insight; see also Larry E. Cable, *Conflict of Myths: The Development of American Counterinsurgency Doctrine and the Vietnam War* (New York: New York University Press, 1986). Lansdale's autobiography, *In the Midst of Wars* (New York: Harper & Row, 1972), as well as a recent biography by Cecil Currey, are less critical of his contribution. On the Philippine policy in the immediate postwar period, see Michael Schaller, *MacArthur: The Far Eastern General* (New York: Oxford University Press, 1989) and Alfred W. McCoy, "The Philippines: Independence Without Decolonisation," in Jeffrey, ed., *Asia—The Winning of Independence*, pp. 23–65.

7. The opinions of the ambassador and the chargé are quoted in Kahin, *Intervention*, p. 78. Diem was among a group of Vietnamese nationalists whom the French wished to jail as "disloyal" in 1943; the Japanese protected them, although at least one claimed he had no choice in the matter. See Huynh Kim Khanh, *Vietnamese Communists*, p. 245.

8. Cited in Kahin, *Intervention*, p. 78.

9. He is also widely assumed to be the model for Alden Pyle in Graham Greene's bitter political novel *The Quiet American*. In 1987, however, Greene explicitly denied this. See Christoper Robbins, Letter to the Editor, *New York Times Book Review*, June 18, 1989, p. 36.

10. Lansdale, *In the Midst of Wars*, p. 127.

11. Quoted in Buttinger, *Vietnam at War,*, p. 841.

12. International agreements over Laos in 1962 removed it from protocol protection as well.

13. Cited in Kahin, *Intervention*, p. 73.

14. Millenarian and syncretic (the eclectic Cao Dai pantheon included Victor Hugo), the sects had commanded the loyalty of significant segments of the rural population since the 1930s. Cao Dai adherents were said to number 2 million, with an armed militia of at least 20,000; Hoa Hao claimed 1 million members and an armed force of 15,000. The Binh Xuyen had 25,000 armed men and the entire police force of Saigon, which Bao Dai was said to have sold to Bay Vien, the Binh Xuyen leader, to pay off his gambling debts. See Ronald H. Spector, *Advice and Support, The Early Years of the U.S. Army in Vietnam, 1941–1960* (New York: The Free Press, 1985), p. 244.

15. Minutes, 218th meeting of the NSC, October 22, 1954, cited in Spector, *The Early Years*, p. 229.

16. Quoted in Gibbons, *The U.S. Government and the Vietnam War*, I, p. 296. Some of Dulles's reluctance came from his knowledge of how strong congressional support for Diem remained. Senator Mike Mansfield and other powerful members of the American Friends of Vietnam had already made it clear they would oppose any aid for Vietnam should Diem be replaced. For more details on the crisis, see Buttinger, *Vietnam at War*, chapter XI; Spector, *The Early Years*, chapter 13; Alfred McCoy, *The Politics of Heroin in Southeast Asia* (New York: Harper & Row, 1972) pp. 121–126. Kahin, *Intervention*, pp. 78ff; and Lansdale's own dramatic rendition of events, *In the Midst of Wars*, pp. 245ff.

17. See J. J. Zasloff, "Political Motivation of the Viet Cong: The Vietminh Regroupees," a report prepared by the RAND Corporation for the Department of Defense in 1966 (RM-4703/2-ISA/ARPA, May 1968). Extensive excerpts from the seventy-one intensive interviews conducted by American social scientists in the South in 1964–65 give an intimate view of the thoughts and feelings of the southerners.

18. Landlords, some 3.2 percent of the population, owned 24.5 percent of the land; middle peasants, 31 percent of the population, owned 29 percent. See Table 8-3 in Edwin E. Moise, *Land Reform in China and North Vietnam: Consolidating the Revolution at the Village Level* (Chapel Hill, N.C.: University of North Carolina Press, 1983), p. 151.

19. Zasloff, "The Vietminh Regroupees," p. 50. Moise suggests five thousand as the "rough order" of those killed during land reform—*Land Reform*, p.

222. See also his interesting analysis in "Class-ism in North Vietnam, 1953–1956," in *Vietnamese Communism in Comparative Perspective,* edited by William S. Turley (Boulder, Colo.: Westview Press, 1980), pp. 91–106. See also Gareth Porter, "The Myth of the Bloodbath: North Vietnam's Land Reform Reconsidered," *Bulletin of Concerned Asian Scholars,* 5:2 (September 1973), pp. 2–15. Christine Pelzer White offers a close view of the profound social and ideological transformation land reform required and engendered in "Mass Mobilization and Ideological Transformation in the Vietnamese Land Reform Campaign," *Journal of Contemporary Asia,* 13:1 (1983), pp. 74–89. See also Alexander Woodside, "Decolonization and Agricultural Reform in North Vietnam," for an especially sensitive reading of the land reform effort. *Asian Survey,* X:8 (August 1970), pp. 705–723.

20. Discomfited, the American interrogator hastens to reassure his Defense Department readers that the prisoner probably found life in the North affluent compared to his mountain home and anyway his views "reflect heavy communist indoctrination." See Zasloff, "The Vietminh Regroupees," p. 65.

21. Initially the economic results of both land reform and the early cooperatives were excellent, with high growth rates, the successful initiation of a number of major irrigation projects, and generally rising incomes. By the early 1970s, however, serious problems in the collective agricultural sector had emerged. See Kolko, *Anatomy of a War,* for a generally sanguine account; see also Melanie Beresford, *Vietnam: Politics, Economics and Society,* (London and New York: Pinter Publishers, 1988), especially chapter 9. An interesting account of the collectivization debates and campaigns can be found in Alec Gordon, "North Vietnam's Collectivisation Campaigns: Class Struggle, Production and the 'Middle-Peasant Problem,'" *Journal of Contemporary Asia,* 11:1 (1981), pp. 19–43.

22. Beresford, *Vietnam,* p. 120, and see chapter 9 passim; see also Kolko, *Anatomy of a War,* pp. 69–71.

23. Dulles to American Embassy, Paris, July 7, 1954. *Pentagon Papers,* Gravel edition (Boston: Beacon Press, 1971; hereinafter cited as *PP.* [Gravel]), Vol. I, pp. 546–547.

24. Cited in Kahin, *Intervention,* p. 89.

25. *PP* (Gravel), I:285.

26. On the referendum, see Buttinger, *Vietnam at War,* p. 891; Lansdale, *In the Midst of Wars,* pp. 331–334; Donald Lancaster, *The Emancipation of French Indochina* (New York: Oxford University Press, 1961). State Department report cited in Kahin, *Intervention,* p. 89.

27. *PP* (Gravel), I:247.

28. Zasloff, "The Vietminh Regroupees," p. 55.

29. Ho Chi Minh, "Letter to the Cadres from South Viet-Nam Regrouped in the North," June 19, 1956, in *Ho Chi Minh on Revolution: Selected Writings, 1920–66,* edited by Bernard B. Fall (New York: New American Library, 1966), pp. 273, 274.

30. Quoted in Jeffrey Race, *War Comes to Long An: Revolutionary Conflict in a Vietnamese Province* (Berkeley, Calif.: University of California Press, 1973), p. 74.

31. Joseph Alsop, "A Man in a Mirror," *The New Yorker,* June 25, 1955, pp. 35–36, 38–39, 43.

32. Race, *War Comes to Long An*, pp. 9–10, 11.

33. See Alfred McCoy, "Land Reform as Counter-Revolution: U.S. Foreign Policy and the Tenant Farmers of Asia," *Bulletin of Concerned Asian Scholars*, 3:1 (Winter–Spring 1971). While the program in the Philippines may have begun with promises of basic social change, by the mid-1950s its focus was far more narrow—just enough reform to keep rural discontent at a manageable level.

34. Quoted in McCoy, "Land Reform," p. 34; see also Robert L. Sansom, *The Economics of Insurgency in the Mekong Delta of Vietnam* (Cambridge, Mass.: MIT Press, 1970), especially chapters 2 and 3; William Bredo (who headed the Stanford study), "Agrarian Reform in Vietnam: Vietcong and Government of Vietnam Strategies in Conflict," *Asian Survey*, X:8 (August 1970), pp. 738–750. See also Spector, *The Early Years*, pp. 309, 311 for CIA report, including an account of the reinstatement of corvée labor.

35. Cited in Gibbons, *The U.S. Government and the Vietnam War*, I, pp. 303–304; n. 74.

36. See Robert Scheer, "How the United States Got Involved in Vietnam" (Report to the Center for the Study of Democratic Institutions, Santa Barbara, California, 1965), reprinted in Gettleman, et al., eds., *Vietnam and America*, pp. 118–131, 136–156.

37. Text of Diem's speech in *The New York Times*, May 10, 1957, p. 12. Russell Baker reported the event in the *Times*, observing that the audience seemed to have trouble following Diem's English but burst into loud applause at his pledge to protect the area's resources from the Communists, pp. 1, 12; May 10, 1957, "Man in the News" profile; visit to New York, May 14, 1957.

Chapter 4

1. French reporter quoted in Buttinger, *Vietnam at War*, p. 1164, n. 157. For "Colegrove" hearings, see Gibbons, *The U.S. Government and the Vietnam War*, I, pp. 321ff.

2. Civic Action goal quoted in Race, *Long An*, p. 27. See also Buttinger, *Vietnam at War*, pp. 975ff. In an interview with a U.S. officer, Buttinger was assured that no "real Commie" ever escaped: they were simply "held under water until they stopped kicking", (p. 1165, n. 158); Civic Action account from Race, *Long An*, pp. 25, 26. A young Vietnamese assigned to such a team explained why it was so difficult to persuade people of the government position: "during the Resistance the communists had been the only ones in the village to fight against the French, so when we tried to explain that communists were evil people, the villagers just wouldn't listen to us." There was a three-way dispute among Diem, General Williams (who agreed with Diem), and the head of the police training group, Leland Barrows, over whether the Civil Guards should operate out of the Ministry of the Interior or the Ministry of Defense. See Spector, *The Early Years*, pp. 321–325.

3. Wilfred Burchett, *Vietnam: Inside Story of a Guerrilla War* (New York: International Publishers, 1965), p. 127; Race, *Long An*, p. 27; W. P. Davison and J. J. Zasloff, "A Profile of Viet Cong Cadres," RAND RM-4983-1-ISA-ARPA, June

1966, p. 7; Nguyen Thi Dinh, *No Other Road to Take,* translated by Mai Elliott, Cornell University Southeast Asia Program, June 1976, pp. 50, 51. Quoted with the permission of the author. "There are two seasons in the South," Nguyen Thi Dinh wrote, "the dry and the rainy season. But under the regime of Ngo Dinh Diem . . . the people were battered by wind and rain all year round" (p. 48).

4. An abridged version of Law 10/59 is reprinted in Gettleman, et al., eds., *Vietnam and America,* pp. 157–161.

5. Davison and Zasloff, "Portrait," p. 7; Race, *Long An,* p. 67.

6. See Carlyle A. Thayer, "Southern Vietnamese Revolutionary Organizations and the Vietnam Workers' Party: Continuity and Change, 1954–1974," in *Communism in Indochina; New Perspectives,* edited by Joseph J. Zasloff and MacAlister Brown (Lexington, Mass.: Heath & Co., 1975), pp. 38ff.; Kahin, *Intervention,* pp. 105ff.

7. Race, *Long An,* pp. 99, 100.

8. Phan Thi Nhu Bang, "Ta Thi Kieu, An heroic girl of Ben Tre" (South Vietnam: Liberation Editions n.d.), p. 18. I am grateful to Christine Pelzer White for bringing this account to my attention.

9. See Thayer, "Southern Vietnamese Revolutionary Organizations," p. 42.

10. Tran Van Tra, *Concluding the 30-Years War,* Vol. 5 of *Vietnam: History of the Bulwark B 2 Theatre* (JPRS 82783, SEA Report 1247, National Technical Information Service, Springfield, Va., February 2, 1983), p. 53.

11. Race, *Long An,* pp. 49, 50–51, 65, 66.

12. See Nguyen Thi Dinh, *No Other Road to Take.* The Ben Tre campaign is described on pp. 62ff.

13. David Hunt, "Organizing for Revolution in Vietnam: Study of a Mekong Delta Province," *Radical America,* 8·1–2 (January–April 1974), pp. 14, 15.

14. Nguyen Thi Dinh, *No Other Road to Take,* pp. 73–74.

15. Household requirements listed in ibid., p. 51; account of noisemaking from Hunt, "Organizing," pp. 31, 34.

16. Race, *Long An,* p. 124, and see n. 17.

17. Sansom, *The Economics of Insurgency,* pp. 58, 59.

18. Donnell, Pauker, Zasloff, "Viet Cong Motivation and Morale in 1964: A Preliminary Report" RAND RM450713, March 1965, pp. 27, 29.

19. For text, see Bernard B. Fall, *The Two Viet-Nams: A Political and Military Analysis* (New York: Frederick Praeger, 1967), pp. 435–441. Years later, Diem's own chief of staff, Tran Van Don, echoed the sentiments of the group. The "use of Gestapo-like police raids and torture were known and descried everywhere. Had they [the Ngo Dinh family] confined themselves to known Communists or proven Communist sympathizers, one could understand their methods. The repression, however, spread to people who simply opposed their regime, such as heads or spokesmen of other political parties, and against individuals who were resisting extortion by some of the government officials" —*Our Endless War: Inside Vietnam* (San Rafael, Calif.: Presidio Press, 1978), p. 66.

20. See "Letter from the Party Committee for South Viet-Nam to Party Chapters," March 28, 1960, in Gareth Porter, ed., *Vietnam: The Definitive Documentation of Human Decisions,* Vol. 2 (Stanfordville, N.Y.: Earl M. Coleman

Enterprises, 1979), pp. 59–68. See also "Lao Dong Study Document on Revolutionary Strategy in the South, 1960," in *ibid.,* pp. 52–53. "Our Party does not advocate guerrilla warfare because our Party realizes that: Peace is the most urgent hope of our people. After many years of war, peace is profitable for the restoration of normal life of the people in the South and to create good conditions for the construction of socialism in the North."

21. For text, see Porter, ed., *Definitive Documentation,* Vol. 2, pp. 86–89.

22. Truong Nhu Tang, *A Viet Cong Memoir,* p. 68.

23. James Walker Trullinger, Jr., *Village at War: An Account of Revolution in Vietnam* (New York: Longman, 1980), pp. 79, 80.

24. Race, *Long An,* p. 116.

25. Central Committee member Hoang Tung, cited in Gareth Porter, *A Peace Denied: The United States, Vietnam, and the Paris Agreement* (Bloomington, Ind.: Indiana University Press, 1975), p. 16. For Party anxiety over the speed of events, see especially "Letter from the Party Committee for South Viet-Nam to Party Chapters, March 28, 1960," in Porter, ed., *Definitive Documentation,* Vol. 2, pp. 59–68. January directive cited in William S. Turley, *The Second Indochina War* (New York: New American Library, 1986), p. 29.

26. See Turley, *Second Indochina War,* p. 31.

27. *Ibid.,* pp. 42, 43.

28. Trullinger, *Village at War,* p. 91.

29. Williams complained to Diem about the unsatisfactory ratio of weapons lost without "corresponding personnel losses." See Spector, *The Early Years,* p. 343.

30. See Cable, *Conflict of Myths,* pp. 33ff. for the Korean model on which Army doctrine was based. Cable however accepts the conventional account of Korea, which has been persuasively challenged in Bruce Cumings and Jon Halliday, *Korea: The Unknown War* (New York: Pantheon Books, 1989).

31. *Ibid.,* p. 361.

32. Durbrow to Secretary of State Christian Herter, September 16 and October 15, 1960 with two enclosures, *U.S.-Vietnam Relations, 1945–1967* (Washington, D.C.: Government Printing Office, 1971; hereinafter cited as *PP* [GPO] 10:1318–22).

33. Kennedy to graduating class at West Point, 1962, quoted in Andrew F. Krepinevich, Jr., *The Army and Vietnam* (Baltimore: Johns Hopkins University, 1986), pp. 29–30.

34. The speech was part of Khrushchev's ongoing polemic against China. For an interesting analysis of the speech and the Kennedy administration's misreading of Khrushchev's intent, see Marek Thee, *Notes of a Witness, Laos and the Second Indochinese War* (New York: Random House, 1973), pp. 19–29. Kennedy insisted that the speech be widely disseminated within the government. See Douglas S. Blaufarb, *The Counterinsurgency Era: U.S. Doctrine and Performance, 1950 to the Present* (New York: The Free Press, 1977), pp. 52–54.

35. Gibbons, *The U.S. Government and the Vietnam War,* Part II, pp. 13, 14, 15.

36. For an astute discussion, see Shafer, *Deadly Paradigms,* chapter 5, "Mao Minus Marx."

37. Arthur Schlesinger, Jr., *A Thousand Days* (Boston: Houghton Mifflin,

1965), p. 339; memorandum to Hilsman, May 11, 1962, *Diplomatic History,* 3:3 (Summer 1979), p. 220.

38. Chester Cooper, *The Lost Crusade: America in Vietnam* (New York: Dodd, Mead, 1970), p. 191. See John Prados, *Presidents' Secret Wars: CIA and Pentagon Covert Operations from World War II Through Iranscam* (New York: William Morrow, 1986), chapter 15, for a concise account of Eisenhower and Kennedy policy as well as the growth of Vang Pao's army.

39. Cooper, *Lost Crusade,* p. 191; William Sullivan interview cited in Gibbons, *The U.S. Government and the Vietnam War,* II, p. 24.

40. Bundy to Lucius D. Battle, Executive Secretary for the State Department, cited in Gibbons, *The U.S. Government and the Vietnam War,* II, p. 33.

41. *Ibid.,* pp. 42, 43.

42. Krepinevich, Jr., *The Army and Vietnam,* p. 58, has a succinct account of the debate in this period.

43. *PP* (Gravel), II:92ff.

44. *Ibid.,* II:88–92.

45. For Komer, see Gibbons, *The U.S. Government and the Vietnam War,* II, p. 81; Chayes memorandum, November 16, 1961, *FRUS Vietnam, 1961,* 1, pp. 629–631; Rostow to President, November 11, 1961, pp. 574–575; Roger Hilsman to President, November 16, 1961, p. 620; McGeorge Bundy to President, November 15, 1961, p. 605; Notes on the National Security Council Meeting, November 15, 1961, pp. 608, 609.

46. For a generally positive view of the subject, see Paul Frederick Cecil, *Herbicidal Warfare: The RANCH HAND Project in Vietnam* (New York: Frederick Praeger, 1986). For the effects of spraying on the Americans who were sent to do the job, see Fred A. Wilcox, *Waiting for an Army to Die: The Tragedy of Agent Orange* (New York: Random House, 1983), and Tod Ensign and Michael Uhl, *GI Guinea Pigs: How the Pentagon Exposed Our Troops to Dangers More Deadly than War* (New York: Playboy Press, 1980). For bibliography on the postwar effects on Vietnamese, see Caroline D. Harnly's annotated bibliography, *Agent Orange and Vietnam,* (Metuchen, N.J.: Scarecrow Press, 1988).

47. See Race, *Long An,* pp. 53–55, for a description of an agroville project in that province which, typically, failed in all its objectives, from security to bringing "the light of civilization" to the relocated population. See also *PP* (Gravel), II:133–134, for an account of agrovilles as the precursor to strategic hamlets. For the Pentagon historians' account of the program, see *ibid.,* II:128–159.

48. See *ibid.,* II:149, and Fall, *The Two Viet-Nams,* pp. 377–380.

49. Roger Hilsman, *To Move a Nation: The Politics of Foreign Policy in the Administration of John F. Kennedy* (Garden City, N.Y.: Doubleday, 1967), p. 436. For Hilsman's self-justifying account of how and why strategic hamlets failed, see pp. 522–526. An excellent analysis of Hilsman is John McDermott's review essay, "Crisis Manager," in *New York Review of Books,* September 14, 1967.

50. Burchett, *Vietnam: Inside Story of the Guerilla War,* pp. 43ff; for an account of the tunnel system at this early stage in the war, see pp. 50ff. On the difference between watch towers and ground-level fire positions, p. 45.

51. The document is included in Michael Charles Conley's *The Communist*

Insurgent Infrastructure in South Vietnam: A Study of Organization and Strategy (Center for Research in Social Systems, the American University, Washington, D.C., 1966). Conley's report was prepared for the Department of the Army.

52. See David Hunt, "Remember the Tet Offensive," for a succinct description of how guerrilla warfare in a densely populated area unfolds over time, so that "morale and political strength, rather than territory occupied, are the keys to victory." *Radical America*, 11–12 (November 1977–February 1978), reprinted in Gettleman, et al., eds., *Vietnam and America*, pp. 355–372. Krepinevich, Jr., *The Army and Vietnam*, is extremely critical of the Army approach to counterinsurgency. On the use and misuse of the Green Berets, see pp. 69–73. Krepinevich argues that the U.S. military consistently lost sight of counterinsurgency, whose goal is the *"defeat* of an insurgent movement, primarily its infrastructure and guerrilla forces." Instead, attention was focused on unconventional warfare, which is concerned with "the *organizing* of partisan and guerrilla forces and their employment . . . to supplement the activities of friendly conventional forces" (pp. 69–70). Krepinevich insists that counterinsurgency never really got a chance in Vietnam. However, his examples of successful counterinsurgency in Vietnam are few and explicable by the special character of the region in which they occurred. He does not explain how Americans could have organized villages along the lines described in the report on XB. Ngo Vinh Long, "The Tet Offensive and Its Aftermath," Part 3. *Indochina Newsletter*, 60 (November–December, 1989), describes the dependence of main force units on village and hamlet guerrilla squads throughout the war.

53. Georges Condominas, *We Have Eaten the Forest* (New York: Hill & Wang, 1977), pp. xiv–xv.

54. David Marr, "The Rise and Fall of Counterinsurgency, 1961–1964," in Gettleman, et al., eds., *Vietnam and America*, p. 206.

Chapter 5

1. *Times Talk*, 16:9 (October 1963). This was brought to my attention by Ellen J. Hammer in *A Death in November: America in Vietnam, 1963* (New York: E. P. Dutton, 1987), pp. 84–85. Twenty years later, Halberstam reflected more somberly on his experiences in Vietnam in an essay he called "Letter to My Daughter." Though still half in love with the "rare camaraderie" of war, he wished that while he reacted with outrage when Marguerite Higgins spread the story that he had wept when shown a photograph of dead NLF, it had in fact been true. *Vietnam Voices: Perspectives on the War Years, 1941–1982,* compiled by John Clark Pratt (New York: Viking/Penguin, 1984), pp. 658–665.

2. Neil Sheehan, *A Bright Shining Lie: John Paul Vann and America in Vietnam* (New York: Random House, 1988), p. 315. Sheehan adds: "Our ignorance and our American ideology kept us from discerning the larger truths of Vietnam beneath the surface reality we could see. Professionally, we were fortunate in our ignorance. Had any reporter been sufficiently knowledgeable and open-minded to have questioned the justice and good sense of U.S. intervention in those years, he would have been fired as a 'subversive.'"

3. The best account of the press in the war is Daniel Hallin, *The "Uncensored War": The Media and Vietnam* (New York: Oxford University Press, 1986). The Kennedy years are discussed in chapter 2. Diem could expel reporters he found particularly difficult. In September 1962, *Newsweek* correspondent François Sully, a French citizen whose bleak account of Operation SUNRISE and generally pessimistic assessments of the war offended Diem and the U.S. mission, was expelled. John Mecklin insisted that the embassy protest, which it did somewhat reluctantly and ultimately unsuccessfully. Mecklin, *Mission in Torment: An Intimate Account of the U.S. Role in Vietnam.* (Garden City, N.Y.: Doubleday, 1965), pp. 134–136, 140.

4. Memorandum from John Mecklin to USIS Vietnamese Staff, May 25, 1962, Mecklin Collection, Baker Library, Dartmouth College. *Newsweek* commented that it might be a good idea to conduct "another contest . . . to find a new name for the Saigon USIA, which would make it look just a little less silly— perhaps a colloquial term implying dismay or bewilderment" (June 18, 1962, p. 35). The prize money was divided three ways with first prize for *giac ho*—Ho pirates. But Mecklin was finally persuaded by Thompson that it was probably unwise to drop the word "Cong," since "the enemy is indeed the Communist world . . . and the word can be made to have a reprehensible meaning"—Mecklin to W. K. Bunce, USIA, August 20, 1962.

5. Memo from Captain McCarthy, PsyWar/CA Advisor, Tuy Hoa, II Corps, June 10, 1963, to Senior PsyWar Advisor; Dave [Sheppard?] to Mecklin, May 14, (no year indicated).

6. Davison and Zasloff, "Profile of Viet Cong Cadre," p. 56.

7. *PP* (Gravel), II:722–723.

8. O'Donnell quoted in Gibbons, *The U.S. Government and the Vietnam War,* II, pp. 138, 137, fn.1.

9. See *ibid.,* pp. 140–141.

10. Hammer, *Death in November,* pp. 121, 122.

11. Nolting to Department of State, April 6, 1963, cited in Kahin, *Intervention,* p. 144.

12. Hammer, *Death in November,* pp. 203, 123.

13. Trullinger, *Village at War,* p. 84.

14. See Hallin, *The "Uncensored War,"* pp. 43–48.

15. David Halberstam, *The Making of a Quagmire: America and Vietnam during the Kennedy Era* (rev. eds., New York: Alfred A. Knopf, 1988), pp. 112–113.

16. Not, apparently, a unique event; the heart of a 1948 Vietnamese Buddhist martyr had also failed to burn. Nor, it is said, did the poet Shelley's.

17. Hammer, *Death in November,* pp. 177, 221ff.; Kahin, *Intervention,* pp. 153ff.; Mieczyslaw Maneli, *War of the Vanquished* (New York: Harper & Row, 1971), pp. 112–152. Maneli, the Polish delegate to the International Control Commission, served as an informal intermediary.

18. Hilsman to Lodge, August 24, 1963, cited in Gibbons, *The U.S. Government and the Vietnam War,* II, p. 149. Kennedy to Lodge, August 29, cable marked "No Other Distribution Whatever," *ibid.,* pp. 158–159.

19. Lodge to Rusk, August 30, 1963, in *ibid.,* p. 160.

20. Interview with Kattenburg, February 16, 1979, in *ibid.,* p. 161. See also

account in Kahin, *Intervention,* pp. 165–166. The memorandum of the August 31 meetings is in *PP* (Gravel), II:741–743.

21. Rusk to Lodge, August 31, cited in Gibbons, *The U.S. Government and the Vietnam War,* II, p. 163.

22. *Ibid.,* p. 175.

23. *Ibid.,* p. 165.

24. White House to Lodge, September 17, 1963; Lodge to Kennedy, September 19, 1963, *PP* (Gravel), II:743–746; 746–748.

25. *PP* (Gravel), II:243, 244.

26. Quoted in Kahin, *Intervention,* p. 168.

27. Report of the McNamara-Taylor Mission, October 2, 1963, *PP* (Gravel), II:751–766.

28. Quoted in Gibbons, *The U.S. Government and the Vietnam War,* II, pp. 189; Lodge to McGeorge Bundy, October 25, 1963, *PP* (Gravel), II:780–781.

29. For the coup planning, see *PP* (Gravel), II:264–270; Gibbons, *The U.S. Government and the Vietnam War,* II, pp. 196, 201, n. 182; U.S. Congress, Senate Committee on Foreign Relations, *U.S. Involvement in the Overthrow of Diem, 1963,* Staff Study, 92d Congress, 2d sess. (Washington, D.C.: Government Printing Office, 1972); Halberstam, *Quagmire;* Hammer, *Death in November,* pp. 169–311.

Chapter 6   ————————

1. Gibbons, *The U.S. Government and the Vietnam War,* II, p. 209.

2. Doris Kearns, *Lyndon Johnson and the American Dream* (New York: Harper & Row, 1976), pp. 251, 259–260.

3. Kahin, *Intervention,* p. 185.

4. Memos from Bundy and Rostow to Johnson, January 6 and 10, 1964, quoted in Kahin, *Intervention,* pp. 191, 192.

5. *PP* (Gravel), II:307.

6. *Ibid.,* 96, 98.

7. See Cable, *Conflict of Myths,* p. 216, for the view that non-Western modes of thought were the key.

8. The most complete account of U.S. involvement in the coup is Kahin, *Intervention,* pp. 194ff.

9. For Khanh's amenability, see *PP* (Gravel), II:309, 310; McNamara report to Johnson, March 8, 1964, *ibid.,* II:312; Kahin, *Intervention,* p. 205.

10. *PP* (Gravel), II:459–461.

11. *Ibid.,* III:155–156.

12. Both Morse and Ford are quoted in Gibbons, *The U.S. Government and the Vietnam War,* II, pp. 224, 227.

13. CBS Reports: "Vietnam: the Deadly Decision," transcript of broadcast, April 1, 1964. Kalischer interviewed an American adviser in "Viet Cong country," Long An Province. The adviser insisted on the importance of the "little farmer" in Vietnam and the need to "win their feelings." The "man who gets the support of this farmer . . . is going to eventually win this war." Asked to describe

how he pursued this goal, the officer replied: "I feel that being humble and putting yourself in their position is a way to do it. I have gone out and helped them pick watermelons. I walk around with my bodyguard . . . and we go visit them and drink tea with them in . . . their houses, and . . . this is an oddity to them, because they can't imagine that an American can put himself in this position."

14. *PP* (Gravel), III:169.

15. Kahin, *Intervention,* p. 207.

16. The January plan had been recommended under NSAM-273, which Johnson approved on November 26, 1963, only a few days after Kennedy's death. There were 2,062 separate operations whose purposes were: "(1) harassment; (2) diversion; (3) political pressures; (4) capture of prisoners; (5) physical destruction; (6) acquisition of intelligence; (7) generation of intelligence; (8) diversion of DRV resources." Included were "selected actions of graduated scope and intensity to include commando type coastal raids," *PP* (Gravel), III:150–151.

17. Lodge suggested that if some "terroristic act" occurred before Seaborn arrived in Hanoi, "a specific target in North Vietnam" should be hit "as a prelude to his arrival." Lodge to LBJ, May 15, 1964, quoted in Cable, *Conflict of Myths,* p. 215.

18. *The Secret Diplomacy of the Vietnam War: The Negotiating Volume of the Pentagon Papers,* edited by George C. Herring (Austin, Tex.: University of Texas Press, 1983), p. 11. See also Wallace J. Thies, *When Governments Collide: Coercion and Diplomacy in the Vietnam Conflict 1964–1968* (Berkeley, Calif.: University of California Press, 1980), pp. 37–38.

19. *PP* (GPO) 3, IV, C:1, 84.

20. See Turley, *Second Indochina War,* pp. 57–60, for a discussion of the heated debate that occurred, and how it reflected and was exacerbated by the Sino-Soviet split.

21. Eugene C. Windchy, *Tonkin Gulf* (Garden City, N.Y.: Doubleday, 1971), pp. 75, 92. This account is drawn from the transcript of hearings conducted by the Senate Foreign Relations Committee in 1968, *The Gulf of Tonkin: the 1964 Incidents;* Joseph C. Goulden, *Truth Is the First Casualty* (Chicago: Rand McNally, 1969); Anthony Austin, *The President's War* (Philadelphia: J. B. Lippincott, 1971); and the extremely useful essay "The 'Phantom Battle' That Led to War" in *U.S. News and World Report,* July 23, 1984. See also the narrative in *PP* (Gravel), V:320–341, and Gibbons, *The U.S. Government and the Vietnam War,* II, chapter 5.

22. Windchy, *Tonkin Gulf,* p. 122.

23. Porter, "Tonkin Gulf Reconsidered,"unpublished paper, n.p.; Notes on NSC Meetings, Gibbons, *The U.S. Government and the Vietnam War,* II, p. 293.

24. James Bond and Sybil B. Stockdale, *In Love and War,* (New York: Harper & Row, 1984), pp. 19, 23. Stockdale gives the same account, in somewhat different words, in Kim Willenson's *The Bad War: An Oral History of the Vietnam War* (New York: New American Library, 1987), pp. 29–35.

25. *Love and War,* p. 25; *Bad War,* p. 31.

26. Text of the resolution reprinted in Gettleman, et al., eds., *Vietnam and America,* p. 250.

27. Goulden, *Truth Is the First Casualty,* p. 48.

28. *Ibid.,* p. 59.

29. Interviews with Katzenbach and Fascell in Gibbons, *The U.S. Government and the Vietnam War,* II, pp. 307, 308.

30. *Ibid.,* pp. 326, 327, 334.

31. Michael Charlton and Anthony Moncrieff, *Many Reasons Why: The American Involvement in Vietnam* (New York: Hill & Wang, 1978), p. 112.

32. Gibbons, *The U.S. Government and the Vietnam War,* II, pp. 322, 300. For a discussion of the theory and practice of coercive diplomacy in Vietnam, see Thies, *When Governments Collide.*

33. For press coverage, see Hallin, *The "Uncensored War,"* pp. 15ff.

34. *PP* (Gravel), III:153.

35. See Porter, "Tonkin Gulf Reconsidered."

36. Herring, ed., *Secret Diplomacy,* p. 12.

Chapter 7

1. Truong Nhu Tang, *A Viet Cong Memoir,* p. 93.

2. CIA, SNIE 53–64, September 8, 1964, cited in Kahin, *Intervention,* p. 234.

3. *PP* (Gravel), III:675 (Memorandum of Meeting on Southeast Asia, November 27, 1964: Rusk, McNamara, Taylor, McCone, Wheeler, Ball, Wm. Bundy, McGeorge Bundy, McNaughton, Forrestal).

4. *Ibid.,* 712.

5. *Ibid.,* II:335–336.

6. The text of the memorandum of October 5, 1964, can be found in "A Light That Failed," *Atlantic Monthly,* 230 (July 1972), pp. 35–49.

7. George Ball, *The Past Has Another Pattern,* (New York: W. W. Norton, 1982), p. 384. In an interview in 1979, McGeorge Bundy expressed his agreement with all of Ball's worries but said the alternative Ball presented was not "very persuasive, or, indeed, persuasive at all." Gibbons, *The U.S. Government and the Vietnam War,* Vol. II, p. 362, n. 47.

8. See Kahin, *Intervention,* pp. 243–245; Walter Johnson, "The U Thant-Stevenson Peace Initiatives in Vietnam, 1964–1965," *Diplomatic History,* I:3 (Summer 1977), pp. 285–290.

9. Cable, *Conflict of Myths,* p. 230; Philip Jones Griffiths, *Vietnam Inc.* (New York: Macmillan, 1971), p. 210. Guenter Lewy, *America in Vietnam* (New York: Oxford University Press, 1978), p. 267, states that CBUs were not used in the South until February 1968, which seems unlikely on the face of it and is flatly contradicted by Cable and by the testimony of Jean-Pierre Vigier, director of research at the National Center for Scientific Research in Paris. See *Against the Crime of Silence: Proceedings of the International War Crimes Tribunal,* edited by Richard A. Falk, et al. (New York: Simon & Schuster, 1970), p. 250. Vigier thought the first use was in February 1965.

10. *PP* (Gravel) III:593, 598, 599–600, 604, 605; on the relationship between negotiations and bombing, see p. 225.

11. The documents of the Working Group are still classified. The best

review of the debates in the Working Group and within the NSC is Gibbons, II, pp. 365ff. Johnson established the Working Group as a subgroup of the NSC shortly after his election. It was chaired by William Bundy and included Marshall Green, Michael Forrestal, and Robert Johnson from the State Department; John McNaughton and Vice Admiral Lloyd Mustin from the Defense Department; Harold Ford and George Carver from the CIA. It reported to Rusk, McNamara, McCone, Wheeler, Ball, and McGeorge Bundy of the NSC.

12. *PP* (Gravel), III:238.

13. *The Air War in Indochina,* edited by Raphael Littauer and Norman Uphoff, Air War Study Group, Cornell University (rev. ed. Boston: Beacon Press, 1972), pp. 25, 55–56. B-52s dropped over half the aerial tonnage on the South over the course of the war.

14. *New York Times,* February 2, 1965; Bernard Fall, " 'This Isn't Munich, It's Spain,' " *Last Reflections on a War* (Garden City, N.Y.: Doubleday, 1967), pp. 227–228.

15. For Johnson's hesitations, see *PP* (Gravel), III:248–251. Kahin, in *Intervention,* stresses Johnson's reluctance (p. 252), while Gibbons, in *The U.S. Government and the Vietnam War,* II, (p. 376), suggests that Johnson on the whole approved the Working Group recommendations. For the draft of Taylor's instructions, see *PP* (Gravel), III:679ff.

16. *PP* (Gravel), II:346ff.

17. Johnson to Taylor, December 30, 1964, quoted in Gibbons, *The U.S. Government and the Vietnam War,* II, p. 383.

18. *Ibid.,* pp. 387–388.

19. William Bundy, memorandum for the Secretary, January 6, 1965, in *ibid.,* III:684–686; McNaughton to McNamara, March 14, 1965, in *PP* (Gravel), III:695.

20. Kahin argues that the whole thing was a set-up, including the timing of Bundy's trip to Vietnam. See *Intervention,* pp. 276–280.

21. McGeorge Bundy, "A Policy of Sustained Reprisal," February 7, 1965, was an appendix to the analysis of the situation which Bundy and the group that had traveled with him in Vietnam drew up as they flew back to Washington. It appears in *PP* (Gravel), III:687–691. These quotations are on pp. 690, 689. Other parts of the memorandum are excerpted on pp. 308–311.

22. Zasloff, "Political Motivation of the Viet Cong: The Vietminh Regroupees," p. 125.

23. Truong Nhu Tang, *Viet Cong Memoir,* pp. 96, 98.

24. McGeorge Bundy, February 7, 1965, in *PP* (Gravel), III:691; 309.

25. This account is drawn from Kahin, *Intervention,* pp. 294ff.

26. Jack Langguth, *The New York Times,* March 3, 1965.

27. Taylor to State Department, February 22, 1965, in *PP* (Gravel), III:418–419.

28. James Clay Thompson, ROLLING THUNDER: *Understanding Program and Policy Failure* p. 71. (Chapel Hill, N.C.: University of North Carolina, 1980).

29. Quoted in *PP* (Gravel), III:354; Gloria Emerson, *Winners and Losers: Battles, Retreats, Gains and Ruins from a Long War* (New York: Random House, 1977), p. 377.

30. Cited in Kahin, *Intervention,* p. 290.On infiltration, see pp. 306–308.

31. Excerpts from the White Paper and Stone's critique are reprinted in Gettleman, et al. eds., *Vietnam and America,* pp. 253–270; Hanson Baldwin, *New York Times,* February 21, 1965.

32. Quoted in Michael Maclear, *The Ten Thousand Day War* (London: Thames Methuen, 1981), pp. 127–128.

33. Hallin, *The "Uncensored War,"* p. 132. Wallace Terry, *Bloods: An Oral History of the Vietnam War by Black Veterans* (New York: Ballantine Books, 1984), pp. 1, 2; Morley Safer was in the Amtrac with him. Safer has described the Cam Ne mission and its aftermath in *Flashbacks: On Returning to Vietnam* (New York: Random House, 1990), pp. 85–97.

34. Johnson was so enraged by the report that he accused Safer and CBS of having "shat on the flag" and demanded that Safer be fired or the White House would expose him as a Communist. Rusk remains convinced the entire incident was staged, and both Rusk and former Ambassador Graham Martin think Safer was a KGB agent—*Flashbacks,* pp. 94–95.

35. Blaufarb, *The Counterinsurgency Era,* p. 216. Chapter 7, "The Revival of Counterinsurgency, Vietnam, 1963–1967," is an excellent account of the various programs, including "Hop Tac," and the problems each new program encountered.

36. Sheehan, *Bright Shining Lie,* pp. 102–103.

37. Lodge's approach to pacification is discussed at length in *PP* (Gravel), II:527ff. The ten-point program is on p. 530.

38. Blaufarb, *Counterinsurgency,* pp. 216–217; John Ranelagh, *The Agency: The Rise and Decline of the CIA* (Simon and Schuster, 1986), pp. 439–440.

39. R. Michael Pearce, "Evolution of a Vietnamese Village—Part I: The present, after eight months of pacification," RAND, RM-4551-1-ARPA, April 1965; "Evolution of a Vietnamese Village—Part III: Duc Lap Since November 1964 and Some Comments on Village Pacification," p. 3, RM-5086-1-ISA/ARPA, February 1967.

40. For Vann in Hau Nghia, see Sheehan, *Bright Shining Lie,* pp. 508–518. For his plan to "harness the social revolution," see *ibid.,* pp. 537–538.

Chapter 8

1. This account of the Dominican intervention is based on Tad Szulc, *Dominican Diary* (New York: Delacorte Press, 1966), John Bartlow Martin, *Overtaken by Events: The Dominican Crisis from the Fall of Trujillo to the Civil War* (Garden City, N.Y.: Doubleday, 1966), and Walter LaFeber, *Inevitable Revolutions: The United States in Central America* (New York: W.W. Norton, 1984). Johnson's opinion of the OAS is quoted in LaFeber, p. 158.

2. John M. Mecklin to Hadley, July 21, 1965, Mecklin Papers.

3. Fred Halstead, *Out Now!: A Participant's Account of the American Movement Against the Vietnam War* (New York: Monad Press, 1978), p. 49.

4. Merle Miller, *Lyndon: An Oral Biography* (New York: G. P. Putnam's Sons, 1980), p. 480.

5. *PP* (Gravel), III:407–408 for chronology. Cooper quoted in Kahin, *Intervention,* p. 324.

6. Kahin, *Intervention,* p. 326. The account which follows is based on *ibid.,* pp. 326–331.

7. Herring, ed., *Secret Diplomacy,* p. 585.

8. Halstead, *Out Now!,* p. 52.

9. Mimeograph text of Kahin's speech, May 15, 1965. Excerpts from the exchange reprinted in Marcus G. Raskin and Bernard B. Fall, editors, *The Viet-Nam Reader* (New York: Random House, 1965), pp. 289–307. American withdrawal from Vietnam, Scalapino insisted, "would reduce American credibility with her allies and the neutrals around the world" and "a green light would be given to the new Communist-dominated National Liberation Movements even now getting underway."

10. Kahin, *Intervention,* p. 335. Ultimately 11,000 Thai, 50,000 Koreans, and 2,200 Filipinos served in Vietnam; as early as March 1966, the number of third-country troops outnumbered those from North Vietnam by 10,000. Patrick Lloyd Hatcher, *Suicide of an Elite: American Internationalists and Vietnam* (Stanford, Calif.: Stanford University Press, 1990) discusses the "more flags" program, pp. 56–57, 61–64. The program was essentially directed at the American public, for whom, Lodge believed, "psychologically it is important that others share with us the casualties of the U.S. effort here."

11. Kearns, *Lyndon Johnson,* p. 283.

12. This account of the decision to send troops is largely drawn from Kahin, *Intervention,* pp. 347–401; *PP* (Gravel), III:433–485. Johnson told Doris Kearns that the day Congress got into a "major debate on the war that day would be the beginning of the end of the Great Society," and he was determined to "keep the war from shattering that dream. . . ." Kearns, *Lyndon Johnson,* p. 281. In their section on the July decision, the authors of the Pentagon history, writing two years later, conclude: "No further proof of the monumental implications of the endorsement in the summer of 1965 of the search and destroy strategy, the 44 battalions, and the 'win' concept is required beyond the present state of the war in Vietnam. At this writing, the U.S. has reached the end of the time frame estimated by General Westmoreland in 1965 to be required to defeat the enemy. It has committed 107 battalions of its own forces and a grand total of 525,000 men. The strategy remains search and destroy, but victory is not in sight"—*PP* (Gravel), III:398. Statistics on the odds offered in *ibid.,* 484, Kahin, *Intervention,* p. 357.

13. Turley, *Second Indochina War,* pp. 75–77; Edward Doyle, Samuel Lipsman, et al., in *America Takes Over* (Boston: Boston Publishing Company, 1982), pp. 20–22, give a more upbeat account of the battle and list confirmed enemy dead as 573; Turley says 599 "VC" died, implying, as one might expect, a number of civilian casualties.

14. See Turley, *Second Indochina War,* pp. 77–78; Sheehan, *Bright Shining Lie,* pp. 571–79, 629–630, 682–683; Colonel David H. Hackworth, *About Face* (New York: Simon & Schuster, 1989), p. 496.

15. *PP* (Gravel), III:397, 452–461.

16. William C. Westmoreland, *A Soldier Remembers* (New York: Dell Publishing, 1980), pp. 104, 105. General William DePuy, who claims to have coined

the phrase, explained its use and misuse to Harry Maurer, in *Strange Ground: Americans in Vietnam 1945–1957; An Oral History* (New York: Henry Holt & Co., 1989), pp. 450–451.

17. Emerson, *Winners and Losers,* p. 84.

18. Sheehan, *Bright Shining Lie,* pp. 580–584; Terrence Maitland and Peter McInerney, eds., *A Contagion of War* (Boston: Boston Publishing Co., 1983), pp. 34–48.

19. Emerson, *Winners and Losers,* p. 84.

20. *The Dellums Committee Hearings on War Crimes in Vietnam: An Inquiry into Command Responsibility in Southeast Asia,* edited by the Citizens Commission of Inquiry (New York: Vintage Books, 1972), p. 174.

21. *Ibid.,* p. 283.

22. Thomas D. Boettcher, *Vietnam: The Valor and the Sorrow: From the Homefront to the Front Lines in Words and Pictures* (Boston: Little, Brown, 1985), p. 303, p. 304. See also Sheehan's exposition of Krulak's position. Krulak was stunned by the U.S. casualties at Ia Drang and thought Giap was trying to "attrit U.S. forces through the process of violent, close-quarters combat" in order to "erode our national will. . . ." He was convinced Westmoreland's war of attrition was a strategy of defeat and proposed instead continuous air attack against main force Communist units in the highlands, bombing and mining Haiphong and other North Vietnamese ports, elimination of rail links from China to Vietnam, and village-level pacification. With the exception of systematic bombing inside China's borders—the fear of provoking Chinese intervention was difficult to overcome—everything Krulak proposed was pursued, though not on his timetable.

23. *PP* (Gravel), IV:622.

24. *Ibid.* IV:623, 624.

25. See McCoy, *Politics of Heroin,* pp. 166–181 for details on the careers, rivalry and involvement in the narcotics trade of Ky and Thieu.

26. Kahin, *Intervention,* p. 413; Charles Mohr, *The New York Times,* October 24, 1966. Saigon authorities believed a cease-fire would be a "nightmare" if it precluded the South Vietnamese from continuing their effort to "destroy the Vietcong political organization."

27. Quoted in Kahin, *Intervention,* p. 416.

28. *Ibid.,* p. 417.

29. *Ibid.,* pp. 420, 421.

30. *Ibid.,* p. 421.

31. *Ibid.,* p. 422, 423.

32. David Halberstam, *The Best and the Brightest* (New York: Random House, 1972), p. 627; Miller, *Lyndon,* p. 413.

33. Kahin, *Intervention,* p. 425; Halberstam, *The Best and the Brightest,* p. 628.

34. Leo Cawley, "Vietnam Memoir," 1989 (unpublished) quoted with the permission of the author; Sheehan quoted in Kahin, *Intervention,* p. 429.

Chapter 9

1. Jonathan Schell, *The Real War: The Classic Reporting on the Vietnam War* (New York: Pantheon Books, 1988), pp. 112, 119, 120, 188.

2. Katsuichi Honda, *Vietnam: A Voice from the Villages*, p. 16. Honda's report was serialized in the *Asahi Shimbun* from September to October 1967. It was translated into English by Fujiko Isono and published in 1968 by a committee representing a number of Japanese anti-war groups.

3. Bryan Alec Floyd, "Corporal Charles Chungtu, U.S.M.C.," in *Carrying the Darkness: American Indochina—The Poetry of the Vietnam War*, edited by W. D. Ehrhart (New York: Avon Books, 1985), pp. 110–111. Quoted with the permission of the author.

4. Samuel P. Huntington, "The Bases of Accommodation," *Foreign Affairs* 46: 4 (July 1968) pp. 653, 650, 649. Civilian pacification advisers shared Huntington's view. One, quoted by Jonathan Schell, believed that refugees had a "better standard of living than they did in the villages." The camps brought people "in closer to the urban centers, where they can have modern experiences and learn modern practices. It's a modernizing experience." *Real War*, p. 393.

5. Westmoreland, *A Soldier Remembers*, p. 368.

6. Doris Kearns, *Lyndon Johnson*, pp. 270–271.

7. Miller, *Lyndon*, p. 490.

8. For DePuy, see Halberstam, *The Best and the Brightest*, p. 613; for Kissinger, see Ngo Vinh Long, "The War and the Vietnamese," in *Vietnam Reconsidered: Lessons from a War*, edited by Harrison E. Salisbury (New York: Harper & Row, 1984), p. 228; Westmoreland is quoted in Lewy, *America in Vietnam*, p. 73; McNamara quote is in Halberstam, p. 633. What made McNamara think the Vietnamese enjoyed the fighting is anyone's guess. Johnson on bombing pauses in Halberstam, p. 624.

9. *PP* (Gravel), IV:33. For the debate on this pause, which lasted from December 24, 1965, to January 31, 1966, see *ibid.*, pp. 32–53.

10. See Thies, *When Governments Collide*, pp. 115–122. See also Porter, *A Peace Denied*, pp. 54–55.

11. Cooper, *Lost Crusade*, pp. 295, 391, 339.

12. Allan E. Goodman, *The Lost Peace: America's Search for a Negotiated Settlement* (Stanford, Calif.: Hoover Institute, 1978), p. 27; David Kraslow and Stuart H. Loory, *The Secret Search for Peace in Vietnam* (New York: Random House, 1968), p. 182.

13. Goodman, *Lost Peace*, p. 26.

14. Cooper, *Lost Crusade*, p. 368.

15. Miller, *Lyndon*, p. 473. This account was drawn from *ibid.*, pp. 472–477. See also Harry S. Ashmore and William C. Baggs, *Mission to Hanoi* (New York: G. P. Putnam's Sons, 1968).

16. *PP* (Gravel), IV:136.

17. *Ibid.*

18. Robert L. Gallucci, *Neither Peace Nor Honor: The Politics of American Military Policy in Viet-Nam* (Baltimore: Johns Hopkins University, 1975), p. 94. See also Gallucci's excellent discussion of the ongoing tension between the JCS

and the Secretary of Defense, pp. 87ff. McNaughton report on bombing, a response to a JCS Memorandum on bombing policy, is in *PP* (Gravel), IV:43.

19. See the excellent discussion of the air war in James William Gibson, *The Perfect War: The War We Couldn't Lose and How We Did* (New York: Vintage Books, 1988), pp. 319–382; for Wheeler, *PP* (Gravel), IV:170.

20. Kahin, *Intervention,* p. 432.

21. Quoted in George Herring, *The Longest War: The United States & Vietnam, 1950–1975,* p. 160. (New York: John Wiley & Sons, 1979), p. 160.

22. Charles A. Joiner, *The Politics of Massacre: Political Processes in South Vietnam* (Philadelphia: Temple University Press, 1974), pp. 131, 158. At the time, Dzu's son, David Truong, was a peace activist in the United States.

23. Gibson, *Perfect War,* p. 109.

24. Lewy, *America in Vietnam,* p. 70.

25. Description of Trail from Sheehan, *Bright Shining Lie,* pp. 675–679; Turley, *Second Indochina War,* pp. 91–96.

26. *PP* (Gravel), IV:136, 171. McNamara also pointed to the high costs in lost pilots and planes: one in every 40 sorties at this point in the war.

27. David W. P. Elliott and W. A. Stewart, "Pacification and the Viet Cong System in Dinh Tuong: 1966–1967," RAND, RM-5788-ISA/ARPA, January 1969, p. 100; D. W. P. Elliott and C. A. H. Thomson, "A Look at the VC Cadres: Dinh Tuong Province, 1965–1966," RM-5114-1-ISA/ARPA, March 1967, pp. 26–27. The aim of both studies was to suggest where the NLF was vulnerable and to make recommendations on how best to exploit those vulnerabilities.

28. David Hunt, "Organizing for Revolution," p. 88.

29. *Ibid.,* pp. 88, 90.

30. *Ibid.,* pp. 148–154.

31. Konrad Kellen, "A View of the VC: Elements of Cohesion in the Enemy Camp in 1966 and 1967," RAND, RM-5462-1-ISA/ARPA, November 1969.

32. Russell Betts and Frank Denton, "An Evaluation of Chemical Crop Destruction in Vietnam," RAND RM-5446-1-ISA/ARPA, October 1967; Cecil, *RANCH HAND,* p. 108; Krepinevich, Jr., *The Army and Vietnam,* pp. 210–213.

33. Littauer, et al eds., *The Air War,* pp. 222–223.

34. Ranelagh, *The Agency,* p. 436, note. The experiment took place in 1970 in Quang Binh Province and was not entirely successful, as the ARVN moved in to attack after the peak of the infection had passed.

Chapter 10

1. Salisbury's first story appeared on Christmas Day, 1966, under the headline "A Visitor to Hanoi Inspects Damage Laid to U.S. Raids" and with the startling dateline, "Hanoi." A good account of Defense Department reaction is Thomas Powers, *Vietnam: The War at Home* (Boston: G. K. Hall, 1984), p. 171.

2. Hallin, *The "Uncensored War,"* pp. 147–148.

3. Frank Harvey, *Air War—Vietnam* (New York: Bantam Books, 1967), pp. 2, 60–63, 83.

4. Todd Gitlin, *The Sixties: Years of Hope, Days of Rage* (New York: Bantam Books, 1989), pp. 265–268. On Women Strike for Peace, see Amy Swerdlow, *Women Strike for Peace: The Politics of Motherhood* (Working title, University of Chicago Press, forthcoming).

5. Quoted in Powers, *The War at Home*, pp. 225–226.

6. Howard Zinn, *Vietnam: The Logic of Withdrawal* (Boston: Beacon Press, 1967), pp. 51–59.

7. Schell, *The Real War*, p. 191. Coverage of the war at ground level was not limited to journals like *The New Yorker*, which published Schell, nor the *New York Review of Books*, which carried vivid accounts and analyses of the war by Noam Chomsky among others. Martha Gellhorn wrote about the napalmed children in the Qui Nhon provincial hospital for the *Ladies' Home Journal*. See Powers, *The War at Home*, p. 226.

8. The text of the "Call to Resist Illegitimate Authority" is in Gettleman, et al., eds., *Vietnam and America*, pp. 304–306; the text of the McComb leaflet is in Michael Ferber and Staughton Lynd, *The Resistance* (Boston: Beacon, 1971), pp. 31–32. For an account of the activities of SNCC, see pp. 29–33.

9. *Ibid.*, p. 127.

10. Text of King's speech in Gettleman, et al., eds., *Vietnam and America*, pp. 306–314.

11. Grace Paley, "Cop Tales," in War Resisters League Calendar (Philadelphia: New Society Publishers, 1989).

12. Paul Lauter and Florence Howe quoted in Ferber and Lynd, *The Resistance*, p. 136.

13. Powers, *The War at Home*, p. 240.

14. See Ferber and Lynd, *The Resistance*, pp. 201–219.

15. Howard Zinn, *A People's History of the United States* (New York: Harper Colophon Books, 1980), p. 492.

16. For details on the Fort Hood Three, see Halstead, *Out Now!*, pp. 174ff. See also *Vietnam Generation* 2:1 (1990) a special issue on resistance in the military edited by Harry W. Haines.

17. Emerson, *Winners and Losers*, p. 129.

18. See Thomas Havens, *Fire Across the Sea: The Vietnam War and Japan, 1965–1975* (Princeton, N.J.: Princeton University Press, 1987), for an account of the impact of the Japanese antiwar movement and the war on Japan and Japanese-American relations.

19. United States Senate, Committee on Foreign Relations, Supplemental Foreign Assistance, Fiscal Year 1966—Vietnam Hearings; January 28; February 4, 8, 10, 17, and 18.

20. Mary McCarthy, *Vietnam* (New York: Harcourt, Brace & World, 1967), pp. 94, 91.

21. George Ball, whose efforts to slow the pace of escalation made him a sympathetic administration figure to the "respectable opposition," called friends and acquaintances "in an attempt to win either their support or their silence." Lecturing Walter Lippmann, James Reston, and dissident senators George McGovern, Abraham Ribicoff, and Joseph Tydings, Ball urged the administration case: ". . . we had no option to do anything other than what we were doing. We faced a situation and not a theory; we had to see the war through, and at the price

of substantial increased effort." William M. Hammond, *Public Affairs: The Military and the Media, 1962–1968* (Center of Military History, United States Army, Washington, D.C., 1988), p. 249; McNaughton to McNamara, *PP* (Gravel), IV:478–479.

22. For NSAM-288, see *ibid.*, II:459; III:50–56; Draft memorandum for the President, May 19, 1967, IV:175, 478–479.

23. *Ibid.*, IV:179. Rostow quoted in Larry Berman, *Lyndon Johnson's War: The Road to Stalemate in Vietnam* (New York: W. W. Norton, 1989), pp. 48–49.

24. Paul Joseph, *Cracks in the Empire* (Boston: South End Press, 1981), p. 222.

25. Townshend Hoopes, *The Limits of Intervention: An Inside Account of How the Johnson Policy of Escalation in Vietnam Was Reversed* (rev. edn. New York: Longman, 1978), p. 90.

26. Miller, *Lyndon*, p. 490.

27. McCarthy, *Vietnam*, p. 94.

Chapter 11

1. *PP* (Gravel), IV:205.

2. Halberstam, *The Best and the Brightest*, p. 769.

3. *Ibid.*, p. 648.

4. See Gibson, *Perfect War*, pp. 290ff; Sheehan, *Bright Shining Lie*, pp. 652–660; Blaufarb, *Counterinsurgency*, pp. 239ff.

5. Among them Felix Rodriguez (née Max Gomez), who has served the CIA from the Bay of Pigs to Iran-Contra dealings.

6. Ranelagh, *The Agency*, pp. 438–439.

7. "Military Intelligence and the Phoenix Program," Statement of K. Barton Osborne, Subcommittee of the Committee on Government Operations, House of Representatives, 92d Congress, 1st sess., July 15–August 2, 1971. See also Osborne's testimony at hearings on the nomination of Colby to head the CIA: Committee on Armed Services, U.S. Senate, 93d Congress, 1st sess., pp. 101–116. See also Stanley Karnow, *Vietnam: A History* (New York: Viking Press, 1983), p. 602.

8. Gibson, *Perfect War*, p. 311.

9. Don Oberdorfer, *Tet!* (Garden City, N.Y.: Doubleday, 1971), p. 105. The account of Tet which follows draws on Oberdorfer; Gabriel Kolko, *Anatomy of War;* David Hunt, "Remembering the Tet Offensive," reprinted in Gettleman, et al., eds., *Vietnam and America;* and Ngo Vinh Long's three-part essay, "The Tet Offensive and Its Aftermath," in *Indochina Newsletter,* nos. 49, 50, and 60. A useful compilation of the two narratives of Tet that appear in Vol. IV of the Gravel edition of the *Pentagon Papers* can be found in Gettleman, et al., eds., pp. 374–394. For a careful account of the numbers controversy as it emerged in the CBS documentary "The Uncounted Enemy: A Vietnam Deception," and the lawsuit that followed, see Edwin E. Moise, "Why Westmoreland Gave Up," *Pacific Affairs,* 58:4 (Winter 1985–86), pp. 663–673.

10. Oberdorfer, *Tet!*, p. 100.

11. Halberstam, *The Best and the Brightest,* p. 434; Oberdorfer, *Tet!,* p. 102.

12. Oberdorfer, *Tet!,* p. 102.

13. Quoted by Ngo Vinh Long, "The Tet Offensive and Its Aftermath," Part II.

14. Porter, *A Peace Denied,* p. 66; Hunt, "Remembering the Tet Offensive," p. 362.

15. Robert Shaplen, "Letter from Vietnam," March 23, 1968, cited in Gareth Porter, "The 1968 'Hue Massacre,'" *Indochina Chronicle,* 33 (June 24, 1974). See also Hunt, "Remembering the Tet Offensive."

16. Griffiths, *Vietnam Inc.,* p. 137. Oberdorfer, *Tet!,* pp. 198–235, believes 2,800 people were deliberately killed by the NLF. He reports as well that in the last stages of the NLF occupation, Saigon government assassination teams operating in Hue began to systematically eliminate those believed to have aided the NLF (pp. 232–233). Richard Falk, "Appropriating Tet," World Order Studies Program, Occasional Papers No. 17, Center of International Studies, Princeton University, 1988, p. 30.

17. Griffiths, *Vietnam Inc.,* describes the looting that took place in the course of retaking the cities: "The looting was staggering. The ARVN, who had entered the area first, had taken everything that could be carried by hand. The GI's, with their APC's, were able to take away refrigerators, TV sets, and other heavy items" (p. 143); Oberdorfer, *Tet!,* pp. 152–153.

18. Tom Mangold and John Penycate, *The Tunnels of Cu Chi* (New York: Berkley Books, 1986), p. 174.

19. Willenson, *The Bad War,* p. 97.

20. Hallin, *The "Uncensored War,"* p. 173.

21. Quoted in Noam Chomsky and Edward S. Herman, *The Washington Connection and Third World Fascism* (Boston: South End Press, 1979), p. 317.

22. Turley, *Second Indochina War,* p. 116. Ngo Vinh Long, "The Tet Offensive and Its Aftermath," Part III. Long also argues that the casualty figures have been inflated in the accounts of both Hanoi and Washington.

23. The account of My Thuy Phuong during Tet 1968 is based on Trullinger, *Village at War,* pp. 126–129; the aftermath is discussed on pp. 133–147.

24. Quoted in Goodman, *Lost Peace,* p. 83.

25. Quoted in Berman, *Johnson's War,* p. 192.

26. Willenson, *The Bad War,* p. 196; Hallin, *The "Uncensored War,"* p. 170.

27. Quoted in Herbert Y. Schandler, *The Unmaking of a President: Lyndon Johnson and Vietnam* (Princeton, N.J.: Princeton University Press, 1972), p. 202.

28. It is often objected that McCarthy's victory rested on Republican crossover votes determined to embarrass the president and push for yet a wider war. However, the political point for Johnson was the massive vote from all sides against the war as he was conducting it. Moreover, the militant slogan "Get in or get out" (commit the country completely to the war or withdraw from it) could be understood literally though not in a simpleminded fashion. The implications of the phrase are similar to the conclusions that some in the Pentagon have drawn since the Vietnam War—that any military effort abroad must be accompanied by a total public commitment on the part of the government, backed by over-

whelming popular support—a condition thus far unmet, however bellicose the occupant of the White House. No president who presided over the Vietnam War was ready to risk the test of a declaration of war.

29. Joseph, *Cracks in the Empire*, p. 259; Kolko, *Anatomy*, p. 315. In an angry interview years after the events, Robert Komer agreed. "The goddamn Chiefs of Staff," Komer complained. "Wheeler's the evil genius of the Vietnam war in my judgment"—Willenson, *The Bad War*, pp. 96–97. See also Schandler, *The Unmaking of a President*, pp. 105ff.

30. Meeting with Special Advisory Group, March 26, 1968, excerpt in Williams, et al., *America in Vietnam*, pp. 271–272.

31. Halberstam's account in *The Best and the Brightest*, pp. 652ff; Clifford quoted in Joseph, *Cracks in the Empire*, pp. 273–274; Kolko, *Anatomy*, p. 320.

32. Cooper, *Lost Crusade*, p. 375.

33. Porter, ed., *Definitive Documentation*, Vol. 2, p. 510.

34. Godfrey Hodgson, *America in Our Time* (Garden City, N.Y.: Doubleday), p. 362.

35. Michael Herr, *Dispatches* (New York: Alfred A. Knopf, 1977), p. 158.

36. Alsop quoted in Hodgson, *America in Our Time*, p. 371; Denise Levertov, "Staying Alive," from *To Stay Alive*. Copyright © 1971, Denise Levertov Goodman. First published in *Poetry*. Reprinted by permission of New Directions Publishing Corp.

Chapter 12

1. Nguyen Tien Hung and Jerrold L. Schecter, *The Palace File* (New York: Harper & Row, 1986), pp. 23–29, 484–485. Nixon offered to reward Chennault with an ambassadorial post, but she declined. Johnson and Humphrey were apparently informed of Chennault's efforts through an illegal wiretap, but decided not to expose them. Hung and Schecter argue that Johnson's reticence stemmed from his reluctance to reveal the illegal source of his knowledge, his friendship for a close associate of Chennault, Thomas Corcoran, and his own ambivalence about Humphrey. Humphrey tried to get Corcoran to call Chennault off, but without success. Humphrey's campaign manager still believes that "if Mrs. Chennault and Nixon had not intervened with Thieu, we might have won the election because the momentum was in Humphrey's favor." See Seymour Hersh, *The Price of Power: Kissinger in the Nixon White House* (New York: Summit Books, 1983), pp. 16–24. Bui Diem, South Vietnam's ambassador to the United States, denies he was involved in any deal but suspects that Anna Chennault "may well have played her own game. . . ." (p. 245). See Bui Diem, *In the Jaws of History* (Boston: Houghton Miflin, 1987), pp. 235–246.

2. *From: The President: Richard Nixon's Secret Files*, edited by Bruce Oudes (New York: Harper & Row, 1989), p. 11.

3. Charles Stevenson, *The End of Nowhere: American Policy Toward Laos since 1954* (Boston: Beacon Press, 1972), frontispiece quotation.

4. *Ibid.*, p. 215.

5. Chapelier is quoted in Fred Branfman, *Voices from the Plain of Jars:*

Life Under an Air War (New York: Harper & Row, 1972), p. 19; for Godley, see Stevenson, *End of Nowhere,* p. 225; on the disappearance of the Plain of Jars, see Branfman, pp. 3, 20, 24, 45.

6. Sorties peaked at eighty-one per day; the Vietnam maximum was sixty. See William Shawcross, *Sideshow: Kissinger, Nixon and the Destruction of Cambodia* (New York: Simon & Schuster, 1981), p. 294, note. For Cooper Amendment, see P. Edward Haley, *Congress and the Fall of South Vietnam and Cambodia* (London & Toronto: Associated University Presses, 1982). On the false targeting, see Earl H. Tilford, Jr., "Air Power in Vietnam: The Hubris of Power," in *The American War in Vietnam: Lessons, Legacies and Implications for Future Conflicts,* edited by Lawrence E. Grinter and Peter M. Dunn (New York: Greenwood Press, 1987), p. 74. See also Hearings of the Senate Committee on Armed Services on the Bombing of Cambodia (93d Congress, 1st sess., July 16, 23, 25, 30; August 7, 8, 9, 1973). The following account draws heavily on Seymour Hersh and William Shawcross.

7. Seymour Hersh, *Price of Power,* pp. 52–53.

8. Shawcross, *Sideshow,* p. 92.

9. Hersh, *Price of Power,* pp. 86–88.

10. Text of Ho's will, as it was released in 1969, is reprinted in Gettleman, et al., *Vietnam and America,* pp. 440–441. Karnow, *Vietnam,* p. 597; for references to the recent complete text of Ho Chi Minh's will, see *Vietnam Update,* 2:1 (Summer 1989), p. 13.

11. Hersh, *Price of Power,* pp. 125–127; p. 134, note.

12. Nancy Zaroulis and Sullivan, *Who Spoke Up? American Protest against the War in Vietnam, 1963–1975* (Garden City, N.Y.: Doubleday, 1984), p. 245.

13. Quoted in Michael Klare, *War Without End: American Planning for the Next Vietnams* (New York: Alfred A. Knopf, 1972), p. 324. Essentially, in Klare's words, "a formula which would permit the United States to survive a protracted war without loss of our Asian empire, and without incurring further upheavals at home" (p. 364). For an extended analysis, see John Dower, "Ten Points of Note: Asia and the Nixon Doctrine," reprinted from the *Bulletin of Concerned Asian Scholars* in Lloyd Gardner, ed., *The Great Nixon Turnaround* (New York: New Viewpoints, 1973).

14. Peter R. Kann, "The Hidden War," *Wall Street Journal,* March 25, 1969.

15. Stevenson, *End of Nowhere,* p. 210.

16. Hersh, *Price of Power,* p. 133.

17. *Ibid.,* p. 129.

18. Zaroulis and Sullivan, *Who Spoke Up?,* pp. 282–283.

19. Seymour Hersh's account was published as *My Lai 4: A Report on the Massacre and Its Aftermath* (New York: Vintage Books, 1970). Hersh discusses the U.S. reaction in chapter 12. The Department of Defense prepared a slide show on the Hue massacre that was intended to put My Lai in proper perspective. Representative Richard Ichord, chairman of the House Internal Security Committee, presented this to interested citizens in a congressional hearing room, but expressed disappointment at the paucity of slides of Hue itself in the thirty-minute show. Efforts to secure additional pictures failed (p. 157). A portion of the Army investigation, conducted by General William Peers, has been published:

Report of the Department of Army Review of Preliminary Investigations into My Lai Incident (Washington, D.C.: Government Printing Office, 1976). Hersh analyzed the cover-up of My Lai and the massacre which occurred on the same day in a neighboring hamlet in *Cover-Up: The Army's Secret Investigation of the Massacre at My Lai 4* (New York: Random House, 1972), as does Richard J. Hammer, *One Morning in the War: The Tragedy at Son My* (New York: Coward-McCann, 1970). See also his account of the Calley trial, *The Court-martial of Lt. Calley* (New York: Coward-McCann & Geoghegan, 1972).

20. Zaroulis and Sullivan, *Who Spoke Up?*, p. 241.

21. Hodgson, *America in Our Time,* p. 378.

22. Shawcross, *Sideshow,* p. 144.

23. Hersh, *Price of Power,* p. 190.

24. On Lon Nol, see Shawcross, *Sideshow,* p. 149; for the domestic reaction, *ibid.,* pp. 152–154.

25. Oudes, ed., *From: The President,* pp. 127–134.

26. Hersh, *Price of Power,* p. 202, note. In Saigon, President Thieu explained the invasion, and the ARVN losses there, as the price that had to be paid for continued U.S. support: "We must . . . take over more combat responsibilities . . . to solve a difficult problem for the Americans who do not want their children's blood spilled." The argument was less than persuasive, and a renewed urban protest movement was met by Thieu's threat to "beat to death the people who are demanding immediate peace." See Ngo Vinh Long, "Tet Offensive and Its Aftermath," Part III. Robert Bly, *The Teeth-Mother Naked at Last* (San Francisco: City Lights Pocket Poet's Series, 1970), quoted by permission.

27. Shawcross, *Sideshow,* p. 159.

28. Haley, *Congress and the Fall of South Vietnam,* p. 93.

29. Shawcross, *Sideshow,* p. 173.

30. Cited in Hersh, *Price of Power,* p. 311, note, and quoted by permission.

Chapter 13

1. The phrase is Roger Morris's, a Kissinger aide who resigned over the invasion of Cambodia. See his *Uncertain Greatness: Henry Kissinger and American Foreign Policy* (New York: Harper & Row, 1977), p. 154.

2. Kingsley's is one of the voices in John Pratt's moving book, *Vietnam Voices, Perspectives on the War Years, 1941–1982,* Compiled by John Clark Pratt, (New York: Penguin Books, 1984), pp. 465–466.

3. *The Winter Soldier Investigation: An Inquiry into American War Crimes,* by the Vietnam Veterans Against the War (Boston: Beacon Press, 1972), pp. 44–45.

4. Colonel Robert D. Heinl, Jr., "The Collapse of the Armed Forces," reprinted in Gettleman, et al., eds., *Vietnam and America,* pp. 322–331.

5. Pratt, comp., *Vietnam Voices,* p. 471.

6. Emerson, *Winners and Losers,* pp. 330, 331. Although Chief Justice Burger had apparently given the "go-ahead," White House aide Pat Buchanan strongly advised moving against the veterans, who were receiving a lot of posi-

tive publicity. "Seriously," he wrote Haldeman on April 21, 1971, " 'the crazies' will be in town soon enough . . . and if we want a confrontation, let's have it with them." Oudes, ed., *From: The President*, p. 240. For Kerry's speech, see Gettleman, et al., eds., *Vietnam and America*, pp. 453–458.

7. Hersh, *Price of Power*, pp. 325ff.

8. William C. Berman, *William Fulbright and the Vietnam War: The Dissent of a Political Realist* (Kent, Ohio: Kent State University Press, 1988), p. 145.

9. Jonathan Schell, *Time of Illusion* (New York: Vintage Books, 1976), p. 152.

10. Oudes, ed., *From: The President*, pp. 270–271.

11. For an account of the legal battle over publication, see Sanford J. Ungar, *The Papers and the Papers: An Account of the Legal and Political Battle over The Pentagon Papers* (New York: E. P. Dutton, 1972); Kissinger is quoted in Hersh, *Price of Power*, p. 384.

12. Oudes, ed., *From: The President*, p. 278.

13. *Ibid.* Colson memorandum, June 25, 1971, p. 284.

14. Schell, *Time of Illusion*, pp. 166–167.

15. For the full transcript of the White House tape of this conversation, see *The New York Times*, September 24, 1981. See also Hersh, *Price of Power*, p. 427, note.

16. Hodgson, *America in Our Time*, p. 378.

17. Tom Oliphant, "War in the Back Pages," *Ramparts* 11:5 (November 1972), p. 43. Oliphant was Washington correspondent for the *Boston Globe*. The Nixon administration, Oliphant observed, had learned how to "bury a fact so no one will really pay attention to it; the most effective technique . . . is not to announce it."

18. Tilford, Jr., "Air Power in Vietnam" in Grinter and Dunn, eds., *The American War in Vietnam*, p. 74.

19. George and Audrey Kahin were in Hanoi with Senator Fulbright's explicit encouragement in order to clarify the Vietnamese position and protect it from the process of distortion already under way. "Nixon and the PRG's Seven Points," George Kahin unpublished paper, November 1988, p. 6.

20. Hersh, *Price of Power*, p. 426.

21. Kahin, "Nixon and the PRG," p. 15.

22. This account is based on Hersh, *Price of Power*, pp. 426 ff.; for the manipulation of the vote in the provinces, see Pratt, comp., *Vietnam Voices*, p. 489. See also George Kahin, "Nixon and the PRG."

23. Speech before the Commonwealth Club of San Francisco, April 2, 1965, cited in Hung and Schecter, *The Palace File*, pp. 8–9.

24. Hersh, *Price of Power*, p. 81.

25. *Ibid.*, pp. 484ff; on Muskie, see pp. 487ff.

26. Trullinger, *Village at War*, p. 178; on the 1972 offensive, see Turley, *Second Indochina War*, pp. 143–149.

27. Abrams quoted in Hersh, *Price of Power*, p. 516.

28. Sheehan, *Bright Shining Lie*, pp. 761, 776, 783.

29. Arnold R. Isaacs, *Without Honor: Defeat in Vietnam & Cambodia* (Baltimore: John Hopkins University Press, 1983), p. 26.

30. Shawcross, *Sideshow*, pp. 218–219.

31. Goodman, *The Lost Peace,* p. 74.

32. The pervasive racism of Kissinger and the Nixon White House is described by Hersh, *Price of Power,* pp. 110–111. On Kissinger's contempt for the Vietnamese, pp. 620, 596, note.

33. *Newsweek,* October 30, 1972; Goodman, *Lost Peace,* pp. 80, 82.

34. Hersh, *Price of Power,* p. 584. Porter, *A Peace Denied,* pp. 126–127.

35. Hersh, *Price of Power,* p. 563; Goodman, *Lost Peace,* p. 83.

36. Isaacs, *Without Honor,* p. 48.

37. Hersh, *Price of Power,* p. 594.

38. Isaacs, *Without Honor,* p. 44.

39. Account drawn from Porter, *A Peace Denied,* pp. 132–133.

40. Hung and Schecter, *The Palace File,* p. 124.

41. For the gifts Kissinger brought, see Hersh, *Price of Power,* p. 613. See Porter, *A Peace Denied,* pp. 144–158, for a detailed analysis of these November-early December negotiations.

42. On Sindlinger, see Hersh, *Price of Power,* p. 606; on the Christmas bombings, see *ibid.,* pp. 610ff; Porter, *A Peace Denied,* pp. 158ff; Hung and Schecter, *The Palace File,* pp. 130ff.; and Isaacs, *Without Honor,* pp. 54–57. Only one B-52 had been shot down prior to December 17, 1972. See Isaacs, *Without Honor,* p. 55, note. For statistics on losses, see Porter, *A Peace Denied,* pp. 161–162. In addition to the problem presented by these losses, the bombing threatened Nixon's larger strategic ambitions as both the Soviet Union and the PRC reaffirmed their support for Vietnam and the Soviet Union increased its military aid.

43. Hersh, *Price of Power,* p. 629, note.

44. Isaacs, *Without Honor,* pp. 133, 138.

45. Porter, *A Peace Denied,* p. 165; Negroponte quoted in Hung and Schecter, *The Palace File,* p. 146.

46. Isaacs, *Without Honor,* p. 58. Hersh, *Price of Power*, p. 634.

47. Thomas C. Thayer, *War Without Fronts: The American Experience in Vietnam* (Boulder, Colo.: Westview Press, 1985), see tables on pp. 104, 106, 107; for civilian estimates, see p. 129.

Chapter 14

1. "Bombing in Cambodia," Hearings before Senate Armed Services Committee, 93d Congress, 1st sess. Greven testified on August 8, pp. 276ff. Quote is on p. 286.

2. Isaacs, *Without Honor,* p. 226.

3. Shawcross, *Sideshow,* pp. 297, 265, 318–319.

4. Quoted in Isaacs, *Without Honor,* p. 229; Ambassador Swank quoted in Shawcross, *Sideshow,* p. 295. According to Noam Chomsky and Edward S. Herman, the bombing and its consequences were under-reported, except for Neak Lung which, because it was an accident and presumably atypical, was acceptable. See *Manufacturing Consent: The Political Economy of the Mass Media* (New York: Pantheon Books, 1988), pp. 276–279.

5. Ben Kiernan, *How Pol Pot Came to Power: A History of Communism in Kampuchea, 1930–1975* (London: Verso, 1985), pp. 390–391.

6. For a brief account of the Dawson case, see Shawcross, *Sideshow,* pp. 291–294; Hungate quoted in *ibid.,* p. 331.

7. Isaacs, *Without Honor,* pp. 125; p. 124 for a description of the dismantling of the base; pp. 71–100. See Porter, *A Peace Denied,* pp. 188–196, for accounts of the cease-fire war.

8. Frank Snepp, *Decent Interval* (New York: Vintage Books, 1978), p. 105, for Tong Le Chan. Of course Markham may have been informed as well, as Snepp's general reflections on his relations with the press imply. See Harry Maurer, *Strange Ground,* p. 566. The following account draws on Kolko, Snepp, Tra, Isaacs, Porter, Turley, James P. Harrison, and Van Tien Dung, *Our Great Spring Victory* (excerpted in Gettleman, et al., eds., *Vietnam and America,* pp. 497–500).

9. All quotes are from Tra, *Concluding the 30-Year War.*

10. Isaacs, *Without Honor,* p. 126. The heaviest Communist use of munitions occurred during the 1972 offensive; even then, it amounted to less than 1 percent of American usage.

11. News stories collected in *Indochina Today,* Indochina Resource Center (May–June 1974).

12. On Thanh, see Snepp, *Decent Interval,* p. 116. For an account of the Saigon army, see Isaacs, *Without Honor,* pp. 109ff.

13. Turley, *Second Indochina War,* p. 180.

14. Snepp, *Decent Interval,* p. 201.

15. Snepp's March analysis, *ibid.,* pp. 232–234; Earl S. Martin, *Reaching the Other Side* (New York: Crown Publishers, 1978), p. 106.

16. Martin, *Reaching the Other Side,* p. 138.

17. Snepp, *Decent Interval,* pp. 248–249; italics in the original.

18. Porter, *A Peace Denied,* p. 275; Isaacs, *Without Honor,* pp. 414, 418.

19. Snepp, *Decent Interval,* pp. 352, 353.

20. *Ibid.,* pp. 416–417.

21. Turley, *Second Indochina War,* p. 185; see Hung and Schecter, *The Palace File,* pp. 331–332, for further excerpts; *Newsweek*, May 5, 1975, p. 26.

22. Harrison, *Endless War,* p. 19.

23. James Fenton, "The Fall of Saigon," in *All the Wrong Places: Adrift in the Politics of the Pacific Rim* (New York: Atlantic Monthly Press, 1988), p. 87.

24. Martin, *Reaching the Other Side,* p. 263.

Chapter 15

1. John Balaban, "After Our War," appears in *Blue Mountain* (Greensboro, N.C.: Unicorn Press, 1982) and is quoted here with the permission of Unicorn Press. Goldwater is quoted in Shawcross, *Sideshow,* p. 476.

2. Quoted in Nayan Chanda, *Brother Enemy: The War After the War: A History of Indochina Since the Fall of Saigon* (New York: Harcourt Brace Javanovich, 1986), p. 143. The following account draws on Chanda, and Kelvin Rowley

and Grant Evans, *Red Brotherhood at War: Indochina Since the Fall of Saigon* (London: Verso, 1984).

3. Unexploded ordnance made farming dangerous in Laos and Cambodia also, lending a certain irony to the American accusation against the Soviet Union for its failure to clear the mines it left behind in Afghanistan. See *The New York Times,* Robert Pear, August 14, 1988. Elizabeth Kempf in *New Scientist,* June 23, 1988 (no. 1618), reports that extensive areas, referred to by the Vietnamese as "Agent Orange Museums," have still not regenerated. But see also her report on Vietnam's efforts at "regreening," in "Re-Greening Vietnam," *Wildlife Conservation* (March–April 1990).

4. Holbrooke quoted in Chanda, *Brother Enemy,* p. 152.

5. *Ibid.,* p. 156. A House Select Committee on Missing Persons in Southeast Asia had learned of the secret aid protocol to the Paris Agreement in December 1975. The discussions in 1973 had been very specific, outlining a five-year aid package that included, among other things, a steel mill, a prefabricated housing factory, and a thermal power station. See Joel Charny and John Spragens, Jr., *Obstacles to Recovery in Vietnam and Kampuchea: U.S. Embargo of Humanitarian Aid* (New York: Oxfam America, 1984), and Porter, *A Peace Denied,* pp. 232–238.

6. The intermediary was David Truong, an anti-war activist and son of a South Vietnamese politician Thieu had jailed; he was sentenced to fifteen years in prison. The Vietnamese ambassador to the UN was expelled from the country. One document marked "top secret" by the FBI and described by their agents as relating to the KGB turned out to be pages from a 1949 book on the Soviet Union available at the public library; other items included a UPI story on the MIAs, books on agriculture and development, U.S. government reports on human rights, and a photograph of Truong and an unidentified friend standing in front of a picture of Ho Chi Minh. For more on the case, see "The War Is Never Over: The Case of 'Agent Keyseat,' " *The Village Voice,* February 3–9, 1982, and Nubar Hovsepian and Stuart Schaar, "Who Wanted David Truong Put Away?" in *The Nation,* March 2, 1985.

7. Christine Pelzer White, "Interview with Nguyen Huu Tho," *Journal of Contemporary Asia,* 11:1 (1981), p. 130.

8. For a brief account, see Evans and Rowley, *Red Brotherhood,* pp. 45, 47, 132, and 154; Porter, "Vietnamese Policy and the Indochina Crisis," in David W. P. Elliott, ed., *The Third Indochina Conflict* (Boulder, Colo.: Westview Press, 1981), p. 71.

9. *Ibid.* See also Alexander Woodside, "Nationalism and Poverty in the Breakdown of Sino-Vietnamese Relations," *Pacific Affairs,* 52:3 (Fall 1979), pp. 381–409.

10. On Khmer Rouge irrendentism, see Chanda, *Brother Enemy,* pp. 56, 96; Evans and Rowley, *Red Brotherhood,* pp. 91, 112.

11. See Evans and Rowley, *Red Brotherhood,* pp. 49–58; Chanda, *Brother Enemy,* pp. 235–247. All of this was made more complicated by Hanoi's effort to compel Hoa to choose Vietnamese citizenship (which carried with it the obligation to serve in the military) while Beijing, in a new activist mode, declared all overseas Chinese "part of the Chinese nation" and urged them to work together against "hegemonism," its code word for the Soviet Union and its allies.

Indeed, everyone of "Chinese descent," whatever their nominal nationality, was invited to return to the motherland. For a sensitive account of the issue, see Charles Benoit, "Vietnam's 'Boat People,' " in Elliott, ed., *Third Indochina Conflict,* pp. 139–162.

12. See Michael Vickery, *Cambodia: 1975–1982* (Boston: South End Press, 1984); Ben Kiernan, *Pol Pot.*

13. Chanda, *Brother Enemy,* p. 256.

14. Grant and Rowley, *Red Brotherhood,* p. 30.

15. See Chanda, *Brother Enemy,* pp. 260–261, for Deng's anti-Vietnamese remarks. At the same time the Chinese decided against sending troops to Cambodia itself for many reasons: a conviction that "the defense of a country's independence and sovereignty is essentially the job of its own people"; the sheer logistical problem of supplying an army as far from China as Cambodia; the danger of Soviet intervention; the fear such a move might arouse in non-Communist Southeast Asian countries; and the cost.

16. Cyrus Vance, *Hard Choices: Critical Years in American Foreign Policy* (New York: Simon & Schuster, 1983), pp. 116, 79.

17. *Ibid.,* p. 78; Chanda, *Brother Enemy,* p. 181; Jimmy Carter, *Keeping Faith: Memoirs of a President* (New York: Bantam Books, 1982), p. 196. Brzezinski may have been seduced as well by visions of shaping internal Chinese political dispositions in favor of Deng Xiaoping over his rivals. See Evans and Rowley, *Red Brotherhood,* p. 160.

18. Evans and Rowley, *Red Brotherhood,* p. 59; Chanda, *Brother Enemy,* p. 281.

19. Chanda, *Brother Enemy,* pp. 272, 266.

20. *Ibid.,* p. 287.

21. Zbigniew Brzezinski, *Power and Principle: Memoirs of the National Security Adviser (1977–1981)* (New York: Farrar, Straus, Giroux, 1983), p. 25.

22. *Ibid.,* p. 414.

23. Quoted in John McAuliff and Mary Byrne McDonnell, "Ending the Cambodian Stalemate," *World Policy Journal* 7:1 (Winter, 1989–90), p. 84.

24. Michael Vickery estimates that between 700,000 and 1 million people died between 1975 and 1979; perhaps half of them "may have been executed, the rest dying of illness, hunger, and overwork." The same essay discusses the amount of American aid to the Khmer Rouge after 1979. "Cambodia (Kampuchea): History, Tragedy, and Uncertain Future," in *Bulletin of Concerned Asian Scholars* 21:2–4 (April–December 1989), p. 48. See also "How Many Died in Pol Pot's Kampuchea," correspondence, *Bulletin of Concerned Asian Scholars* 20:1 (January–March, 1988), pp. 70–73.

25. Willenson, *The Bad War,* p. 423.

26. Japan voted with the United States. See Susumu Awanohara, "Fiscal Interdiction," *Far Eastern Economic Review,* September 28, 1989, pp. 22–23.

27. "Cambodia and Vietnam: Trapped in an Eddy of History?" Address to the International Symposium on the Future of US-Indochina relations, September 8, 1989, Los Angeles, CA.

28. Noam Chomsky, "Visions of Righteousness," *Cultural Critique,* 3 (Spring 1986), pp. 10–43, argues that the continuity of U.S. policy is evidence

that, contrary to popular opinion across the political spectrum, the United States won at least a partial victory in Vietnam.

29. Willenson, *The Bad War*, p. 147.

30. "If I recall correctly, when France gave up Indochina as a colony, the leading nations of the world met in Geneva with regard to helping those colonies become independent nations. And since North and South Vietnam had been, previous to colonization, two separate countries, provisions were made that these two countries could by a vote of all their people together, decide whether they wanted to be one country or not. And there wasn't anything surreptitious about it, that when Ho Chi Minh refused to participate in such an election. . . ." Reprinted in Gettleman, et al., eds., *Vietnam and America*, p. xiii.

31. *Discriminate Deterrence*, Report of the Commission on Integrated Long-Term Strategy, January 1988, pp. 13, 14. Eugene Luttwack, in an editorial essay in *The New York Times* (October 17, 1989), worried as well about the reluctance to use force to defend non-vital interests: "We should not be fobbed off by sentimental protestations that the lives of young Americans can only be risked for 'vital interests.' The reason we have such a large military establishment is precisely to protect non-vital interests as well."

32. Michael Klare and Peter Kornbluh, eds., *Low Intensity Warfare* (New York: Pantheon Books, 1988), p. 3.

33. Brecht quote from Robert Jay Lifton, *Home from the War. Vietnam Veterans: Neither Victims nor Executioners* (New York: Simon & Schuster, 1973), p. 14. Kirkpatrick quoted in Shafer, *Deadly Paradigms*, p. 288.

Epilogue

1. Lawrence Baskir and William A. Strauss, *Chance and Circumstance: The Draft, the War and the Vietnam Generation* (New York: Vintage Books, 1978), pp. 8, 9, 10.

2. *Ibid.*, pp. 124, 125–126; see also Lisa Hsiao, "Project 100,000: The Great Society's Answer to Military Manpower Needs in Vietnam," *Vietnam Generation*, 1:2 (Spring 1989), pp. 14–37.

3. See Bob Greene, *Homecoming: When the Soldiers Returned from Vietnam*, (New York: Putnam, 1989), pp. 10–11.

4. Ellen Frey-Wouters and Robert S. Laufer, *Legacy of a War: The American Soldier in Vietnam* (Armonk, N.Y.: M.E. Sharpe, Inc., 1986), p. 52.

5. Robert J. Lifton, *Home from the War*, pp. 39–40.

6. *Ibid.*, p. 40.

7. Larry Rottman, "What Kind of War?," originally published in *Winning Hearts and Minds: War Poems by Vietnam Veterans* (Brooklyn, N.Y.: 1st Casualty Press, 1972); appears here with the permission of the author.

8. See Renny Christopher, " 'I never really became a woman veteran until I saw the wall': A review of oral histories and personal narratives by women veterans of the Vietnam war," *Vietnam Generation* 1:3–4 (Summer–Fall, 1989), pp. 33–45. In addition to the titles Christopher discusses, see Patricia Walsh, *Forever Sad the Hearts*, and interview with Peggy Perri in *Let Me Tell You Where*

I've Been, photographs and interviews with Seven Vietnam Veterans by Janice Rogovin (Boston: Joiner Center for Study of War and Social Consequences, 1988).

9. Quotes are from Kathryn Marshall, *In the Combat Zone: Vivid Personal Recollections of the Vietnam War from the Women Who Served There* (New York: Viking/Penguin, 1987), pp. 130, 178, 58.

10. Quoted in Christopher, " 'I never really . . .' ", p. 41.

11. Marilyn M. McMahon, "Wounds of War," from *Works in Progress* (Seattle, 1988), quoted with permission of the author.

12. Tamar Lewin, "Nation's Homeless Veterans Battle a New Foe: Defeatism," *The New York Times,* December 30, 1987; Myra MacPherson, *Long Time Passing: Vietnam and the Haunted Generation* (Garden City, New York: Doubleday, 1984), p. 185.

13. Jon Nordheimer, "From Dakto to Detroit: Death of a Troubled Hero," *New York Times,* May 16, 1971. The story was brought to my attention by Lifton, *Home from the War,* p. 39, note.

14. George Swiers, " 'Demented Vets' and Other Myths: The Moral Obligation of Veterans," *Vietnam Reconsidered: Lessons from a War,* ed. Harrison E. Salisbury, pp. 196–197.

15. "Interviews with Vietnam Vets," by Bloomfield College students; MacPherson, *Long Time,* p. 597.

16. Bruce Weigl, "Song of Napalm," from *The Monkey Wars* (Athens, Georgia: University of Georgia Press, 1985), copyright 1985 by Bruce Weigl. Reprinted by permission of the University of Georgia Press.

17. William Ehrhart, "Making Children Behave," reprinted from *To Those Who Have Gone Home Tired: New and Selected Poems* (New York: Thunder's Mouth Press, 1984), by the permission of the author. Vietnamese poem and conversation from William Ehrhart, *Going Back: An Ex-Marine Returns to Vietnam* (Jefferson, N.C.: McFarland, 1987).

18. Thomas McGrath, "Ode to the American Dead in Asia" (original title: "Ode to the American Dead in Korea"), from *Selected Poems, 1938–1988* (Copper Canyon Press, P.O. Box 171, Port Townsend, WA. 98368), reprinted with permission of Copper Canyon Press.

19. Bruce Weigl, "Welcome Home," *The Nation,* 235:549, November 17, 1982.

20. Harry Haines, " 'What Kind of War?': An Analysis of the Vietnam Veterans Memorial," *Critical Studies in Mass Communication,* 3:1 (March, 1986), p. 17.

21. Peter Marin, "What the Vietnam Vets Can Teach Us," *The Nation,* November 17, 1982; Tim O'Brien, *The Things They Carried* (Boston: Houghton Mifflin, 1990), p. 76.

22. Michael Herr, *Dispatches,* p. 20.

Additional Bibliography

In addition to the works cited in the footnotes, I consulted the following books.

Adams, Nina S., and Alfred W. McCoy, eds. *Laos: War and Revolution.* New York: Harper & Row, 1970.

Aulich, James, and Jeffrey Walsh, eds. *Vietnam Images: War and Representation.* New York: St. Martin's Press, 1989.

Bain, David Haward. *Aftershocks: A Tale of Two Victims.* New York: Penguin Books, 1980.

Balaban, John, text, and Geoffrey Clifford, photographs. *Vietnam: The Land We Never Knew.* San Francisco: Chronicle Books, 1989.

Baritz, Loren. *Backfire: A History of How American Culture Led Us into Vietnam and Made Us Fight the Way We Did.* Morrow, 1985.

Barnet, Richard J. *Roots of War: The Men and Institutions Behind U.S. Foreign Policy.* New York: Atheneum, 1972.

Braestrup, Peter. *Big Story: How the American Press and Television Reported and Interpreted the Crisis of Tet 1968 in Vietnam and Washington.* Boulder, Colo.: Westview Press, 1977.

———, ed., *Vietnam as History: Ten Years after the Paris Peace Accords.* Washington, D.C.: University Press of America, 1984.

Brewin, Bob, and Sydney Shaw. *Vietnam on Trial: Westmoreland vs. CBS.* New York: Atheneum, 1987.

Brown, Frederick Z. *Second Chance: The United States and Indochina in the 1990s.* New York: Council on Foreign Relations Press, 1989.

Browne, Malcolm. *The New Face of War.* Indianapolis: Bobbs-Merrill, 1965.

Broyles, William, Jr. *Brothers in Arms.* New York: Alfred A. Knopf, 1986.

Butler, Robert Olen. *Alleys of Eden.* New York: Ballantine Books, 1983.

Caputo, Philip. *Indian Country.* New York: Bantam Books, 1987.

———. *A Rumor of War.* New York: Holt, Rinehart & Winston, 1977.

Chaliand, Gerard. *The Peasants of North Vietnam.* Baltimore, Md.: Penguin Books, 1969.

Chandler, David P., and Ben Kiernan, eds. *Revolution and Its Aftermath in Kampuchea: Eight Essays.* New Haven: Monograph Series No. 25, Yale University Southeast Asia Studies, 1983.

Chanoff, David, and Doan Van Toai. *Portrait of an Enemy.* New York: Random House, 1986.

Chomsky, Noam. *At War in Asia.* New York: Pantheon Books, 1970.

———. *For Reasons of State.* New York: Vintage Books, 1973.

Colby, William, and Peter Forbath. *Honorable Men: My Life in the CIA.* New York: Simon & Schuster, 1978.

Committee of Concerned Asian Scholars. *The Indochina Story.* New York: Bantam, 1970.

Committee on Foreign Relations, U.S. Senate. *Background Information Relating to Southeast Asia and Vietnam,* 7th Revised edition, Washington, D.C.: U.S. Government Printing Office, December 1974.

———. *Bombing as a Policy Tool in Vietnam: Effectiveness.* Staff Study No. 5, October 12, 1972.

———. *Causes, Origins and Lessons of the Vietnam War,* Hearings, May 9, 10, 11, 1972. Washington, D.C.: U.S. Government Printing Office.

———. *Foreign Assistance Act of 1968. Part 1: Vietnam.* Hearings, March 11, 12, 1968. Washington, D.C.: U.S. Government Printing Office.

———. Staff Report. *Vietnam: May 1972.* Washington, D.C.: U.S. Government Printing Office, June 19, 1972.

———. Staff Report. *Vietnam: May 1974.* Washington, D.C.: U.S. Government Printing Office, August 5, 1974.

———. *Vietnam: Policy and Prospects: 1970.* Hearings, February 17, 18, 19 and 20; March 3, 14, 17, 19, 1970. Washington, D.C.: U.S. Government Printing Office.

Committee on the Judiciary, House of Representatives. Final Report, *Impeachment of Richard M. Nixon.* New York: Viking Press, 1975.

Corson, William. *The Betrayal.* New York: Norton, 1968.

Cortright, David. *Soldiers in Revolt: The American Military Today.* Garden City, N.Y.: Doubleday, 1975.

Dawson, Alan. *55 Days: The Fall of South Vietnam.* Englewood, N.J.: Prentice-Hall, 1977.

Del Vecchio, John M. *The 13th Valley.* New York: Bantam, 1982.

Dellinger, David. *Vietnam Revisited: From Covert Action to Invasion to Reconstruction.* Boston: South End Press, 1986.

Dommen, Arthur J. *Conflict in Laos: The Politics of Neutralization.* New York: Praeger, 1971.

Duiker, William. *The Communist Road to Power in Vietnam.* Boulder, Colo.: Westview Press, 1981.

Ehrhart, W. D. *Passing Time: Memoir of a Vietnam Vet Against the War.* Jefferson, N.C.: McFarland and Company, 1989.

———. *Vietnam—Perkasie: A Combat Marine's Memoir.* New York: Zebra Books/Kensington Publishing Company, 1983.

Ellsberg, Daniel. *Papers on the War.* New York: Simon & Schuster, 1972.

Ewell, Julian J., and Hunt, Ira A., Jr. *Sharpening the Combat Edge: The Use of Analysis to Reinforce Military Judgment.* Washington, D.C.: Department of the Army, 1974.

Fall, Bernard. *Last Reflections on a War.* Garden City, N.Y.: Doubleday, 1967.

Fitzgerald, Frances. *Fire in the Lake: The Vietnamese and the Americans in Vietnam.* New York: Random House, 1972.

Fulbright, J. William. *The Arrogance of Power.* New York: Random House, 1966.

———, with Seth P. Tillman. *The Price of Empire.* New York: Pantheon Books, 1989.

Gardner, Lloyd. *A Covenant with Power: America and World Order from Wilson to Reagan.* New York: Oxford University Press, 1984.

Gelb, Leslie H., with Richard K. Betts. *The Irony of Vietnam: The System Worked.* Washington: The Brookings Institute, 1979.

Glasser, Ronald J., M.D. *365 Days.* New York: George Braziller, 1971.

Goodwin, Richard. *Remembering America: A Voice from the Sixties.* Boston: Little Brown, 1988.

Halberstam, David. *One Very Hot Day.* Boston: Houghton Mifflin, 1968.

Halperin, Morton H., et al. *The Lawless State: The Crimes of the U.S. Intelligence Agencies.* New York: Penguin Books, 1976.

Hammel, Eric. *Khe Sanh: Siege in the Clouds: An Oral History.* New York: Crown Publishers, 1989.

Hassler, Alfred. *Saigon, U.S.A..* New York: Richard W. Baron, 1970.

Heinemann, Larry. *Close Quarters.* New York: Farrar, Straus, & Giroux, 1977.

———. *Paco's Story.* New York: Farrar, Straus, & Giroux, 1986.

Hellman, John. *American Myth and the Legacy of Vietnam.* New York: Columbia University Press, 1986.

Herrington, Stuart A. *Silence Was a Weapon: The Vietnam War in the Villages.* New York: Ivy Books, 1987.

Hickey, Gerald C. *Free in the Forest: Ethnohistory of the Vietnamese Central Highlands, 1954–1976.* New Haven: Yale University Press, 1982.

———. *Village in Vietnam.* New Haven: Yale University Press, 1960.

Hilsman, Roger. *To Move a Nation.* New York: Doubleday, 1967.

Hoopes, Townsend. *The Limits of Intervention (an Inside Account of How the Johnson Policy of Escalation in Vietnam Was Reversed).* New York: David McKay, 1969.

Horne, A.D., ed. *The Wounded Generation: America After Vietnam.* Englewood Cliffs, N.J.: Prentice-Hall, 1981.

Jackson, Karl D., ed. *Cambodia: 1975–1978. Rendezvous with Death.* Princeton: Princeton University Press, 1989.

Johnson, Lyndon Baines. *The Vantage Point: Perspectives of the Presidency, 1963–1969.* New York: Holt, Rinehart & Winston, 1971.

Just, Ward. *To What End: Report from Vietnam.* Boston: Houghton Mifflin, 1968.

Karnow, Stanley. *Vietnam: A History.* New York: Viking, 1983

Ketwig, John. *And a Hard Rain Fell.* New York: Pocket Books, 1986.

Kinnard, Douglas. *The War Managers.* Hanover, N.H.: University Press of New England, 1977.

Kirk, Donald. *Tell It to the Dead: Memories of a War.* Chicago: Nelson-Hall, 1975.

Kissinger, Henry. *White House Years.* Boston: Little, Brown, 1979.

———. *Years of Upheaval.* Boston: Little, Brown, 1982.

Knoebl, Kuno. *Victory Charlie: The Face of War in Vietnam.* New York: Praeger, 1967.

Komer, R. W. *Bureaucracy Does Its Thing: Institutional Constraints on U.S.–G.V.N. Performance in Vietnam.* Santa Monica, Calif.: Rand Corporation, 1972.

Krulak, Victor H. *The First to Fight: An Inside View of the U.S. Marine Corps.* Annapolis, Md.: Naval Institute Press, 1984.

Lacouture, Jean. *Vietnam: Between Two Truces.* New York: Vintage, 1966.

Lake, Anthony, ed. *The Vietnam Legacy: The War, American Society, and the Future of American Foreign Policy.* New York: New York University Press, 1975.

Landau, David. *Kissinger: The Uses of Power.* Boston: Houghton Mifflin, 1984.

Lang, Daniel. *A Backward Look: Germans Remember.* New York: McGraw-Hill, 1979.

———. *Casualties of War.* New York: McGraw-Hill, 1969.

———. *Patriotism Without Flags.* New York: W.W. Norton, 1974.

Le Ly Hayslip, with Jay Wurts. *When Heaven and Earth Changed Places: A Vietnamese Woman's Journey from War to Peace.* New York: Doubleday, 1989.

Lomperis, Timothy, J. *Reading the Wind: The Literature of the Vietnam War.* Durham, N.C.: Duke University Press, 1987.

———. *The War Everyone Lost and Won: America's Intervention in Vietnam's Twin Struggles.* Baton Rouge, La: Louisiana State University Press, 1984.

Luce, Don, and John Sommer. *Vietnam: The Unheard Voices.* Ithaca: Cornell University Press, 1969.

Lukas, J. Anthony. *Night-mare: The Underside of the Nixon Years.* New York: Viking, 1976.

McAlister, John T., Jr., and Paul Mus. *The Vietnamese and Their Revolution.* New York: Harper & Row, 1970.

McCormick, Thomas. *America's Half Century: United States Foreign Policy in the Cold War.* Baltimore, Md.: Johns Hopkins University Press, 1989.

McCoy, Alfred W., ed. *Southeast Asia Under Japanese Occupation.* New Haven: Monograph Series No. 22, Yale University Southeast Asia Studies, 1980.

McGehee, Ralph. *Deadly Deceits: My 25 Years in the CIA.* New York: Sheridan Square Publications, 1983.

Mailer, Norman. *Armies of the Night.* New York: Signet, 1968.

Marchetti, Victor, and John D. Marks. *The CIA and the Cult of Intelligence.* New York: Alfred A. Knopf, 1974.

Marr, David. *Vietnamese Anticolonialism, 1885–1925.* Berkeley, Calif.: University of California, 1971.

———. *Vietnamese Tradition on Trial, 1920–1945.* Berkeley, Calif.: University of California Press, 1981.

———, and Christine Pelzer White, eds., *Postwar Vietnam: Dilemmas in Socialist Development.* Ithaca, N.Y.: Cornell University Southeast Asia Program Series No. 3, 1989.

Mason, Bobbie Ann. *In Country.* New York: Harper & Row, 1985.

Mason, Robert. *Chickenhawk.* New York: Viking, 1983.

Melman, Seymour. *In the Name of America.* Commissioned and published by Clergy and Laymen Concerned About Vietnam. New York: Distributed by E. P. Dutton, 1968.

Menashe, Louis, and Ron Radosh. *Teach-ins, USA.* New York: Frederick A. Praeger, 1967.

Murray, Martin. *The Development of Capitalism in Colonial Indochina, 1870–1940.* Berkeley, Calif.: University of California Press, 1980.

Nelson, Jack, and Ronald J. Ostrow. *The FBI and the Berrigans: The Making of a Conspiracy,* New York: Coward, McCann and Geoghegan, 1972.

New York Times, The. The Pentagon Papers. New York: Quadrangle Books, 1971.

Ngo Vinh Long. *Before the Revolution: The Vietnamese Peasants Under the French.* Cambridge, Ma.: MIT Press, 1973.

Nguyen Du. *Tale of Kieu.* New York: Random House, 1973.

Nguyen Khac Vien. *The Long Resistance (1858–1975).* Hanoi, 1975.

————. *Tradition and Revolution.* Berkeley, Calif.: Indochina Resource Center, 1974.

Nixon, Richard. *RN: The Memoirs of Richard Nixon.* New York: Grosset & Dunlap, 1978.

O'Brien, Tim. *Going After Cacciato.* New York: Delacorte, 1978.

————. *If I Die in a Combat Zone: Box Me Up and Ship Me Home.* New York: Delacorte Press, 1973.

Olson, James S. *Dictionary of the Vietnam War.* New York: Greenwood Press, 1988.

Page, Tim. *Nam.* New York: Alfred A. Knopf, 1983.

Palmer, Bruce, Jr. *The 25-Year War: America's Military Role in Vietnam.* Lexington, Ky: University of Kentucky Press, 1984.

Phillips, Jayne Anne. *Machine Dreams.* New York: Dutton, 1984.

Pilger, John. *The Last Day: America's Final Hours in Vietnam.* New York: Random House, 1975.

Pisor, Robert. *The End of the Line: The Siege of Khe Sanh.* New York: W.W. Norton, 1982.

Polner, Murray. *No Victory Parades: The Return of the Vietnam Veteran.* New York: Holt, Rinehart & Winston, 1971.

————. ed. *When Can I Come Home? A Debate on Amnesty for Exiles, Antiwar Prisoners and Others.* Garden City: Anchor Books, 1972.

Powers, Thomas. *The Man Who Kept the Secrets: Richard Helms and the CIA.* New York: Alfred A. Knopf, 1979.

Rotter, Andrew. *The Path to Vietnam.* Ithaca: Cornell University Press, 1987.

Salisbury, Harrison E. *Behind the Lines—Hanoi.* New York: Harper & Row, 1967.

————, ed. *Vietnam Reconsidered: Lessons from a War.* New York: Harper & Row, 1984.

Scigliano, Robert. *South Vietnam: Nation Under Stress.* Boston: Houghton Mifflin, 1963.

Severo, Richard, and Lewis Milford. *The Wages of War: When America's Soldiers Came Home from Valley Forge to Vietnam.* New York: Simon & Schuster, 1989.

Shaplen, Robert. *Bitter Victory.* New York: Harper & Row, 1986.

Sheehan, Neil. *The Arnheiter Affair.* New York: Dell Publishing Co., 1971.

Sheehan, Susan. *Ten Vietnamese.* New York: Alfred A. Knopf, 1967.

Smith, Joseph B. *Portrait of a Cold Warrior.* New York: Ballantine, 1981.

Sorenson, Theodore C. *Kennedy.* New York: Harper & Row, 1965.

Stockwell, John. *In Search of Enemies: A CIA Story.* New York: W. W. Norton, 1978.

Stone, Robert. *Dog Soldiers.* Boston: Houghton Mifflin, 1974.

Summers, Harry Jr. *On Strategy: A Critical Analysis of the Vietnam War.* Novato, Calif.: Presidio Press, 1982.

Surrey, David S. *Choice of Conscience: Vietnam War Military and Draft Resisters in Canada.* New York: Praeger Publishers, 1982.

Taylor, Maxwell. *Swords and Ploughshares.* New York: W.W. Norton, 1972.

Terzani, Tiziano. *Giai Phong! The Fall and Liberation of Saigon.* New York: St. Martin's Press, 1976.

Thich Nhat Hanh. *Vietnam: The Lotus in the Sea of Fire.* London: SCM Press, Ltd., 1967.

Thompson, W. Scott, and Donaldson Frizzell, eds. *The Lessons of Vietnam.* New York: Crane, Russak, 1977.

Walton, Richard J. *Cold War and Counter-Revolution: The Foreign Policy of John F. Kennedy.* New York: Viking, 1972.

Warner, Denis. *The Last Confucian: Vietnam, Southeast Asia, and the West.* Baltimore: Penguin Books, 1964.

Waterhouse, Larry G., and Mariann G. Wizard. *Turning the Guns Around: Notes on the GI Movement.* New York: Praeger, 1971.

Werner, Jayne. *Peasant Politics and Religious Sectarianism: Peasant and Priest in the Cao Dai in Vietnam.* New Haven: Yale University Southeast Asian Studies, 1981.

———. "A Short History of the War in Vietnam." *Monthly Review* 37:2 (June 1985), pp. 14–21.

Whiting, Allen. *The Chinese Calculus of Deterrence: India and Indochina.* Ann Arbor, Mich.: Michigan Studies on China, University of Michigan Press, 1975.

Wills, Gary. *Nixon Agonistes, The Crisis of the Self-made Man.* New York: New American Library, 1971.

Wright, Stephen. *Meditations in Green.* New York: Charles Scribner's Sons, 1983.

Woodside, Alexander. *Community and Revolution in Modern Vietnam.* Boston: Houghon Mifflin, 1976.

Zinn, Howard. *A People's History of the United States.* New York: Harper & Row, 1980.

There are two journals of exceptional interest: *Vietnam Forum* and *Vietnam Generation.* The former, published by the Yale Center for International and Area Studies, carries important translations of Vietnamese literature as well as essays on its history and culture. *Vietnam Generation* encourages an interdisciplinary study of the Vietnam War. Its special issues (on Kent State and Jackson State, the experience of blacks in the military, for example) are invaluable.

Grateful acknowledgment is made for permission to reprint excerpts from the following sources:

"A Time to Break Silence" by Martin Luther King, Jr. Copyright © 1967 by Martin Luther King, Jr. Reprinted by permission of Joan Daves.

The papers of John M. Mecklin are reprinted by permission of Mary Mecklin Jenkins.

"Corporal Charles Chungtu, U.S.M.C." by Bryan Alec Floyd is reprinted by permission of the author.

"Song of Napalm" from *The Monkey Wars* by Bruce Weigl. Copyright © 1985 by Bruce Weigl. Reprinted by permission of The University of Georgia Press.

"After Our War" from *Blue Mountain* by John Balaban. Copyright © 1982 by John Balaban. Reprinted by permission of Unicorn Press.

"What Kind of War?" by Larry Rottmann from *Winning Hearts and Minds: War Poems by Vietnam Veterans.* Reprinted by permission of the author.

"Ode to the American Dead in Korea" by Thomas McGrath. Reprinted by permission of Copper Canyon Press.

"Wounds of War" by Marilyn M. McMahon. Reprinted by permission of the author.

"Making the Children Behave" from *To Those Who Have Gone Home Tired: New and Selected Poems* by W. D. Ehrhart. Copyright © 1984 by W. D. Ehrhart, and published by Thunder's Mouth Press. Reprinted by permission of the author.

"Staying Alive" from *To Stay Alive* by Denise Levertov. Copyright © 1971 by Denise Levertov Goodman. First published in *Poetry.* Reprinted by permission of New Directions Publishing Corporation.

Grateful acknowledgment is made for permission to reprint maps from the following sources:

From *Vietnam: A Country Study* edited by Ronald J. Cima. Copyright © 1989 by the United States Government as represented by the Secretary of the Army. Reprinted by permission of the Library of Congress.

From *Vietnam: A Study* by Stanley Karnow. Copyright © 1983 by WGBH Educational Foundation and Stanley Karnow. Reprinted by permission of Viking Penguin USA.

From *Intervention: How America Became Involved in Vietnam* by George McT. Kahin. Copyright © 1986 by George McT. Kahin. Reprinted by permission of Alfred A. Knopf, Inc.

From *A Bright Shining Lie: John Paul Vann and America in Vietnam* by Neil Sheehan. Copyright © 1988 by Neil Sheehan. Cartography copyright © 1988 by John Paul Tremblay. Reprinted by permission of Random House, Inc.

From *The Tunnels of Cu Chi* by Tom Mangold and John Penycate. Copyright © 1985 by Tom Mangold and John Penycate. Reprinted by permission of Random House, Inc.

From "Anti-U.S. Protest Around the World This Month," February 21, 1965. Reprinted by permission of *The New York Times.*

From "The Communist Takeover: How Breakthrough in South Vietnam Developed After the Paris Accord," May 1, 1975. Reprinted by permission of *The New York Times.*

Index